THE PUNIC WARS

HAMPSHIRE COUNTY LIBRARY
WITHDRAWN

TO THE BRITISH ARMY

THE PUNIC WARS

NIGEL BAGNALL

HUTCHINSON
LONDON   SYDNEY   AUCKLAND   JOHANNESBURG

Copyright © Nigel Bagnall 1990

The right of Nigel Bagnall to be identified as Author of this work
has been asserted by Nigel Bagnall in accordance with the
Copyright, Designs and Patents Act, 1988

All rights reserved

This edition first published in 1990 by
Hutchinson

Random Century Group Ltd
20 Vauxhall Bridge Road, London SW1V 2SA

Random Century Australia (Pty) Ltd
20 Alfred Street, Milsons Point, Sydney, NSW 2061, Australia

Random Century (NZ) Ltd
PO Box 40–086, Glenfield, Auckland 10, New Zealand

Random Century South Africa (Pty) Ltd
PO Box 337, Bergvlei, 2012 South Africa

British Library Cataloguing in Publication Data
Bagnall, Nigel
 The Punic wars
 1. Punic wars
 I. Title
 937.04

ISBN 0–09–174421–0

Set in Bembo by Speedset Ltd, Ellesmere Port
Printed and bound in Great Britain by Mackays of Chatham PLC

CONTENTS

Principal Characters   vii
Introduction   xi

PART ONE   THE BACKGROUND

I	Carthage	3
II	Rome	19
III	Sicily	35

PART TWO   THE FIRST PUNIC WAR 264–242 BC

IV	The Opening Round in Sicily 264–261 BC	49
V	The Maritime Dimension 261–256 BC	60
VI	The African Campaign 256–255 BC	70
VII	The Return to Sicily 254–242 BC	79
VIII	Commentary	100

PART THREE   STRIFE BETWEEN WARS 241–218 BC

IX	The Mercenary Revolt 240–237 BC	111
X	The Gallic Invasion 241–220 BC	127
XI	The Illyrian Expeditions 229–227 BC	135
XII	The Conquest of Spain 237–219 BC	142

CONTENTS

PART FOUR   THE SECOND PUNIC WAR 218–201 BC

XIII	From the Ebro to the Alps 218 BC	155
XIV	The Epic Years 218–216 BC	168
XV	The War Expands 215–206 BC	198
XVI	Sardinia, Sicily and Illyria 215–205 BC	218
XVII	The Waning Years 216–211 BC	233
XVIII	Hannibal in Retreat 211–205 BC	253
XIX	The Romans Carry the War to Africa 205–203 BC	267
XX	Victory in Africa 205–201 BC	286
XXI	Political Ferment 201–149 BC	300

PART FIVE   THE THIRD PUNIC WAR 149–148 BC

XXII	The Destruction of Carthage 149–148 BC	313

Epilogue	321
Select Bibliography	342
Index	344

LIST OF MAPS

The Carthaginian Empire and Dependencies	4
Sicily – To illustrate the First Punic War	50
Carthage and its Neighbourhood	71
Italy – To illustrate the Second Punic War	156
The Battle of Lake Trasimene (217 BC)	181
The Battle of Cannae (216 BC)	190
Illyria, Southern Italy and the Peloponnese	219

PRINCIPAL CHARACTERS

FIRST PUNIC WAR 264–242 BC
SECOND PUNIC WAR 218–201 BC
THIRD PUNIC WAR 149–148 BC

ADHUBAL Carthaginian admiral who defeated the Roman fleet commanded by Publius Claudius Pulcher at the battle of Drepana in 249 BC.
AGATHOCLES 361–289 BC. Tyrant of Syracuse who eluded the Carthaginian siege of the city and carried the war into their North African homeland.
ARCHIMEDES The most famous mathematician in antiquity. Native of Syracuse, whose war machines devastated the Roman fleet during the siege in which he was killed when the city fell in 212 BC.
BOMILCAR Carthaginian admiral who failed to relieve Syracuse during the Second Punic War.
CATO Roman senator who had fought in Spain. His implacable hatred of Carthage was a major cause of the Third Punic War and the city's destruction.
DEMETRIUS OF PHARUS An Illyrian adventurer, who vacillated in his attitude towards Rome after first espousing their cause in 229 BC.
FABIUS MAXIMUS, QUINTUS (Cunctator) Roman consul who shadowed Hannibal during the Second Punic War, hoping to wear him down without giving battle.
FLAMINIUS, GAIUS Roman consul killed with most of his men at the battle of Lake Trasimene in 217 BC when trapped by Hannibal.
HAMILCAR BARCA Father of Hannibal. Commanded the Carthaginian

forces in Sicily during the First Punic War. Suppressed the Mercenary Revolt in Africa (240–237 BC). Created an independent base in Spain where he was killed fighting in 228 BC.

HANNIBAL Son of Hamilcar Barca. Secured the family base in Spain after the death of his father. Led his army from Spain over the Alps into Italy to begin the Second Punic War. After withdrawing to North Africa he was defeated by Scipio Africanus at Zama in 202 BC.

HANNO Carthaginian general sent to Sicily at the outbreak of the First Punic War. Defeated at the naval battle of Ecnomus in 256 BC.

HANNO (The Great) Leader of the aristocratic party in Carthage from 240–200 BC. Favoured development of the African provinces, so was the chief opponent of Hannibal and the Barcid party seeking overseas expansion.

HASDRUBAL BARCA Left in command in Spain when his brother Hannibal crossed the Alps to campaign in Italy at the outbreak of the Second Punic War. Later tried to join Hannibal but was killed on the Metaurus in 207 BC.

HASDRUBAL GISCO Carthaginian general who served victoriously with Hasdrubal Barca in Spain until defeated on the Ilipa in 206 BC. Finally defeated by Scipio Africanus in North Africa in 203 BC.

HASDRUBAL HANNO Leader of the Popular Party in Carthage and son-in-law of Hamilcar Barca. Signed the Treaty of Ebro with the Romans defining the extent of the Carthaginian empire in Spain. Assassinated in 221 BC.

HIERO King of Syracuse. Sided with the Carthaginians over the Mamertine problem in 254 BC, but after being defeated by the Romans changed his allegiance to them. Thereafter remained a faithful Roman ally until his death in about 214 BC.

MAGO BARCA Brother of Hannibal, accompanied him to Italy at the beginning of the Second Punic War. Returned to Spain where he defeated the two Scipios, before himself being vanquished at the battle of Ilipa in 206 BC. Recalled to Italy where he was mortally wounded in 203 BC.

MAHARBAL Numidian cavalry general who crossed the Alps with Hannibal in 218 BC. Fought at the battles of Trasimene in 217 BC and Cannae in 216 BC.

MARCELLUS, MARCUS CLAUDIUS Four times consul, and Rome's most vigorous field commander in Sicily and Italy during the Second Punic War. Took Syracuse but was killed in battle in 208 BC.

MASINISSA Numidian prince who fought with the Carthaginians in Spain during the Second Punic War but changed his allegiance to Rome. Fought with Scipio Africanus in North Africa and was subsequently recognised as King of Numidia by the Romans.

PAULLUS, LUCIUS AEMILIUS Roman consul sharing dual command with Varro at the Battle of Cannae where he fell in 216 BC.

PRINCIPAL CHARACTERS

PHILIP V King of Macedonia who entered into an alliance with Hannibal during the Second Punic War in 215 BC. Driven out of Illyria by the Romans and finally defeated during the Second Macedonian War in 192 BC.

REGULUS, MARCUS ATILIUS Roman consul who defeated the Carthaginian fleet at the battle of Ecnomus in 256 BC. Invaded North Africa where he was defeated by Xanthippus in the following year.

SCIPIO, GNAEUS CORNELIUS Uncle of Scipio Africanus. Killed with his brother Publius Cornelius Scipio in Spain in 211 BC.

SCIPIO, PUBLIUS CORNELIUS Roman consul and father of Scipio Africanus. Carried the campaign to Spain during the Second Punic War where he was defeated and killed in 211 BC.

SCIPIO, PUBLIUS CORNELIUS (Africanus) After the deaths of his father and uncle in battle, given command of the Roman army in Spain in 209 BC and captured New Carthage. Landed in Africa in 204 BC and defeated Hannibal at Zama two years later.

SCIPIO, AEMILIANUS PUBLIUS CORNELIUS Adopted by Publius Scipio, son of Scipio Africanus. Captured Carthage in the Third Punic War.

SPENDIUS Roman deserter who, with the Libyan Matho, led the Mercenary Revolt in 240 BC.

SYPHAX King of Numidia who sided with the Carthaginians and was defeated in the battle of the Great Plains by Scipio Africanus and Masinissa in 203 BC.

VARRO, MARCUS TERENTIUS Roman consul sharing dual command with Lucius Aemilius Paullus but under whose direction the battle of Cannae was fought in 216 BC.

XANTHIPPUS Spartan mercenary who trained and led the Carthaginian army which defeated the Romans under Marcus Atilius Regulus in North Africa in 255 BC.

INTRODUCTION

One of the difficulties besetting successive generations is to accept the fact that we may not all be pioneers in space, but we are the inheritors of other's experiences. As the Roman historian Polybius wrote, 'There are only two sources from which any benefit can be derived; our own misfortunes and those that have happened to other men.'

So, bearing Polybius' words in mind, we can turn with advantage to those three major human misfortunes known as the Punic Wars: in spite of their remoteness they possess a remarkable contemporary relevance. Two largely incompatible civilisations confronted one another in a rivalry which quickly developed into a to-the-death struggle for supremacy, and the lessons of that struggle are clear enough: it demonstrates the need for a positive and consistent national political direction, the consequences of failing to adapt military force structures and thinking to changed circumstances, and the battlefield applications of principles which remain constant and common to all times.

As well as those of the Ancients, a number of more recent histories have been written about the Punic Wars, and without the scholarly research which has gone into them this book would be all the poorer. My aim has been to look at the wars through the eyes of a professional soldier, and to comment accordingly. I do not claim to have drawn out all the lessons, nor even to have identified the most important ones. I hope rather that others will read with care and then be able to form their own opinions. This is what the study of military history is all about.

There are basically two different ways to have written this book.

INTRODUCTION

Either I could present an across-the-board chronological account, or I could examine the different campaigns sequentially, each in its entirety. There are advantages and disadvantages to both but I chose the latter because I consider any difficulty in interrelating events occurring at the same time in different theatres to be far outweighed by the ability to follow through the developments of each separate campaign in an unbroken sequence. And I have tried to reduce the disadvantages of this approach by summarising major events taking place elsewhere whenever this appeared helpful.

In analysing the various campaigns, I have considered them at the strategic, operational and tactical levels. By first portraying the broad politico–military objectives, their implementation at the operational level will be easier to follow, together with the tactics which evolved.

I have also written a concluding chapter, pulling together the various lessons and deductions that can be drawn, and showing their contemporary relevance. This then provides a basis for comment on the present and speculation about the future. Any conclusions arrived at in this manner are bound to be controversial, but it has been my overriding intention simply to link past, present and future coherently and usefully.

I am indebted to John Andrews, head librarian at the Ministry of Defence, for his invaluable assistance and advice. He and his staff could not have been more patiently understanding and helpful. I am furthermore very aware of my indebtedness to the Fellows of Balliol who permitted me to spend a year among them, and to Professor Sir Michael Howard for the guidance he gave me at that time. I was provided with an undisturbed twelve months for reflection and learning, the value of which has been incalculable.

Finally, I am profoundly grateful to the British Army, from which I have received such a wealth of experience, and to which I now dedicate this book.

PART ONE

THE BACKGROUND

CHAPTER ONE

CARTHAGE

The Founding

It was Phoenician settlers from Tyre who founded Carthage in about 814 BC, not far north of modern Tunis. Their ancestors had come from Asia between 1200 and 1000 BC in one of those great and largely unexplained population explosions of ancient times, which in this case produced two major migratory movements and eventually spread into Northern Italy and the Eastern Mediterranean. Those who settled in Tyre were given the name Phoenician by the Greeks, meaning dark-skinned. The Romans then called them Poeni, from which the name Punic was derived. They were a Semitic race and a seafaring people, thought to have originated from the Persian Gulf. According to Herodotus, after the Egyptian King Neco had failed in his attempt to construct a canal between the Nile and the Arabian Gulf, he sent a fleet manned by a Phoenician crew down the Gulf with orders to sail round Africa and return to Egypt and the Mediterranean by way of the Straits of Gibraltar. The Phoenicians set off and when autumn came put in at some convenient spot on the coast, sowed a patch of ground, and waited for next year's harvest before continuing their journey. After two full years they returned to Egypt.

It seems unlikely that all those who settled on the Syrio-Palestine coast, broadly equating to modern Lebanon and northern Israel, made this hazardous and protracted journey, but rather followed the established caravan routes leading overland to the Eastern Mediterranean seaboard. Here on the coastal strip lying between the Lebanon mountain range and the sea were founded the first settlements that grew into the Phoenician cities of Aradus (Ruad), Byblos, Berytus,

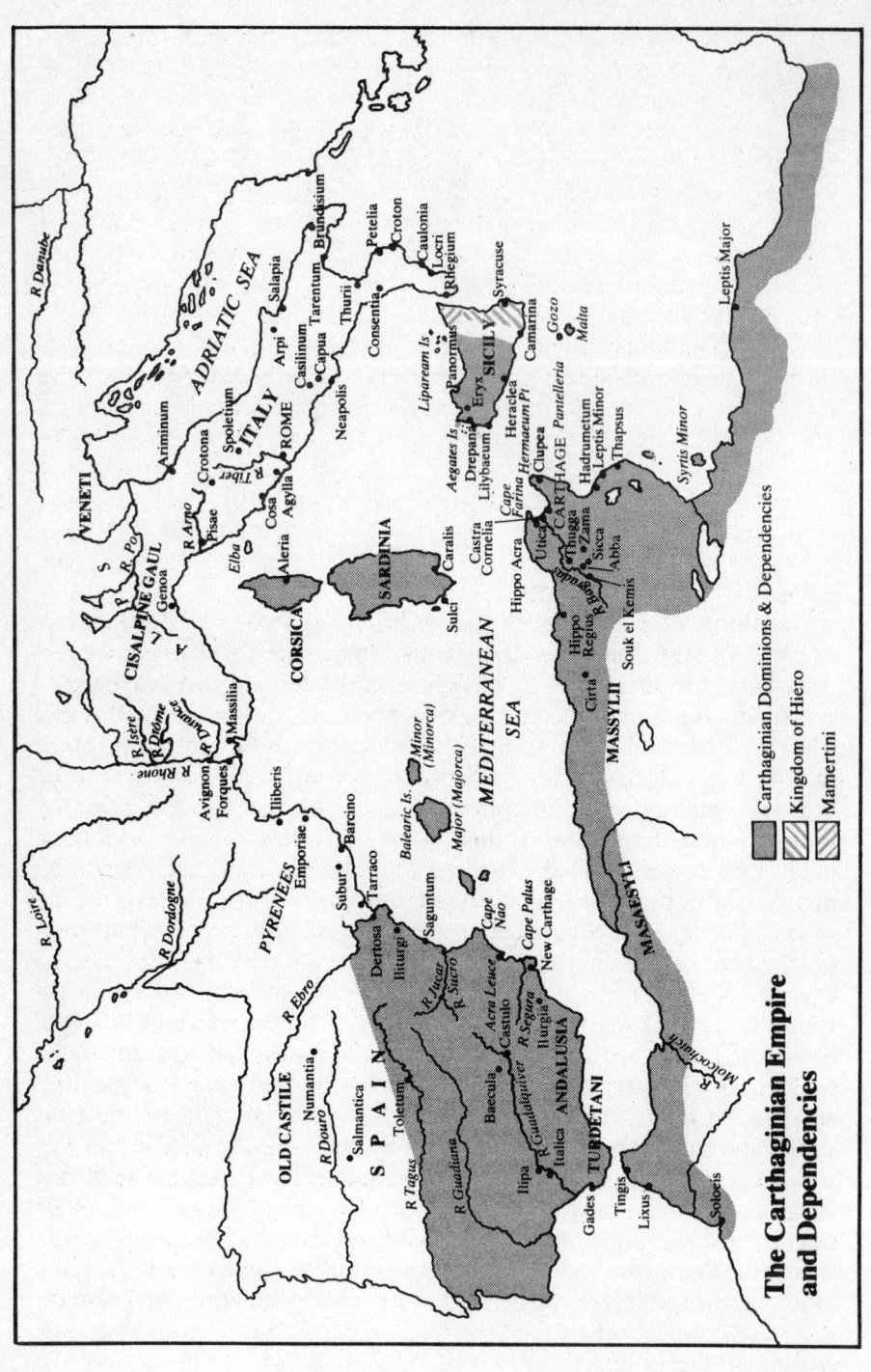

The Carthaginian Empire and Dependencies

Sidon, Serepta and Tyre. With a hinterland of varying depth, a few miles in many places and nowhere more than about thirty-five, crossed by mountain spurs sometimes running out into the sea as promontories, the cities were inevitably separated from one another. Though forming a homogeneous region sharing the same language, religious beliefs, artistic styles and political and administrative organisation, the cities tended to develop in an autonomous and largely self-contained manner, assuming a predominance over one another at different periods of their history. A seafaring people, the Phoenicians selected rocky promontories for their settlements, since these enabled them to shelter their ships and develop harbours on both the north and south sides. In this way they could seek shelter and take advantage of the winds in most seasons of the year. Alternatively, small islands lying off the coast which could be easily fortified were used – as in the case of Tyre to which Alexander the Great was obliged to build a causeway when he set about its capture. The land behind the cities was fertile enough and readily cultivated, while cedar woods flourished on the mountain slopes and provided a plentiful supply of timber for ship building.

Once they had established themselves, the Phoenicians began to search for trade along the shores of the Mediterranean, a movement made easier following the collapse of the Minoan and Mycenaean civilisations in about 1200 BC, together with those of the Hittites to the north of Tyre and the Egyptians to the south. The races who then inhabited the North African coast were in a relatively primitive state of development, probably due at least in part to their being isolated by the waterless Sahara desert to the south and by the sea to the west and north. Phoenician trading posts were therefore established with little opposition. In the centuries immediately before Christ, North Africa was very different from today, being thickly wooded and supporting a multitude of game, such as elephants, lions, panthers and bears, much of which has now moved elsewhere. As we have already seen, the coast itself, which the Phoenician traders would have followed as they spread westwards, provided harbours for their ships and open beaches for their settlements. Though the hinterland was generally inhospitable, it contained gold and other minerals which could be worked by the indigenous tribes who were rounded up as slaves. One of the larger trading posts established was Carthage, near the head of a peninsula of sandstone hills running eastwards parallel to the Mediterranean coast and providing shelter from north and west winds. There were two harbours, the inner one reserved for ships of war and the outer one for merchant vessels, and the two isthmuses joining the ends of the peninsula to the mainland formed the Lake of Tunis between them.

The northern isthmus, which ran due west from the city for about three miles, was by far the larger and, being some three thousand yards wide and almost level, it offered the most obvious and direct approach. It was consequently well protected, with three layers of defences. First there was a ditch, backed by an earth rampart, a low wall packed into shape from the excavated soil, which would probably only have been manned by skirmishers ready to withdraw in the face of a major assault. The second wall, constructed of stone, dominated the outer defences and enabled the defenders to shower down a hail of missiles onto their assailants as they scrambled forward until, coming within range, large fishing nets were cast down to entangle entire groups like so many thrashing fish. Behind this second wall stood an even more formidable third wall, forty-five feet high and at least thirty feet wide, punctuated by some fifteen towers spaced at two-hundred-yard intervals. Behind this wall were the stables for what is estimated to have been 300 elephants and 4000 horses, together with storage space for all their provisions and harnesses. There was also barrack accommodation, again based on an estimate, for some 20,000 soldiers.

Encircling the city on its seabound perimeter beyond the northern isthmus was a single wall, which did not extend down to the water's edge in its entirety. This was to prove of considerable significance during the Mercenary Revolt which followed the First Punic War.

The southern isthmus was narrow, no more than a hundred yards wide in places, little more than a sand bar which separated the lake of Tunis from the open sea. This southern isthmus was to figure prominently during the final Roman assault that led to the destruction of Carthage.

In his historical novel *Salammbo* Gustave Flaubert, who spent a considerable amount of time researching topographical and archaeological details during his several visits to North Africa, paints this picture of Carthage.

Behind [the battlements] extended the city, its tall, cube-shaped houses rising in tiers like an amphitheatre. They were made of stone, planks, pebbles, rushes, sea shells, trodden earth. The temple groves stood out like lakes of greenery in their mountain of multi-coloured blocks. Public squares levelled it out at irregular intervals; countless intersecting alleys cut it from top to bottom, the walls of the three old quarters, now mixed together, were still distinguishable; they rose here and there like great reefs, or extended huge sections – half-covered with flowers, blackened, widely streaked where rubbish had been thrown down, and streets passed through their gaping apertures like rivers under bridges.

The Acropolic hill, in the centre of Byrsa, was covered over with a litter of monuments. There were temples with twisted pillars, bronze capitals, and metal chains, cones of dry stone with azure stripes, copper cupolas, marble architraves, Babylonian buttresses, obelisks balancing on their points like upturned torches. Peristyles reached to pediments; scrolls unfolded between colonnades; granite walls supported file partitions; in all this one thing was piled on another, half hiding it, in a marvellous and unintelligible way. There was a feeling of successive ages and, as it were, memories of forgotten lands.

Behind the Acropolis, where the land was red earth, the Mapalian Way, with tombs on either side, ran straight from the shore to the catacombs; then came large dwellings spaced out amid gardens, and this third quarter, Megara, the new tower, went up to the edge of the cliff, where stood a giant light house which blazed out every night.

Though Flaubert's description was based on the best archaeological evidence at the time of writing in 1858, whether it is factually correct in all its detail is not of great consequence. What he provides is a picture upon which the imagination can build in trying to visualise this crowded, bustling city, influenced in its culture and customs by the wide range of its commercial contacts and the diversity of its population.

To round off the description, since there was then no aqueduct, the supply of water to the city was always a problem. Though there were natural springs which flowed for at least part of the year, these were not sufficient to meet the demands of the population, estimated to number some 700,000 at the time of the city's destruction in 148 BC. A series of giant cisterns were constructed, into which water from the heavy winter rains was channelled and stored.

Initially the mainland area under cultivation was comparatively small, but trade and prosperity brought a steadily rising increase to the population over the centuries, so there was a matching increase in the demand for food. The cultivated areas were therefore gradually extended to include the whole of what now forms the northern part of Tunis. It was mainly arable land providing wheat, barley and grapes, predominantly farmed by negroes and Berbers.

Though Carthage was by far the largest city, there were others, such as the coastal towns of Utica, Hippo Acra (Bizerta) and Tunis, as well as a number of inland towns, all of which depended to a varying extent on the inland produce.

Beyond the African continent, further trading posts which had been established along the coasts of Spain, Sardinia, Cyprus, Malta and Sicily gradually developed into colonies, themselves seeking territorial expansion. Indeed, by about 500 BC the Carthaginians themselves had acquired supremacy over the whole of southern Spain with its rich silver, gold and copper mines, and in Sicily the Carthaginians' expansion was eventually checked only by Greek settlements in the east of the Island. The situation in Sicily will be considered further in an examination of the role of the Greek cities during the First Punic War. The principal difference between them and those of the Carthaginians was that the former, though fiercely loyal to their cultural heritage, were independent of one another and Greece itself, whereas the Phoenician settlements were more like colonies. They had their own governments but relied on Carthage for their defence since they possessed no military forces. Also Carthaginian subject territories in Africa were expected to pay a heavy annual tribute, some of which was paid in kind, which resulted in considerable resentment and later led to desertions and open revolt.

The Army and Navy

Carthage was primarily a trading nation seeking to extend its commercial connections, sphere of influence and empire. In support of this expansion was a military force which enabled Carthage to maintain her role and trading monopolies for three centuries; mainly through her unequalled navy which was not averse to sinking rival trading vessels – incidents which were then not regarded as acts of war, especially since many of these losses were probably attributed to natural disasters in the absence of any survivors to testify to the contrary.

The Carthaginian army consisted mainly of mercenaries, recruited from the various subject territories, who seldom served in their own country, and remained isolated from one another by differences of language and religion. They were dependent upon the Carthaginian fleet for the majority of supplies and discipline was uncompromisingly enforced by a strict code which included capital punishment. Each territory provided special military skills: Numidia supplied a nimble, bold, impetuous and indefatigable cavalry armed with a spear and javelins, lightly clad, unequalled horsemen who rode without saddle or bridle. These finest of light cavalry were capable of fighting in the hills or the plains with equal facility, manoeuvring like flocks of starlings that wheel and change direction as though by instinct. Threatening and enticing, surprising with the suddenness and unexpectedness of their moves, there was no other cavalry on the battlefield that could match them.

From the Balearic Islands came the formidable slingers, organised into corps of two thousand men armed with two types of slings, one for long-range engagements against a densely packed enemy and the other for close-quarter, individual targets. Their delivery of stones or lead, which could penetrate a helmet or light protective armour, matched contemporary archers' rate of fire and accuracy. They were trained to whirl their slings once about their heads and hit a bundle of straw or faggots at 600 feet. They were savage fighters who were often paid in women rather than gold or silver.

Tough infantry soldiers were recruited from backward Spanish hill tribes: in perpetual conflict with one another, this disharmony had simplified their defeat by the Carthaginians, and the conquest of Spain. They were experts at guerrilla warfare but of temperamental disposition and at times loyalty, so that they were not best suited to set-piece battles of prolonged intensity. Their basic weapon was a short sword equally suitable for cutting and thrusting, the effectiveness of which is borne out by the fact that the Romans adopted it in the Second Punic War. Also recruited from Spain were a lightly armed cavalry who could carry a second rider ready to dismount and fight as an infantryman.

The largest group of mercenaries who served in the Carthaginian army, however, were the Libyans of Tunisia. Hardened by the harsh conditions of their country, they were versatile fighters who served both as light infantry skirmishers and in the heavy, massively concentrated infantry of the line. There were also some Gauls but they were relatively few, until Hannibal's invasion of Italy encouraged them to join in substantial numbers to fight against their traditional enemies, the Romans. They fought without armour and showed great dash in the attack but were unreliable, especially when hard pressed.

Then there were the elephants. Initially the Carthaginians only used the African elephant found in the forests around Carthage at the foot of the Atlas mountains and the coast of Morocco, but later it seems probable that Hannibal obtained some of the larger Indian elephants from Egypt. Until tactics had been developed to counter them on the battlefield, elephants struck terror into men and horses alike and their small numbers had a disproportionate effect. They could however be a two-edged weapon since when frightened they sometimes wreaked devastation in their own ranks by turning and fleeing.

There were of course also native Carthaginians in the army, but the numbers were never very great. It was considered more economical to hire mercenaries, rather than employ their own limited manpower at the expense of commercial activities. In the 4th century BC a small all-Carthaginian force of some 3000 was raised to fight as heavy infantry, an elite corps called the Sacred Band, from whom the long-term professional leadership of the army was selected. In this way the Carthaginians ensured that the generals who commanded their mercenary army came from amongst their own citizens, since only the more junior officers were recruited from the ranks of the mercenaries. To be a Carthaginian general, however, carried considerable risks. As Diodorus Siculus, the 1st century BC Greek historian relates:

They advance the most eminent persons to be Generals in their Wars, because they conclude that they will fight with more resolution than others, when all lies at stake; but after the Wars are ended, and peace concluded, then they bring false accusations against them, and most unjustly, through envy, put them to death; and therefore some Generals, out of fear of those unjust sentences, either give up their Commissions, or seek to become absolute Monarchs.

There was the occasional non-Carthaginian commander: Xanthippus, for example, a Spartan whose generalship saved Carthage from defeat when the Romans landed in North Africa during the First Punic War. Little is known about him, but he must have been not only a thoroughly competent soldier but one displaying a remarkable degree of good sense; as soon as he had defeated a Roman army before Carthage and so saved the city from destruction, he returned to Sparta before jealousy and intrigue could tarnish his reputation. His reorganisation of the Carthaginian army was based on Greek military methods.

The basic Greek fighting formation was the phalanx, a solid body of 4000 heavy infantry standing shoulder to shoulder in 256 files, each sixteen men deep. The soldiers wore body armour, were armed with a pike and carried a heavy shield; when advancing the pikes of the first five ranks were held forward and were of such a length that even those of the men in the fifth rank extended beyond the leading one. In the succeeding ranks the soldiers rested their spears on the shoulders of the men in front with their points slanting upwards; in this way they formed a kind of rampart above their heads which served to protect them from the enemy's missiles. Renouncing flexibility in order to achieve shock through mass, the phalanx was a formidable formation on any ground which permitted its orderly deployment and unimpeded advance, since its momentum was almost certain to break the opposing ranks. But on less favourable ground or when taken in the flank, its very mass became a hindrance, preventing any orderly adjustment to face in another direction.

Historians differ as to the effectiveness of the Carthaginian mercenary army. Those who tend to take the side of Rome point out that the mercenaries were not united by any common and reciprocal interest, and had no long-term concern for the wellbeing of those they served, who were largely indifferent to them anyway. They then could not be relied upon or expected to face extremes of danger with zeal, or disasters with resolution, since they served solely for money. Others point out that though there were incidents of desertion and cowardice, as well as a bloody rebellion by the Libyan mercenaries in 240 BC when they were not paid after the First Punic War, such incidents were not exclusive to mercenaries. It would belittle Roman feats of arms to suggest they were opposed by an enemy significantly less courageous and resolute than themselves and, on balance, the defects and inadequacies of the mercenary system seem to have been exaggerated. Like most soldiers, in the final count they owed their allegiance to their commander. Given a great one such as Hannibal, for the majority their loyalty knew no bounds.

The navy played a vital part in the Carthaginian war machine and unlike the army, it was manned entirely by Carthaginians. There were three basic types of ships: transports, warships and small general purpose vessels. The transports had rounded hulls to provide capacious cargo holds and were about four times as long as their width. The warships, needing speed rather than capacity, were narrow and long in order to accommodate the greatest possible number of oarsmen, their length being seven times greater than their width, and they had two masts. The central main mast provided propulsion and the smaller mast, mounted on the prow, allowed the ship to be manoeuvred in a cross-wind. Each warship had at least three officers, one of whom was the navigator, and there were some thirty to forty sailors who handled the sails and worked on deck. The number of oarsmen depended upon the size of the ship: a trireme had 150, a quadrireme about 240 and quinquereme some 300. The sails were used for normal travelling and when approaching the battle area, but before battle was joined the masts were lowered and the ships were rowed. The basic tactical unit consisted of twelve ships, which could be grouped together to form a fleet of varying size, though 120 ships, or ten tactical units, was the normal number.

The general purpose vessels were smaller, swift and easily manoeuvrable, and were mainly employed on reconnaissance and communication tasks. Two such vessels have been found off the western coast of Sicily and provide an insight into how the Phoenicians constructed their ships. Both were built of wooden components prefabricated separately and assembled later. This discovery helps to explain how, as will later be related, when the Romans captured a Carthaginian ship, they were able to dismantle it so that it could be copied. Battles mainly took place near the coast where the ships could be handled in relatively calm water. There were two basic battle tactics: in both instances the fleet was initially deployed in line ahead but the subsequent action depended on the enemy's dispositions. If there was sufficient space, the Carthaginian ships would move alongside those of the enemy and by suddenly turning, ram them amidships. If there was not enough room to operate in this manner, then the Carthaginian vessels would break through gaps in the enemy line and turn sharply about to take them in the rear. In the meantime the small craft manoeuvred round the battle area ready to help a damaged ship, or tow away captured enemy vessels.

To conclude, the Carthaginians' mastery of the sea with its emphasis on maritime trade took them not only throughout the Mediterranean but beyond the Pillars of Hercules to the Atlantic coast of Africa and Europe. They therefore possessed a strategic mobility that potentially gave them a unique advantage over any opponent, especially one attempting to challenge them beyond the confines of their own strictly limited geographical area.

The Constitution

The most striking aspect of the Carthaginian constitution was its stability. A century after the extinction of the city, Cicero was to write in his treatise on governments, 'Carthage could not have maintained her pre-eminent position for six hundred years had she not been governed with wisdom and statesmanship.' A rare tribute from a Roman when the bitter legacies of the long struggle of the Punic Wars must have still been very much to the forefront of his compatriots' minds. Professor Bosworth Smith in his book *Carthage and the Carthaginians*, suggests that although we know little about the circumstances which produced such estimable results, these results are undeniable and may in part be attributed to the nature of Carthaginian aristocracy. Although there was no parallel with the iron discipline of Spartan education which subordinated all other considerations to that of the military greatness of the state, and the patriciate of Carthage was never as hereditary as that of early Rome, the interminable constitutional struggles which racked the Roman political and social scene were relatively unknown in Carthage. Elevation to the aristocracy was by wealth, and when wealth could be relatively easily acquired by those prepared to take advantage of the commercial opportunities offered by the state, the aristocracy cannot have lacked a steady flow of enterprising families joining it as new members. Also until towards the end of Carthage's history, its discontented masses could largely be satisfied, unlike the Roman plebeians, by offering them new and fertile land along the Mediterranean coastline, where further settlements were created and the Carthaginian trading empire extended.

Thus the citizens of Carthage appeared to have been far more homogeneous in their attitudes than for example the heterogeneous population of the Greek cities in Sicily with their incessant internecine squabbles. Certainly this was so until the end of the First Punic War, when the social turmoil which followed resulted both in a crisis between Carthage and its colonial empire. There was also a new phenomenon; class antagonism within the city, engendered by growing disparities in wealth, and the apparent cessation of immigration during a period of bitter colonial unrest.

Our knowledge of the government of Carthage is derived mainly from Aristotle. Originally a monarchy, the constitution eventually developed into something akin to those of Sparta and Rome. Three different authorities, the Suffetes, Senate and the People, were united in such a way that they counterbalanced one another while at the same time providing mutual support. The Suffetes, who were the two supreme magistrates, held office only for a year. They equated to the consuls of Rome, though they have been variously referred to as kings, dictators and consuls because they combined and exercised the functions of all three. They presided over the Senate and their authority was supreme in all matters relating to the city and civil affairs. The only limitation apparently imposed upon them was that they did not hold command of the army. Perhaps this was to ensure that they did not become complete dictators rather than because they lacked military competence.

The Senate consisted of men distinguished on account of their age, birth, wealth and experience but above all, merit. They formed the Council of State and were the main outlet for public debate. It was before the Senate that complaints from the provinces were heard, ambassadors received and declarations of war determined. When the vote was unanimous, there was no appeal against the Senate's decision but when their voices were divided, the matter was referred to the people. Being jealous of their authority, however, they usually avoided this latter course. Within the Senate were sub-committees, consisting of five members, responsible for particular legislative activities. Also, a hundred of the senators formed a separate Assembly of the People, appropriately called the Hundred, designed to counter excessive aristocratic power and at the same time to suppress any rebellion against the established order. By all accounts they in fact wielded near-despotic power.

The most broadly representative body in Carthage was the People's Assembly, which was basically only consulted in case of disagreement between the Suffetes and the Senate. It is not clear how election to the Assembly was made but certainly slaves, foreigners and those below a certain level of income were excluded. Initially the people were generally content to leave the management of public affairs to the Senate, but as time went by they increasingly claimed a greater share of responsibility for themselves. Jealous perhaps of the élitism and oligarchic character of the Senate, the people eventually obtained virtual control but soon became divided among themselves into cabals and factions. This effectively precluded the exercise of positive leadership, a fundamental requirement for the prosection of any successful war.

The administration of the African territories was based on districts under officials appointed by Carthage. Though there was a degree of autonomy in domestic matters, the whole metropolitan area was subject to tribute, which extended from taxation levied on farm produce to customs duties. Similar arrangements existed in the colonial territories of Spain and Sardinia, but in Sicily the Punic cities were entirely responsible for their own internal administration, only acknowledging Carthage's authority for defence and foreign affairs. The fundamental weakness of the Carthaginian administration of its widespread and diverse colonial possessions was that, although it achieved a remarkable degree of military, commercial and fiscal coordination, it failed to provide a unified commitment to an empire possessing any shared sense of belonging and so common identity. The needs of commercial exploitation predominated over any sort of political freedom or reciprocal loyalties so that, when the authority, let alone the existence, of Carthage was threatened, the edifice of the empire crumbled and collapsed.

Polybius in his assessment of the Carthaginian constitution considers it 'originally to have been well contrived in three most important particulars: they had Kings (Suffetes), and Aristocracy and the People who were supreme in matters affecting them'. He goes on to say, however, that 'in everybody, polity or business a natural stage of growth, zenith and decay occurs'. When comparing the constitutions of Rome and Carthage, he concludes that Rome was at its zenith when the Senate was at the height of its power and that its decisions were usually sound because they were being made by the best men available. Carthage on the other hand, because its strength and prosperity had preceded that of Rome, was past its prime by the time of the Punic Wars, and the people had gained too much power. In making this assessment. Polybius, however, appears to have only considered the constitution as it affected a city state and to have overlooked the wider fact that, whereas Rome had forged a confederation of states which held together even when gravely threatened, Carthage had merely created a feudal empire with no sense of corporate loyalty.

Religion

Particular caution needs to be exercised in making any assessment of the Phoenician religion and that of the Carthaginians in particular, not only because the available evidence is far from complete, but because much of even what is available is dependent upon indirect sources and archaeological interpretations. As Sergio Ribichini says when writing in *The Phoenicians*:

The enthusiasm of archaeologists embarking on successful missions and excavations in Cyprus, Phoenicia and the whole of North Africa, was counter-balanced by the scepticism of scholars who regarded with suspicion the variety of documentation available, which offered a picture of Phoenician religion that was full of contradictions and gaps.

As he goes on to explain, the Phoenician religion was polytheistic in nature, characterised by the worship of a number of deities who controlled the totality of man's and society's needs and interests. In this respect there was nothing dissimilar from the basic religious beliefs of several other civilisations, with their pantheons of major and minor superhuman beings who had to be propitiated and placated in accordance with established rites. What was different, however, was the way in which the political independence of the city states along the Phoenician coastline enabled them to develop a diversity of religious interpretations. Each city organised its own form of worship, creating individual traditions and assigning prominence to a range of elected deities of their own choosing.

In Tyre, Melgarth was the principle deity. His name meant 'King of the City', he was originally regarded as the founder and lord of Tyre, but later he became its protector. Alongside Melgarth ruled the female deity Astarte, who had a somewhat diverse background. In Tyre she was associated with the stars but elsewhere she was variously held to be a warrior deity and connected with Aphrodite; the latter association possibly arising from the temple prostitution involved in her worship, a ritual that temple slaves and other women fulfilled on payment, particularly for foreign visitors.

Thus Carthage, while initially preserving the cults of her mother city Tyre, from the 5th century BC began to adopt an increasingly independent theology and liturgy – a development which may have been given an additional impetus by the 480 BC Greek defeat of the Carthaginians at Himera in Sicily. In the ensuing political upheaval, political relations with Tyre were broken off and this act of independence was apparently reflected in the city's religious observances. The worship of Melgarth and Astarte was replaced by that of Baal Hammon and another female deity, Tanit. This new divine couple were not unknown in Phoenicia but it was not until they had been adopted and elevated in the Carthaginian pantheon that they obtained a position of pre-eminence. Thereafter, as Carthage rose in importance and power to create her own empire, so Baal Hammon and Tanit came to figure more prominently throughout the Western Mediterranean.

THE BACKGROUND

The origins of Baal (Lord) Hammon are obscure and those of Tanit's were relatively insignificant, although like Astarte, she was connected with the stars. But with the precedence accorded to Baal Hammon, Carthaginian religion took a sinister turn since the god was associated with human sacrifice. That human sacrifice was practised among Mediterranean civilisations other than the Phoenicians is borne out by the Biblical prophet Jeremiah, who tells how the children of Judah did evil in that they built tophets 'to burn their sons and daughters in the fire', a custom which was continued among the Canaanites, from whom it was adopted by the Israelites.

How prevalent the sacrifice of children was is not known for certain, but Diodorus describes what occurred in Carthage during Agathocles', tyrant of Syracuse, advance on the city.

In former times they offered to the God the sons of the most eminent persons; but of later times they secretly bought and bred children for this purpose; and upon strict search being made, there were found amongst those to be sacrificed some children that had been changed and put in the place of others. Weighing these things in their minds and now seeing that the enemy lay before their walls, they were seized with such a pang of superstition, as if they had utterly forsaken the religion of their fathers. That they might then, without delay, reform what was amiss, they offered as a public sacrifice two hundred of the sons of the nobility; and no fewer than three hundred more, who were liable to censure, voluntarily offered themselves up. For amongst the Carthaginians there was a brazen statue putting forth the palms of its hands bending in such a manner towards the earth, so that the boy to be sacrificed who was laid upon them would roll off and fall into a deep fiery furnace.

Writing in the early 19th century the French historian, M. Rollin, more emotionally describes how

the cries of the unhappy victims were drowned by the uninterrupted noise of drums and trumpets. Mothers made it a merit, and a part of their religion, to view this barbarous spectacle with dry eyes, and without so much as a groan; and if a tear or a sigh stole from them, the sacrifice was less acceptable to the deity and all the effects of it were entirely lost.

That the sacrifice of children by fire seems to have been widespread and on a substantial scale is confirmed by archaeological excavations. Tophets, the sacred place where the cremated remains of sacrificed children were interred in urns, have been found near all the major Carthaginian settlements throughout the Western Mediterranean. Though the practice was continued by a decreasing number of fanatics until all traces of the Carthaginian empire had been obliterated, from the 4th century BC onwards there was a gradual Hellenisation of the Carthaginian religion. In 396 BC the gentler cult of Demeter and Kore was introduced into the city by the land-owning aristocracy. Though this move by the wealthy upper class initially only affected a small proportion of the population, it heralded what has been described as a reformation, a significant religious break with the past. During the 3rd century BC the sacrifice of children was increasingly replaced by that of animals: these were offered to Tanit, rather than Baal Hammon, and as a personal thanksgiving instead of a propitiatory dedication. The benefits bestowed by Tanit, as the source of life, extended beyond this world into an eternity after death.

That the religious practices of the Carthaginians were factors of any significance in determining their conduct on the battlefield, or the attitudes of their enemies, seems unlikely. Though Diodorus gives an account of how on one occasion the Carthaginians sacrificed their prisoners in a religious ceremony, such cruelty was widely practised, so that such an incident cannot be considered to have had any particular influence on the relationship between the two opponents.

The People

Historical assessments of the Carthaginian character come from Roman sources, and so can appear to be prejudiced. Polybius refers to the superior Roman customs and principles over money matters, whereby wealth obtained from unlawful transactions was widely disapproved of and bribery was punished by death. The Carthaginians, on the other hand, obtained office by open bribery and nothing was thought disgraceful which resulted in a profit. Cicero identifies the Carthaginians' most distinguishing characteristics as being craft, skill, industry and cunning. All of which in moderation can reasonably be associated with people who made their living through trade. It is alleged, however, that the Carthaginians combined craft and cunning to an inordinate degree. 'Punic honour' and 'a Carthaginian mind' were derogatory terms in Roman times. Rollin in his *History of the Carthaginians* is equally partisan and as an example of their perfidy, quotes a truce granted by Scipio Africanus which had been earnestly entreated by the Carthaginians, during which some Roman ships, driven by a storm on to the coast of Carthage, were pillaged. He maintains that the Carthaginians had something 'austere and savage in their disposition and genius, a haughty and imperious air, a sort of ferocity which was deaf to either reason or remonstrances and plunged brutally into excesses of violence'.

Michelet, the French 19th century historian of the Roman Republic, paints an equally unfavourable picture when he writes:

Carthage represented its metropolis but on an enormous scale. Situated in the centre of the Mediterranean, commanding the coast of the West, oppressing her sister Utica, and all the Phoenician Colonies of Africa, she mingled conquest with commerce everywhere establishing herself at the sword's point, founding factories in spite of the natives, imposing duties and taxes upon them, forcing them at one time to buy, and at another to sell.

The trouble with this description is that, to some extent, it could be applied to almost any country during a period of colonial expansion, be it Spain or England, or even his own beloved France.

Yet Herodotus tells us, admittedly with the Carthaginians themselves as his source, how they traded with a race who lived in Libya beyond the Pillars of Hercules.

On reaching this country, they unloaded their goods, arranged them tidily along the beach and after returning to their boats raised smoke. Seeing the smoke the natives then came down to the beach, placed a certain amount of gold on the ground in exchange for the goods and then withdrew. The Carthaginians then came ashore and if they thought the gold represented a fair price, they collected it and took it and went away; if on the other hand they thought it too little, they would go back on board and wait. The natives would then come and add to the gold until they were satisfied. There was perfect honesty on both sides; the Carthaginians never touched the gold until it equalled in value what they had offered for sale, and the natives never touched the goods until the gold had been taken away.

Whatever one may think about this story, Herodotus himself, who lived in the 5th century BC and travelled as far west as Sicily and Italy, must certainly have known some Carthaginians – and even if his acquaintances were too few to justify a wider assessment of them, he would surely have known about their reputation from the others. It therefore seems improbable that he would have related such an incident without comment, had the Carthaginians really been as perfidious as some later writers have suggested. Rollin's condemnation of them in particular may have reflected his devoutly Christian abhorrence of their religious barbarities, rather than his measured assessment of their character.

It would seem reasonable to conclude that the Carthaginians were like all mortals, neither wholly good nor wholly bad. They were traders who lived by profit in a time when their political institution was in decline and their earlier religious fanaticism a cause for general loathing. Their personal and collective conduct would then probably have appeared corrupt to the Romans who, at the particular period we are considering, were in an earlier, more austere and virtuous but no less crude stage of their evolutionary development.

CHAPTER TWO

ROME

The Founding

The development of Rome into the dominating power throughout the Italian peninsula can be considered as having occurred during three broad periods. The first lasted from the traditional date of the city's founding in about 750 BC, until its absorption by the Etruscans about 100 years later; the period of Etruscan colonisation lasted some 250 years, until about 400 BC; then, after its brief occupation by the Gauls in 386 BC, Rome's own expansion gradually began, so forming the third and final period of growth, which was completed in 270 BC with the surrender of Rhegium (Reggio).

An Indo-European people, among whom were the Latins, Sabines and Samanites, crossed over the Alps between 1200 and 1000 BC to establish themselves south of the river Tiber in Latium and Campania, some of the Latins building pastoral settlements on the Palatine Hills adjacent to crossing places over the Tiber. During this period other migrants came by sea from Asia Minor and occupied land to the north which became known as Etruria (Tuscany) between the rivers Arno and Tiber, to the east of which rose the Apennines like a great dorsal fin. It is not known when the Etruscans first started to contest the Tiber crossing places, but as they infiltrated south to the fertile district of Campania the Latin villages on the Palatine Hills gradually merged to form the city of Rome under Etruscan suzerainty. The actual date for the founding of the city is unknown, though there is no shortage of patriotic myths and legends to choose from. Archaeological excavations, however, suggest that by the early 7th century BC the hill communities had begun to merge, becoming a city. At a slightly later date the low-lying area, which was to become known as the Forum, was drained, enabling the city's expansion steadily to increase.

By the end of the 6th century BC the Etruscans had founded a number of cities in Campania, including Pompeii and Salerno, but had failed to capture the Greek city of Cumae, which marked the limit for their southern expansion. Some twelve years after this defeat, while the Etruscans were heavily engaged with the Gauls on their northern frontier, the Greeks took the offensive and drove them out of Campania. This was a signal for a general uprising by the Latins, during which Rome rid itself of its kings and became a republic. The city was then briefly freed from Etruscan domination, but in spite of the myth of Horatus' heroic defence, it was retaken under the leadership of Lars Porsena. The Etruscan period is difficult to unravel with its endless succession of wars and fluctuating fortunes, but its influence on Rome was profound and enduring. Rome remained virtually an Etruscan city, not only by right of occupation but in every important sphere of human activity, political, religious, cultural or economic, until the Gauls swept over the Alps in 386 BC to defeat a disorganised Roman army and seize the city.

At this time there was another important development, which was to be of political significance during the First Punic War some 200 years later. The ruling family of the Fabii gained a position of dominating influence in the Roman Republic and, being temperamentally northerners, with some 300 members of the clan being killed defending the northern frontiers, they continued to favour Rome's northern interests and never encouraged the southern expansion which eventually brought Rome into conflict with Carthage.

After the Gallic invasion Rome was rebuilt and its defences strengthened by the construction of an encircling wall. From this secure base a Roman territorial expansion began which led to a series of conflicts; and some of them involved closely-related Latin tribes such as the Sabines and the Samanites, but others were against the Etruscans and the Gauls, and finally the Greek cities of Magna Graecia in southern Italy. As the Romans spread southwards they inevitably found themselves having to contend with a series of Gallic invasions from the north, which they countered by annexing Sabine territory and settling colonies on the Adriatic coast as well as at strategic points inland. Roman supremacy was finally assured following the battle of Sentinum in 295 BC when a coalition of Samanites, Etruscans and Gauls was defeated, thus ending any attempt by Rome's enemies from the north and the south to confront her in combination. The Samanites' opposition continued, however, until they were finally subdued five years later, which was an important victory since it brought about their incorporation into the Roman Confederacy.

Rome now controlled all central Italy and the great consular roads started spanning the country, so facilitating Rome's rapid domination of the entire peninsula. The composition of the resulting Confederation was, however, very varied. There were the twenty-eight Latin colonies forming the hard core, settled at strategic points and given arable land around a readily defensible site, but the remainder of the Confederation consisted of cities and tribes only loosely allied to Rome by a diversity of treaties, a diversity which reflected the sometimes tenuous circumstance under which the allies had joined; some had done so voluntarily, others had been constrained to do so by force of circumstances, and yet others as a consequence of divided loyalties within them. It is important to note the apparent fragility of the Roman Confederation, since it was to be a factor of fundamental significance when Hannibal came to determine strategic objectives for his campaign in Italy.

But now, as Rome extended her hegemony, the Greek cities began to regard her with growing apprehension. One of these cities, Tarentum (Taranto), became involved in a disagreement between Rome and Etruria, which led to them sinking four Roman ships after they had crossed an established navigational limit into the bay of Tarentum. Rejecting the Romans' demands for compensation, the Tarentines sent a request for help to Pyrrhus, King of Epirus, a kinsman of Alexander the Great and an able tactician but perhaps not such an accomplished strategist, who quickly responded and crossed the Adriatic, together with his elephants. After the Romans had refused to accept him as a mediator between themselves and the Greeks in Italy, Pyrrhus brought them to a battle on the plains near Heraclea in 280 BC. In a hard fought contest the Romans were defeated, so encouraging the Lucanians and the Samanites, together with a number of Greek cities, to join Pyrrhus. He then advanced within forty miles of Rome itself, but, after having had his proposals for a treaty of peace and friendship rejected, he withdrew to Asculum. There he won another costly battle; this prompted him to exclaim, 'another such victory and we are undone', thus giving rise to the immortal expression, a *Pyrrhic victory*.

Ambassadors then reached him from Sicily, offering to put Agrigentum and Syracuse in his hands if he would drive out the Carthaginians. Nothing loath for adventure and tempted by the prospect of being able to extend the campaign to Africa, Pyrrhus crossed to Sicily in 278 BC and was soon in possession of most of the island. But his high-handedness and his excessive demands for ships and crews to transport his army over to Africa eventually alienated the

Sicilians to such an extent that he was glad to abandon the island in answer to another request. In his absence the Romans had taken the opportunity to revenge themselves on the Samanites and Tarentines: being hard pressed, these peoples had urgently addressed themselves to Pyrrhus. Now, as he set sail for Italy, he looked back on the receding Sicilian coastline and made the prophetic observation: 'What a field we are leaving to the Carthaginians and the Romans to exercise their arms.'

After losing a number of his ships to attacks during the crossing, Pyrrhus at length gained the Italian shore where he was able to brush aside the light resistance he encountered. But after a difficult night march which caused a considerable amount of disorganisation, he found himself faced by a Roman army intent on battle. Since their last encounter with Pyrrhus, the Romans had devised tactics for dealing with his elephants. Confronted by a new combination of javelins and flaming torches, the startled animals turned and tore through their own ranks. This unexpected blow brought about the disintegration of the already hard-pressed Carthaginian army. Deserted by the Samanites, who had been virtually crushed during his absence in Sicily, in 275 BC Pyrrhus returned to Epirus, abandoning the Greek cities which over the next five years capitulated separately to Rome. Following the final surrender of Rhegium in 270 BC, the experiment within Magna Graecia of the political state in miniature ended; too diverse and divided to cooperate effectively and too small to survive singly, the cities became victims of their own strife-torn independence. Their disappearance left the Romans in possession of the whole of Italy, but with only the Straits of Messana to separate them from the Carthaginians. This was not to prove an adequate barrier.

The Army

All Roman citizens were liable for selection into the army except, according to Polybius, those whose wealth rated below 400 asses (about £32 today) and so, curiously, were only employable in the navy – except in times of emergency when standards were lowered and they could be recruited into the army. From about the middle of the 6th century BC following the introduction of body armour, the infantry had been selected from the wealthier classes who alone could afford to pay for this and other accoutrements. What had started as an economic necessity appears to have become a social distinction by the 3rd century BC. Four hundred asses represented a fairly substantial sum when related to the pay soldiers received which, again according to Polybius was $5\frac{1}{3}$ asses (about 45p) a day for an infantry soldier while a centurion received $10\frac{2}{3}$ (about 90p). Both of them, moreover, had to pay for their food and clothes from these amounts, as well as any additional arms they might require.

Under normal conditions, all males between the ages of eighteen and forty-six who satisfied the property criteria were eligible for military service and were recruited into either the cavalry or the infantry. The infantry, who were by far the more important arm and comprised the main element of the principal fighting formation, the legion, were expected to serve for twenty years, while selection for the cavalry was even more heavily dependent upon wealth, but only carried a commitment for only two years. Each legion consisted of 4200 infantry, except in times of special danger when the number was increased to 5000, and 300 cavalry, divided into ten squadrons, the selection process ensuring that the quality of all those enrolled was evenly spread. Military service was regarded as a mark of honour without which public recognition and advancement were virtually impossible, especially since it was only after ten years' duty that a man could hold public office.

The legion consisted of ten cohorts and had been developed from the Greek phalanx into a more flexible formation, better able to manoeuvre over broken ground and face the highly mobile Gauls. It was organised into three *maniples* comprising soldiers of different ages. Forming the first rank was the *hastati*, 120 young men in twelve well-spaced files each ten men deep; behind the *hastati* at a distance equivalent to the frontage of the *maniple*, came the *principes* of 120 slightly older men, again organised into twelve files of ten men deep, so disposed that they faced the gaps between the files of the leading *maniple* to form a chequerboard pattern. In this way the *maniples* could either advance or withdraw to create a solid line without any complicated manoeuvring. When adopting this more compact order, a legionary standing to arms occupied three feet and unlike the Greek in the phalanx, three further feet separated him from the men on either side, thus enabling him to use his sword freely and change the position of his shield. The third *maniple* of sixty older men, usually veterans, was called the *triarii*. They were also deployed to cover the gaps between the files of the *maniple* in front of them, but were in six files each ten men deep. In addition, each cohort had a squadron of cavalry and 120 *velites*, or light infantry used as skirmishers, who could fall back when pressed through the intervals between the files of the leading *maniple*. The light infantry were also used to provide flank protection or form a rearguard.

The *hastati* in the leading *maniple* were equipped with a short cutting and thrusting sword, together with two javelins to be thrown on approaching the enemy. The shields they carried were some four feet long and two and a half feet wide, bound with iron at the upper edge to withstand a sword blow and at the bottom to enable it to be rested on the ground without damage. The legionaries wore body armour and a helmet, but though the *principes* and the *triari* were similarly protected, they carried a spear instead of the two javelins. The light infantry, the *velites*, were armed with a spear for thrusting or throwing, a sword and round shield three feet in diameter. Not much attention was paid to the cavalry, in spite of their aristocratic associations. There was only one thirty-strong squadron in each cohort, poorly armed and wearing no body armour. The Romans never considered their cavalry much more than an adjunct to the main infantry force. As far back as 496 BC, when they defeated the Sabines at Lake Regillus, Livy recounts how the cavalry dismounted to join the infantry slogging match when this reached a critical stage, and only remounted when it was time for the pursuit.

Command was exercised at the different levels by centurions, tribunes and consuls. The centurions were long-service professional officers equating to company commanders, two of whom were selected by merit to command each *maniple*, which was divided into two *centuries*, the commander of the right-hand one being the senior. According to Polybius, the reason for having two centurions was to provide a degree of insurance against the *maniple* being leaderless in the event of battle casualties. The cohorts were commanded by tribunes who had either been promoted from among the centurions, in which case they would have been thoroughly professional officers, or were magistrates, who had been posted to the army to serve for a few years before returning to another civilian appointment. A legion, which in modern terms could be compared with a division, was commanded by a legate, another temporary civilian appointment, but of senatorial rank. An army was formed by combining two legions and was commanded by a consul appointed by the Senate, though sometimes two were nominated. One of the legions was invariably Roman but the other was generally recruited from one of the allied cities forming the Roman federation. Each commander was accompanied by two specially selected standard bearers and the standards themselves served a dual purpose; first, they showed where the commander was and so acted as a rallying point and second, they were used to signal orders, such as a change of formation or direction. The standards then came to symbolise the honour of the *maniple*, cohort or legion. Since their loss was a disgrace, some of the severest fighting was centred upon them. To have been selected as a standard bearer was viewed as a distinction, however brief its duration.

It seems fairly certain that the legion must have been too unwieldy to permit it to manoeuvre as a formation and that tactical flexibility was therefore restricted to the legion's components. Though to have attempted anything overcomplicated would have resulted in chaos, the Romans clearly introduced a considerable degree of delegated authority, as is borne out by what occurred at the battle of Cynoscephalae, during the Macedonian War in 197 BC. Polybius recounts how a tribune saw that a Macedonian phalanx had advanced far ahead of the rest of the army and was pressing the Roman left flank backwards. On his own initiative, the tribune detached his cohort and made a circuit to fall upon the Macedonians in their rear and so rout them.

A further example of tactical flexibility occurred at the battle of the Great Plains in Africa in 203 BC. On this occasion Scipio Africanus, refining the tactics developed by Hannibal, and after introducing his own tactical and organisational innovations, deployed the army in the usual manner with the *hastati* in the front rank, followed by the *principes* and the *triarii*. After the two wings of the Carthaginians had been broken, the *principes* and *triarii* wheeled round and enveloped the Carthaginian centre on both flanks, using the space equivalent to their frontage which separated them from the preceding rank.

Tactical flexibility could also be achieved by the *maniples* advancing or withdrawing to fill the chequerboard gaps that had been left, or they could be used to reinforce fallen ranks. All this manoeuvring was conducted as well-rehearsed drills carried out on the orders of the tribunes and centurions; the legates do not appear to have exercised tactical command, if only because the legions were too big to handle in this overall manner. This slow progression towards improving tactical flexibility was disastrously discarded at the battle of Cannae in 216 BC when, as will be seen, the Romans for some reason reverted to massing as in a phalanx.

Once he had made his dispositions and given his orders, the consul commanding an army usually seems to have taken up a position from where he could observe the battle and influence it by his personal intervention, or through the commitment of his reserves. Scipio Africanus at the battle of Zama in 202 BC remained mounted on horseback so that he could get around the battlefield, and Scipio Aemilianus in 146 BC is described as touring the battlefield conspicuously clad in a red toga with only three shield bearers. Admittedly Plutarch, when commenting on the life of Fabius Maximus who lived in the 3rd century BC, tells us how the Senate refused to provide him with a horse, presumably because he was expected to lead his men into battle on foot, but the evidence points strongly to the commander of a consular army remaining detached from the battle, until the critical moment when his personal intervention could produce a decisive result, or when he was required to rally a faltering part of the line. Much, of course, would depend on the calibre of the consul himself, and they varied greatly. Many of them were inexperienced and devoid of professional knowledge – but even so, as long as they did not do anything particularly foolish they could probably rely on the competence of their centurions to see them through. But the chief weakness of the Roman system arose from the custom of appointing two consuls to exercise command on alternate days; often with predictable consequences. The Romans, however, were nothing if not pragmatic and the right to command in this manner does not seem to have always been exercised. Certainly in the First Punic War the consuls either undertook separate duties or accepted that one of them should play a more prominent role in the common task.

Discipline was strict and unforgiving, with those offences which endangered the lives of others usually resulting in death. After being found guilty by a court martial, the culprit was made to run the gauntlet through a hail of stones and cudgel blows delivered by his erstwhile comrades. Few survived such an experience, but those who did lived as outcasts, banned from their own country and homes. Lesser crimes were punished by flogging, seizure of personal goods or fines. When a large number of men were involved in an offence, for example if an entire *maniple* had deserted its battle position, then a different procedure was adopted. The tribune assembled the legion, called the defaulters to the front and after rebuking them, selected about a tenth of them by lot to run the gauntlet; the remainder were then fed on a diet of barley rather than wheat and made to take up quarters outside the protection of the camp. The Roman soldier therefore usually found the prospect of the certain punishment he would receive for cowardice more fearful than the possibility of death on the battlefield. Bravery and victory on the other hand brought rewards, a triumph for the consul, spoil and public esteem for those who had shared in his achievements. The Romans do not appear to have been any braver than their opponents; if they showed greater courage over a longer period, it was because of their training and their social conditioning.

The Constitution

In the early 6th century BC the kings were displaced by consuls, two of whom exercised power together for a year and were then replaced by a further two. At first, the people themselves had no say in public affairs, but this eventually led to such resentment that two tribunes were appointed specifically to represent them. This period came to be known as the Succession of the Plebeians and, in turn, led to conflict between them and the Patricians, the hereditary aristocracy.

Following a long period of political, economic and military upheaval, a more stable and durable constitution evolved; described by Herodotus as having three elements, consuls, senators and people, each element possessed sovereign powers which were regulated with such scrupulous regard for equality and equilibrium that no one could say for certain whether the constitution was democratic, despotic or aristocratic: the consuls could be regarded as despotic, the senators as aristocratic and the people as democratic.

The consuls were despotic in that they had complete control of the administration, received foreign ambassadors, summoned the people to meetings when any matter of state required their authorisation, raised levies on Rome's allies, appointed the military tribunes and had the authority to spend public money as they chose. They also, as has been related, commanded the legions when the army took to the field. On the other hand, the consuls' authority was undeniably restricted. First, since they were elected only for a year, the account of their stewardship which would be demanded from them on leaving office stood close at hand. Second, being a pair they were subject to one another's vetoes, which no doubt both curbed some of their more wayward ideas, and also gravely impeded the taking of timely decisions. But, when considering the full range of a consul's responsibilities outside the military field, a shared social background among those appointed and a training common to their class generally ensured a consensus of opinion and a consistency of policy.

The Senate, which numbered about 300, came to be largely hereditary and aristocratic. Because it held the right to exercise authority in many public areas, without paying attention to the views of the people, it was also to some extent despotic. The hereditary nature of the Senate inevitably led also to the perpetuation of factional party interests, represented by three influential family clans, the Aemilii, Claudii and Fabii, whose fluctuating fortunes powerfully influenced Roman policy and strategic thinking.

The Senate controlled all state expenditure except that which the consuls elected to disburse, and investigated such major crimes as treason, murder and conspiracy, all of which when committed in Italy required public investigation. The Senate also settled disputes between Rome's allies, reconciled warring communities and prepared the replies to be given to foreign ambassadors who presented demands or petitions.

The part left for the people looked small but in fact they had a number of important functions. Besides exercising their powers through a number of assemblies, they were also the sole authority for deciding honours, ratifying or refusing peace treaties, passing sentences of death, and imposing major fines. Honour and punishment were then in the hands of the people and, in the view of

Herodotus, it is these two things and these alone that hold human society together. He then goes on to give an example as to how the three elements interacted. A consul possessed full power when leading an expedition but remained dependent on the Senate for the provision of supplies; furthermore, at the end of his year in office, it was the Senate who decided whether he should continue in command or be replaced. As for the people, it was before them that a consul had to give an account of his administration when giving up his office.

Cicero, writing shortly before his death in 43 BC and looking back at the period which covered the Punic Wars, had this to say about the Roman form of government:

I cannot but observe this much, that so long as our empire supported itself, not by the methods of injustice and violence, but rather by actions of kindness and gentleness, wars were undertaken to protect its allies, or defend its honour; and accordingly their issues were attended with mercy, or at least no more rigour than was absolutely necessary. The Senate then was a kind of port and refuge for princes and nations to have recourse to in their need; and our officers and commanders made it their greatest glory to defend their provinces, and assist their allies, with justice and fidelity. The city, therefore, was not then the empress so properly as the protectress of all the world. This conduct and method of managing the state began little by little to wear off, but utterly vanished immediately after the victory of Sylla, for people began to think nothing would be unjust to their confederates and allies, when once they had seen so great cruelties exercised even on their very fellow citizens.

However idealistic Cicero's interpretation of Rome's earlier days may have been, he obviously considered them to have been part of an era when high standards of virtue were expected and practised. The dramatic change to which Cicero refers as occurring after Sylla's victory, may require some explanation. Sulla (Sylla) lived between 138 and 78 BC and was a competent but unscrupulously ruthless general who, according to Plutarch, was totally immoral in both his private and public life. After many years' campaigning in Asia he seized power in Rome, unmercifully butchered his opponents and ruled as a tyrannical dictator until, somewhat uncharacteristically, he went into voluntary retirement. He then died from putrescence of the flesh, brought about by his gregarious sexual appetites.

The position of the states allied to Rome by treaties was this: after they had been defeated in battle, Rome treated them with liberal generosity. They were allowed to retain their independence, except in their foreign policy, and they paid no tribute. Their land was seldom encroached upon after the 4th century BC, except for the establishment of Roman garrisons at strategic points, and they were free to maintain their own political parties. They were expected, however, to provide troops and these would be organised on Roman lines and grouped alongside a Roman legion to form a consular army. When they were called upon to provide troops in excess of their treaty obligations, they received special payment from Rome. Additionally, allied soldiers did not have to pay for their food and weapons, and in this way Rome was able to field a substantially greater number of men than her otherwise limited manpower would have allowed.

Religion

As the Romans extended their conquests, so they absorbed the religion and culture of the races they had subjected and in the process, modified their own earlier animistic worship. It was the influence of the Greek cities in southern Italy and Sicily which made the greatest impact. By the 3rd century BC the Greek gods and goddesses had been assimilated by the Romans to overlay and largely replace the Etruscan, Samanite and Latium deities. Greek names were Romanised; Demeter became Ceres; Poseidon and Ares, Neptune and Mars; Zeus and Hera, Jupiter and Juno; Aphrodite and Hestia, Venus and Vesta, though this retitling did not change their fickle natures. The influence of mystic Greek cults received a particular impulse during the closing stages of the Second Punic, or as the Romans called it, Hannibalic War. Returning soldiers from southern Italy, especially those who had spent long years in garrison duties or as prisoners of war, together with the freed slaves, had been strongly influenced by the cults of Dionysius and Proserpine. The devotees were organised into secret societies, largely formed in Rome and on the great growing plantations of Campania and Etruscany, as well as the new ranches of Apulia. Secret societies being prohibited by law, they and the orgies associated with the Bacchic cults were vigorously oppressed when the scale of their activities became known.

There was no established church as we know it, with its own hierarchy, creed and moral code. Nor was there a truly single all-powerful god, but rather a multiplicity of deities interfering with and squabbling over their different interests and mortal protégés. To the majority of Romans the mythology which we regard as no more than a collection of diverting fables was, in varying degrees, a portrayal of immortals to whom established rights were due and who had to be propitiated. The correct fulfilment of these obligations would ensure victory in battle by Mars or the safe return of mariners by Neptune, while Ceres would provide an abundant harvest and Jupiter rain. Neglect on the other hand would lead to abandonment, if not the purposeful infliction of disaster. Though there were a few hardy souls like the consul Publius Claudius Pulcher who, before the battle of Drepana off Sicily, lost patience when the sacred chickens would not provide a favourable omen by eating, and flung the cosseted birds overboard with the short-tempered advice, 'If you won't eat, then drink instead.' For most Romans, however, their relationship with the gods was strong and personal. In many ways it resembled a legal contract, far removed from spiritual or moral judgements involving pangs of tortured conscience, or holding out prospects of paradisical rewards. Rather it was a case of reciprocal responsibility; homage having been paid, a favourable divination amounting to an assurance of assistance could reasonably be anticipated.

In view of the diversity of the traditional rights due to the gods and the complexity of the ceremonies, however, it must have been conveniently easy for the religious authorities to account for the gods' failure to fulfil their side of the bargain; attribution could be made to either the inadequacy of the sacrificial offerings, or the neglect of some ritualistic punctilio. The details of the ceremonial procedures were meticulously prescribed; every movement at the altar, every phrase of respectful subservience and propitiation, and even the modes of dress were all of supreme importance demanding unswerving observance which, if neglected, invalidated the whole ceremony. Plutarch tells us how two priests of the noblest families were deprived of office; one because he failed to observe the proper procedures in presenting the entrails of a sacrificial victim, the other because his peaked cap fell off during such a ceremony. Furthermore Minucius the dictator, together with his master-of-horse whom he was initiating, were immediately deprived of their positions by the people when a shrew mouse was suddenly heard to interrupt the proceedings. Plutarch adds, perhaps somewhat illogically, that 'Although they were so scrupulous in observing these minute details, they (the people) did not indulge in any kind of superstition, because they never permitted any change or departure from their ancient rites.'

As there was no church, responsibility for the form and observance of these official religious ceremonies was a function of the state, the chief officials being the College of Pontiffs, under its head the Pontifex Maximus, who were the judges and arbiters of divine and human affairs, the interpreters of portents, augurs and omens. This role was of great significance since the gods could only make their wishes known through coded messages. Divination, however, was not confined to officials alone: so long as he could afford to do so, no citizen entered into an undertaking of any importance without having offered a sacrifice and read the signs in the victim's entrails for himself.

An indication of the reverent respect in which Auguries were held is given by Plutarch in his life of Marcellus (271–208 BC), when writing about an incident which occurred during the recrudescence of the Gallic Wars following the First Punic War in 241 BC. Two consuls,

Gaius Flaminius and Furius, had led an army against the Insubres but just as they set out, a river was seen to be running with blood and a report was received that three moons had appeared simultaneously. Additionally the Augurs, whose duty it was to observe the flight of birds during consular elections, insisted that the omens had been inauspicious when the victorious candidates' names had been announced. The Senate immediately despatched letters ordering the consuls to return and expressly forbidding them from starting the campaign. Flaminius, however, refused to open the letters until he had defeated the Insubres. When he returned to Rome laden with booty, the people would not go out to meet him, and because he had not complied with the order recalling him at first they even considered denying him a triumph. Though they eventually relented, as soon as the celebrations were completed both he and Furius were made to renounce their consulship. As Plutarch commented:

Such were the scruples of the Romans in referring all their affairs to the Will of the Gods, nor would they tolerate the smallest oversight in the observation of omens and traditional rites, even if the omission were followed by the most brilliant success. In short they regarded as more important for the safety of the state that their magistrates should honour religious observances than that they should defeat their enemies.

As an example of this belief Plutarch relates the case of Tiberius Sempronius Longus who, having announced the names of two newly appointed consuls, discovered that whenever a consul had hired a house outside the city to take the Auspices from the flight of birds, but had to return before any sure signs appeared, proper religious observances demanded that he give up the original house and begin his observations afresh in a new one. Being unaware of this requirement, Sempronius Longus had twice used the same house before proclaiming the new consuls, and when he later reported his misdemeanour to the Senate it was decided that such negligence could not be lightly overlooked. The two consuls were at once recalled from the posts they had already taken up and obliged to resign their appointments.

Apart from the more formal observance of religious ceremonies, there was also a less specific side to the Romans' belief in the influence of their deities; a wider consciousness of supernatural power that determined their actions in everyday life. This spiritual element could be called mere superstition but however categorised, it permeated most citizens' lives and significantly influenced their decisions. A passing bird, an ill-omened action or expression, or the counselling spirit of a departed ancestor were all sufficient causes for postponing a voyage, or delaying an undertaking. Again, it was not only the public officials who were capable of divination, every individual citizen might give his own interpretation of events as they affected him personally.

Since beliefs varied considerably, however, religion and its role in determining the course of men's lives was as varied as it is now. Even so, after allowing for this individual disparity of conviction, which must have been reflected in the consciousness of social and military groups, there can still be little doubt that religion influenced military decisions. As will be seen major ventures could frequently not be undertaken without favourable portents, thus causing delay and hesitancy. Among the soldiers, too, individual interpretations inevitably had some bearing on the way they faced an impending battle. A favourable omen could raise morale but an unfavourable one could equally be the cause of uncertainty.

The People

The generally accepted view of the Romans at the outbreak of the Punic Wars is that they were still largely a rural society, the attitudes and conduct of which reflected their way of life. They had not yet been greatly affected by the spoils of conquest or the sight of the unprecedented and unimagined luxury which they had found in the vanquished Greek cities. Nor had their intellectual horizons been widened by close contact with others possessing more questioning minds and more sophisticated beliefs. The loosening of their strict, simplistic code of behaviour had hardly begun. Cicero commended the age when he wrote,

There is nothing in which our ancestors took greater care than that the obligation of an oath should always be held as most sacred and invaluable. This appears plainly from the Twelve Tables, [the oldest code of Roman laws, engraved on twelve copper tables dating from the 5th century BC] it appears from those laws which are called sacred; it appears from the strict observation of leagues, by which we are obliged to keep faith even with the enemies, and lastly it appears from the punishments and the penalties which have been inflicted by the Censors, who in no one thing have been more severe, than in punishing those who have transgressed their oaths.

This adherence to an oath can be traced back to the 5th century BC, when the Romans defeated the Sabines and adopted one of their gods who was responsible for watching over oaths and good faith (*fides*) between nations. But following the social and moral pressures of the First Punic War, the sanctity of good faith began to be broken, or came at least to be regarded as being inapplicable to non-Italians. As an example, total disregard was shown for the peace treaty which had been drawn up with Carthage when Sardinia and Corsica were forcibly annexed.

Polybius believed that the reason behind Rome's seeming invincibility was that her traditions and standards were superior to those of other people. Austerity, discipline and faithfulness in honouring her undertakings, together with the strict honesty of her citizens, put her in a class of her own. The severe training which moulded the Roman character began at infancy. The Roman paterfamilias ruled his family as an autocrat, instilling obedience, loyalty and integrity with a severity that can only have been surpassed by the institutionalised training of Spartan youth under state direction. A school education was not universal and very limited in scope, so much instruction was given at home by the parents.

The result of this upbringing, upheld and fortified by the rigorous demands of public opinion, was that the Romans displayed high moral standards and set themselves an ideal of virtue based on willpower, self-restraint, a seriousness devoid of frivolity, perseverance, and a binding sense of duty to the family, social group or military unit; all established within the hierarchy of state authority. The importance of the individual was subordinated to his corporate responsibilities, and a willingness to sacrifice his own interests of his life for the good of his group was accepted as the normal standard of personal conduct.

There is one important aspect of Roman life which, because it is virtually unknown today, is easily overlooked. This was the system of patronage, which constituted a vital link in the social fabric binding the poorer classes to powerful patrons in a reciprocal bond of loyalty. As an institution the system was known as *clientela*; the clients were free men who put themselves under the patronage of a leading figure, doing all that they could to advance their patrons' political ambitions, general wellbeing and particular interests. In return the patron looked after his client, a care which extended into all aspects of his life including the provision of financial and legal support, together with protection against other powerful groups threatening his freedom of livelihood. Such an arrangement cut through the constitutional divisions of Roman society and formed power groups within the political system, not unlike today's trade union block vote for certain politicians, even if on a much smaller scale.

Though as a free man a client could change his patron, *clientela* was fundamentally a hereditary system binding its participants with the all-pervasive moral force of *fides* which, in spite of not being legally enforceable, was of such strength that it transcended the obligations of blood relationship. There was a religious dimension to this loyalty; as we have seen, 'Good Faith' was worshipped as a goddess adopted from the Sabines who exerted a cogent influence over moral attitudes. There was also *pietas*, the dutiful respect due to gods, parents and, of course, patrons. Though there must have been some conflict between these not infrequently incompatible loyalties, lending itself to selectivity and opportunism, *clientela* provided the poorer classes with a degree of security and a sense of belonging which contributed strongly to the cohesiveness of the Roman social fabric. Even if it was not particularly democratic, it was a further example of Roman pragmatism and realism in arranging their affairs.

The rustic ideal placed a particular emphasis on permanence as an expression of virtue. The regular rhythms of life, the cycle of the seasons and crop rotation, sowing and harvesting, fertility and decay, all of these were seen to demonstrate a dependence on a superior cosmic order that sustained a predictable sequence of familiar, accepted ways. Natural disasters such as floods, hurricanes or droughts broke the established pattern to bring misery and famine in their wake. Such disasters came to be associated with the unexpected, with change and innovation, all of which disrupted the state's social and political order. Critical attitudes and attempts at reform were therefore considered to be inherently bad, since their consequences were unpredictable. Permanence ensured stability and confined the hazards of life within reasonable bounds.

As a result of all these influences a pragmatic, dour and persistent breed of men was fostered which held no doubts about the moral rectitude of the state's policies and which, in the main, were deeply conservative; probably not very imaginative though profoundly superstitious; certainly parochially minded but hard working; bound together by a powerful moral code of reciprocal loyalty; brave through training and fear of punishment; cruel and hardened mentally and physically by the vicissitudes of nature and life of laborious toil. They made hardy, courageous and disciplined soldiers, tempered only in their resolution by superstition and a fair measure of human shortcomings.

CHAPTER THREE

SICILY

There is evidence that in the 3rd century BC the climate of Sicily was a lot pleasanter than today and the correspondingly more fertile soil produced an abundance of wheat, vines and honey. According to Thucydides, the Sicels who had come from Italy were the earliest inhabitants. Then, after the fall of Troy in the mid-13th century BC, some of the Trojans escaped by sea from the Achaeans to settle alongside the Sicels. Archaeological excavations in the last hundred years, however, have shown that man first arrived on the island in about 5000 BC and that successive waves of settlers crossed over from Italy, replacing the earlier migrants and spreading out westwards until sometime around 1500 BC the whole island was settled, though very sparsely. In about 1300 BC a series of disasters appear to have occurred, resulting in a dark age which was not ended until 500 years later when a new wave of migrants arrived, this time the Phoenicians. To quote Thucydides:

There were also Phoenicians living all around Sicily, who occupied the headlands and the small islands round the coast and used them for trading with the Sicels. But when the Greeks began to come in by sea in great numbers, the Phoenicians abandoned most of the settlements and concentrated on the towns of Motya, Soluntum and Panormus where they lived together with the neighbouring Elymians, partly because they relied on an alliance with them and partly because the voyage from here to Carthage is the shortest.

From this account and the archaeological evidence, it seems therefore that the Phoenicians were not forcibly evicted by the Greeks, but merely abandoned what were no more than trading posts. It was not until they settled in the towns mentioned by Thucydides that any permanent construction was carried out.

The first Greeks to arrive were no more than traders also, but as reports of the island's natural wealth filtered back to the overpopulated and relatively barren mainland, Greek immigrants began to establish flourishing agriculturally-based settlements both in Sicily and southern Italy. Although in many cases these new communities had originally been sponsored by a Greek mainland city, they were politically independent, retaining only ties of heritage and sentiment. Nor did they have any sense of collective loyalty to one another, except in brief moments of crisis, but remained fiercely independent. Yet this independence did not result in them seeking security through cohesion within their individual communities. They were as divided internally as they were in their external relationships, factions and classes schemed and fought with one another for power, and were not above betraying their communities to outsiders if this offered the prospect of bettering their own cause. One of the basic reasons for their disunity was that their origins were mixed, either Ionic or Doric, so that this behaviour reflected the racial distinctions and antagonism existing between Athens and Sparta. Indeed, during the Peloponnesian War between these two cities in the 5th century BC, both Athens and Sparta sought dominance in Sicily not only as a source of grain, wealth and manpower, but also simply as an extension of their rivalry.

The Greeks founded some fifteen cities, including Syracuse, Naxos, Agrigentum and Messana. Though originally aristocratic, the constitutions of these settlements gradually became despotic as power-seeking individuals, later to be described as tyrants, seized control in most of them. By the 5th century BC Doric Syracuse had become the dominant power under Gelon, who soundly defeated the Carthaginians at Himera in 480 BC and effectively removed their influence from the island for seventy years. A period of unparalleled prosperity and tranquillity followed before the seemingly inevitable self-destructive urge between Greek and Greek broke out anew. During the Peloponnesian War, the inhabitants of the Ionian city of Egesta sent a delegation to Athens imploring assistance against Doric Syracuse, justly claiming that should they be abandoned, Syracuse would dominate the entire island. As the Athenians' enemy Sparta was receiving grain supplies from Sicily at that time, the prospect of being able to inflict a severe economic blow against their opponents and extend their own domination over this important area overcame the Athenians' hesitancy about undertaking such a hazardous adventure. Attracted by promises of great wealth as payment, which eventually proved illusory, an Athenian expedition set sail in 415 BC under the command of Nicias, who was later reinforced by further troops and ships under Demosthenes. It was an ambitious endeavour that ended in disaster, as Thucydides relates:

> Of all the Hellenic actions which took place in this War or any other, this was the greatest, the most glorious to the victors and the most ruinous to the vanquished, for they were utterly defeated and their sufferings were prodigious. Fleet and Army perished from the face of the Earth; nothing was saved and of the many who went forth, few returned home.

The significance of this defeat was that though the Athenians continued to sustain the war for another nine years, they were deserted by their allies and the confederation they had led dissolved once again into disparate factions. Doric Syracuse on the other hand, under the rule of Dionysius from 405 to 367 BC, confirmed its position as the dominant and most prestigious city in Sicily. During this period there occurred a resurgence of Carthaginian influence which led to a war of dramatically fluctuating fortunes, beset by plagues, desertions and rebellions, all of which afflicted Greek and Carthaginian equally, until hostilities were ended, leaving Carthage in possession of most of western Sicily. But an opportunity for them again to extend their influence occurred shortly afterwards with the death of Dionysius and the succession of his son. These two events in fact initiated such a period of anarchy throughout the island as rival cities and classes fought for ascendancy, that two competing liberators arrived: Timoleon, a Corinthian who came with a small force at the invitation of a group of disgruntled aristocrats, and the Carthaginians, whose intervention had been delayed by their usual need to raise a mercenary army before engaging in a major conflict. After a period of relative peace following Timoleon's victory over the Carthaginians, during which he imposed a series of major political reforms amongst the Greek cities including the ending of tyranny, this great peacemaker went into voluntary retirement and obscurity. Agathocles of Syracuse then led a revolt against the new rulers in 320 BC and reinstated despotic rule in Syracuse, massacred the aristocrats, courted public favour and started to expand his domain.

But in doing so he aroused the antagonism of the Carthaginians who, after some initial hesitancy, despatched a large expeditionary force under Hamilcar. This drove Agathocles back into Syracuse and the city began to face starvation. He eluded the Carthaginian fleet blockading the town, however, and landed in North Africa at Cap Bon in 310 BC with 14,000 troops in sixty warships. After burning his ships, which he had too few men to protect, he marched to within a few miles of Carthage. Diodorus Siculus describes the scene:

> The whole country through which they marched was beautiful and gardens planted with all sorts of fruits trees and sluices and canals were cut all along

for the convenience of water, by which that whole tract was everywhere abundantly watered. Their part of the country was likewise full of towns and villages, adorned with stately houses, the roofs of which were curiously wrought, all setting forth the wealth and riches of their owners. The houses were full of all manner of provision of everything that was needful; for the inhabitants, through a long peace, had stored up their treasures in great abundance. The country is planted partly with vines, and partly with olive trees, and furnished likewise with many other fruit trees; in another part, the fields are pastured with flocks of sheep, and herds of cows and oxen; and in the neighbouring Pens run great herds of breeding mares. And what shall I say more? Those places abounded with plenty of all things for the use of man, and the rulers so, because they were the possessions of the nobility of Carthage, who laid out much of their estates and wealth with more than ordinary curiosity to improve them for their delight and pleasure; so that the feasibility and sweetness of the country was the admiration of the Sicilians, and roused up their drooping spirits in the view they had of these rewards and rich returns, which they judged well worthy the hazards to be run by the conquerors to obtain them.

Though this rich prize lay close to hand, it eluded Agathocles. After a largely inconclusive battle which left the Carthaginians unwilling or unable to continue fighting without reinforcements, and left Agathocles too weak to take their city by storm, a lull set in for the combatants. Inside Carthage there was consternation, if not panic, at this sudden turn of events. As has already been mentioned, fearful of divine wrath for their failure to offer their own children for sacrifice, the nobles sought to placate their fearful god Baal Hammon with the slaughter of their grown-up offspring.

Meanwhile, in Sicily the garrison of Syracuse had sallied forth and surprised Hamilcar's investing troops in the middle of their redeployment around the city. The resulting victory acted as a signal for other towns to rise against the Carthaginians who now found themselves hard-pressed both in Africa and Sicily. But then the Libyans, whom Agathocles had recruited, deserted to their former overlords and obliged him to abandon his North African campaign. Eventually a peace treaty was signed in Sicily which left the Carthaginians in occupation of the western part of the island. Agathocles' campaign in North Africa had not led to the general uprising against Carthage he had probably hoped for; though there had been some defections among the Libyans, other tribes had sent contingents to Carthage when requested, perhaps indicating how strong a hold the City had over its possessions. Following the death of Agathocles some twenty years after he had been forced to flee from from North Africa, anarchy broke out yet again amongst the Greek cities in Sicily. Carthage once more sought to reassert her domination over the entire island, and bring about the final conquest of Greek Sicily.

SICILY

It was in the interests of both Rome and Carthage at this period to eradicate western Hellenism. The Carthaginians had opened negotiations with the Romans to try and persuade them to continue their campaign against Pyrrhus and the Greek cities on the mainland of Italy, while they campaigned in Sicily, but the enterprise failed and Pyrrhus crossed over to assist the Syracusans with 1000 troops. He was greeted as a liberator throughout the island except in Messana, which was held by former mercenaries of Agathocles, and Lilybaeum (Marsala) in the extreme west where the Carthaginians maintained their hold. Having thus suffered a series of punishing defeats, the Carthaginians sought peace and were prepared to relinquish all their possessions in Sicily except for Lilybaeum, conditions which were unacceptable to Pyrrhus and a number of the Greek cities. But as has been related, when called upon to provide ships to transport Pyrrhus to North Africa, and furnish support for the reduction of the remaining Carthaginian strongholds, dissension broke out between the Greeks who resented Pyrrhus' haughty demands and lacked the will to make a final and conclusive effort. Summoned back to fight in Italy, Pyrrhus was obliged to abandon his campaign to win Sicily for western Hellenium.

The role the Greek cities played in establishing the balance of power during this early period was of fundamental importance. While Rome was still under attack from the Gauls and fighting for its very existence, had Syracuse fallen, instead of twice surviving as a bastion of Greek independence in 410 and 397 BC, Sicily would have been secured as a Carthaginian province. A further extension of the Carthaginian empire into southern Italy could have forestalled Roman conquests by well over a century, with consequences of unpredictable significance. As it was, however, after the departure of Pyrrhus the strife-ridden island, as he had predicted, was left to be a future battlefield between the Romans and Carthaginians.

There were in fact no compelling reasons for Carthage and Rome to have gone to war with one another; there had been three treaties between them establishing certain rules governing their relationship, with nothing one-sided or obviously objectionable in any of their clauses. Polybius gives 509 BC as the date for the first treaty which, after stating that there shall be friendship between the Romans and their allies, and the Carthaginians and their allies, stipulated a number of not unreasonable conditions. The more interesting ones can be summarised as prohibiting the Romans and their allies from sailing beyond the Fair Promontory (that is, west of what was probably Cape Bon) but permitting trade with Sardinia, Libya, Sicily and Carthage itself. The Carthaginians were clearly speaking of the first two as belonging to them, but referring only to that part of Sicily which was under their domination. Similarly, when barring the Carthaginians from a number of coastal cities the Romans only referred to Latium, making no reference to the rest of Italy which was not under their authority.

A second treaty was signed some 150 years later, in the 4th century BC, setting out much the same conditions, confirming the Roman attitude towards Sardinia, Libya and Sicily but effectively excluding them from the Carthaginian preserves in the western extremity of the Mediterranean, the Romans for their part again naming certain cities on the seaboard which were barred to the Carthaginians.

The third treaty was drawn up in 279 BC, at the time of Pyrrhus' campaign in Italy, when the Carthaginians wished to ensure that the Romans did not make peace with him, so leaving them to stand alone. Not only did they pay the Romans handsomely but, having confirmed the earlier treaties of friendship, the following significant clause was added:

If either of the signatories shall make a treaty that they will go to the aid of the other in whichever country they are attacked, whichever one may need help the Carthaginians shall provide the ships for transport and attack, but each shall provide the pay for its own men. The Carthaginians shall also aid the Romans by sea if need be, but no one shall compel the crews to land against their will.

The two cities had then entered into an alliance which enabled the Romans to call on Carthaginian naval support against Pyrrhus, either in Italy or to transport their army to Sicily in aid of the Carthaginians should this be required. This clause shows that in spite of all three treaties restraining Roman ships from Carthaginian preserves, their fleet must have been of insignificant proportions. This situation continued until the outbreak of the First Punic War, though by then the Romans had established an auxiliary system whereby the ships from the coastal cities of Italy, especially the Greek cities, provided small contingents. These contingents are estimated by Thiel, the Dutch naval historian, to have numbered no more than some forty to fifty ships, so were greatly inferior to the Carthaginian fleet but this was not only a matter of numbers, they were also qualitatively inferior, possessing only triremes while the Carthaginians had the far more formidable quinqueremes.

It is clear that the Romans had not appreciated the importance of naval power. Their conquest of southern Italy had been achieved by their army alone and no attempt had been made to reduce cities like Tarentum and Rhegium by a combination of land and sea assault, or even by blockade. Instead they had had to depend on traitors within Tarentum before they could breach its defences, and later the capture of Rhegium was only achieved with the assistance of Syracusan naval forces. That the Romans attached little importance to the naval arm is further borne out by the low priority they accorded to the standard of their recruits who, it will be remembered, they largely drew from those unfit for service in the legions. Even after four of their ships had been sunk in the conflict with Tarentum, which had led to the intervention of Pyrrhus, the Romans still made no effort to rectify what was a clearly visible inadequacy.

This negative attitude was in strict contrast to that of the Carthaginians whose fleet not only secured their trading interests, but also projected their power throughout the western Mediterranean by transporting their armies wherever they were required. The Carthaginians also understood the importance of combined operations by land and sea, and on the three occasions when their possessions in Sicily had been reduced to the key city of Lilybaeum, they had been able to sustain it by sea. But in spite of their important naval forces, there is no reason to think that the Carthaginians had any intention of countering Roman territorial conquests in Italy with landings of their own. Certainly they had established themselves in Sardinia and Corsica, but this principal preoccupation was to preserve their monopoly of trade in the western Mediterranean, especially in Spain, and so they bound themselves by treaty to renounce any ambitions of gaining a foothold in Latium, recognising it to be a Roman sphere of influence.

Although this was not sanctified by treaty, as the Romans extended their hegemony down the peninsula, the Carthaginians still maintained their policy of non-intervention. Whether this was primarily because they were already occupied in Sicily and had no wish to enter simultaneously into a new and potentially hazardous undertaking, or whether they thought their overall interests were best secured by not antagonising this emerging but apparently land-bound power, is not known. But the result remains the same; the Carthaginians did not provoke the Romans, any more than the fleetless Romans directly challenged Carthaginian interests. What then were the causes for them going to war?

A modern strategist could point out that the possession of Sicily would have brought untold advantages; strategically placed between Africa and Italy, it provided an important springboard for military operations in either direction, while dominating east/west trade routes across the Mediterranean at its narrowest point. In the case of the Romans, it also offered a forward operating base from where the sea communications between Carthage, Sardinia and Spain could be interdicted. But clearly such an analysis played no part in Roman thinking, since Rome lacked a fleet for its implementation. That the Carthaginians could have pursued such reasoning is more plausible. But as they had shown no wish to renew their earlier endeavours to conquer Sicily as a step towards further exploitation, their goal seems to have been limited to achieving a monopoly of trade throughout the island. There are two other considerations which support this contention. Spain was by far the most important source of wealth for the Carthaginians and their attention must have been drawn westwards, rather than towards an area in which they had much difficulty in establishing a presence. Secondly, whenever the Carthaginians had mounted an expedition to Sicily, it had been in response to the loss of their existing possessions, not in direct search of further conquests. This hardly supports the idea that they had any long-term ambitions towards Italy. We must, then, look for less dynamic reasons for war.

The actual catalyst for hostilities was the request by the Mamertines of Messana for admission into the Roman federation and the provision of a garrison. The Mamertines had previously been Italian mercenaries, recruited by Agathocles during his war against the Carthaginians. After being welcomed by the inhabitants of Messana on his death in 289 BC, the Mamertines massacred the leading citizens, appropriated their wives and property, and then set about creating a vassal empire around the city, which extended over the north-east corner of the island. But in so doing they came into conflict with Hiero of Syracuse, who was building an empire to succeed that of Agathocles. Adopting a high moral tone, Hiero condemned the Mamertines for the treacherous manner by which they had obtained Messana, though this had occurred fifteen years earlier, and marching north with his army he brought them to battle on the Longanus River where he decisively defeated them.

Before Hiero could reap the full rewards of this victory, however, the Carthaginians moved swiftly to assist the Mamertines by placing a garrison in Messana. This prompt action did not of course arise from any concern for the Mamertines, but rather from a determination that the Syracusans, against whom the Carthaginians had waged war for so many years, should not obtain possession of the harbour of Messana and so be in a position to dominate the narrow straits between Sicily and Italy.

Although they had been saved from Hiero, who quickly realised he was no match for the Carthaginians and withdrew to Syracuse, the Mamertines had no desire to be subjected to a regime which put the orderly conduct of trade above their own self-interest.

Furthermore, since the Carthaginians had not displayed great consistency of purpose or undisputed skill in their military campaigns, the wheel of fortune might take a less favourable turn and leave the city once again exposed to the ambitious tyrant of Syracuse. An alliance with the Romans looked a better bet; they were after all fellow Italians with whom they shared a common heritage, and who allowed a considerable degree of independence to the cities and tribes they assimilated into their empire. Envoys were therefore despatched to Rome, seeking an alliance and Roman protection.

This request put the Roman senators on the horns of a dilemma. Agreeing to it would clearly risk war with Carthage. There were those, led by the Claudii, who believed that the future of Rome lay in the south, while the group headed by the Fabii – whose estates extended along the banks of the Tiber – saw Roman and their own interests being best served by a northern expansion, coupled with a policy of moderation and cooperation with Carthage. There were also the Aemilii, a senatorial faction rather more indiscriminately favouring overseas expansion but later inclining towards the Western Mediterranean.

The Senate was also probably divided in its attitude towards the prospect of a war on account of its changing social composition. The old families who had once dominated the Senate by aristocratic right, were now seeing their position progressively weakened by the promotion of a new class of men who had either won distinction on the battlefield, or recognition in the democratic assembly of the people. Another war would threaten the Senate with a renewed influx of candidates borne in on the wave of public favour. Additionally, the popular assembly had acquired increasing influence and power by means of its ultimate right to declare war and approve terms of peace, while the Senate was still left responsible for the direction of the war and any consequential failures. The people had thus acquired power without responsibility, while the Senate was attempting to combine in a single assembly two diverse factions, one based on the inherited privilege of aristocratic birth and the other on plebeian approval.

Apart from these conflicting interests, in which those of the Claudii prevailed, there were also obvious attractions in responding positively to the Mamertines' request. While the Carthaginians held Messana they were in a position to dominate the Straits with their vastly superior fleet and, more menacingly, they might be tempted to extend their conquests onto the mainland of Italy itself. Thus the occupation of Messana by a Roman garrison would not only provide a foothold for further expansion, but also ensure that the two key cities either side of the straits were in Roman hands. No doubt there were those whose unbridled imagination and ambitions saw an opportunity here to secure the whole of Sicily as a Roman province, but the inherent dangers of such a project probably damped the ardour of all but the most ardent.

There must have been considerable debate over the recently reaffirmed treaty with Carthage, declaring friendship and a readiness for military cooperation; any unprovoked breach of this treaty would be seen to be an act of flagrant aggression. The argument that the dispatch of Roman troops would be only in response to an appeal for protection against Syracuse and not directed against Carthage, was sheer sophistry: a Carthaginian garrison was already installed and would have to be evicted. For Rome to be portrayed as an aggressor would not only be a contradiction of the virtuous standards so purposefully inculcated into her people and society generally, but would also endanger her dealings with other states which were, at least in public-relations terms based on equally noble ideals. There was a further moral problem facing those in the Senate who were pressing for the occupation of Messana. A few years earlier the Roman garrison in Rhegium had seized control of the city and established a tyrannical government similar to the one which the Mamertines, probably in imitation, were now practising. When Rhegium had eventually been recaptured the mutinous survivors were assembled in the Forum in Rome, flogged and then beheaded. What then was the moral justification in responding to a call for assistance from criminals in Messana who had been fortunate in preserving their skins, if not their possessions, under Carthaginian protection? The answer was self-evidently none.

At the time of the Mamertine request, there is nothing to suggest that the Romans had anything to fear from the Carthaginians in their foreseeable future. The garrison was small and the subsequent hesitancy of its commander Hanno in resisting the Romans when they eventually landed, which resulted in his crucifixion, hardly suggests that he or his troops were preparing for a Carthaginian invasion of Italy. Even the Carthaginian fleet was absent from the harbour of Messana and had done nothing to contravene the treaty, let alone attempt to dominate the straits. Surprisingly however, although lacking both provocation and a fleet to transport and sustain their army, the Senate could not sufficiently overcome its contesting factions to determine a rational policy, and instead delegated the responsibility for reaching a decision to the popular assembly.

Though constitutionally correct, this resulted in the Roman response being based on a popular vote, probably even more heavily influenced by powerful voices with vested interest, than would have been the case within the Senate itself. This does not mean that Rome and Carthage would not have eventually fought for supremacy in the Mediterranean – this was a seemingly inevitable development given

Rome's bludgeoning imperialistic ambitions and Carthaginian preoccupations with their commercial empire – but in 264 BC there was no reason for these two powers to have become embroiled in a major and costly war. The fact that they did so, and over such a minor and unworthy cause, was unequivocally the fault of the Romans.

PART TWO

THE FIRST PUNIC WAR
264–242 BC

CHAPTER FOUR

THE OPENING ROUND IN SICILY
264–261 BC

Although the accounts as to what exactly occurred are sometimes conflicting, there can be little doubt that once the decision had been taken to aid the Mamertines, it was necessary to act promptly before the Carthaginians were alerted and moved their fleet to intercept the Romans and forestall their landing. The problem for the Romans was that they had not yet assembled an army, and simply to send an embassy ahead to Messana to proclaim their intentions and make the necessary preparations would obviously have jeopardised the whole operation. What appears to have happened is that Appius Claudius, on being appointed to command the expedition, realised that to wait until he had assembled his two legions and then march them south for 400 miles to the embarkation point in Rhegium, would run the risk of reports about his preparations reaching the Carthaginians. He accordingly dispatched a smaller force under a tribune and relation, C. Claudius, to move by sea and secure Messana until reinforced by the main body.

It was a risky venture. Even if C. Claudius' force could elude the Carthaginian ships, it might not be strong enough to evict the garrison holed up in the formidable citadel and then hang on until reinforced. There was also the possibility that the Carthaginians would intercept the main body as it crossed the straits, and then blockade Messana, forcing the Romans to accept a humiliating surrender on top of an ignominious defeat. That the Romans were prepared to accept such risks must have been the result of a particularly favourable omen and an assessment, possibly from reports made by the Mamertines, that the state of readiness of the Carthaginians was low and that their

Sicily – To illustrate the First Punic War

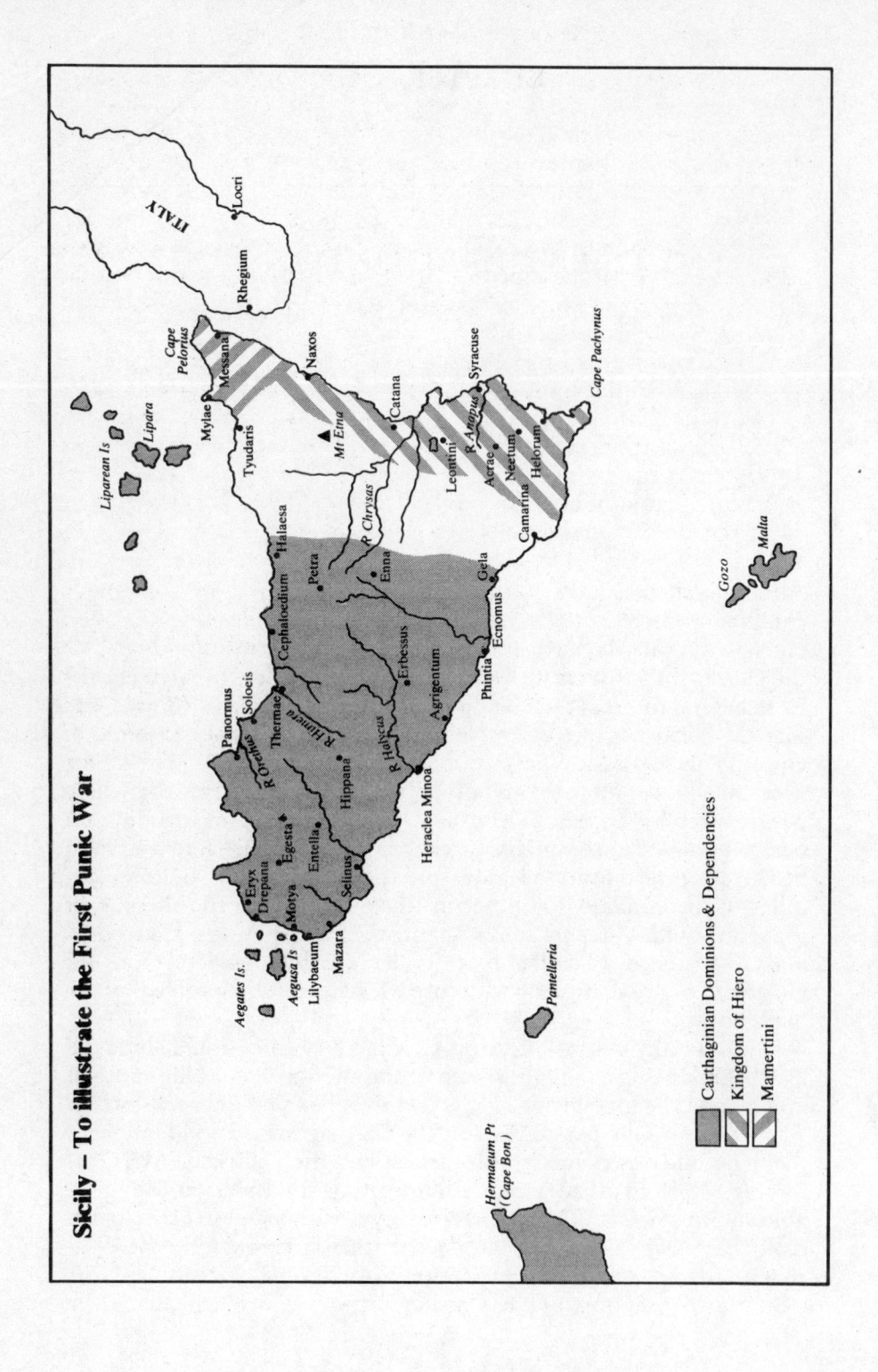

- Carthaginian Dominions & Dependencies
- Kingdom of Hiero
- Mamertini

reaction was likely to be hesitant on account of their uncertainty as to how Hiero of Syracuse would react. After all, in spite of the fact that the Romans would be acting as aggressors against the Carthaginians, the Mamertines themselves still surely had a right to decide who was to protect them? Whatever Hiero might think about these alliances directed against himself, he could have considered that in accepting Roman possession of Messana, he would be better placed to advance his own interests at the expense of the Carthaginians elsewhere in the island. In short, the situation was inherently unstable and so lent itself to opportunistic adventurism.

C. Claudius seems, surprisingly, to have been able to land his force at Messana without incident. This may have been due to the commander of the Carthaginian ships, which were at sea, not having received clear instructions as to what he should do in the event of the Romans attempting to enter the harbour – to have engaged them on his own initiative could have resulted in a war with Rome, so a more prudent course would have been to let them alone and merely report what he had sighted. The same uncertainty may have been responsible for the Carthaginian commander Hanno's irresolute conduct. Although according to Polybius, 'the Mamertines drove Hanno out of the citadel partly by open force and partly by fraud and delivered the city to the Romans', later historians have suggested that, seeing the Romans greeted with open arms by the Mamertines, Hanno capitulated without a fight. At any rate, the Romans secured the town and the Punic garrison was allowed to leave unmolested, though the unfortunate Hanno was later crucified by the Carthaginians for his pusillanimity.

After recovering from their initial surprise, the Carthaginians collected their forces and, stationing their fleet at Cape Pelorias, closed in on Messana with Hiero who had agreed to assist them. Meanwhile Appius Claudius had arrived at Rhegium with his two legions and managed to get them across the straits at night by using auxiliary ships provided by the neighbouring cities, and by Rhegium itself. That he should have been able to avoid the Carthaginian fleet is clearly due to the difficulty of intercepting ships at night. And since there is no record of any of the Carthaginian commanders being put to death or even more mildly punished for dereliction of duty, it is reasonable to conclude that there were excusable reasons at the time for the Romans having eluded them. Some sort of engagement occurred, however, as is confirmed by Polybius who, when relating how the Romans started to construct a fleet some four years later, states that the design of their ships was based on a Carthaginian decked vessel which, at the time of Claudius' crossing, 'charged so furiously that it ran aground and fell into Roman hands'.

Though there had been no formal declaration of war and there is every indication that the Carthaginians still acted with considerable restraint, the First Punic War had broken out. This can be considered under four phases: the opening campaign in Sicily, which lasted for three years; the struggle for maritime supremacy, which continued for five years; the brief one-year campaign in North Africa; and the second Sicilian campaign which endured for twelve years until 242 BC.

After successfully getting into Messana, Appius Claudius was faced with the prospect of having to fight both the Carthaginians and the Syracusans who were investing the city. His first act was to enter into negotiations with the two commanders, Hanno and Hiero, but when this proved fruitless he decided to defeat them separately. That this was considered possible suggests that when Claudius or his envoys were attempting to negotiate a settlement they discovered that their two opponents had not yet coordinated their operation, let alone concentrated their forces.

Appius Claudius attacked Hiero first and quickly drove him back into Syracuse. In spite of the fact that there are widely conflicting claims about what actually occurred, Hiero undoubtedly deserted the battlefield with such precipitation that the Romans were able to turn on the Carthaginians almost immediately afterwards. This suggests that the fighting cannot have been of any great severity. Additionally, this would have been a prudent course for Hiero to have adopted. He had no particular reason to support the Carthaginians; they had forestalled his earlier ambition to obtain Messana for himself, they had displayed no great determination in preventing the Romans from landing and capturing the city, and now they were showing themselves either reluctant or unable to come to his assistance. Hiero would in fact have been profoundly unwise to have committed his army whole-heartedly to a decisive battle under such circumstances.

The Syracusans having withdrawn, Appius Claudius turned on the Carthaginians and, though he also drove them from the field, they were able to effect an orderly withdrawal into the neighbouring cities. Thereafter they restricted themselves for a time to holding strongpoints, as they had done during the war against Pyrrhus. The Romans now dominated the open ground and were free to manoeuvre so long as they could assure their supplies, and since the harvest was due to be gathered they would be able to live off the land in the event of the Carthaginian fleet being able to blockade the harbour of Messana.

Claudius now decided to march south. According to Polybius, he intended to lay siege to Syracuse and afterwards Echetla, a city standing on the frontier between the Carthaginian and Syracusan territories about fifty miles west of Syracuse. Modern historians have largely discounted Polybius' account on the grounds that the fortifications of Syracuse were far too formidable for the Romans to have attempted to take by storm, and a prolonged siege was impossible since supplies could have been brought in by sea. But such reasoning seems to miss the point that Claudius could quite justifiably have hoped to induce Hiero to come to terms by merely investing and threatening the city. The Syracusans had had a taste of Roman military might, and the Carthaginians had just been defeated outside Messana; it then does not seem unreasonable to think that Claudius should have 'laid siege' to Syracuse as Polybius relates.

The Romans' subsequent foray to Echetla can only have been of secondary importance and may have been no more than a diversion; the city was of no strategic importance, but possibly its garrison had been interfering with Roman activities around Syracuse, or the area may have represented a source of supply. Whatever the reasons for their attack on Echetla, Syracuse must have been the main Roman objective. In consequence, when Hiero refused to be intimidated, they had no alternative but to withdraw to Messana. To have remained dispersed between Messana and the Syracuse-Echetla area would have risked defeat in detail and entailed passing a winter without adequate quarters.

After his audaciously successful crossing of the straits, therefore, Claudius had not been able to achieve decisive results against either the Carthaginians or the Syracusans. Considering the Senate's hesitancy over occupying Messana in the first place, and the unlikelihood that they would have authorised Claudius to extend his campaign southwards in the manner he did, it is not surprising that he did not receive a triumph on his return to Rome and was replaced in command by two new consuls, Manius Otacilius Crassus, a plebeian of Samanite origins, and Manius Valerius Maximus, who were given two more legions to reinforce those still in Messana.

The appointment of Otacilius in particular typified the shift of power from the aristocratic families to the plebeian group within the Senate. Appius Claudius had belonged to the Claudii, and while their influence had been eclipsed following his unsuccessful campaign, the Fabii had clearly not been able to assert their own authority instead. Although the conquest of the whole of Sicily does not seem to have been decided upon at this stage, this political adjustment brought in its wake a populist determination to consolidate the Roman foothold in Sicily. To achieve this Hiero had to be eliminated as an opponent.

That the two consuls and their armies shared the Senate's apparent intent to pursue only limited objectives, seems most improbable. Manius Valerius appreciated that the campaign was likely to develop into a much wider conflict, even if he did not actually intend that this should occur. He saw the need for the Romans to acquire a fleet, and it seems that he may have retained a small one to blockade Syracuse from the vessels he had assembled to cross the straits. His soldiers were certainly interested in the spoils of war and it is not difficult to imagine how their enthusiasm for a wider-ranging campaign could have been aroused. These views could well have been shared by Otacilius, since there is no record of any dissension between him and Valerius over their plans. After crossing the Straits of Messana, the consuls marched with their two armies of four legions directly into Syracusan territory, taking a frontier post by storm. According to Diodorus, this display of Roman determination and overwhelming force quickly persuaded sixty-seven Syracusan and Punic cities that an accommodation with Rome was preferable to ineffective resistance. Offers of submission were made and accepted, leaving Syracuse itself isolated and once again abandoned by the Carthaginians. But its formidable fortifications defeated the Romans' first assault and without a fleet to blockade the city, there was no question of their being able to reduce it by siege.

With no desire to become entangled in a protracted conflict, the Syracusans now entered into negotiations to secure the most favourable conditions they could; while for their part the Romans were no doubt thankful to have secured their primary objectives at so little cost. After Hiero had released his Roman prisoners, an alliance was entered into which recognised Hiero as King of Syracuse and all the former cities which had been under his jurisdiction. These included Acrae, Leontini, Megara, Neetum and Helorum, all of which lay within a semi-circle about Syracuse within a radius of some thirty miles. There were also a few other cities like Tauromenium lying on the high plateau between Messana and Catana, which were restored to Hiero; perhaps indicating that the Romans had no territorial ambitions at his expense and considered his active support essential for any extension of the campaign in other directions.

The alliance with Hiero was confirmed by the Senate, after which Valerius returned to Rome to receive a triumph and the cognomen of 'Messana'. He was also permitted to have a battle scene painted on the wall of the Senate House portraying him as a conquering hero; all of which indicated the measure of the Senate's approval for his achievements. The burden of the war on the Roman exchequer had been considerable lightened, and although they must have been aware that the Carthaginians would be most unlikely to accept the situation without a struggle, the Senate decided to maintain only two legions in Sicily. They claimed that this was because of difficulties in provisioning a larger force when they could not guarantee their sea communications, but if this was genuine and not just a cover for parsimony, it is surprising that they felt unable to rely on local supplies.

The Carthaginians in the meanwhile had not been inactive. Though they had made only one belated and seemingly not very determined attempt to come to Hiero's assistance – which was quickly abandoned when they discovered that he had reached a settlement with the Romans – they had been busy raising a mercenary army. Unable to stand against the Romans while Hiero was still alongside them, there was no question of them being able to do so alone without first building up their strength. The new army under formation drew many of its recruits from Liguria and Gaul, but it was from Spain that the greatest number were enlisted. It was a slow business; recruits had to be found, assembled, equipped and trained, and when the weather was favourable, transported to Sicily, disembarked, and deployed for battle. The first contingent to arrive, under another Hannibal, entered the great Greek city of Agrigentum, one of the most formidable fortresses on the island, founded in 582 BC by colonists from Gela. The city lay on rising ground which reached its peak two to three miles from the sea, before falling away precipitously on the northern and eastern slopes, and more gradually to the west. Its natural defences were further strengthened by the rivers Acragas (Biagio) to the east and the Hypas (Drago) to the west, which almost surrounded the town to meet just below it to the south. Diodorus relates how Hanno had fortified the citadel of Agrigentum in 264 BC and, after winning over its population to the Carthaginians, had incorporated the city into their Confederacy. As one of the principal Greek colonies lying on the southern coast of Sicily facing the African continent and well acquainted with the Punic customs and culture, the Greek population would have found it quite natural to associate themselves with the Carthaginian cause. Though Hannibal had been able to secure the city before the Romans had begun to threaten it, he was in no position to do more than defend what he had gained. The best he could hope for was to block the Romans' further advance westwards by forcing them to besiege the city, thus preserving Carthaginian-held territory until the main body of the new Punic army arrived.

With some 40,000 men the two new Roman consuls, Lucius Postumius Megellus and Quintus Mamilius Vitulus, who had taken over from their predecessors following the conclusion of the treaty with Hiero of Syracuse, marched directly on Agrigentum, which they reached as the crops were ripening. After establishing their camp some two miles from the city, the legionaries were dispatched into the fields to gather in the harvest. Spread widely over the countryside with scant regard for security, the Roman foragers were surprised by a sudden Carthaginian foray and were driven back into their camp in considerable disarray. But they managed to stage a rally and after a sharp and at times critical fight, they forced the Carthaginians to withdraw back behind their city walls.

The Romans now earnestly prepared to besiege Agrigentum, and to that end established a forward supply base at Erbessus, probably to the north-east of the city. Polybius speaks of it as standing no great distance from the Roman positions, and being regularly provisioned by allied convoys, which must have originated from the eastern part of the island which was now either allied to, or occupied by, the Romans. Two fortified camps were then constructed near the coast, one on either side of Agrigentum, connected by a double line of defence works around the city, with smaller fortifications being sited so that they were able to cover their entire length. The inner line confined the Carthaginian garrison closely within the city walls, while the outer line countered any Carthaginian relieving force. For the next five months the siege was maintained, with the Carthaginian garrison doing no more than mount limited forays. Inside the city itself the situation was becoming critical as supplies became exhausted and disease started to spread through the congested and physically weakened population.

In the meantime the Carthaginians had managed to assemble a substantial army, numbering some 50,000 infantry, 600 cavalry and sixty elephants, under Hanno at Heraclea Minoa, a coastal town some twelve miles west of Agrigentum. In view of their poor state of training and the difficulty of welding disparate mercenary troops into a cohesive fighting force, Hanno was still understandably wary of taking the field for a major confrontation. The most he felt capable of for the next two months was a few minor tactical engagements and the encirclement of the Romans who, though always able to break out of the Carthaginian rings, could not bring them to battle by pursuit or assault their base at Heraclea, without risking raising the siege of Agrigentum.

In order to lay close siege to Agrigentum and defend their rear, the Romans were therefore obliged to keep their forces widely dispersed, a situation Hanno was quick to exploit. Shortly after occupying Heraclea, he advanced towards Agrigentum, sending his Numidian cavalry ahead with orders to provoke the garrison of the Roman camp lying to the west of the city into an intemperate response. The Numidians were then to retire as though in precipitous retreat, and so lure their pursuers into a trap prepared by the infantry. The action went as planned, with the Roman cavalry suffering heavily as they blundered into the ambush. The opening round had gone well for the Carthaginians, who followed up their success by establishing an advanced camp on a hill adjacent to the Romans. Profiting from the dispersion of the Romans as they maintained the siege, Hanno sent a part of his force to destroy their recently established supply base at Erbessus, and then cut off any alternative supplies by his Numidians, who roamed the countryside at will.

Under the circumstances the Carthaginian tactics appear to have been thoroughly sound; they were applying force indirectly in a manner which would have made the Romans raise the siege had it not been for two considerations. First, Hiero of Syracuse showed great zeal and skill in getting provisions through to the hard-pressed Romans. Second, and more importantly, after a siege that had now lasted for seven months, the situation in Agrigentum was becoming desperate; desertions were increasing and both population and garrison were on the point of starvation. Continual signals were made by fire which left Hanno in no doubt that the end was near. He had no alternative, therefore, but to change his tactics and face the Romans in a set piece battle.

Accepting the challenge, the Romans deployed on to the open ground that separated the two opponents' camps, which were probably to the west of Agrigentum. The battle was hard fought and for some time the Carthaginians held their own, but eventually the Romans' superior discipline and fighting ability began to tell, and a part of the Carthaginian line started to crumble. As the infantry in the forward rank fell back on to those behind them, confusion began to set in, until all order was lost and panic overtook the whole army. Hanno and rather less than half his troops managed to regain Heraclea. But although he had shown himself to be a skilful tactician who had been unavoidably drawn into a battle for which his army was inadequately trained, he was relieved of his command and heavily fined.

The Romans had not gone unscathed either, however: after months of hardship and privation, carelessness appears to have overcome them as darkness cloaked the battlefield, and within the city Hannibal seized his chance. Towards midnight, muffling the sound of his troops' movement with sacks filled with chaff, he silently abandoned Agrigentum and passed undetected through the Roman lines. Only his rearguard was discovered and harried, but the Romans soon broke off their pursuit and fell instead upon the now unprotected city which they then proceeded to plunder with a ruthless abandon matched only by the unconstrained cruelty they visited upon the civilian Greek population.

Until the capture of Agrigentum, the Romans had drawn a distinction between the citizens and the garrisons of foreign cities, but with the ferocious reprisals that had now been taken, an example was set which possibly was intended to serve as a warning to others contemplating siding with Carthage. The effects of this new policy are not clear. Some inland cities went over to the Romans, but those on the coast which could be sustained by the Carthaginian fleet stood firm, while still others rose to declare their Punic allegiance. A repetition of the generous terms extended to Hiero of Syracuse, which had ensured his loyalty throughout the recent crises and would endure until his death some fifty years later, would have been far more likely to have swung the Greek cities behind the Roman cause. It is not perhaps irrelevant to note that although the successful outcome of the year's campaign as a whole aroused the Senate's enthusiasm for an extension of the war, no triumph was awarded to either of the victorious generals.

While the Carthaginians had been making their main effort in Sicily, they had not been inactive elsewhere. Early in 262 BC a part of their fleet had been moved to Sardinia, from where they raided and harried the Italian coastline. Whether this activity was intended to discourage the Romans from dispatching troops to Sicily and instead tie them down in defence of the mainland, or whether it was no more than an annoying diversion, is not known. But this Carthaginian display of sea power in Roman home waters must certainly have affected the Senate's attitude and become a factor in later influencing them to create a fleet of their own.

Even if the long-term political objectives of the Romans' involvement in Sicily had been unclear, for the first three years of the war their field commanders had at least few doubts concerning their primary objectives: the occupation of Messana, the subjugation of Syracuse and the reduction of Agrigentum. These precise objectives had enabled the Romans to take the offensive, and also to achieve a concentration of force at the operational level – even if a degree of tactical dispersion had proved unavoidable, both before Agrigentum and elsewhere in the island. Though there had been periods of stagnation in the campaign the Romans had taken and held the initiative.

In 261 BC, however, the situation was reversed. Although things had gone too far and imperialistic appetites had been too whetted for the ultimate political objective to be anything less than the total expulsion of the Carthaginians from Sicily, how this was to be achieved militarily was far from clear. Rome's strength lay in the set-piece battle, the decisive clash of opposing armies that decided the issue one way or another; in this case the possession of Sicily. But the Carthaginian commander replacing Hanno was to prove as circumspect as his predecessor. Hamilcar used the flexibility bestowed on him by his fleet to dominate the seaboard and its cities. Although the Romans held two-thirds of the island from Cephaloedium on the north coast to Heraclea on the south, the fighting became diffuse and reactive as city after city flared into revolt or declared for Carthage – with notable exceptions such as Segesta and Halicyae, which defected to the Romans from deep within Carthaginian-held territory. The problem facing the Romans was that, even if they were to seek a conclusive action by concentrating their army and marching on the main Carthaginian base at Lilybaeum on the extreme west coast, they would be unable to reduce it by siege unless they were also able to prevent provisions coming in by sea. Meanwhile they would incur the risk of being cut off from their own supplies, as had nearly occurred at Agrigentum. An entirely land-based strategy had thus become patently inadequate and the need for a fleet was now self-evident.

CHAPTER FIVE

THE MARITIME DIMENSION
261–256 BC

Polybius wrote that, 'among the motives which induced me to enter into a more minute description of the war in Sicily, this was not the least: that I might take occasion to explain the time and manner in which the Romans first equipped a naval ornament'. He had a remarkable story to tell, the authenticity of which has been convincingly argued by Thiel in his *History of Roman Sea Power*. It is a story that bears repeating.

As will be recalled, the Romans possessed no ships of their own and had been obliged to borrow them from their allies in barely sufficient numbers to effect the crossing of their legions to Messana. During the subsequent brush with the Carthaginians, one of the latter's quinqueremes had run aground and now served as an indispensable model for the Romans. The construction of a fleet was an ambitious and massive undertaking, the sheer scale and scope of which strongly suggests that a decision was taken and planning had begun some considerable time before the actual work was put in hand. But to keep to the recorded facts, 100 quinqueremes and twenty triremes were ordered to be ready in two months and while the workmen were busy building and fitting out the ships, recruiting and training the sailors proceeded apace. A quinquereme required five men on each oar, a trireme only one, so the larger vessels would have had a crew of at least 250 and it must have taken every day of the allotted two months to weld the 30,000 rowers into some semblance of order. This was done by constructing along the shore skeleton ship frames with benches and drilling the rowers under the command of their officers. Once the ships were ready, a further period of preparatory training was carried out at sea. According to Polybius, the ships proved slow and heavy in their motions because they had been built with little skill, but the inexperience of the crews must also have been a contributory cause.

The Romans' first encounter with the Carthaginians was not auspicious. In 260 BC two new consuls had been appointed, Cornelius Scipio Asina and Caius Duilius, to command the fleet and the army respectively. The consular army destined for Sicily was to consist of only two legions, perhaps reflecting the heavy demands on manpower and other resources which the naval programme required. After completing their sea training the main body of the fleet started to move down the Italian coast, Scipio Asina going ahead by a few days with seventeen ships to prepare for their arrival at Messana. Here he received a report which tempted him into trying to take the town of Lipara by surprise. The Carthaginian naval commander, Hannibal, had however learned of Scipio's intentions and dispatched twenty of his ships, led by a Senator Boodes, from Panormus (Palermo) to deal with him. Boodes sailed at night and bottled-in the Roman ships lying at anchor in Lipara's nearby port. At daybreak, when the Roman crews discovered their plight, they abandoned their ships and fled ashore, leaving Scipio Asina and his officers to surrender to the Carthaginians and be taken back to Hannibal, together with their ships now manned by their captors.

Not many days after this incident, however, Hannibal himself suffered a reverse. News had reached him of the movement of the main Roman fleet down the coast of Italy, so he decided to go and investigate their numbers and disposition – possibly with a view to intercepting them since he cannot have held them in much regard after their performance at Lipara. But he had scarcely rounded Cape Pelorias with his fifty ships when he blundered into them. The Romans were deployed in good order and Hannibal suffered severely, being fortunate to escape himself with a part of his fleet. This engagement must have done much to restore Roman confidence in their ability to confront the Carthaginians at sea.

The Romans were well aware of their inadequacies, however, and they adopted a technical innovation to compensate for their lack of nautical expertise, so enabling them to exploit their legionaries' aptitude for close-quarter combat. During the ill-fated Athenian expedition to Syracuse during the Peloponnesian War, a grappling machine had been constructed on a number of ships. The Romans now developed this device, possibly with the assistance of Syracusan craftsmen, and added a boarding bridge, or corvus. A twelve-foot pillar of wood with a pulley on the top was fitted to the prow of every vessel. To this pillar the eighteen-foot long and four-foot wide boarding bridge was attached, which could be hoisted up and swung round in the required direction. At the end of the bridge there was a large pointed spike which, when the corvus was released, drove itself into the deck of the opposing vessel so locking the two ships together. On the quinqueremes were some eighty soldiers, with a lesser number on the triremes, who then stormed aboard. Skill at arms then replaced seamanship.

In 260 BC, Scipio Asina having been taken prisoner, Duilius left the conduct of the land campaign to the tribunes and took command of the fleet himself. Shortly after all his ships had been fitted out reports were received that the Carthaginians were ravaging the land around Mylae (Milayyo), on the north coast near Messana, and openly challenging the Romans to show that they were capable of facing them in battle. Though the Carthaginian fleet was numerically inferior to that of the Romans, 130 ships against the latters' 145, the Carthaginians confidently expected to compensate for this by their superior seamanship. A naval engagement consisted principally of manoeuvre, ships being handled so that they cut through their opponent's banks of oars and so immobilised them. Alternatively, they would simply turn sharply and ram their opponent, cleaving through the exposed timber with their metal clad prows.

An impression of such a naval engagement can be gained from the vivid account Thucydides gives of the battle between the Athenian and Syracusan fleets when the Athenians attempted to seize Syracuse during the Peloponnesian War:

When the Athenians approached the closed mouth of the harbour the violence of their onset overpowered the ships which were stationed there; they then attempted to loosen the fastenings. Whereupon from all sides the Syracusans and their allies came bearing down upon them, and the conflict was no longer confined to the entrance, but extended throughout the harbour. No previous encounter had been so fierce and obstinate. Great was the eagerness with which the rowers on both sides rushed upon their enemies whenever the word of command was given; and keen was the contest between the pilots as they manoeuvred one against another. The soldiers too were full of anxiety that, when ship struck ship, the service on deck should not fall short of the rest; every one in the place assigned to him was eager to be foremost amongst his fellows. Many vessels meeting, and never did so many fight in so small a space, for the two fleets together amounted to nearly two hundred, they were seldom able to strike in the regular manner, because they had no opportunity of first retiring or breaking the line; they generally fouled one another as ship dashed against ship in the hurry of flight or pursuit. All the time that another vessel was bearing down, the men on deck poured showers of javelins, arrows and stones upon the enemy; and when the two closed, the soldiers fought hand to hand, and endeavoured to board. In many places, owing to the want of room, they who had struck another found that they were struck themselves; often two or more vessels were unavoidably entangled about one, and the pilots had to make plans of attack and defence, not against one adversary only, but several coming from different sides. The crash of so many ships dashing against one another took away the wits of the crew, and made it impossible to hear the boatswain, whose voices in both fleets rose high, as they gave directions to the rowers, or cheered them, or the excitement of the struggle . . . at length the Syracusans and their allies, after a protracted struggle, put the Athenians to flight, and triumphantly bearing down upon them, drove them ashore where the crews abandoned their ships.

At Mylae the Carthaginian commander, the same Hannibal who had escaped from Agrigentum, shared his sailors' contempt for the inexperienced Romans and their clumsily handled ships. Disdaining even to pause to form them into battle formation, as soon as they sighted the Romans he let them race towards the enemy individually, fearful of missing the spoils of such an easy killing. As they approached the Roman fleet, however, there was a moment's hesitation and bewilderment at the sight of the strange construction rearing up on the prows of every ship. But contempt soon overcame hesitancy and they closed for action, whereupon they were immediately grappled, boarded and overcome.

Seeing their first thirty ships becoming locked to their opponents' in this manner, the remainder of the Carthaginian squadron turned aside to elude the corvi and then, exploiting their superior seamanship, swung round to approach the Roman ships from astern or from a flank. But from whichever direction they attempted to close, the corvi pivoted round to hang menacingly over them. Most of the Carthaginian ships veered off in time, but a further twenty were grappled, probably some of them by the second Roman line, and boarded in their turn before Hannibal and the survivors broke off the engagement. Duilius made no attempt to pursue the Carthaginian survivors, who were too fleet for him anyway, and they made their escape to Carthage. More urgently, he sailed to the western extremity of Sicily where he landed his troops just in time to relieve Segesta, which was under seige from Hamilcar and in the last stage of distress. When news of the naval success reached Rome, a victory column was raised in the Forum to Duilius, bearing the names of captured vessels and a fulsome inscription listing the honours bestowed upon him. A fragment of a copy of this inscription is to be found in the Capitoline Museum.

Their victory at Mylae gave the Romans an opportunity to extend the war beyond the narrow confines of Sicily. What until now had been a geographically-limited and land-based campaign, could in future be given a wider strategic dimension. There were two broad courses of action open to the Romans. First, they could pursue the Sicilian campaign but extend the theatre of operations to include Corsica and Sardinia. By coordinating land and sea operations against the key coastal cities they could sever their communications with Carthage and starve them into submission. In this manner the islands would fall to Rome and from a position of strength, a favourable peace treaty could be concluded. Against this had to be set the danger that sooner or later, the Carthaginians would reassert themselves. They then posed a long-term threat which could materialise at any time, but most menacingly when the Romans were engaged elsewhere, against other enemies, such as the Gauls.

Alternatively, the Romans could go on to the defensive in Sicily, ignore Corsica and Sardinia as being of no immediate consequence, and instead concentrate their forces for an assault on the African mainland, eventually leading to the destruction of Carthage. No doubt recalling the near success Agathocles of Syracuse had achieved when adopting this course under much more constrained circumstances, the Romans must have been tempted to follow his example. After one audacious and eliminating stroke against the heart of the Carthaginian empire, the then defenceless colonial territories could be incorporated into the Roman Confederation at little cost. Undoubtedly the risks were high. The Carthaginian fleet, though reduced, was still a potent force and its losses were being replaced. There was also no guarantee that the successful Roman tactics which had secured the victory of Mylae could be repeated under different circumstances. In the event caution prevailed and an enterprise of great moment was rejected in favour of the more meagre, localised operation.

Having established a clear strategic objective, the Romans now had to decide their operational priorities. The expulsion of the Carthaginians from Sicily could not be achieved by a purely land-based campaign. The ports of the strongly-fortified coastal cities had to be blocked and the sea lanes dominated. Naval supremacy was also necessary if the Romans were to secure the coastal ports of Sardinia and Corsica, though their defences were not nearly as formidable as those found in Sicily.

Now, the Romans had energetically sought to enlarge and improve their fleet, but it was still, like the Roman army, not sufficiently powerful to be split between widely spread objectives. Yet in 258 BC, this is exactly what was ordered. Instead of concentrating their resources against either Sicily or Sardinia and Corsica, the Romans attempted to conduct both campaigns simultaneously. Militarily, Sicily was by far the most important island; once it had been secured Sardinia and Corsica would have been isolated and their garrisons quickly destroyed. But either the military advice given was particularly inept, or political priorities appear to have prevailed: although Carthaginian raids on the Italian coastal regions from their bases in

Sardina had been of little military significance, their proximity to Rome was probably a matter of considerable concern. In this case political and military priorities must have come into conflict. But whatever the cause, no sensible operational plan was developed, and one consul, Cornelius Scipio, sailed for Corsica and Sardinia while the other, Cornelius Florus Aquilius, went to Sicily.

Scipio captured the port of Aleria in Corsica and so provided the Romans with a base for operations against Sardinia. There was no need to attempt to occupy the whole of the island; there were no other Carthaginians present and the island's inhabitants, who mainly lived in the near-impenetrable mountainous interior, did not pose a serious threat to Aleria. Leaving a part of his force to garrison the town, Scipio then attempted to establish a foothold in Ulbia, on the northern coast of Sardinia. He failed to capture the town because he did not have enough troops to engage the Carthaginian garrison. This shortage of troops probably also explains why, when he then encountered a Carthaginian naval squadron of slightly smaller size, he avoided giving battle for fear of not being able to board their ships. Scipio then withdrew to Aleria and in due course was replaced by Sulpicius Paterculus, who received substantial reinforcements.

Though the strength of his fleet was increased and the confidence with which he handled it suggests that his ships carried a full complement of troops, Sulpicius Paterculus did not feel strong enough to land on Sardinia, and certainly not until he had destroyed the Carthaginian fleet. He therefore concentrated on establishing Roman maritime supremacy. At the head of some 300 ships he made as though he was sailing to Africa, and in this way lured the much smaller Carthaginian fleet into giving battle. The Romans won a conclusive victory. Though the details are obscure it seems certain that the Carthaginians fared badly as much as a result of faulty leadership as from numerical inferiority, since Hannibal, their commander, was subsequently crucified by the enraged survivors. After this victory Sulpicius Paterculus continued to raid Sardinia but achieved nothing conclusive and the new campaign became bogged down through a lack of resources; a situation which was paralleled in Sicily.

Indeed, except for ending the politically sensitive Carthaginian raids against their own exposed coastline, there was no hope of the Romans being able to accomplish anything of significance. In fact the situation in Sicily had deteriorated. Dissension had arisen between the Romans and their allies, which had caused so much ill feeling that the decision was taken to separate their camps and live apart. News of this move reached Hamilcar, the Carthaginian commander-in-chief, while he was at Panormus and he now acted with determination.

Moving swiftly, he caught his opponents in the process of breaking camp and killed 4000 of them – though Diodorus puts the figure at 6000 and implies that they were all Romans, in which case their allies must have already distanced themselves. Diodorus then relates how some cities fell to the Romans and others to the Carthaginians as for two years the land war continued with revolts and desertions, each side occasionally obtaining some local success but unable to achieve anything decisive. Polybius gives a similar account but portrays a situation generally more favourable to the Romans, specifically mentioning the capture of Enna situated in the middle of the island. But the overall picture was the same, neither side possessed the means to do more than undertake a series of isolated, tactical battles. And the situation was very similar at sea; another indecisive naval encounter took place at Tyndaris, only a few miles from Mylae, in 257 BC, during which both fleets suffered near equal losses before Hamilcar made good his escape to Lipara.

At this stage of the war neither the Carthaginians nor the Romans had a continental strategy; they were engaged in a war of islands which depended upon sea power for its successful prosecution. At the outset of hostilities the Carthaginians already had a substantial fleet, and must have appreciated the significant advantage this gave them if used offensively in conjunction with their army. Initially, however, they were constrained by the fact that they had an insufficient army to face the Romans on land, and by the time their mercenary army had been raised and deployed, the Romans had largely redressed their maritime inferiority. Thus the two opponents who had started the war with unbalanced forces, by now had largely rectified their respective deficiencies and were seeking to achieve supremacy where the priority clearly lay, at sea.

Whether the decision to change the strategic direction of the war was a cause or a consequence of the Romans' greatly enlarging their fleet, is not known. But in all probability a growing disenchantment with the existing strategy, combined with an increasing acceptance of those advocating a more adventurous course, led to the construction of a fleet and the pragmatic introduction of new strategic thinking. In the meanwhile the Carthaginians, who could not have been unaware of Roman preparations and possibly of their intentions, had also been greatly increasing the size of their fleet. The stage was now set for what was to be one of the largest naval battles in the history of maritime warfare, that of Ecnomus. There had been a more consequential encounter at Salamis, where Greek civilisation was saved from possible extinction by Xerxes in the 5th century BC, and others were to come, such as Lepanto when the expansion of the Ottoman empire was checked in the 16th century, and Trafalgar in the

19th century, but for sheer size, Ecnomus stands alone. Ecnomus did not even decide the outcome of a campaign, let alone a war; it was no more than a battle which allowed an expedition to get under way. But in spite of its relatively limited consequences, it remains of historical interest in that it serves as an example, conceptually pre- dating Cannae, of land tactics being applied at sea. According to Polybius, the Romans had 330 ships, about 250 of which were probably quinqueremes and the remainder transports. To man this fleet would have required 100,000 men, with each quinquereme now having 300 rowers and 120 soldiers. The Carthaginian fleet was rather smaller but since it did not include any transports, its fighting strength was broadly comparable.

In the summer of 256 BC the Roman fleet set sail from Messana southwards along the eastern coast of Sicily, this time genuinely bound for Africa. A substantial part of the southern coast was in their hands and it was at Phintias, a port lying under Mount Ecnomus, that the two legions which had been carefully selected for the African expedition, were waiting to begin embarkation.

It may appear surprising that the Romans did not attempt to seek out the Carthaginian fleet and defeat it before taking their troops on board, especially when such substantial numbers of transports were involved. The vulnerability of these vessels which had to be towed is obvious enough, and the Romans must have had compelling reasons for risking their destruction. A possible explanation may be that the Romans recognised that the Carthaginians would not give battle until they saw that their army had been embarked. After all, there were two courses of action open to the Carthaginians: either they could withdraw to the African coastline and so be near their own bases, while correspondingly disadvantaging the Romans should the battle go against them; or they could adopt what in modern parlance is termed a 'forward defence' posture and force a decision off Sicily. As for the Romans, had they set sail for Africa without their transports, there was no reason why the Carthaginians should pursue their warships which, by themselves, posed no great threat. Alternatively, had the Romans sought a naval engagement in Sicilian waters, they could have found themselves lured away by the greater part of the Punic fleet, so that in either instance, the Romans' empty but vital transports lying defenceless off Phintias would have been an easy prey to even a small number of Carthaginian fighting ships. It is then readily understandable why the Roman fleet and their expeditionary force in fact set sail together.

While the Romans had been completing their preparations and final deployment, the Punic fleet under Hamilcar had sailed in the summer of 256 BC from Carthage and after reaching Lilybaeum, had moved eastwards along the southern coast to their forward base at Heraclea. This fortress, which had featured so prominently during the seige of Agrigentum, was no more than fifty miles from Phintias. From here Hamilcar must have been able to keep the Romans under close observation. It seems probable that the Romans would have had to undertake some final training at sea to perfect the handling of such a large number of ships. Whether or not this was the case, Hamilcar was not surprised at the Romans' eventual deployment and had devised his own countermeasures.

The Romans divided their fighting ships into four squadrons. Two squadrons formed the sides of a triangle with the two huge six-banked oared ships of the consuls Marcus Atilius Regulus and Lucius Manlius Vulso at the apex. The third squadron formed the base of the triangle and had the transports in tow. Behind them came the fourth squadron; also deployed into a single line but so extended as to cover the flanks of the third squadron and the transports.

The Carthaginians also divided their fleet into four squadrons; three of them were placed in line from the shore so that the one on the extreme seaward right did not directly face the Roman wedge, but remained free to advance and attack their left flank. The fourth Carthaginian squadron was deployed forward of the others, parallel to the shore, so that it was already in a position to attack the Roman right flank without having to change direction.

The Roman wedge drove forward towards the Punic fleet but as they approached the two squadrons directly facing them, the Carthaginians turned in accordance with the orders they had received, and withdrew. Enthused by their opponents' apparent flight, the Romans quickened their pace in pursuit, but in doing so lost formation; the third squadron towing the transports could not keep up with the two leading ones and soon became widely separated. At a signal from Hamilcar, the two squadrons which had been withdrawing suddenly turned upon their pursuers, while the one which had been deployed beyond the tightly formed Roman wedge, now advanced and fell upon the Roman rear. Simultaneously, the Carthaginian vessels which had been posted along the shore, advanced to attack the Roman squadron towing the transports. Three separate battles now raged, while the hapless transports were cast off and left to drift unattended. For a while both contestants held their own but eventually, despite their brilliant initial tactics, the Carthaginian squadrons engaging the apex of the Roman wedge were forced to give way and finally flee in earnest. Instead of giving pursuit, the Romans returned to assist their third and fourth squadrons, which were being heavily pressed, and the Carthaginians there were eventually totally broken.

The corvi had again proved their usefulness and though nearly as many Roman ships were sunk as Carthaginian, 24 and 30 respectively, 64 Carthaginian ships were captured.

Although the Romans were now free to cross over to Africa some delay occurred while essential repairs were completed, not only to their own vessels but also to those which had been captured and were now pressed into service. When all was ready the Romans put to sea for the second time. Abandoning any attempt to hold forward and dominate the seas around Sicily and Sardinia, the Carthaginians had fallen back to the Gulf of Carthage, where, in spite of their considerable losses, they were still a potent force and prepared to give battle a second time. But instead of sailing into the gulf on the western side of Cape Bon, the Romans disembarked at Aspis, called Clupea by the Romans and now known as Kelibia, on the eastern seaboard. The bay of Clupea provided secure anchorage and an excellent harbour, while the town, which lay close to the sea on high ground dominating the surrounding plain, formed a natural defensive position.

There was an element of inevitability in the Carthaginian fleet's failure to intercept that of the Romans and so prevent the disembarkation of their army. The most direct and obvious course for the Romans to have adopted was to have entered the Gulf of Carthage and land in close proximity to the city. But this would have necessitated another sea battle which, though it was one the Romans could have confidently expected to win, carried the risk of incurring heavy losses. They therefore chose an indirect approach, as had Agathocles of Syracuse, and accepted the greater natural land obstacles that would have to be overcome in marching on Carthage. Even without the precedent of Agathocles, the Carthaginians must have appreciated this possibility; the trouble was they could do nothing about it. To have divided their fleet would have invited defeat in detail, while to have covered the eastern approaches only would have exposed Carthage. The difficulty of implementing a purely defensive posture is well illustrated and the Carthaginians' previous forward deployment fully justified. Only the side possessing by far the greater strength and fighting ability can sit back and wait to be attacked; a fact that raises the question whether there are ever circumstances under which this could conceivably occur.

CHAPTER SIX

THE AFRICAN CAMPAIGN
256–255 BC

The Carthaginians did not have enough troops in Africa to do more than defend Carthage, so the Romans disembarked without hindrance and soon forced Clupea, some forty miles due east of Carthage, to surrender. They then set about putting its defences in order, while dispatching messages back to Rome reporting their success and requesting further instructions. That they had not been given clear orders before setting out, or were not prepared to act on their own initiative, may appear surprising. But presumably the delay following the battle of Ecnomus had so thrown out the Roman plans that a reappraisal of their original instructions was necessary. The Romans had probably assessed that Carthage, like the fortress cities of Sicily, could only be taken if blockaded by both sea and land, but winter was now approaching and it was too late to undertake such an enterprise. There was also the problem of what to do with the fleet; if it were to winter at Clupea, an enormous logistic problem would be created through having to feed some 75,000 rowers, who outnumbered the soldiers by three to one. In these circumstances it is readily understandable that existing plans would require revision.

While awaiting the return of their messengers and having completed the defences of the town, the Romans set out to plunder the surrounding countryside. They rounded up 20,000 slaves and great herds of cattle, and brought them back to Clupea. By then the messengers had returned from Rome with new instructions. One consul, Marcus Atilius Regulus, was to stay in Africa with 15,000 infantry, 500 cavalry and 40 ships. The other consul, Lucius Manlius Vulso, was to return to Rome with the majority of the fleet, including all the transports.

Carthage and its Neighbourhood

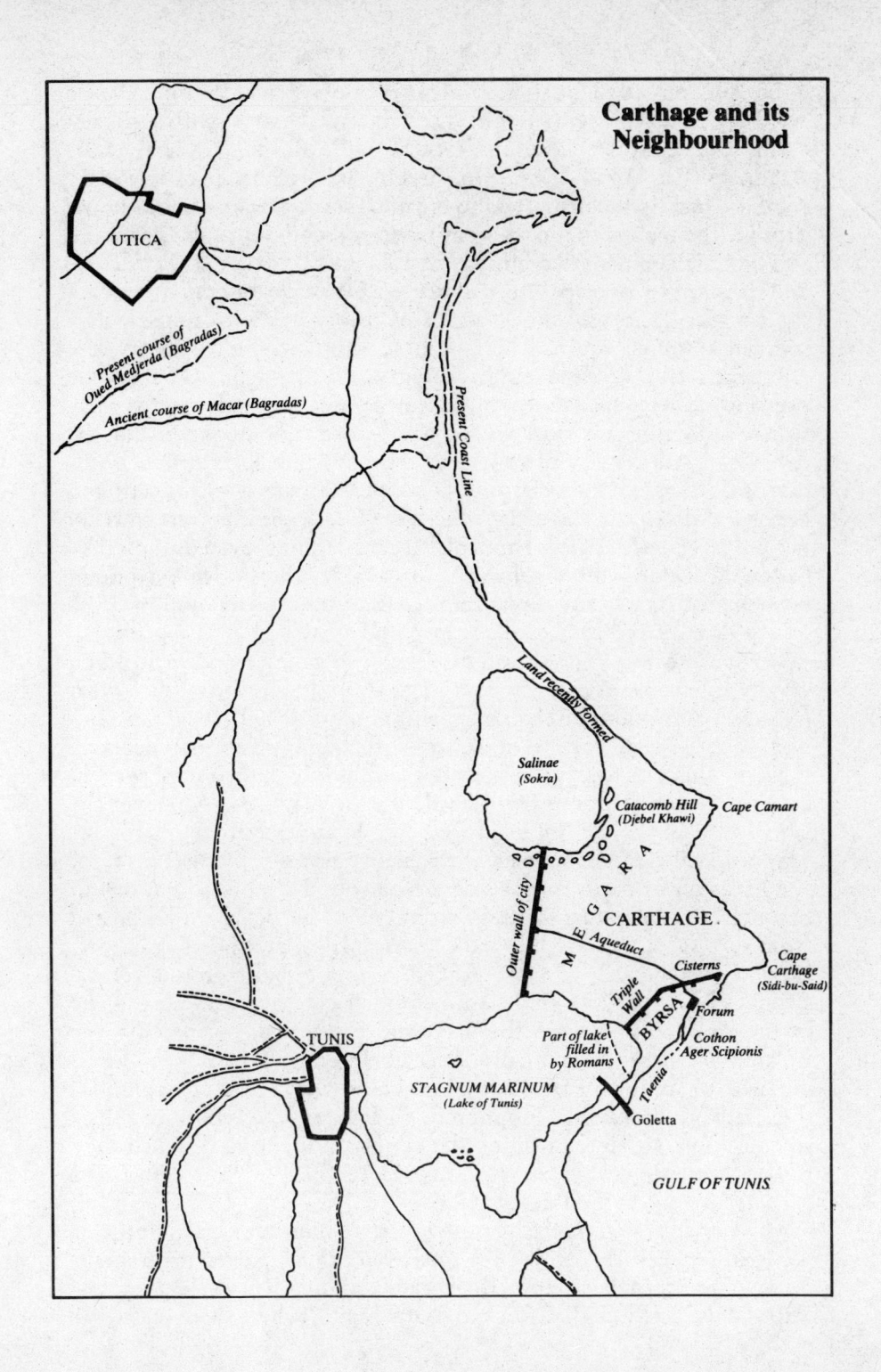

UTICA

Present course of Oued Medjerda (Bagradas)

Ancient course of Macar (Bagradas)

Present Coast Line

Land recently formed

Salinae (Sokra)

Catacomb Hill (Djebel Khawi)

Cape Camart

Outer wall of city

MEGARA

CARTHAGE

Aqueduct

Cisterns

Cape Carthage (Sidi-bu-Said)

Triple Wall

BYRSA

Forum

TUNIS

Part of lake filled in by Romans

Cothon

Ager Scipionis

STAGNUM MARINUM (Lake of Tunis)

Taenia

Goletta

GULF OF TUNIS

Loading on board the slaves and other booty, Lucius Manlius Vulso went on his way, leaving Regulus and the two legions, with sufficient ships to keep open communications with Rome. He was more fortunate than Agathocles who, in similar circumstances it will be recalled, had been constrained to burn his ships, because he could not provide the troops to guard them when marching into the interior.

The Carthaginians had initially appointed two generals, Hasdrubal and Bostar, to oversee the defence of Carthage but now, fearing their inadequacies and the shortage of troops at their disposal, they recalled Hamilcar from Sicily, with 5000 infantry and 500 cavalry. After the arrival of these reinforcements the Carthaginians felt able to prevent the Romans from ranging unopposed through the countryside, plundering at will. They therefore set about organising the defence of Adis, a city of some importance about forty miles southeast of Carthage, which early in 255 BC, the Romans were preparing to besiege. Adis lay on the plain, where the Carthaginians were initially not prepared to face the formidable Roman legions, even though they had with them some elephants and cavalry, the two most potent elements of their army. Accordingly they took possession of a hill which overlooked the Roman camp and provided a strong natural defensive position, cut through with steep ravines and protruding craggy outcrops. Whatever advantage this gave to their infantry, it effectively immobilised their elephants and cavalry. Tactical mobility was sacrificed in search of security through positional defence. Possibly this was to have been only the first move, the establishment of a secure base before giving battle on the plain; but whatever the Carthaginians' long-term intentions, the Romans were quick to take advantage of the predicament their enemy had got themselves into. Under cover of darkness they deployed round the hill and at dawn, before the Carthaginians could descend on to the plain, they attacked from two sides. For a while the Carthaginian mercenaries held their ground courageously and even forced one of the legions to withdraw, so that their elephants and cavalry, which had taken no part in the battle, were able to reach the plain and make their escape. But the isolated infantry were finally overwhelmed and broke in flight, pursued for some time by the Romans before they returned to plunder the Carthaginian camp. Unopposed, the Romans then continued their advance on Carthage, ravaging the countryside through which they passed until they arrived at Tunis. Here they pitched camp and prepared to invest the Punic capital.

The Carthaginians were by now in a state of near despair. Some of the Numidians had risen in revolt and were causing even greater and more widespread devastation than the marauding Roman legionaries. Thousands of refuges had flocked to the capital where there was soon an acute shortage of food, as well as the usual threat of disease breaking out among the overcrowded population. The mercenary troops had fought bravely and resolutely, but these soldierly qualities had not been matched by the competence of their generals, on sea or land.

The superiority of the Romans was then firmly established. They were strongly encamped within a few miles of Carthage in a position from where they dominated the surrounding countryside, the riches of which provided them with provisions in abundant quantities. Their sea communications to Rome were secure and the Libyans, if not actively helping them, had risen in revolt against their former overlords. The glorious prospect of a triumph stood before Marcus Atilius Regulus. After winning a notable victory at sea and now the sole consul at the head of no more than two legions, he had accomplished in one year's vigorous campaigning in a distant, hitherto unknown fearsome continent, more than any of his predecessors in nine years of costly warfare. Fame lay within his grasp: all that was required of him was the reduction of tottering Carthage.

But there was the rub. Desperate though its plight might be, Carthage was still a formidable city to take by storm and time was pressing. Regulus' replacement as commander of the consular army could shortly be expected to arrive from Rome and it would be intolerable if that man were to be accorded the glory of final conquest. The thought was too much for him and Polybius maintained that Regulus decided to negotiate with the Carthaginians, an offer which was gladly accepted. Diodorus and others, however, state that the initiative came from the Carthaginians which, under the circumstances, would not have been surprising. But in his desire to obtain through negotiations all that could have been accomplished by victory, Regulus' vanity overreached itself. He demanded that they cede Sicily, Sardinia and Corsica, renounce a fleet of their own, provide ships for Roman use, pay a large war indemnity, and sign a humiliating treaty of alliance which would have placed Carthage under Roman sovereignty at a level comparable to such minor cities as Tarentum and Neapolis (Naples). Such demands were too preposterous for even the despairing Carthaginians to accept. Negotiations were abruptly broken off.

It has to be admitted, however, that even if Regulus had attempted a more reasonable settlement it is still open to doubt whether acceptable terms could have been agreed. The Roman Senate could well have demanded the withdrawal of all Carthaginian troops from Sicily as a minimum requirement – a condition which would have been unlikely to have gained acceptance, since it would have required the abandonment of the great Carthaginian fortress cities in the western part of the island. Be as that may, the greatest mistake Regulus made was not to have solicited the assistance of the Numidians. It seems that the Romans did not yet appreciate the need for a mobile arm. Had they done so, it is inconceivable that they would have made no attempt to recruit these most versatile of horsemen and form a cavalry wing. It was a lost opportunity for which they were to pay dearly; the chance was not to occur again until over fifty years later, when Scipio landed in Africa.

But this failure may also have been attributable to the arrogance of Regulus. Diodorus, when commenting on him said,

> I look upon it as the duty of an historian diligently to observe the stratagems and management of affairs by generals on both sides; for by laying open and criticising other men's fault, the like miscarriage may be prevented in them that come after. And on the other side, by commending things which are done well, others are stimulated to virtuous actions. For who can but utterly condemn the pride, folly, madness and insolence of Atilius Regulus who, not able to bear the weight of this prosperous fortune, both lost his own reputation, and brought many great mischiefs and calamities upon the country. For when he might have concluded a peace with the Carthaginians, honourable and advantageous to the Romans, but base and dishonourable to the other, and his name might for ever have been renowned amongst all men for his clemency and humanity, he had no regard for any of these things; but proudly insulting the distresses of the afflicted, stood upon such terms which not only provoked the Gods to anger, but forced the conquered, by reason of these unreasonable conditions, to stand it out resolutely to the utmost extremity: so that the face of the affairs was suddenly changed . . . But he who was the author and occasion of so many miseries, had himself no small share in the calamity; since the present dishonour and disgrace far overbalanced his former glory and reputation; and by his misfortune others are taught not to be proud in prosperity.

Unfortunately for themselves, and for the many others who suffer from the consequences of their egocentricity, few such people ever believe they have anything to learn from history.

The firmness displayed by the Carthaginians in rejecting the Roman terms may in part have been because they knew assistance was on its way. When the plight of Carthage had prevented the recruitment and training of a new army from their traditional sources, the Carthaginians must have appreciated that professional soldiers, ready to take the field without delay, were urgently needed. Agents had accordingly been sent to Greece and what Polybius describes as 'a large body of troops' were recruited there and quickly shipped to Carthage, under the command of Xanthippus, a Spartan general who had received the thorough and disciplined military schooling associated with the Lacedaemonians. He was to prove himself a thoroughly competent soldier.

Incidentally, that such a substantial relief force could enter Carthage throws doubt on the severity of the famine inflicting the city portrayed by Polybius. If troops could get in, then so could have food and other provisions at an earlier date. Additionally, since there are no reports of the city being kept on short rations after the mercenaries arrival, and as there is no further mention of famine during Carthaginian preparations throughout the winter months, the situation was in fact probably less than critical.

During this preparatory period, Xanthippus closely questioned those who had been present at the defeat of Clupea. He then inspected the Carthaginian troops, paying particular attention to the elephants and the cavalry with which he was considerably impressed. He soon came to the conclusion that the fault lay not with the soldiers themselves, but with their generals. Although the Carthaginians had recruited Xanthippus because of his professional qualities, what remained of tarnished reputations had to be jealously preserved and, they could not bring themselves to put this mercenary soldier at the head of their army. But his views soon became known and were passed round until they finally reached the ears of the Senate, or perhaps the formidable Hundred. Xanthippus was summoned before them and gave his assessment clearly and convincingly. It had been a mistake to try to compensate for the weakness of their infantry by positioning them on broken ground. The respite gained had been brief and their mobile arms incapacitated. Since the Carthaginian strength lay primarily with their cavalry and elephants, they should exploit the superior mobility these provided by fighting the next battle on the plains. The Senate was convinced and according to Polybius, 'the care of the army was given to him'. But this care only extended to its training: when it eventually took the field, command was shared by what appears to have been a consortium of generals – at any rate until the troops themselves demanded that Xanthippus alone should lead them.

The preliminary winter training which Xanthippus had given the Carthaginian army had taken place outside the city walls, a sure indication that the Romans had not maintained the siege during the winter months but had retired into winter quarters. Furthermore, in the spring of 255 BC, before any reinforcements could reach the Romans, the Carthaginians marched out determined to give battle. In all they now mustered some 12,000 infantry and 4000 cavalry together with an unspecified number of elephants, and kept boldly to the plains. The Romans were initially surprised at this new-found Carthaginian audacity, but they quickly took up the challenge and had closed to within about a mile of their opponents before darkness started to fall and both sides camped for the night. At dawn the next morning Xanthippus, exercising his popularly-declared right of unfettered command, deployed his army in a thoroughly professional battle formation. He placed the elephants in a single line some way ahead of his infantry phalanx, with the cavalry equally distributed on the two wings. As Regulus was particularly concerned with the elephants, he drew up his Roman legions in deep and close order behind his light troops, positioning his cavalry on the wings like the Carthaginians. The result of these dispositions was that the Romans decreased the breadth of their front in order to achieve greater depth. In this way they hoped to be able to prevent the elephants from breaking through – but in fact, since their cavalry was outnumbered by at least six to one, it was courting disaster so to restrict the tactical mobility of their legions by compressing them into an unwieldy mass, so abandoning the open chequerboard formation which permitted the maniples to wheel within the legions to face a threatened flank. The Romans were to pay dearly for renouncing this flexibility, as they were also to do forty years later, at Cannae.

After completing their dispositions the two armies faced one another waiting for their commanders to give the signal to engage. Xanthippus made the first move. His elephants advanced to break the Roman ranks; he then unleashed the cavalry on both wings with orders to scatter their opponents' horse and swing round onto the exposed flanks of the infantry before surrounding them. The Romans for their part did not wait to receive the elephants, but ran forward clashing their swords against their shields and roaring their battle cry in an endeavour to scare man and beast alike. On the flanks, as was only to be expected, the Roman cavalry was soon swept off the battlefield and the survivors fled for their lives. Initially the infantry in the centre were more successful. In spite of their shortened front, the Roman left wing still extended beyond the elephants and so were able to close with the Carthaginian infantry immediately behind them who, unable to withstand the onslaught, broke and fled into their very camp, pursued by the Romans. But elsewhere unmistakable signs of an impending Roman disaster started to unfold. The elephants were not affected by the clamour raised by Regulus' centre and right wing but continued their lumbering gait, smashing into the Roman legionaries and trampling them underfoot in crumpled heaps. Confusion began to set in but, in spite of their heavy losses, the disciplined Romans held firm until the Numidian cavalry started to assail them from the rear, forcing those at the back to turn about in order to defend themselves. All semblance of order slowly disintegrated leaving each man to fight desperately for his own survival.

Waiting for the critical moment, Xanthippus then ordered forward his as yet unengaged phalanx lying behind the elephants. The disorganised Romans, by now attacked on all sides, could offer only a token resistance; forced yet more closely onto one another they were slaughtered where they stood. We are told that only 2000 escaped back to Clupea, though this figure presumably included some of the surviving cavalry from the Roman left wing which, when breaking the Carthaginian right, had become detached from the main army. Some 500 prisoners were taken, including Marcus Atilius Regulus himself. This suggests that if the Romans' total strength had remained the same as when they first landed, they must have lost at least 12,000 men, against the Carthaginians' 800, most of whom came from their right wing.

A later story tells how Regulus was sent by his captors to Rome to negotiate, but instead of trying to persuade the Senate to accept the Carthaginian peace terms, he urged them to continue the war. He then honourably returned to Carthage where, it is alleged, he was put to death with the greatest barbarity. Since neither Polybius nor Diodorus makes any mention of this incident, it appears to have been an attempt by the Romans at a later date to create a legend of honour in place of the shameful truth. When news of the defeat reached Rome, plans for the summer season's campaigning were radically revised, and new consuls were appointed. But all this delayed the fleet's sailing and the original intention to lay seige to Carthage by both land and sea had to be abandoned in favour of a more modest objective. As far as the Romans were concerned, there was after all no certainty even that Clupea would be able to hold out and remain available as a port of disembarkation for a renewed campaign in Africa. Without knowing all the circumstances, it is difficult to comment sensibly on the Roman decision to discontinue their African adventure, but in view of the magnitude of the reverse they had suffered, and the improved circumstances of the Carthaginians, it does not seem surprising that the Romans decided to limit their year's campaigning to recovering their troops from Clupea and then to change the strategic direction of the war back to Sicily. Even this undertaking was evidently only entered into after considerable debate. The Carthaginians had been making strenuous efforts to reconstruct their fleet, and the risk of engaging in a major sea battle off the distant coast of Africa must have seemed to the Romans hardly justified for the sake of rescuing the relatively small number of troops still holding out in Clupea – especially since the Carthaginians might in fact already have overwhelmed them.

Polybius deals briefly with what occurred: in the early summer a Roman fleet of 350 ships, under command of the consuls M. Aemilius and Servius Fulvius, sailed along the coast of Sicily to Hermaeum, on the tip of Cape Bon. Here they encountered the Carthaginian fleet and defeated it with ease, though there must be some doubt about the number of ships Polybius claims the Romans captured. He gives a figure of 114, which he later confirms when referring to a total of 464 vessels as eventually returning from Africa, compared to the original 350 which left Italy. Diodorus however, admittedly while commenting on the battle in an even more perfunctory manner, claims only twenty-four. But whether or not their ships were captured in such numbers, the Carthaginians clearly lost a large proportion of their fleet in one way or another, since they made no further attempt to interfere with the Romans.

Meanwhile, on land the Carthaginians had been besieging Clupea but the small garrison had held firm and the Romans were able to embark their men with hindrance, and, if later Roman historians are to be believed, also marched into the interior as a final demonstration of strength. This suggests that no very vigorous attempt had been make to take the city by storm and that following the defeat of their fleet, the Carthaginians probably raised the siege through fear of a direct threat to Carthage.

The relief felt by the survivors of Regulus' legions in Clupea was to be short-lived, since yet another devastating catastrophe faced them, this time at sea. The Roman fleet took its usual course when making its way back to Rome and sailed along the southern coast of Sicily. Polybius tells us that this was against the pressing advice of the pilots, who feared the sudden summer storms which were frequent at this time of year, but there may have been sound reasons for avoiding the Carthaginian-held cities on the western shore of the island. But in any event, the fleet was caught in a violent storm off Camarina and all but eighty ships were lost, together with their crews and the soldiers they were transporting. It has been estimated that 100,000 men may have drowned, though Thiel, without quoting any figures, implies that it could have been considerably less as the ships were undermanned. Whatever the figure, it was an appalling setback, coming as it did closely upon the débâcle on the African mainland.

As the year 255 BC drew to a close, both the Romans and the Carthaginians must have reviewed their respective positions with concern. The critical situation facing the Romans was obvious enough: either the war would have to be discontinued or another enormous effort made to replace their losses. The latter course was in fact adopted and in the space of some seven or eight months a new fleet was constructed and fresh legions raised. For the Carthaginians' part, although they had driven the Romans out of Africa, they too had to rebuild their fleet, as well as contend with widespread uprisings throughout their African possessions. Punic primacy and overlordship had been challenged. It would have to be re-established before Carthage could confidently resume the struggle.

CHAPTER SEVEN

THE RETURN TO SICILY
254–242 BC

In the spring of 254 BC two new consuls, Atilius Calatinus and Cornelius Scipio Asina left Italy for Messana with two fresh armies and 220 new ships. Here they joined up with the survivors from the disastrous storm off Camarina, who had been cared for and re-provisioned by Hiero of Syracuse before being assisted on their way to Messana. The eighty ships that managed to weather the storm now joined the newly-arrived fleet. Once the necessary preparations had been completed, all 300 vessels sailed round Cape Pelorias, along the north coast of Sicily to Cephaloedium, which was delivered up to the Romans by treachery. The armies then marched to Drepana but their attempt to besiege the city had to be abandoned due to the energetic efforts of the talented Carthaginian general Carthalo. Though the depleted forces which he had been left with in Sicily were no match for the new Roman armies, he was at least able to deflect them. The Romans then re-embarked their troops and sailed to Panormus, one of the largest and richest of the Carthaginian cities lying on the sea and possessing a good harbour. The city had grown with prosperity, becoming economically the most important in the Punic area, and the old town with its retaining wall had not been able to contain the expanding population, so a new town had been built round the original site, enclosed within a new fortified wall. Though modern historians speak of less than half the number, according to Diodorus, there were nearly 70,000 people living in Panormus, and since he refers to the heavily wooded countryside coming up to the very city gates, most of these cannot have depended to any great extent on agriculture for living.

Casting anchor in the harbour, the Romans landed under the walls of the city which they then set about investing by digging a surrounding trench and constructing timbered mounds and bulwarks. Once this work had been completed they placed their siege weapons in position and without great difficulty battered down one of the forts standing nearest to the sea. Entering the breach, the Romans quickly secured the new outer town and gave little quarter to those they found there. No doubt intimidated by the ease and ruthlessness with which the Romans had secured their first objective, those sheltering in the old town immediately surrendered. Such of the population who could afford to purchase their freedom for 200 drachmas a head did so; the remainder were sold into slavery.

It has been suggested that Carthalo did not attempt to relieve Panormus as he had relieved Drepana because he was prevented by one of the Roman consular armies detached from the assault on Panormus. Whatever the cause, Carthalo must then have decided that he would do better by attacking the Romans elsewhere. Marching suddenly to the south, therefore, he seized Agrigentum and burnt the much-fought-over city to the ground. In the meantime, the two successful Roman consuls at Panormus had left a strong garrison in the town, which was to remain a Roman base for the rest of the war, and then returned to Rome at the end of the year's campaigning.

The immediate consequences of the fall of Panormus was that several other cities – notably Tyndaris and Solus on the north coast, and the inland city of Petra lying midway between them – rose against their Punic garrisons and declared for Rome. Carthaginian possessions in Sicily were now mainly reduced to those in the western extremity, principally around Lilybaeum and Drepana and on the south coast, Heraclea, which had served as a forward operating base during the Roman siege of Agrigentum eight years previously. Thermae was the only city on the north coast not already taken that remained loyal to Carthage, but its relative isolation made it of little practical consequence. All seemed to be going well for the Romans after the return to Sicily as their major theatre of operations, but in the following year there was a shift of policy.

According to Polybius, in 253 BC the consuls Cornelius Servilius Caepio and Cornelius Sempronius Blaesus at the head of their armies only staged through Sicily before setting sail to Africa, where they did not attempt to threaten Carthage directly but contented themselves with raiding the Libyan coast line some 200 miles to the south. The decision to undertake this campaign seems quite extraordinary. Even though subsequent events indicate that the Romans did not actually send more than a part of their army on the African expedition, and there would still have been some hard fighting ahead before all the remaining cities in Sicily could be taken, there was certainly every prospect of being able seriously to compress the Carthaginian possessions during the year's campaigning.

What may have caused the Romans to change the direction of the campaign was the fear that they would not be able to secure the whole of Sicily before the Carthaginians had quelled the unrest in Africa and restored their authority over the Libyans, and so been free to send a relieving expeditionary force to Sicily. Carthalo had proved himself a worthy opponent two years previously, when he had been left to manage with only those troops remaining after the major withdrawals made for the defence of Carthage. Were he to be substantially reinforced, the problems for the Romans in reducing such formidable cities as Lilybaeum and Drepana would be greatly increased. The need to provoke more trouble on the mainland and sustain the unrest among the Libyans and the Numidians had probably appeared more urgent than pressing forward with the campaign in Sicily.

However logical the reasoning, this sudden change of policy both caused confusion by dividing Roman resources in the attempt to pursue a double aim and also, in the event, proved ineffectual. The early authorities, Polybius and Diodorus, are agreed in stating that the Romans accomplished nothing, the latter going so far as to say that they were prevented even from making a landing. Later sources, favoured by some modern historians, give a somewhat different account, alleging that though Servilius Caepio remained in Sicily with the army, Sempronius Blaesus was so successful in taking the fleet on its raiding expedition that he was awarded a triumph. If this honour really was granted, he seems to have been most fortunate. Polybius describes, perhaps somewhat charitably, how through ignorance of the Libyan coast, his fleet was nearly lost when it became ignominiously stranded off the island of Meninx on an ebb tide, the Romans saving themselves only by throwing overboard all their baggage and furniture. But worse still was to befall them; after putting in at Panormus on their return, they were caught in a storm on passage to Rome and lost 150 of their 220 ships, together with their crews. After such episodes it seems improbable that Sempronius Blaesus should have celebrated a triumph – especially since the claim of success in Africa seems equally doubtful as the Carthaginians were able to send reinforcements to Sicily shortly afterwards.

Although many of Sempronius Blaesus' crews came from among the allies, and at least a proportion of those lost could have been impressed rowers from the subjected cities of Sicily, or other slaves, the drain on Roman manpower must have been becoming acute. In consequence, perhaps, the Senate took no immediate steps to replace their naval losses. Instead they sent two new consuls to Sicily the following year with sixty ships, sufficient only for a holding operation there, to convey the necessary provisions and provide an element of local protection. Except for the capture of the isolated town of Thermae and the occupation of the principal islands of Liparae, the latter only made possible through the help of Hiero who provided an auxiliary naval contingent, the following two years saw little developments of consequence.

Behind the scenes, however, there was much activity. Shortly after Sempronius Blaesus' abortive expedition to Africa, the Carthaginians re-established their sovereignty over the dissident Libyans and, in late 252 or early 251 BC, sent fresh troops to Sicily under Hasdrubal, son of Hanno, who had been one of the Carthaginian generals with Xanthippus at the defeat of Marcus Atilius Regulus. He seems to have learned a lot from his experiences but, as events were to show, not enough to save his life.

Polybius relates how for two years Hasdrubal, although probably numerically the inferior, dominated the plains and in particular the countryside around Lilybaeum and Silenus, the latter lying on the south coast. Perhaps because the survivors of Regulus' disastrous defeat had brought back horrific stories about the Numidian cavalry and the elephants that had trampled through their ranks, the Roman army was not prepared to face either again in open battle, and kept to the high ground instead. The Carthaginians for their part were unwilling to engage the Romans unsupported by their most effective arm. Thus the situation which had existed at the battle of Adis was now reversed: the Carthaginians sought battle on the plains and the Romans had taken to the hills for protection, and neither was prepared to challenge the other except on ground of his own choosing. The stalemate had to be broken and once more the Roman Senate turned to the sea for a solution. In 250 BC they started constructing another fleet, though on this occasion of more modest proportions, an additional fifty ships. Once these were ready two new consuls were appointed, Cornelius Atilius Regulus and Lucius Manlius Vulso, both of whom had previous experience in the field. But long before they could arrive in Sicily, the situation there had changed dramatically.

The previous autumn, encouraged by the news that one of the consuls of the previous year had returned to Italy with half the Roman troops and that the remaining consul, Lucius Cecilius Metellus, had left the protection of Panormus to gather in the harvest, Hasdrubal had decided to give battle. No doubt he was further influenced by the knowledge that, should he not act now, two new consular armies would be dispatched the following year, so tilting the balance of strength decisively against him. Confident in his moral and physical superiority over the Romans, Hasdrubal marched his army from Lilybaeum to Panormus and camped with his elephants at the head of what was probably the Orethus Valley. Metellus, seeing the confidence with which the Carthaginians had entered this hitherto Roman-dominated territory, made no effort to protect the harvest which was now being systematically ravaged, but instead retired temptingly behind the city walls.

Hasdrubal was deceived by this appearance of timidity, boldly advanced his army through the pass, and continued wasting the countryside and destroying the harvest. Metellus held his men back until the Carthaginians had crossed the river flowing into the sea just south of the city. Then he sent forward his light troops to harass the Carthaginian vanguards, so forcing them to deploy into the entrenchments which surrounded the city walls – possibly those dug by the Romans when besieging the city four years previously – with orders to discharge their javelins at the elephants as they advanced but if hard-pressed, to take refuge in the ditches. The light troops were kept well supplied with weapons by artificers who were drawn up at the front of the city walls, and Metellus himself stood concealed with the legions outside the gate that faced the Carthaginian left wing, from time to time dispatching detachments to help them. The commander of the Carthaginian elephants pressed forward the advance to scatter this seemingly feeble opposition, but in doing so he exposed the animals to such a hail of missiles from the walls and the trenches that they became enraged and, being unable to cross the entrenchments, turned about and tore through the ranks of their own infantry behind them. At this moment Metellus ordered the legions to advance and fall upon the left flank of the outwitted Carthaginians, who either fell where they stood, or fled in total disorder. The Romans wisely made no attempt to pursue them but instead rounded up the elephants, of which ten were taken together with their Indian mahouts, the remainder being collected later by their drivers who had been thrown but miraculously had survived the ensuing butchery. The elephants were later sent back to Rome to grace the triumph accorded to Metellus before being slaughtered in the circus. Nor was Hasdrubal himself any more fortunate; he escaped from the battlefield only to be recalled to Carthage and executed. He was replaced by Adhubal who considered it no longer possible to garrison Silenus; now that their elephants had been lost the Carthaginians could not dominate the low-lying countryside, so the town was destroyed and its inhabitants moved to Lilybaeum.

Shortly after Hasdrubal's defeat, Regulus and Lucius Manlius Vulso arrived at Panormus and disembarked their legions before marching them to invest Lilybaeum. There is some dispute as to the number of ships the two consuls brought with them; Polybius refers to 240, Diodorus adds 'sixty round vessels and all other sorts of shipping' to the number while Thiel, after some fairly abstruse calculations and reasoning, arrives convincingly enough at the figure of 120. The significance of the lower estimate is that the Romans had a fleet of sufficient size to support their land operations, but not to dominate the sea approaches to Lilybaeum or to retain overall maritime supremacy, should the Carthaginians increase their own numbers beyond the seventy ships they had remaining to them. Meanwhile, their fleet was sheltered at Drepana, lying between Lilybaeum and Panormus, from where it seems to have had little difficulty in running the Roman blockade of Lilybaeum.

On land the besieging Romans had four legions but they also employed the crews of their ships in a variety of ways, such as in the construction of siege works and manning the siege engines. This diversion of naval manpower must have been largely responsible for the relative ineffectiveness of the blockade. It also resulted in so many deaths through battle casualties, exposure and probably disease, that 10,000 replacements were required the following year. But we do not know the facts, and the enormity of the task in constructing the siege works may have justified such a seemingly wasteful sacrifice.

Within Lilybaeum the Carthaginian garrison, mainly Greek and Celtic mercenaries, had been reduced following the defeat of Hasdrubal to some 7000 infantry and 700 cavalry. Their morale must have been low. Indeed, after the Romans had begun their assault in earnest, some mercenary officers attempted to betray the city by crossing the lines by night. That they were prevented from doing so was due to the loyalty of a Greek officer called Alexon, who had already rendered a similar service at Agrigentum when the Syracusans had turned traitor. So Himilco, the Carthaginian commander, having been warned, was able to rally the garrison by personal exhortation, and when the traitors returned with Roman peace terms, they were driven back from the walls with stones and javelins.

The Romans faced a herculean task in trying to reduce Lilybaeum. The city lay on a promontory which formed the western extremity of the island, and was secured by a massive wall and a deep ditch. Additionally, the approach to the harbour lay through a number of tidal inlets, so that only those closely acquainted with the shifting shoals could safely make the passage. Following their usual practice, the Romans' first action was to establish two camps on either side of the promontory and then fortify the ground lying between them. Having done this, they then started constructing earth and timber works which were extended towards the fort on the southern, or African, side of the promontory. By using battering rams and siege engines to hurl massive boulders, they succeeded in demolishing six of the outer towers. In spite of the energetic leadership of Himilco, the destructive force of the Romans' siege weapons and the relentless pressure of their assaults began to wear down and demoralise the garrison. It was at this critical moment that Hannibal, son of Hanno, who had been waiting at sea between Carthage and Lilybaeum for a favourable wind, sped through the surprised Roman blockading force with fifty ships under full sail. According to Polybius, he brought with him 10,000 reinforcements, as well as ample provisions. Though Diodorus reduces the number to 4000, whatever the figure, the garrison gained new heart from the presence of these fresh troops, and the display of determination on the part of Carthage which their arrival represented. As for the Romans, they attempted to prevent any recurrence of such an exploit by closing the harbour mouth with a massive timber boom, firmly anchored to the sea bed. But high winds soon combined with the surging sea to smash it, and although further attempts were made an effective barrier was in fact never created. For most of the siege, therefore, skilfully-handled Carthaginian ships came and went almost at will. Eventually, however, the Romans captured one which had run aground at night on an artificial bank they had constructed and manning this vessel with a specially-selected crew, they overhauled and took another of these fleeting quinqueremes captained by a legendary figure called Rhodian, who had pioneered the blockade-running. With two such vessels in their possession, the Romans were at last able to put an end to such traffic.

Prompted by the arrival of reinforcements and the rising confidence of his troops, Himilco meanwhile had decided to try and destroy the Roman siege works which were so relentlessly demolishing the city's fortifications. He therefore assembled his soldiers and after promising substantial rewards and high honours to those displaying marked courage, he dismissed them with orders to rest before the coming battle. At dawn the Carthaginians mounted their foray but the Romans, whether as a result of intelligent anticipation or through the betrayal of a deserter, were standing to arms and fully prepared. The Carthaginians attacked with desperate ferocity and some of them succeeding in cutting their way through the Roman ranks bearing flaming torches, but before they could fire the siege works they too perished. Seeing his troops being annihilated to no advantage, Himilco sounded the retreat and the engagement was broken off, but at great cost.

The Carthaginians then gave up all hope of being able to destroy the Roman siege works, and instead were concentrating their energies on repairing the damage they wrought when an unexpected opportunity suddenly presented itself. A violent wind blew down several of the wooden towers protecting the Roman siege machinery. Some Greek mercenaries saw their chance and, after receiving Himilco's permission, again sailed out. Three separate fires were started among the fallen towers and as their timbers were old they were soon well ablaze. Fanned by a high wind the fire spread rapidly, engulfing the siege machines as well as the remaining towers and other engineering works. Blinded by the flames, flying sparks and billowing smoke that rolled towards them, the Romans were unable either to save anything from the inferno or confront the Carthaginians who, with the wind behind them, took every opportunity to complete the destruction; all the towers were burnt to their foundations and even the metal heads of the great battering rams melted in the fire. Following such a setback, the Romans gave up trying to take the city by storm and, after improving their own entrenchments and protective fortifications, settled down to starve Lilybaeum into submission. But eight years later when the First Punic War ended, it still stood unconquered.

Undeterred by the magnitude of the reverse that had been suffered, in 249 BC the Senate dispatched two new consuls to Sicily, Publius Claudius Pulcher and Pullus Junius, together with the 10,000 new rowers required to replace those lost in the siege. When Claudius Pulcher arrived at the Roman camp before Lilybaeum, he assembled the tribunes and put forward an audacious plan to destroy the Carthaginian fleet while it was at anchor in Drepana. Adhubal, he argued, would be quite unprepared since he knew nothing about the new levies which he, Claudius Pulcher, had brought with him to crew the fleet. Convinced by his eloquence, the tribunes approved the proposal and the sailors were immediately ordered to embark. Allured by the prospect of an easy killing, volunteers from the legions were also taken on board. If they really were volunteers as Polybius declares, in view of what must have been the obviously poor state of training among the hastily assembled and inexperienced crews they would have been wiser to remain ashore.

Though the Romans still relied on closing with enemy ships and boarding them, they no longer employed the corvus which had given them such an advantage until the battle of Ecnomus. The reason for this appears to be twofold: first, the awkward construction on the prows of the ships undoubtedly adversely affected their handling, especially in bad weather; second, having got over their initial surprise, the Carthaginians had developed tactics which reduced the effectiveness of the corvus.

Setting sail at midnight, the Roman fleet of 120 ships hugged the shore in line astern, timing their arrival as near to dawn as possible so as to achieve the maximum surprise; the intention being to catch the Carthaginian fleet while still at anchor in the harbour. But as so often happens with even the best of plans, nothing worked out quite as intended. As a start, either the passage of some twenty miles must have taken longer than expected or Adhubal had forward lookouts or scouting ships in position. But in either case he saw the van of the Roman fleet in good time. At first he could not believe that the ships belonged to the Romans, but once they had been correctly identified, Adhubal was able both to evacuate the harbour without undue haste and to harangue his crews on the prospects of an easy victory. Claudius Pulcher made his own positive contribution to the pending disaster by taking station during the night move at the rear of the fleet. Evidently this was normal practice, to ensure there were no laggards, but as a result, when the Carthaginians sailed out of Drepana, he must have been about the last person to have known what was happening and was unable to adjust his plans. In the absence of any fresh orders, the leading Roman ships entered the harbour. Orders to turn about then reached them, but in turning the ships already in the harbour fouled those still attempting to enter; oars were broken and total confusion arose among those forming the van.

At last however, the officers managed to form up all the ships as ordered, into a line along the shore with the prows facing out to sea. The Carthaginians meanwhile had cleared the two small islands lying across the approaches to the harbour and, swinging round behind them, formed a corresponding line facing the shore, with their right wing extending slightly beyond that of the Romans' left, where Claudius Pulcher had stationed himself. The Romans were now effectively trapped with the shore behind them, the sickle-like promontory to their right and the Carthaginians to their front and left.

When all his ships were in position, Adhubal gave the order to attack. To begin with, when the two lines of ships clashed and the close in-fighting started, both sides held their own, but after a while the disadvantages from which the Romans suffered began to tell. As a start the Roman ships were heavier and clumsier, while their crews were relatively inexperienced and unskilled. They were also restricted through having the shore so close behind then, leaving no room to manoeuvre or, if hard-pressed, to withdraw. The Carthaginian vessels on the other hand were lighter, better crewed, more agile, and free to manoeuvre at will. It was not long before the Roman fleet started to disintegrate. Some of their vessels were smashed against the shore, other grounded on the shallows, while still others were taken or destroyed by the Carthaginians. Claudius Pulcher managed to escape with about thirty of his ships on the left flank, but the remainder, numbering at least ninety, together with the majority of their crews and the soldiers on board, either perished at sea or were taken by the Carthaginians. Only a few managed to run their ships ashore in such a manner that they could make their escape. As for Claudius Pulcher, after being roundly abused on the spot for his gross imprudence he was returned to Rome in disgrace to face a heavy fine. He had been responsible for a disaster in which, though Polybius gives no figures, according to Diodorus 20,000 lives were lost.

There is little to mitigate the scorn that has been poured upon Claudius Pulcher; Thiel in particular is positively savage in his condemnation. The fortunes of war can be very fickle, however. In view of Claudius Pulcher's impiety towards the sacred chickens which, it will be remembered, he flung overboard because they would not eat, the gods perhaps could not reasonably have been expected to exhibit much favour, but circumstances generally could have been kinder. Had he been able to achieve his planned surprise, his adventurism would have gone down instead in history as an example of inspired daring. Still, it has to be admitted that he was a particularly arrogant member of the already proud Claudius family, as two stories related by Livy suggest. The first tells that when Claudius Pulcher's sister was taking part as a Vestal Virgin in a procession, the crowd pressed in more closely than she considered appropriate and she was heard to say that 'she wished her brother was still alive to get rid of more of them at sea'. The second claims that when Claudius Pulcher was recalled, without authority he named a dictator in his stead, a freed man of his family, Claudius Glycia. Though his nominee was shortly afterwards disposed of, it was an act of true Claudian effrontery.

After he had dispatched the Roman prisoners and captured ships to Carthage, Adhubal was joined at Drepana by seventy more vessels commanded by Carthalo. He added thirty of his own ships to these reinforcements, thus dividing his forces, and dispatched them to Lilybaeum with instructions to destroy the remainder of the Roman fleet sheltering there. Carthalo, with the timing and element of surprise Claudius Pulcher had failed to achieve when sailing in the opposite direction, arrived under cover of darkness and after entering the Roman anchorage before it was even light, seized or destroyed all the ships which he found there. Himilco, seeing the confusion which reigned in the Roman camp as a result of this sudden attack, sallied out from behind the city walls to add to the Romans' disarray. After reassembling his triumphant fleet, Carthalo then set sail from Lilybaeum to Heraclea where, for the moment, it is necessary to leave him.

While these dramatic events had been unfolding around the western limits of Sicily, Claudius Pulcher's fellow consul Pullus Junius had been active at the other end of the island. His task was to collect the supplies so badly needed by the Roman legions besieging Lilybaeum and transport them there by sea. For this purpose Junius had been given sixty-six ships in Italy, with which he sailed to Messana. Here he was joined by a further 120 ships of war and 800 transports, gleaned from every available source in and around Sicily. Junius then moved his massive fleet further down the coast to Syracuse, where, like Adhubal in Drepana, he divided it into two. Placing one half under command of the quaestors, he dispatched it to bring immediate relief to the army at Lilybaeum. Retaining command of the other half himself, Junius remained at Syracuse to gather in the corn being supplied by the allies from the inland parts of the island. There were also a number of ships that had not been able to reach Messana in time but were beginning to arrive at Syracuse.

It is necessary now to try and understand what the Romans and the Carthaginian naval commanders' assessment of the situation was. It seems reasonable to suppose from the account given by Polybius that by the time Junius had reached Messana, news of Claudius Pulcher's defeat had reached him. The transfer of his fleet to Syracuse was then probably his first step in reaching a decision to follow the southern coast of Lilybaeum, so as to avoid the Carthaginian fleet lying at Drepana. Though Syracuse's superior harbour and the convenience of assembling and loading supplies was an important factor, there may also have been others which had been taken into account. That Junius then divided his fleet has been roundly condemned by modern historians, but these criticisms should be moderated. How urgently did the Roman army standing before Lilybaeum require reprovisioning? How could the port there receive and shelter an assembled fleet numbering nearly 1000 vessels? Was it possible to control such a vast armada during its passage along the exposed southern coast? Did Junius know, as seems highly improbable, that Carthalo was sailing south to Heraclea? These and other questions need to be answered before untempered criticisms are levelled. All we do know for certain is that the situation of the army at Lilybaeum cannot in fact have been all that desperate, since it held out until resupplied by land some considerable time later.

As for the Carthaginians, Adhubal's fleet must have taken a buffeting during the battle off Drepana, and the thirty ships he detached to accompany Carthalo may have been the only ones immediately available in a seaworthy condition. Was this then the reason for his dividing his fleet, or was he uncertain as to whether the Romans would come round the northern or southern coast? According to Diodorus, it was only following Carthalo's raid at Lilybaeum that news of the Romans' intentions to move round the south coast reached the Carthaginians. After holding a council of war, the decision was taken by Carthalo to sail to Heraclea and intercept them. There is some confusion over the number of Punic ships available for this operation; we know Carthalo had a hundred when he left Drepana, seventy of his own and thirty of Adhubal's, but Diodorus now refers to him sailing with 220 which, if correct, means that he had been reinforced from Carthage or Drepana. As no mention is made of this occurring by either Polybius or Diodorus, it seems probable that the figure had been inflated. It can, then, be assumed that Adhubal remained at Drepana with most of his ships as there was still some uncertainty about Roman intentions; they had after all also divided their fleet.

When Carthalo and Junius set out from Lilybaeum and Syracuse respectively, they both kept close to the southern coastline, the former sailing east in full anticipation of another victory, the latter sailing west in ignorance of any danger. Near Gela the scouting frigates saw one another and when the Romans realised that they were faced with a superior Carthaginian fleet, they ran for shelter at Phintias. This is somewhat surprising, as Phintias lay some twelve to fifteen miles further west of Gela. The accounts of what then occurred differ in detail but the main course of events is clear. Phintias was a small fortified town which had sided with Rome. It did not have a harbour but there were a number of creeks enclosed by promontories that extended for some way into the sea, and it was here that the Roman ships took shelter and the troops disembarked. The Carthaginians pressed home their attack, but after a stiff fight in which an uncertain number of Roman ships were destroyed or captured, they withdrew to the adjacent river Alycus where they cast anchor, tended their wounded and awaited developments.

Junius by now had finished loading the supplies which had been collected at Syracuse. He set sail and, after rounding Cape Pachynus (Cape Passero), proceeded along the coast towards Lilybaeum in all ignorance as to what had happened to the quaestors. It then came as a total surprise to him to find the Carthaginian fleet blocking his passage off Phintias. Accounts differ as to whether Junius turned and fled, or took refuge near a particularly dangerous stretch of the coast where Carthalo, not being prepared to hazard his own ships, stood and waited, knowing that the Romans could not remain there indefinitely. But in the event it was nature which decided Junius' fate. The experienced Carthaginian coastal pilots recognised the signs of an impending storm and urged their commander to take shelter in the lee of Cape Pachynus without delay. Although Carthalo promptly took their advice, it was only with the greatest of difficulty that the Carthaginian fleet rounded the promontory and was able to ride out the storm in its shelter. The Roman fleet never had a chance to escape the tempest that hit them: only two vessels escaped, the remainder were shattered on the rocks. Miraculously Junius numbered among the survivors and managed to make his way to Lilybaeum without further mishap. Here the siege was reinforced and the legions were sustained in food and other provisions by means of great overland pack trains supplied by the allies.

In spite of his failure at sea Junius now showed himself to be a vigorous and even enterprising commander on land. He appreciated that there was no way of actually taking Lilybaeum, now that the Carthaginians dominated the sea. Dividing his force, therefore, and leaving one part to maintain the siege, he marched to the mountain of Eryx, on the coast between Drepana and Panormus. On its level summit at that time there stood a temple of great antiquity which, though dedicated to Venus, betrayed by its system of temple prostitution, an eastern origin. Its importance to the Romans, however, was derived from its dominating position at the approaches to Drepana. By seizing the mountain, they were able to contain the Carthaginian garrison in Drepana as well as Lilybaeum.

In spite of this tactical coup, ill fortune appears to have dogged poor Junius. He was captured soon afterwards when leading a foray and, when returned to Rome two years later in an exchange of prisoners, he committed suicide rather than face the humiliation and condemnation which had befallen Claudius Pulcher.

Meanwhile, their succession of maritime disasters had brought the war to a low ebb for the Romans. Not only had at least 500 fully-manned vessels of war and a thousand transports been lost, but the state faced bankruptcy and exhaustion. The census of citizens had fallen by some 17 per cent of the total, not counting their allies. To call for new taxes and further levies of manpower risked social unrest, and in 247 BC political changes became inevitable. The Fabii who had traditionally favoured a policy of moderation towards Carthage, so that their own landed interests in the north could be extended, had been rebuilding their political alliances and exerting an increasing influence on public opinion. The Claudii, who had stood to gain more by a southern expansion, were becoming discredited and faced accusations of impiety; after all the chicken-drowner Claudius Pulcher was a member of the Claudian clan.

Nor was the situation in Carthage all that much better. Success at sea had been nullified by impotence on land. Following the ousting of the war party by the great landowners, therefore, attention was diverted from Sicily to interests nearer home. Two of the most successful generals – Himilco the heroic defender of Lilybaeum, and Adhubal the victor, were relieved of their command – they were replaced by Hanno the Great, appointed by the landowning party, and Hamilcar Barca. Barca represented the Carthaginian war party's interests and, being energetic and resourceful, he was not prepared to accept the situation he found on arriving in Sicily – disaffection among the mercenary troops who had served under Carthalo and a passive acceptance of being bottled up in the static defence of besieged Lilybaeum and Drepana. He dealt severely with the malcontents, and by his leadership, earned their unwavering allegiance throughout the remainder of the war. His next intention was to take the offensive, but his resources were slim, limited basically to the existing garrisons within the two besieged cities.

Hanno the Great, meanwhile, had been given orders to pursue the campaign against the Saharan tribes and exploit the Carthaginian agrarian empire in Africa. Backed by greater support than Hamilcar Barca's, these orders resulted in the capture of Theveste, the furthest point Carthaginian conquests ever reached.

But the Carthaginians were growing short of money. The demands placed upon their resources in simultaneously maintaining a powerful fleet, sustaining her troops in Sicily, subduing the Numidians, and extending her Libyan conquests still further, were proving too much for even their well-stocked treasury. When an attempt was made to negotiate a loan from Ptolemy II of Egypt and he sagaciously declined on the grounds that he was a friend of both Rome and Carthage, the Carthaginian fleet was withdrawn from Sicily altogether.

It was at this time that Rome's treaty with Hiero of Syracuse expired: he had been a loyal ally, providing supplies not only on a regular basis but also in times of crisis when the Romans had faced starvation before the cities of Agrigentum and Lilybaeum. He had also harboured the survivors of two naval catastrophes off the southern coast of Sicily. In consequence a permanent treaty of friendship was offered him and he was freed from any further instalments of the war indemnity that had been imposed upon him seventeen years before. He was also granted more land, and as his kingdom already extended over about a quarter of Sicily and included some of the richest parts, his power base was now very significant.

With the Romans resuming their colonisation of southern Etruria and the Carthaginians that of Africa, Sicily then became something of a backwater. In both Carthage and Rome it would appear that there were two political currents running their conflicting courses: these resulted in peace feelers being extended, while simultaneously preparations for continuing the war between the two great nations were also put in hand. That there was an exchange of prisoners is known from the fact of Junius's return to Rome. There is also the story about Marcus Atilius Regulus being sent to Rome by the Carthaginians in about 247 BC to plead for peace, and instead urging the Romans to continue the struggle.

The Romans for their part had dispatched the consuls Metellus,

THE RETURN TO SICILY

who had been the victor of Panormus, and Buteo to Sicily; both of whom represented the moderate, Fabian clan. Their orders cannot have been very ambitious, since without a fleet it had been repeatedly and conclusively shown that it was impossible to subdue the Carthaginian garrisons. The assault on Lilybaeum, which had been by far the greatest effort to take a city in this manner by the Romans, had failed. The only course open to them was to continue the sieges of Lilybaeum and Drepana while strengthening their hold on the remainder of the island. Not a particularly inspiring or challenging task, it represented the political mood of Rome at that time; the war would continue but no great effort would be made to bring it to an early conclusion. The price of earlier Sicilian endeavours had been too high and other interests in the north of Italy prevailed. The unusual situation had developed whereby the central stage of the Roman and Carthaginian struggle for supremacy had been largely abandoned in favour of conquests pursued in diametrically opposite directions.

Hamilcar Barca was, however, to give the Romans a livelier time than they had anticipated, while injecting a sense of purpose into his own dispirited troops. Since he did not possess the strength directly to challenge the Roman legions besieging Lilybaeum and Drepana, his intention appears to have been indirect, to loosen their hold by raiding Italy itself, attacking the areas of Alsium, Brundisium (Brindisi) and Fleganae south of Ostia. There was no question of his attempting to launch a major land campaign: he lacked the means and, although he did manage to inflict some damage to the countryside around Locri, on the toe of Italy, in fact he failed to take the town or gain any support. The only response the Romans made was to take the first steps in forming new colonies in the three threatened areas, which they garrisoned with troops raised for this purpose locally.

On his return to Sicily, Hamilcar Barca found that as well as the Romans continuing the sieges of Lilybaeum and Drepana, consul Buteo had also captured the island of Pelias at the mouth of Drepana harbour and now held it firmly. Hamilcar therefore landed on the north coast and seized the fortress-like stronghold of Mt Heirkte probably as a counter move to the Roman occupation. Today Mt Heirkte is thought to have been either Mt Pellegrino, an isolated 600 metre- high hill to the north of Panormus, or Mt Castellacio standing somewhat higher at 890 metres, about seven miles northwest of Panormus. But whichever it was, the mountain was craggy with steep slopes on every side. The only approaches to the actual Carthaginian position, which seems to have been on a spur or saddle, were so straight and narrow that they could be easily watched and defended. Surrounding the mountain lay rich agricultural land off which the

Carthaginians lived, and an adjacent harbour provided shelter from which raiding parties of ships continued to harry the Italian coast as far north as Cumae.

Though the Romans no longer had a fleet, they responded to these raids by encouraging privateers to respond in kind along the African coastline. One such enterprise was undertaken in 247 BC when the Romans suddenly descended on a seaport lying to the west of Carthage, and set fire to the ships anchored there, as well as some of the buildings lining the shore. But – like their Carthaginian equivalents – these raids achieved nothing of consequence.

The land fighting in Sicily was not dissimilar. Hamilcar Barca could not risk a full-scale encounter and the Romans were unable to bring him to one. This is not to say that he or the Romans were inactive: for almost three years Hamilcar was able to maintain his position on Mt Heirkte and from there wage a guerrilla war of great intensity. Every stratagem and ruse was employed to inflict casualties on the Romans or to destroy their outlying camps, and whenever the fighting became too intense the Carthaginians withdrew to their mountain stronghold and prepared for the next venture. Though nothing decisive was achieved, the Carthaginians posed a perpetual threat to Panormus in particular and severely impeded Roman land and sea communications to their legions investing Lilybaeum and Drepana. As seen from Rome or Carthage the war may well have appeared something of a sideshow – except for the continual drain on money and manpower – but this was far from being the case for those on the spot.

Hamilcar's next move, in 244 BC, was audaciously directed at Mt Eryx, where the Romans maintained a garrison on the summit together with some outposts around the foothills. The town in the valley was not occupied by any troops, however, and it was this town that Hamilcar now seized. Celtic deserters from the Carthaginian army were stationed on the summit, and these defended the temple there with the desperate courage of men who know no quarter can be expected if they are taken alive. It is clear the supplies and reinforcements could reach the Celts as well as the Carthaginians, since both contestants maintained their positions for another two years before the war ended. Although it is not absolutely clear that this was so, it seems that Hamilcar was forced to abandon Mt Heirkte when establishing himself on Mt Eryx. After he had made the move, nearly the whole of the Carthaginian fleet was withdrawn from Sicilian waters. Why this occurred is not known, but after three years of constant use the ships themselves may not have been seaworthy. But in any case, not to have replaced them was to prove a calamitous mistake as will be seen.

THE RETURN TO SICILY

The wheel of fortune was now to make an abrupt and decisive turn. Probably in 243 BC, the Roman Senate decided it was both necessary and possible to settle the war in Sicily that had been dragging on for the last four years around the last remaining Carthaginian footholds in the extreme northeast of the island. Successive consular armies had failed to achieve decisive results and the unremitting drain on Rome's already depleted human and financial resources was becoming unsustainable. If it was not politically possible to negotiate a peace – this inevitably would have left the Carthaginians in possession of their two formidable bases – it was still very clear that no military solution would be possible by merely pursuing a land campaign. If no Roman consul could match the tactical skills of Hamilcar Barca and no Roman army could overcome the seemingly unassailable defences of the two Punic coastal cities, a new fleet would have to be raised to besiege and starve the obstinate Carthaginians into submission. The trouble was that the states' finances were exhausted, and any attempt to raise taxes would have risked incurring unrest and even rebellion amongst the sorely oppressed Roman citizens and allies.

Even so, the decision to build a fleet could not be avoided, so instead of levying a tax on the whole population, the wealthiest families were prevailed upon to make substantial loans, with promises of repayment from a war indemnity to be imposed upon the defeated Carthaginians. In this manner 200 new vessels were financed, modelled on the pattern of the light, highly manoeuvrable quinqueremes captured off Lilybaeum from the Carthaginian blockade-runner Rhodian. (Though Mommsen describes this act of private subscription, which had been resorted to before, in Athens, but not on such a magnificent scale, as standing perhaps unparalleled in history, there may have been no small element of duress, not to mention the possibility of long-term gain, associated with it.)

In 242 BC, the year following the decision to begin the fleet's construction, the consul Lutatius Catulus sailed it to Sicily, where he gained possession of the ports and bays of Lilybaeum and Drepana without difficulty, and then energetically pressed the siege against Drepana. Recognising that the main purpose of his expedition was to achieve maritime supremacy, however, he did not misemploy his sailors as had previously occurred before Lilybaeum, but trained them rigorously for the inevitable naval battle that lay ahead. Now that sea access to Hamilcar's embattled army had been severed, the Carthaginians, who had been totally surprised by the sudden appearance of a Roman fleet, attempted to restore their earlier undisputed control of the coastline. The provisions and ships that had been so parsimoniously denied to Hamilcar for the last four years, were now hastily assembled under Hanno. This was a stupendous undertaking which matched that of the Romans, involving not only the construction of a large number of new vessels but the recruitment and training of around 75,000 rowers. The only significant difference between the two fleets was that the Romans had had time to train their crews, whereas the Carthaginians, though there were undoubtedly many experienced individuals amongst them, had found little time for collective training. Since there were only eight months between the appearance of the Roman fleet and the sailing of the re-created Carthaginian one, this would barely have allowed time for the Carthaginians to build the ships, assemble the stores and recruit the crews, let alone undertake a period of thorough training.

When Hanno in 241 BC sailed with his enormous fleet, which according to Diodorus consisted of 1000 assorted ships, his intention was to arrive near Eryx undiscovered and after unloading the stores, take on board Hamilcar with some of his best troops, then sail back to engage the Roman fleet off Drepana. He put in at Hiera, an outer island of the Aegates group lying some thirty miles west of Drepana, and waited there for a favourable wind which would enable him to dodge the Roman blockade and make a landfall near Eryx. But the consul Catulus got news of Hanno's movements and, divining his intentions, embarked some picked legionaries before sailing out to the island of Aegura that lay opposite Lilybaeum.

The next morning there was a stiff westerly wind which favoured the Carthaginians. If the Romans were to intercept them as Catulus had planned, they would have to face both the wind and a strongly running sea. For some time he hesitated about risking his ships in such unfavourable conditions, but he at length decided that to let the Carthaginians reach shore and unload their stores, presented an even greater risk. He then stripped his ships for action and put to sea, extending them into a single line with their prows into the wind. Hanno had no alternative but to accept battle. Striking the sails, he closed on the Romans. The battle did not last long: the better-trained Roman fleet soon got the upper hand, sinking fifty of the Carthaginian ships and capturing seventy more with all their crews. It was only a sudden change of wind that saved the Carthaginians from complete destruction; they were then able to raise their masts and sail away from the Romans who, having stripped their ships, did not have their masts with them.

But even so the Carthaginian defeat was decisive and the scattered remnants of their fleet fled back to Carthage, where the unfortunate Hanno was crucified. The Romans returned to the port of Lilybaeum to disembarrass themselves of the 10,000 prisoners and the seventy ships they had taken; all for the loss of what was probably no more than a dozen vessels.

Polybius tells us that this unexpected defeat did nothing to abate the zeal and ardour of the Carthaginians, but they had no competent general or army left and as the enemy were masters of the sea, it was anyway no longer in their power to send supplies and troops to Sicily. They left it to Hamilcar, therefore, to negotiate the best terms he could. But even after allowing for all this, if the Carthaginian zeal for the war was as unabated as Polybius maintains, there is no obvious reason why it should not have been continued even if Sicily were lost. Nor, in view of the determined line Hamilcar Barca took during the subsequent peace negotiations, does it seem that he and his troops resisting around Mt Eryx and in the cities of Lilybaeum and Drepana were in such a desperate situation that there was no alternative to immediate surrender. Rather it seems likely that the powerful landowning classes held the political ascendancy, and were determined to put an end to a costly and futile war; they had more pressing and potentially more rewarding matters with which to concern themselves nearer home. They were probably only too glad to wash their hands of Hamilcar Barca and let him fend for himself.

Hamilcar was fortunate in having Catulus to deal with, rather than a Regulus, but even so the negotiations were tough and protracted. Admittedly the Romans themselves had every reason to want to end the war, but Catulus' achievement would not be complete if it had to be left to his replacement the following year to snuff out the final vestiges of Carthaginian resistance. Moreover, the divided political ambitions and consequent policies of the Senate would have had to be taken into account, so that the expulsion of the Carthaginians from Sicily, and the extraction of a war indemnity to reimburse those who had raised the shipbuilding loan, must have been minimum requirements necessary to satisfy the Claudii. On the other hand, any quibbling over subsidiary issues, such as the exchange of prisoners, that risked not being able to reach an early peace settlement, and the consequent need to furnish fresh legions for what would then have become a guerrilla war, would have alienated the Fabii.

In the event, both Hamilcar Barca and Catulus showed themselves realistic and reasonable in their demands and a treaty was concluded in the following terms:

There shall be peace between the Carthaginians and the Romans, subject to approval by the Roman people, upon these conditions. The Carthaginians shall relinquish every part of Sicily. They shall not make war against Hiero; nor do anything to disturb the Syracusans, or their allies. All the Roman prisoners will be returned without ransom and a tribute of two hundred talents of silver paid within twenty years.

When these conditions were received in Rome, the people at first refused to confirm the treaty and sent ten commissioners to resume the negotiations. But Hamilcar's refusal to cede much more, in particular the handing back of Roman deserters or any surrender of arms, was finally respected. The only additional requirements were an increase of a thousand talents to the indemnity, which was to be paid in a shorter time, and the evacuation of Lipara and the Aegates Islands. As Lipara was already in Roman hands and possession of the Aegates would have little meaning for the Carthaginians following the loss of Sicily, these conditions were accepted by Hamilcar. After twenty-four years of fluctuating fortunes which had resulted in a heavy expenditure of human lives and resources, a peace was at last concluded, the acquisition of Sicily had important administrative consequences for Rome, changing the entire conception of government so that for the first time a theory of state ownership was introduced. Previously the Romans had never exacted a tribute from subjected territories: instead of payments in kind or cash, they had demanded military service from those they termed as allies and with whom they shared the spoils of war. Sicily now confronted the Romans with a major administrative problem; should they impose the methods they had used hitherto, or should they maintain the forms of administration which the Sicilians had already accepted during the rule of Carthage and Syracuse? To begin with the Romans continued their established policy, entering into their traditional treaties with Messana and Syracuse, but as they extended their conquests they found it more convenient not to demand military service but to impose a tribute, permit self-administration through bureaucratically appointed councils, and to provide the military garrisons themselves. These measures changed Rome from the leader merely of an Italian confederation into being an imperial power which was ultimately to dominate the western world.

There were also important internal political consequences. As had occurred in the past, new plebeian families who had distinguished themselves in the war were elevated into the Senate. Though this did not lead to the creation of a powerful military faction, or produce effective military leadership, the result may have been that consulships were at least distributed with commendable political and social evenness. There was, however, a price to be paid. Of the forty-eight consuls, only twelve held office a second time and few extended their service for a second year. It is then not surprising that there was such a degree of inconsistency in the future direction of the government.

The effects of the war on Carthage were both immediate and far more devastating. When a predictable mercenary uprising broke out the policy of the wealthy landowning families, which had always favoured territorial expansion in Africa, was adopted out of necessity by nearly all sections of the community.

But if Diodorus is correct in saying it was only in time of war that the Carthaginians selected their most eminent citizens to be generals, it is not surprising that tactical incompetence may at least in part be responsible even in Africa for a lack of clearly defined strategic and operational objectives. And in any case, the peacetime officer corps training cannot have been well founded or rigorous. One suspects that they may have been more concerned with low-level colonial wars against a relatively unsophisticated enemy, than studying for a longer and more complex conflict – an Imperial situation not unknown to the British army during the 20th century.

The practice of crucifying unsuccessful generals may only have been a wartime measure also, in which case it was probably accepted as a practical and effective means of encouraging them all to try harder, a technique applied by others in more recent times; Stalin, for example, summarily shot his generals by the score when they failed during World War II. What is surprising, nevertheless, is the number of Carthaginian generals who fled from the battlefield, particularly at sea, in full knowledge of the fate that awaited them; but perhaps that is no more surprising than that the Carthaginians were able to find commanders for their forces in the first place.

CHAPTER EIGHT

COMMENTARY

The causes of war are seldom explicit or simple, nor do they lend themselves to broad generalisations, such as commercial rivalry, social unrest, or religious fanaticism. Usually there are also other interacting, if subsidiary, factors. These can include national or individual ambitions, prejudices and fears, all heightened by a generous measure of misunderstanding and miscalculation. To isolate one of these factors risks arriving at an oversimplification, while to follow several can result in confusion. Furthermore, to rely on subsequent statements by those directly involved is notoriously dangerous: memories become clouded and perhaps even adjusted, if subconsciously, in the light of hindsight.

Then there are the theorists: some consider war to be a cyclical process, the revulsion of a generation which has participated in a prolonged conflict being replaced by the romantic ardour of the next. Others put forward the theory of delinquency: nations are human beings writ large who inevitably squabble and then fight. A third group believes that wars arise from ignorance which, through increased commercial, personal, cultural and other contacts can be abolished. Although such explanations all contain elements of truth, in the light of experience none has given grounds for thinking that it is capable of standing alone.

If so much contemporary analysis and theorising has been devoted to determining the causes of war, it may well be asked what purpose will be served by considering what occurred over 2000 years ago. The available evidence is fragmentary, the opinions expressed are hearsay and the relevance of such distant conditions is questionable. Even so,

COMMENTARY

although there will admittedly never be any way of determining exactly why Carthage and Rome went to war, there are nevertheless two clearly identifiable factors which made such a war more probable. First, that the Romans saw an opportunity to advantage themselves, and second, that because they saw that the Carthaginians were unprepared militarily they succumbed to this temptation. Nothing appears to have changed in human nature during the last twenty centuries. Whether as individuals, or collectively, most of the human race displays an unfortunate proclivity for opportunism unless deterred by the threat of sufficiently painful consequences.

To recapitulate briefly the sequence of events which led to the First Punic War. A gang of ex-mercenaries turned brigands seized Messana to exploit its people and its natural resources for their own enrichment. Faced with the threat of falling under the domination of Hiero of Syracuse and losing their privileged status, the Mamertines turned to the Carthaginians for help. Soon finding this arrangement unsatisfactory, they invited the Romans to help them instead. The Romans had recently recovered one of their own cities, Rhegium, from a similar band of adventurers whom they considered so reprehensible that they had taken them to Rome for public execution. But in spite of this, they accepted the Mamertines' invitation and occupied Messana. The temptation to acquire a foothold in Sicily and secure the straits in the face of Carthaginian unpreparedness clearly overcame all moral considerations. It was an example of blatant opportunism. Though they gravely underestimated the consequences, the Romans had the muscle and they used it.

The Terminology of War

In commenting on the Punic Wars, it is not intended to suggest that either Carthage or Rome possessed a military vocabulary similar to that which is used in this commentary. Apart from the words themselves, the conceptual distinctions between strategic, operational and tactical levels had not been recognised. Roman and Carthaginian planners did not sit round a table spread with maps and specifically determine strategic objectives and the operational plans necessary for their implementation. When discussion was held on such matters, the questions would have been phrased in more general terms. For instance, the Romans would have not claimed that strategic priorities had changed. Instead they would have recognised that they were not going to defeat the Carthaginians by just fighting them in Sicily – as fast as they killed them the Carthaginians sent in more mercenaries, and their fortified cities were almost impossible to capture anyway –

and that the best alternative was to send an army to Africa and attack Carthage itself.

But although the terminology is today's, it will still be helpful at this point briefly to distinguish between the three levels of war:

Strategic Level The definition of strategic objectives to be achieved in fulfilment of government policy.

Operational Level The planning and execution of military operations to achieve stated strategic objectives.

Tactical Level The planning and conduct of battles in pursuit of the operational aim.

In nontechnical language: having decided what you want to do, you plan how this is to be achieved and coordinate the actual battles to be fought in its fulfilment.

The Conduct of the War

Though many of those Romans holding positions of authority, as well as other influential individuals and powerful groups with vested interests, knew what they hoped to achieve as a result of the decision to occupy Messana, the Romans had no stated policy helping them to formulate their strategic objectives. An opportunistic act had been taken without any rational appreciation of the likely consequences; preparations for a major confrontation with Carthage were woefully inadequate, the need to win over Hiero or Syracuse was not initially recognised, and the mood of the Carthaginians themselves was either ignored or misread. The war that then broke out was entered into haphazardly, the field commanders – though undoubtedly subjected to a variety of pressures – being left free to decide for themselves what action should be taken. Policy was determined by the sword and a major military campaign was entered into without any clear political objectives, and therefore with no strategic objectives either.

As the campaign developed into a full-scale war, so the inadequacies of the Romans' preparations and the limitations of their capability became painfully apparent to them. Without a fleet to protect them, their initial crossing of the straits to Messana was a hazardous enough undertaking, while the subsequent movement of supplies remained in considerable jeopardy. But having successfully braved and surmounted these dangers, the Romans then found themselves stalemated through a lack of sea power. The fortified Carthaginian-held coastal cities were impregnable to direct assault and could only be forced into submission by starvation, but this required them to be both besieged by land and blockaded by sea. Until their ports were closed, not only could these cities by reprovisioned at will, but an unrestricted flow of reinforcements could sustain the Carthaginian army and the inland cities of their allies. The Romans lacked not only the means to implement the necessary operational measures, but also the flexibility to adjust their strategic objectives. They therefore found themselves in a straitjacket both strategically and operationally.

The Romans were largely victims of their own successes elsewhere. The legions had thrown back the invading Gauls without requiring the assistance of a fleet, nor had one been necessary for the conquest of sea-girt southern Italy. In spite of their elaborate fortifications and free-ranging ships, the great Greek cities ringing the Aegean had fallen in quick succession. Obviously, therefore, the same would occur were the legions to confront the Carthaginians and their allies in Sicily. The invincibility of the consular armies was an established fact: nobody could stand before them and survive. Overconfidence thus precluded any critical examination of what in fact occurred once the Sicilian campaign got under way. Defects and deficiencies remained concealed and changed circumstances were not identified – especially the fact that the Carthaginian fleet possessed a completely different dimension of capability from the fleets of the Greek cities. Hubris brought its inevitable nemesis. The legions were not all-conquering: they suffered severely and, in spite of being able to dominate the open battlefield, were stalemated by the particular circumstances that prevailed in Sicily.

By constructing a fleet the Romans then reaffirmed their intention to expel the Carthaginians from Sicily, but this time they also included Sardinia and Corsica. Although they now possessed the means to achieve this intent, their operational planning was at fault and the stalemate continued. Eventually the intractability of the situation resulted in another reappraisal of the conduct of the war and the destruction of Carthage itself was decided upon. Naval supremacy and the successful landing of the expeditionary force on the continent of Africa, paved the way for a negotiated peace treaty on favourable terms, if not outright victory, but the Romans were to fail again, this time as a result of the faulty execution of operational plans rather than of the planning itself. After being decisively defeated they were forced to call off their African adventure and revert to their earlier objective, the capture of Sicily, which undertaking they eventually accomplished.

The Carthaginians for their part had been unprepared and accordingly were quickly thrown into disarray. Having little alternative to abandoning the open countryside to the Romans, they sought refuge behind the walls of the cities remaining loyal to them. Having raised a mercenary army, the Carthaginians set out to recover their lost territory and evict the Romans by campaigning in Sicily. This remained their consistent policy throughout the war, but was it the right one? Obviously their hard-pressed garrison on the island had to be reinforced but, once they had done this, the Carthaginians did not attempt to use the initially unchallenged mobility given to them by their fleet. Instead of using this capability offensively, they restricted themselves to raiding the Italian coast.

The Carthaginian operational planning is clearly open to severe criticism. By inserting their army into their own part of the island and successfully resupplying the coastal cities they effectively stalemated the Romans but did not succeed in making them withdraw; nor could they have done, since they were being purely defensive in their thinking. At best, war weariness might eventually have brought the Romans round to accepting a peace settlement, though it is difficult even then to imagine that this would not have resulted in their retaining a strong foothold on the island. The Carthaginians' faulty operational planning may, at least in part, have been due to their failure to master the tactical battle, and this shortcoming arose entirely as a result of bad generalship. The Carthaginian generals did not believe they could face the Romans on the battlefield so, except for occasional local opportunities which they seized upon, they avoided decisive actions. An example of this failure to exploit their own strength and take advantage of the Romans' weakness, was provided by Xanthippus. At the battle of Adis, it will be remembered, the Carthaginians were defeated because they attempted to compensate for the weakness of their infantry by occupying broken ground which afforded them a greater degree of protection. But in so doing they rendered their mobile arm impotent. Instead of taking the offensive, they had adopted a passive and ineffectual defence. Xanthippus then arrived and gave a convincing demonstration of what should have occurred in the first place. He annihilated the Roman consular army in the open plains by using the superiority of his cavalry and the fear induced by his elephants.

If good generalship could give the Carthaginians such a convincing victory in Africa, there is no obvious reason why this should not have also occurred in Sicily, or elsewhere. To argue from the particular of a single battle to the general tactical arena can be grossly misleading, but Xanthippus' achievement was not due to fortuitous circumstances – such as the particular bravery of his troops, a fundamental error of judgement on the part of the Romans, or unique battlefield conditions. The battle was won quite simply because of the superior mobility of the Carthaginians which gave them an overwhelming advantage in open country. All they needed was to choose their battlefield, a limitation largely dealt with by that same mobility. Except for poor generalship, there is then no reason why the Carthaginians should not have dominated every battlefield, until the Romans changed the composition of their legions – an opportunity Marcus Atilius Regulus missed on first landing in Africa when he failed to raise a potent cavalry arm from the disaffected Numidians.

The Carthaginians' initial mastery of the sea also gave them a distinct advantage, strategically and operationally. They could have given a wider operational dimension to the war by landing an army in Italy and, in so doing, quite probably would have forced the Romans to withdraw their troops from Sicily in order to defend the homeland. Had the Carthaginians adopted this course, the disaffected Greek cities of Magna Graecia could well have risen also, and the whole of southern Italy would have become a battlefield, allowing the Romans little scope for an expansionist policy abroad. Against this possibility, admittedly, must be set the fact that since Hiero of Syracuse had sided with the Romans and remained loyal to them throughout their fluctuating fortunes, other Greek cities might have done the same in Italy. Nevertheless, the opportunity for the Carthaginians to take the offensive and force the Romans on to the defensive presented itself but was not exploited. Less ambitiously, the Carthaginians could alternatively have used their fleet to deploy their army at selected points around Sicily and in so doing, again would have forced the Romans to react. As they must have known of Rome's strenuous efforts to build and man a fleet, even limited operations to disrupt these would have enabled them to maintain their maritime supremacy. As it was however, the Carthaginians left the strategic and operational initiative almost exclusively to the Romans throughout the First Punic War.

Following their decision to close down the campaign in North Africa, if the Romans were to continue the war they only had one strategic choice open to them, the conquest of Sicily. Aware that their earlier planning had dissipated their resources throughout the island, resulting in a tactical stalemate, the Romans now concentrated both their naval and land forces for a coordinated offensive against the northwest of the island. The objective was to secure the main Carthaginian bases of Lilybaeum, Panormus and Drepana. Once this had been accomplished, it would be relatively simple to overrun the remaining southwestern region still under Carthaginian sovereignty. But this perfectly reasonable strategic plan was never backed up with a consistent operational plan.

Panormus was successfully assaulted and captured. But then, the following year, instead of concentrating both their naval and land forces against the two remaining but far more formidable strongholds of Lilybaeum and Drepana, the new consuls took the navy and army on two divergent operations in Africa and Sicily, neither of which could possibly hope to succeed in isolation from one another. The same lack of consistency in pursuing a single clearly defined aim was manifested during the siege of Lilybaeum. Having appreciated that the major fortress cities could only be starved into submission and accordingly raised a fleet in order to this, the Romans then disembarked the crews and employed them on land to try and take the principal city by storm. Obliged to replace these decimated sailors with raw recruits, the Romans then attempted to gain a naval victory through a surprise night passage to Drepana, an operation that could only have been successful if undertaken with fully trained and experienced crews.

This inconsistency of purpose can be attributed to the system of annually appointing new consuls, who arrived with fresh ideas and ambitions but apparently with no direction from the Senate as to the basic purpose of the campaign. Nor were these frequently untrained and inexperienced political appointees prepared to listen to the advice of their professional subordinates on the spot. In the absence of a general staff, which was not to be introduced by any nation until the advent of the Prussian general staff in the early 19th century, there was no system whereby the hard-learned lessons of the previous year's fighting could be studied and applied to the current situation. This limitation not only prevented the purposeful conduct of the war, but also inhibited the development of the army's organisational structure. The principal shortcoming was the lack of tactical mobility. The legions were designed for set piece battles against an enemy who employed similar tactics, and they could only contend with the Carthaginian cavalry and elephants by restricting their confrontations to hilly and broken ground.

Achieving the right force structure in peacetime is a very difficult task, especially for a country which is trying to reconcile a number of conflicting political requirements. As we have seen, before the Punic Wars broke out the Romans were almost exclusively concerned with land campaigns to extend their frontiers north and south of Rome along the Italian peninsula. The fighting was characterized by predominantly infantry-to-infantry combat, and innovation on the part of the Romans was confined to minor structural modifications to the legions, required to counter the more flexible tactics of the Gauls. The cavalry was very much a subordinate arm, useful for scouting, skirmishing and pursuit but not for coordinated and decisive action. Although elephants had been encountered and tactics developed to reduce their effectiveness during the war against Pyrrhus, the lessons learnt from that experience appear to have been neglected. When confronted with them again by Xanthippus in Africa, the Romans merely attempted to counter mass with mass, which would only have been an acceptable measure if their opponents' momentum and numbers had been matched in density and quantity.

But it was not just at the tactical level that the Romans failed to get their own and their allies' force structure right, either before or during the First Punic War. Though more understandably they did not foresee the need for a navy, and when they did acquire one it was not properly handled until the consul Lutatius Catulus showed a willingness to adhere to the aim of the campaign, and to coordinate land and maritime operations. He also appreciated the need for thorough training; and his crews were fully prepared when the final encounter came. No single nation has a monopoly of bravery, battles are won by those whose armed forces are better organised, trained and equipped. Good training helps identify and develop leaders, as well as pointing the way to organisational adjustments to meet new weapons and technological changes. Those who neglect training in peacetime or restrict it for reasons of financial stringency cannot expect their armed forces to be able to respond effectively in an emergency.

The organisational adjustments which need to be made following assessments of training exercise results are of course only relevant to the internal composition of an individual service. The overall force structure of a nation's defence forces is arrived at very differently. For a warring state in the First Punic Wars it was based on clearly-perceived national requirements; for the Carthaginians these were for a powerful fleet in being and the ability to mobilise a mercenary army in a crisis; for the Romans it was a home-based army with no overseas commitments. When brought into conflict over the possession of Sicily, the Carthaginians could not mobilise an army in time to offer resolute resistance and the Romans could not project power effectively beyond their own shores. Both states had based their military requirements simply on past experience.

PART THREE

STRIFE BETWEEN WARS
241–218 BC

CHAPTER NINE

THE MERCENARY REVOLT
240–237 BC

Although the treaty between Lutatius Catulus and Hamilcar Barca that had ended the First Punic War introduced an era of reconciliation between Carthage and Rome, it did not herald a period of peace for either. Both soon found themselves engaged in bitter fighting against other opponents. In the case of Carthage it was a death struggle with her mutinous mercenaries and the winning of an empire in Spain; for Rome it was a renewal of her age-long conflict with the Gauls and an extension of her power across the Adriatic into Illyria. The twenty-three years which separated the First from the Second Punic War brought about intense activity and change for the two states, involving territorial expansion and constitutional adjustments, both of which eventually brought them once again into open conflict. Since many of these events unfolded over the whole period under consideration and interacted upon one another, they cannot be related chronologically without danger of confusion. Instead they are presented here in a sequence intended to explain how it was that the Carthaginians were able to create a powerful new empire in Spain without drawing upon themselves the early intervention of Rome.

After the peace treaty had been concluded, Hamilcar led his army from Eryx to Lilybaeum where he handed over its command to Gisco, the governor of the city. Fully alive to the extent of the potential problem of repatriating the mercenaries, Gisco dispatched them to Carthage in manageable groups over a period of some months. In this way he intended that the pay arrears of each group could be settled and the different national contingents dispatched to their several countries before the succeeding group arrived – a thoroughly sensible plan which would have kept the resettlement problem in manageable proportions. But the Carthaginian authorities thought otherwise. Hoping to avoid the drain on an already depleted treasury, they decided to quarter the mercenaries in the city itself, and so entertain them that they would renounce, at least in part, the money due to them. It was a naive and short-sighted policy.

Following upon years of hard campaigning during which their carnal appetites had either been unrequited or forcefully satisfied, the mercenaries gladly made free use of all that the city had to offer. Alarmed by the consequent disorders and tumultuous licentiousness that raged by day and night, the Carthaginians sought another approach. The mercenaries' officers were approached and asked to move their men to the isolated town of Sicca (Le Kef), which was conveniently removed from Carthage. In return enough gold was to be advanced to defray the mercenaries' immediate expenses; the remainder would follow as soon as it could be raised. The proposal was accepted and the move completed but, once the soldiers were settled in Sicca and freed from any last restraints of discipline, inactivity and boredom soon lead to dissatisfaction. Speculation grew among the troops as to just how much was owing to them. There was more than just an arrears of pay involved; high rewards had been promised by senior Carthaginian officers during the many periods of extraordinary difficulty and danger that had been experienced. Just when expectations were at their most inflated, Hanno the Great, who was responsible for affairs in Africa, arrived at Sicca. Instead of making the anticipated payments, or even announcing exactly what arrangements were being made, he explained the parlous state of the Carthaginian economy and offered a settlement on greatly reduced terms. The effect on the already highly charged atmosphere was electric. The mercenary army consisted of some Spaniards, Gauls, slingers from the Balearic Islands and a few Greek fugitives and slaves. The majority, however, were Africans and, meeting together first as tribes and national contingents, the men found this general resentment breaking through the barriers of language to gain expression in angry collective assemblies.

The problem facing Hanno was how to appease their wrath and abate their demands. The course he adopted was to try and persuade their officers to act as mediators, but as they were of mixed education, intelligence and partiality, his message became distorted. Rumours abounded and suspicion turned into outright distrust; the more so because it was not one of their own generals who had come to negotiate with them, but a stranger who had not even served in Sicily.

Despising the authority of Hanno and mistrustful of their officers, over 20,000 of the mercenaries marched on Carthage, establishing themselves at Tunis some fourteen miles to the south.

Thoroughly alarmed, the Carthaginians were now cravenly ready to adopt any expedient to placate the lawless troops. Provisions of every kind were dispatched in abundance to their camp, while deputations from the Senate itself promised to consent to their demands. But the result was only to increase the confidence and insolence of the mercenaries: sensing victory, they made totally unreasonable demands. The Carthaginians therefore arranged that one of the generals who had served in Sicily would act as a mediator. Hamilcar Barca was not acceptable to the troops: they felt he had handed over his command too precipitously and, by thus showing a lack of interest in their fate, was the cause of their present difficulties. Gisco on the other hand, having handled their departure from Sicily with care and consideration, being held in esteem and even favour; the troops accordingly agreed to refer the dispute to his decision.

Gisco sailed to Tunis and after explaining the straitened circumstances of the republic first to the officers and then to the soldiers in their several national groups, he then appealed to their loyalty and started to distribute the money he had brought with him. This was sufficient to settle the arrears of pay but not the additional claims – for instance for corn and horses – which would, he said, be paid at a later date. The majority of the mercenaries would probably have been prepared to accept this arrangement, had it not been for two rabble-rousers who had personal reasons for not acceding to the Carthaginian terms. The first was a fugitive Roman slave called Spendius, who had been a courageous soldier, but who now feared the prospect of being returned to the Romans to face certain death by torture. The other was Matho, an African, who, as the chief instigator of the present trouble and so acutely aware of the similar fate likely to overtake him should he fall into Carthaginian hands, sided with Spendius. The two together played upon the anxieties and suspicions of their fellows. In particular they suggested to the Africans that, once the other nationalities had been returned to their various countries, they would be left behind to suffer the full vengeance of the Carthaginians. Mob rule then took over and those who attempted to advocate moderation, whether they were officers or soldiers, were set upon and stoned to death.

On a swell of popular fervour, Spendius and Matho were declared generals, and to cement their authority and ensure that there would be no turning back they seized the money Gisco had brought with him and he, together with his companions, were put in chains and imprisoned. What Polybius described as a truceless war was then declared against Carthage. Messengers were dispatched to all the occupied cities urging them to join the revolt and recover their liberty. Utica and Hippo Acra lying on the coast to the northwest of Carthage, refused, but the great majority consented readily enough, sending both troops and supplies so that the ranks of the mercenaries were swollen by a further 70,000 men. Spendius and Matho then divided their army: while firmly holding their camp at Tunis, Matho mounted attacks on Utica and Hippo, and Spendius set siege to Carthage, cutting the city off and confining the garrison within its walls.

The enthusiasm with which the African cities had turned against Carthage in joining the revolt was largely due to the harshness of the treatment they had received during the closing years of the war. Persuaded that the exigencies of the situation justified such measures, the Carthaginians had commandeered one half of the annual produce of the lands throughout their subject territories, and doubled the annual tribute imposed upon the cities. No compunction was shown in extracting these dues, regardless of the devastating consequences for those living in no more than a subsistence economy. There was therefore little need for the mercenaries to be urged to revolt; a simple message sufficed to fire their resentment and desire for revenge. The young men flocked to swell the ranks, while the women and those others who remained behind met together and solemnly swore not to conceal any of their possessions but to offer them all to the common cause. As a result, Spendius and Matho were not only able to complete the payment of the arrears of pay due to their soldiers but from that time on were able to defray all the expenses of the uprising – a situation which suggests that the cause of such deep resentment, had not been so much the actual raising of money by the Carthaginians as the brutality with which it was conducted.

According to Polybius the Carthaginians, cut off from supplies, and already worn down to near exhaustion by the length and demands of the recent war, were also deprived of an effective fleet following its rout off Sicily and found themselves devoid of any revenue to support an army and without a single ally or friend to whom they could turn. Their lot looked hopeless, and after the cruelties they had practised on their African subjects, little mercy would be expected from them should the city gates be opened.

But the situation cannot have been quite so forlorn as Polybius suggests, since the Carthaginians were able to break out and take the field shortly afterwards, and in considerable strength. They obtained new mercenaries, perhaps some of them from non-African contingents who had, in the final count, remained loyal. They also refitted the surviving triremes and vessels of fifty oars, armed all their able-bodied citizens, raised a new force of cavalry and mustered the hundred elephants still remaining in their possession. Responsibility for this feat is attributed by Polybius to Hanno who, as the Military Governor of Africa, had suppressed the earlier Libyan and Numidian revolts following the expedition of Marcus Atilius Regulus. If this attribution is correct, his subsequent incompetence as a field commander appears in striking contrast.

In 240 BC, Hanno marched on Utica, taking his siege train with him – though for what reason remains obscure, since he was relieving not besieging the city, and to assault the mercenary camp can hardly have required such machines. As it was, the elephants more than adequately broke through the encircling entrenchments and devastated the camp, forcing the mercenaries to flee into the surrounding hills. Conditioned by his earlier experience of fighting the Numidians and Libyans, Hanno assumed that they would continue their flight until well out of harm's way. But he was dealing with Hamilcar's old Sicilian veterans who, though they had broken before the elephants, reformed themselves in the security of the hills. They did not take long to discover that the Carthaginians camping round the outskirts of Utica had relaxed their vigilance and discipline. Deserted by Hanno, who had entered the city to indulge himself in its luxuries, the leaderless soldiers were surprised and overrun by an attack mounted by the mercenaries in close order. Many of the Carthaginians were killed, the remainder abandoning their baggage and siege trains as they sought safety in ignominious flight. Hanno escaped with them. He subsequently twice missed opportunities to force the mercenaries into accepting battle under unfavourable conditions, and on two other occasions failed to grasp the chance to take them by surprise. He would appear fortunate finally only to have been relieved of his command as a consequence of his failure and not, in accordance with normal Carthaginian practice, crucified. But as he had established his reputation previously and had strong political backing, he was undoubtedly more secure than most of those appointed to high command.

Hamilcar Barca, the intrepid general of Mt Eryx, was now entrusted with the prosecution of the war. His army in Carthage consisted of some 10,000 men, made up from the mercenaries' deserters, as well as Carthaginian cavalry, together with seventy elephants. With this greatly outnumbered and not obviously proficient force, Hamilcar decided to take the offensive with the minimum of delay. The difficulty lay in how this was to be achieved. At the extremity of the 2000-yard-wide isthmus which joined Carthage to the mainland, there rose to the south an easily defensible range of rough and craggy hills, the roads over which were strongly guarded by Matho's troops. While it was possible to move round the lagoon to the north by hugging the sea shore and wading through the intersecting pools, further northerly progress was barred by the swift-running river Macar (Medjerda) which in those days flowed just north of Carthage before emptying into the sea. The single bridge which spanned the river was, like the hill passes, firmly held by the mercenaries. If he were to break out into the open countryside, Hamilcar would have to achieve surprise, since his force was far too small to attempt a conventional passage through the hill passes, or over the Macar bridge.

The prospects for achieving this, however, looked remote until a quirk of tide and weather came to Hamilcar's notice. When the wind blew in a westerly direction and the tide was out, a sand bar was partly exposed across the salt flats at the river mouth, enabling it to be forded. As soon as the appropriate conditions reoccurred, Hamilcar led his men out of the city gate under cover of darkness, and completed the crossing before dawn without having been detected. He then turned inland along the course of the Macar to secure the bridge and advance in extended line northwards across the plain with the elephants in the lead, followed by the light troops and cavalry, while his heavy infantry brought up the rear.

Once Spendius had recovered from his initial surprise at the unexpected turn of events, he advanced to meet Hamilcar at the head of the 10,000 men who had been encamped around the bridge, together with another 15,000 who joined him from Utica. With such superior numbers Spendius closed confidently on the Carthaginians, extending his left flank so as to overlap and then encircle them against the river. The mercenaries' confidence grew as they saw the leading Carthaginians wheel off to their right flank, turn about and make as though to withdraw. There has been much speculation about this manoeuvre but what probably occurred is that the head of the column wheeled right until in line, then made as to withdraw, before once again facing their front. The effect was to cause the mercenaries to rush forward in the mistaken belief that the Carthaginians were retreating. They quickly discovered they had been duped. Hamilcar had skilfully inverted his dispositions so that his leading troops withdrew only until the heavy infantry had marched forward into the van, and the elephants, cavalry and light troops then turned about to face their front and come into line alongside the heavy infantry.

No longer overlapping the Carthaginians' right flank and disorganised by their ill-disciplined advance, the leading mercenary troops were in no position to face the regular ranks of their opponents. They then fell back; but did so in such precipitous disorder that the succeeding ranks of their army were thrown into confusion. Seizing the opportunity, Hamilcar released his elephants and cavalry, who mercilessly trod or rode down the mercenaries in piled heaps. About 6000 were killed and a further 2000 taken prisoner. The remainder either fled to Utica, or sought temporary refuge in the camp around the bridge before being driven back to Tunis. It had been a neatly executed operation twice achieving success in a masterly manner; first through the unexpectedness of the night river crossing and secondly as a result of a well-executed tactical manoeuvre. Such a convincing display of superior leadership and martial superiority brought in its turn a further battle-winning factor, high morale. Virtually unknown and overshadowed by the great battles to follow, Hamilcar Barca's victory on the banks of the Macar river in fact provides a classic example of imaginative and skilful leadership.

Instead of attempting to join up with Hanno, who was now opposing Matho at Hippo Acra with the troops left to him after his disaster at Utica, Hamilcar next advanced through the surrounding countryside either reducing by force those cities which opposed him or persuading the less resolute to submit peacefully. As the Carthaginians progressed into the interior the mercenaries, of whom only about a third had even been remotely engaged at the Macar, shadowed them under the command of Spendius and the Gauls' general Autaritus. Avoiding the plains and so the Punic elephants and cavalry, the mercenaries made their way among the foothills of the mountainous terrain, waiting for further reinforcements to reach them and an opportunity to engage the Carthaginians. Such a moment occurred when Hamilcar, having ill-advisedly entered a valley hemmed in by hills, found himself surrounded by mercenaries who by then had been heavily reinforced. Blocking his further advance were the Libyans, while Spendius threatened his flanks and the Numidians covered his rear; a seemingly desperate situation from which Hamilcar was only relieved by an unexpected development. Naravas, a young Numidian prince, who had forged close family links with the Carthaginians and later married one of Hamilcar's daughters, reflecting the rivalries between the Numidian kingdoms and tribes, decided to desert. Approaching the Carthaginian entrenchments with an escort of a hundred horsemen, he signalled with his hands that he wished to parley. Suspicious and doubtful, the Carthaginians remained irresolute until Naravas, dismounting and handing over his horse and weapons to his attendants, advanced on foot alone into the Carthaginian camp. When brought before Hamilcar he pledged his loyalty and friendship with such candour and sincerity that he soon won Hamilcar's trust and a plan of action was agreed between them. Naravas was to return to his own camp, and bring over to the Carthaginians the 2000 men under his command. This was accomplished and in consequence when both opponents were ready for battle, the Carthaginians eventually emerged victorious. Some 10,000 mercenaries were left on the battlefield where they had fallen, and a further 4000 taken prisoner. Hamilcar now displayed well-considered magnanimity; he enlisted those prisoners into his own army who were prepared to serve under him, and the remainder he assembled in their national contingents, informing them that they would be pardoned and allowed to go where they pleased. He added, however, the warning that should they take up arms against Carthage again no mercy would be shown to them. They were then dismissed.

Fearful that Hamilcar's display of clemency towards his prisoners would weaken the determination of the other mercenaries to continue the revolt, Spendius and Autaritus sought an excuse to commit an act of such atrocious barbarity that the pardon extended by the Carthaginian general would be revoked. A sense of revulsion so deep as to allow no forgiveness on the part of the Carthaginians was essential if the mercenary army was not to dissolve through desertion. The word was accordingly spread round that Hamilcar's promises were no more than a trick to disarm them, and that once they were impotent and dispersed, a terrible vengeance would be wrought throughout the subject territories. In particular it was reported that warnings had been received from Tunis and as far away as Sardinia that there were traitors in the mercenary camp, plotting with the Carthaginians to set Gisco and the other prisoners free. The escape of such an eminent and accomplished commander would do much to raise the spirits of the Carthaginians while posing a dangerous threat to the mercenaries themselves. Having thus aroused suspicion and fear throughout the army, Autaritus proposed that not only should Gisco and his fellow prisoners be put to death, but the same fate should be meted out in future to any Carthaginian who fell into their hands.

Some of the troops who had served with Gisco in Sicily and who remembered his courageous and humane leadership, attempted to remonstrate but, being either misunderstood or misrepresented when their words were translated, they were suspected of being the rumoured traitors and were promptly killed. Gisco and the 100 odd Carthaginian prisoners were then seized and after being scalped and having their limbs broken and mutilated, were thrown into a common pit with what little life still remained to them. To eradicate any last hope of reaching a negotiated peace with the Carthaginians, Spendius and Autaritus then announced officially that in future all Carthaginian prisoners would be put to death by torture, while their allies, if captured, would have their hands cut off before being returned to their own lines.

These measures had the desired effect. Incensed by what had occurred, Hamilcar issued orders of equal ferocity; no mercy was to be shown on the battlefield, and any prisoners that were by chance taken, were to be cast alive to the elephants. Determined to eradicate the mercenary scourge as quickly as possible, Hamilcar approached Hanno and suggested that they should join together in a united campaign. The attempted reconciliation was a failure, no common ground could be found between them, and the situation became so critical that the Assembly of the Hundred was forced to intervene. But being either unable or unwilling to determine the issue themselves, the Tribunal left it to the troops to elect their own commander. This seemingly democratic decision was to have important consequences; for the first time a general was to receive his authority not from the politicians, but from the army itself. With the election of Hamilcar Barca as their commander by the troops, the first seeds for the subsequent establishment of a Barcid empire in Spain had been sown.

While these developments were taking place, the Carthaginians suffered a triple reverse. First, the ships which usually drew supplies from the district of Emporia, the granary of Carthage some 200 miles to the south around Syrtis Minor, were sunk in a sudden storm. Then the mercenary garrison in Sardinia rose in revolt, slaughtered all the Carthaginians they could lay hands on and established themselves in control of the island until at a later date, having antagonised the local people, they were forced to flee to Italy. Finally, and most disastrously, the cities of Utica and Hippo Acra declared for the mercenaries. This was an unexpected development; both communities had remained consistently loyal to Carthage, not only during the present unrest, but when first Agathocles and then the Romans under Marcus Atilius Regulus had stood before the walls of Carthage. Now the inhabitants of the two cities seized the Carthaginian garrison, put them to death and flung their corpses over the walls. Over 500 Punic troops died in this manner and all requests on the part of the Carthaginians to bury them were received with curt refusal.

The Carthaginians were now too weak to attempt to recover the lost cities, or to bring the mercenaries to battle. Instead Hamilcar Barca, assisted by Hannibal, a commander who had replaced Hanno, concentrated on trying to prevent supplies from reaching their enemies, a task greatly aided by Naravas and his Numidian cavalry. Without their earlier defection to Hamilcar, the relative immobility of the bulk of his army would have greatly restricted the scope of his operations. But however vigorously Hamilcar pursued the campaign, the Carthaginians began to fear that without outside help, there was little prospect of being able to bring the increasingly bitter struggle to an end. They accordingly appealed to 'those states that were in alliance with them', to use Polybius' words.

Hiero of Syracuse, who had already been meeting the Carthaginians' hitherto fairly modest needs, now redoubled his efforts. His reasons for doing so appear to have been twofold. First, as has been related, Roman policy towards Carthage after the First Punic War had been characterised by reasonableness and restraint. It would have been appropriate for Hiero to adopt a similar approach. Second, as Polybius suggests, he may not have wished to see an end to the balance to Roman power which Carthage represented. His own position with regard to the Romans depended to some extent on their assessment of his worth as an ally. Remove this value to them and he became no more than a minor power whose wishes and requirements could be ignored, or forcibly subordinated should they ever conflict with those of Rome. Hiero could never divide and rule, but he could at least try and preserve a balance of power to ensure his own survival.

Beyond his direct reference to Hiero, Polybius does not enlarge upon his assertion that the Carthaginians appealed for help from those in alliance with them: when he refers to the Romans, there is nothing to suggest that the events he relates resulted from any special alliance or treaty obligations. What seems more probable is that the Romans were willing to help because it served their interests to preserve Carthaginian authority, rather than have to deal with unpredictable revolutionaries. Especially as many of these were deserters from their own ranks whom when negotiating for a peace settlement in Sicily, Hamilcar had refused to hand over in compliance with Roman demands.

Whatever understanding existed between Rome and Carthage, their relationship was put under considerable strain only a year or two after peace had been concluded. A few Roman traders, who had been supplying the mercenaries, fell into Carthaginian hands and were promptly thrown into prison. This arbitrary and high-handed treatment of Roman citizens nearly led to a serious breach between the two states, but the Carthaginians wisely acceded to Roman demands for their early release. Mollified by this recognition of their authority, the Romans reciprocated by returning the Punic prisoners whom they still held. They also showed their desire for good relations by encouraging direct trade with Carthage, while prohibiting any dealings with the mercenaries. Even more significantly, the Romans refused to respond to an appeal for help which had been received from the Carthaginian mercenaries in Sardinia who, in emulation of their former comrades in Africa, had also risen in revolt to rid themselves of their Punic officers. Likewise, when Utica unexpectedly sided with the mercenaries and invited the Romans into the city, so recreating the situation which had occurred at Messana, the request was firmly declined.

Whether these restrained responses were motivated by self-interest or resulted from treaty obligations, is open to question. But as will be seen, Rome had her own problems and to have embarked on another costly and uncertain contest with Carthage at this stage can have held out few attractions. Nor would a renewal of hostilities have received any political support from the ascendently powerful Fabii, who were engrossed in a northerly expansion. But in any case, sustained by the supplies which had been sent by Hiero or traded with the Romans, Hamilcar was now free to pursue his campaign against the mercenaries, secure in the knowledge that there would be no hostile outside interference.

The mercenaries had divided their forces. While Matho maintained his position in Tunis, Spendius and Autaritus persevered with their earlier tactic; they kept to the high ground in order to avoid the Carthaginian superiority in open warfare given to them by their elephants and, one suspects, superior generalship. Though Hamilcar sought every opportunity to bring his opponents to battle, he only succeeded in cutting off or ambushing relatively small numbers of men, and was unable to achieve any conclusive results from this battle of mutual harassment and continual manoeuvre. The evasive tactics adopted by Spendius and Autaritus in many ways predated those of Fabius Maximus, the Cunctator (Delayer), which would gain such renown in the Second Punic War.

Hamilcar was eventually able to trap the mercenary army against a mountain barrier, no longer identifiable today, which was named the Saw because of the sharp indentations of its deep probing valleys. Unable to scale the Carthaginian-held peaks to their rear, hemmed in on the plain by encircling entrenchments and fearful of the elephants, the mercenaries put their faith in Matho marching from Tunis to their relief. Sustained by this hope, they held out even when their supplies were exhausted. But as famine started to set in, they were forced to adopt the most extreme measures in their struggle to survive. Their pack animals and cavalry horses were first to go, then came the prisoners and the slaves until, faced with the prospect of dying from slow starvation or devouring one another, the men rose against their commanders who had no alternative but to throw themselves upon the mercy of Hamilcar. After dispatching a herald, Spendius and Autaritus, together with a number of their higher-ranking officers were summoned into the Carthaginian camp. The terms Hamilcar offered appeared remarkably lenient: 'the Carthaginians would choose from their enemy ten persons, whomsoever they thought proper; and that the rest should be dismissed, each with a single garment.' These conditions having been agreed, Hamilcar elected to detain those with whom he had negotiated the surrender. Deprived of their leaders and unaware of the circumstances under which this had occurred, the mercenaries suspected treachery and sought death in battle, rather than through starvation. Forty thousand of them died in a massacre from which there was no escape, and no mercy shown.

Hamilcar then marched with the combined forces of Hannibal and Naravas on Tunis, where Matho and the remainder of the mercenaries were still holding out. On arriving, Hamilcar positioned himself to the south and Hannibal to the north, so completing the city's encirclement. Spendius and the other hostages who had been detained by Hamilcar were then led forward to an exposed position under the eyes of the beleaguered garrison and crucified. Having completed this act of intimidation, the Carthaginians retired to their camps to await events. It was not however a deputation from Matho seeking to negotiate peace terms who approached them, but a party of thirty prominent citizens of Carthage who had come to investigate the situation for themselves. It was an unfortunate coincidence. Having observed Hannibal's troops become negligent, their attention distracted by this delegation, Matho seized the opportunity to mount a sudden foray. Many Carthaginians were killed on the spot and the remainder fled, abandoning their baggage. Hannibal and the visiting elders, however, were promptly taken prisoner, marched to the site where Spendius and his compatriots had been executed, and tortured and nailed up in their place.

Following this major reversal of Carthaginian fortunes, Hamilcar was obliged to raise the siege of Tunis and withdraw to near the mouth of the Macar. Once again the very survival of Carthage was threatened just when victory had appeared assured. Desperate to bring the protracted revolt to a final conclusion, the Senate at last prevailed upon Hanno and Hamilcar to agree to a reconciliation. This time the two generals put the future wellbeing of the state before their own discordant rivalries, and took the field together. In the meantime, Matho had abandoned Tunis and withdrawn to near the coastal town of Leptis Minor (Monastir), some eighty miles to the south. Mustering their full strength and calling upon their various allies for support, Hamilcar Barca and Matho prepared for what they both recognised as the final decisive encounter. When all was ready, both armies deployed into their battle formations. No details of what happened are known, but the Carthaginians carried the day and in so doing, broke all effective resistance. Isolated with no hope of support, Utica and Hippo held out for a while, fearful of the terrible revenge awaiting them for the atrocities they had committed against the Carthaginian garrisons, but both cities were eventually forced to surrender. Meanwhile Matho and any other prisoners taken at Leptis

Minor had been paraded through the streets of Carthage, then handed over to the people and tortured to death.

After three years and four months the mercenary uprising had been quelled, but at a heavy cost. The loss of life and material resources had been enormous, while years of outrageous cruelty had added to the sum of human suffering, all of which would have been avoided had the Carthaginians honoured their debts in the first place. The payment of the arrears of salaries due to the Sicilian veterans was paltry in comparison to the sums involved in the final reckoning. As for the mercenary leaders, they suffered deaths which matched anything they had inflicted on their Carthaginian captives. If ever the lessons that perfidious ingratitude destroys loyalty and that terror breeds terror require illustration, then the crimes of both the Carthaginians and the mercenaries provide frightful evidence.

The Seizure of Sardinia 238–225 BC

Rome had rejected the appeal for help made by the Carthaginian mercenaries in Sardinia who had followed the example of the mercenary revolt in Africa in 240 BC, and had murdered their officers. The Carthaginians responded by sending an expeditionary force to recover the island in 239 BC, but the troops joined the rebels, crucified their commander and slaughtered all the Carthaginians they could hunt down. Even so their numbers were not sufficient to do more than secure the principal towns and it was not long before the natives rose in revolt against them. Worsted in the subsequent fighting, the mercenaries fled to Italy and appealed for the second time to Rome.

After the loss of Sicily, the strategically well-placed, fertile and populous island of Sardinia had acquired great significance in Carthaginian eyes, both psychologically and economically. Preparations were therefore put in hand for the island's recapture by Hamilcar as soon as the mercenary revolt had finally been crushed; an action they were fully entitled to take in accordance with Catulus' treaty, which had implicitly confirmed Carthaginian possession of the island. The Romans, however, attempted another interpretation of the treaty, arguing that Sardinia was one of the islands, referred to as lying between Sicily and Italy, which were ceded to Rome. It was an unconvincing claim, as was their claim that the Carthaginian preparations to reoccupy Sardinia were directed primarily against the Romans themselves. The fact of the matter was that Sardinia was of strategic importance to Rome, lying alongside and dominating her western seaboard, and its occupation by a hostile power threatened her sea communications and coastal cities. Weakened by their long internal struggle and with their offer to negotiate rejected out of hand, the Carthaginians had no alternative but to accede to Roman demands. Two additional clauses were added to the peace treaty: any claim to Sardinia (and so implicitly to Corsica) was renounced, and an indemnity payment of 1200 talents was agreed.

This unscrupulous act on the part of the Romans may have brought them an immediate strategic gain, while weakening Carthage yet further both militarily and economically, but it contained the seeds of renewed conflict in the longer term. Deeply resentful of Rome's blatantly unjust conduct, which was condemned by such disinterested people as the Greeks, the Carthaginians harboured thoughts of revenge. Most particularly Hamilcar Barca, still smarting from the indignity of his enforced surrender in Sicily, was determined to reassert Carthaginian power at the expense of Rome. But he was not just motivated by personal bitterness, he was also inspired by a mystical zeal that brought exaltation in its wake. In an emotive sacrificial ceremony devoted to Jupiter, his son Hannibal, then aged nine, was brought to the altar after the libations were completed and swore eternal hatred to the Romans, while Hamilcar dedicated his life to avenging Carthage's defeats and humiliation. Father and son were to prove formidable opponents, and their insatiable enmity arose as a direct, if not sole, consequence of Rome's cynical seizure of Sardinia. Although it may have been inevitable that Carthage and Rome would come into open conflict again at some future date, one of the underlying causes of the Second Punic War can be traced back twenty years to the Romans' conduct in 238 BC. That a smarting injustice imposed upon a defeated but resilient enemy carries the seeds of further conflict, is a lesson which successive generations of political leaders could have recalled with advantage.

It was not only trouble in the longer term which the Romans stored up for themselves when occupying Sardinia and Corsica; there were also some more immediate difficulties. The Carthaginians had never attempted to subdue the whole of the islands: all they had been interested in was trading with the natives, for which purpose the occupation or establishment of coastal towns had been sufficient. Although there had inevitably been clashes, basically the barter trade conducted by the Carthaginians had benefited the natives. Left alone in the mountainous interior of the islands, there had been little cause for discontent and it was only when the established patterns of trade had broken down, following the mercenary uprising, that the natives had risen in their turn. The Romans, however, were not interested in trade, they demanded tribute.

Envoys were dispatched to the various tribes who, probably not even understanding and certainly not accepting this new form of overlordship, refused to pay up. A military campaign was then launched which, though ultimately successful, was to cost the Romans heavily. The warlike tribes resisted fiercely and Roman casualties were high. It was not until 227 BC that the two islands were constituted as provinces of the Roman federation in the same manner as Sicily, and not until two years after that, when a final revolt was quelled, that they were pacified and tribute could be collected on a regular basis. It would appear that the Romans treated the Sardinians in particular with the greatest severity, many were taken as slaves to be employed on hard labour with little hope of being freed. Such an attitude suggests that, even without the Sicilian precedent, the Romans could never have regarded the Sardinians as potential allies.

Carthaginian Constitutional Developments – 238 BC

At the end of the mercenary revolt the great Carthaginian landowning classes, favouring good relations with Rome and the restriction of territorial expansion to Africa, were firmly in power. Confident of their authority they started proceedings against Hamilcar Barca, whom they saw as the rallying point and natural leader of the opposing faction, favouring hostility to Rome and the extension of the Carthaginian colonial empire. He was summoned to appear before the Assembly of the Hundred, where he was to answer charges of being responsible for the Mercenary War. But although the ruling party's position looked strong enough, powerful currents of discontent were running beneath the surface.

Those classes who had formerly profited by trade now saw the riches of Sicily flowing into the Roman treasury and the secure sea routes, which had connected their trading posts throughout the Mediterranean, threatened if not actually broken. The commercial domination, which they had enjoyed and enriched themselves upon, was dissolving before their eyes. Their disquiet provided strong, if for the moment discreet, support for those like Hamilcar who proposed an expansionist policy overseas. Also, it was not only the merchant classes who were discontented: the war with Rome had done more than just disrupt trade, it had also virtually destroyed the navy and had put a large number of already impoverished Carthaginian citizens, connected with maritime activities, out of work. The political leader who emerged to give expression to this general discontent was Hasdrubal. Though he was probably a member of the aristocracy, he represented the people's faction who lent their support to Hamilcar, an alliance which was strengthened by Hasdrubal's marriage to one of Hamilcar's daughters. In consequence Hasbrubal must have been able to restrict the fearsome power of the Hundred since, from then on, there were no more cases of generals being arraigned before this body.

Moreover, the people once more claimed the right to select their generals, though this authority would appear to have been largely exercised by the lower ranks of the army.

The loss of Sardinia and the evidence it provided of Roman untrustworthiness, emphasised the need for Carthage to restore her previous wealth and military strength, if only to be able to resist further Roman aggression. Though many Carthaginians may have still hoped to live in peace with Rome, Hamilcar and his closest supporters undoubtedly regarded the restoration of Carthaginian power as a useful means both to humble Rome and to recover their former possessions. The party that favoured peace, led by Hanno the Great, had been replaced by one which, under the relentlessly vengeful leadership of Hamilcar, was set on war. How these constitutional changes led to the creation of a new and prodigiously wealthy empire in Spain, must wait until consideration has been given to the parallel developments which were taking place in Rome.

CHAPTER TEN

THE GALLIC INVASION
241–220 BC

With no established boundaries between them, the various tribes who surrounded and divided the fertile northern plains had for long been in almost perpetual conflict, not only with one another but also with Rome during her territorial expansion. There can be little doubt that the Romans, spearheaded by the Fabii, at this period regarded the Alps as forming Rome's natural northern boundary; they had incorporated the Etruscans into their federation and annexed Ager Gallicus, on the Adriatic coast south of the Po, from the Gauls. Sparsely settled at first, Ager Gallicus became increasingly more populated as the reforms of the plebeian consul Gaius Flaminius, designed to restore the link between the proletariat and the land, were introduced in spite of strong opposition from the Senate. In particular soldiers returning from the First Punic War were settled there instead of back in their own farms which had been ruined in their absence.

During the war, however, it seems that the Boii had started to drift back into the area and the Ligurians had driven Rome's Etruscan allies out of the Arno valley and captured Pisae. It is not clear exactly when the Ligurians, whose territory had once extended along the French Alps, the head waters of the Po, and down the Italian Riviera, were forced by local pressure to withdraw from their conquests but it appears to have been shortly after the end of the First Punic War. This first open revolt came from the Boii in 241 BC and though swiftly suppressed it was an indication of more serious trouble to come.

In 236 BC a serious threat of war arose when Boii chieftains, without consulting their people, invited some transalpine tribes to join in an attack on Ariminum (Rimini). But when the Romans dispatched an army to counter these moves, dissension among their opponents led to them withdrawing and the attack on Ariminum being abandoned. For the next few years Rome's attention was diverted to Illyria across the Adriatic, an account of which operation will be recorded separately, but in 226 BC the Gauls united and storm clouds again started to gather along the northern frontier. Most historians suggest that this was caused by the Romans' increasing settlement and expansion of the Ager Gallicus. After all, the Boii, who were the most directly threatened by this encroachment, had already attempted to gain support for an attack on Ariminum ten years previously and, whatever their motives, obviously regarded the Romans with hostility. And in any case it would have taken a long time to consult and persuade the various tribes to join in a major campaign without there being a rallying cause, so that if the Roman land encroachment did not serve this purpose, there is no other identifiable reason for the Gauls to unite in this manner. When assembled, the Gallic army consisted of some 50,000 foot soldiers and 20,000 cavalry and chariots, all fully armed and eager for the coming struggle. This number would have been even greater had it not been for the Venetians and the Cenomani, a Celtic tribe who lived between the middle Po and the Alps, maintaining their traditional loyalty to Rome. As a result, the Gauls had to leave a part of their force to cover these potentially hostile and treaty-bound tribes.

It was at this critical moment that news of the Carthaginian conquests in Spain reached the Romans and, as Polybius relates in measured terms, 'they were seized with no small consternation'. Unwilling to limit Carthaginian advances by measures that would have risked war, the Romans had to content themselves with making a treaty with Hasdrubal in 226 BC which, to quote Polybius again, 'set some bounds to the progress of the Carthaginians' before turning their full attention to the crisis posed by the Gauls. In fact the prospect of war with the Gauls had long haunted the Romans. Not only did they dread them more than any of their other opponents, but they could not fail to recollect that in 390 BC, barely 170 years previously, these same barbaric warriors had devastated their city. The most extreme measures were now taken to avoid the recurrence of such a disaster; a law exempting priests from military service was even amended so that in the event of a Gallic invasion, they would be expected to serve. In their consternation, the Romans consulted the Sibylline Books and anxiously hoped to satisfy the oracular pronouncement that Rome 'must twice be held by a foreign enemy' by burying alive two Gauls, a man and a woman, likewise two Greeks, in the Forum. More practically, they mobilised, and put in hand preparations for war.

As soon as the Romans learned that the Gauls had crossed the Alps, the consul Lucius Aemilius Papus was sent with a consular army to cover the Gauls' immediate objective, Ariminum. The other consul, Cornelius Atilius Regulus, had sailed shortly before to Sardinia, so a praetor was sent with the second consular army to block the central mountain passes leading into Etruria. These preliminary deployments having been made, troops from outlying garrisons were recalled; new levies were raised from all the men eligible by age to bear arms; appeals for help were sent to their allies; while magazines and warehouses were stocked with military stores and corn in quantities that had never previously been seen. The general alarm had spread throughout the various states in Italy. These, regarding the Gallic invasion as a threat to the Republic, met the Romans requests in full.

The Romans and their allies were thus able to mobilise 700,000 infantry and 70,000 cavalry. Not all these were first-line troops: they included many reservists, held back primarily as garrison troops in defence of their own homeland, and although many were capable of bearing arms, they were beyond the age of military service, probably not fully equipped and therefore of limited value. But in any event the problems of maintaining large contingents in the field would have excluded the possibility of concentrating them. In accordance with normal practice, therefore, it was the young men who filled the ranks of the legions deployed in the field; the older men served in the reserve legions and formed a source of reinforcements when the age of active service had to be raised to replace heavy casualties.

The deployment of the various armies can be categorised into four broad groups. First, there were the two consular armies, which in view of the crises each consisted of two overstrength legions, numbering 5200 infantry and 200 cavalry deployed on the northern frontier as has already been described. They were reinforced by the Sabines and Etruscans, who had raised more than 50,000 infantry and 4000 cavalry. The second group was formed by the Umbrians and Sasinates, coming from the Apennines north and south of Rome respectively, who provided 20,000 men, as did the Genoans and Venetians, all of whom were deployed along the Boian border to threaten invasion, and so force the Boii to protect their homeland by withdrawing their contingent from the invading Gallic army. The third group acted as a general reserve, and had the specific task of defending Rome: it consisted of 20,000 Roman infantry and 1500 cavalry, with 30,000 infantry and 2000 cavalry provided by the allies. The exact deployment and task of the fourth group is less clear, but since it was dispersed throughout Italy, as well as Sicily, Sardinia and Corsica, its function seems to have been to ensure security within the Republic, act as a local reserve, and provide a source of reinforcements.

The Gauls' first move was to invade Etruria and plunder the countryside as they advanced on Rome. That they apparently had no difficulty in avoiding the two Rome consular armies covering Ariminum and the central Apennine passes is perhaps understandable; Ariminum lay on the east coast and there are other passes over the Apennines which the Gauls must have used. What does seem inexplicable, however, is that the substantial Etruscan and Sabine forces, numbering over 50,000, evidently failed to offer any resistance. Be as that may, when the Gauls had reached Clusium (Chiusi) just over 100 miles from Rome on the road to Arretium, they learned that the Roman army guarding the central passes was close on their heels, so they turned about and when night came they lit their camp fires as usual and then withdrew towards Faesulae (Fiesole) some eighty miles to the south, leaving only their cavalry behind with orders to show themselves to the Romans at dawn.

The next morning the Romans pressed forward as intended. Lured on by the withdrawing Gallic cavalry, they suddenly found themselves assailed from all sides by infantry near Montepulciano in the Val di Chiana. Six thousand Romans fell in the engagement, with the majority of those who survived escaping to a nearby hill which they immediately prepared to defend. But the Gauls merely encircled the hill with their cavalry overnight, while their hard-fought infantry rested, looted and prepared for a final assault the next day. The Gauls' reaction was understandable, but it led to the escape of the Romans. Lucius Aemilius Papus, commanding the army on the Adriatic coast, had heard of the Gauls' advance on Rome, and as night fell his legions arrived in the vicinity of the battlefield. The Gauls held a council of war at which it was decided that in view of the immense quantities of booty they had accumulated it would be highly imprudent to risk their loss in accepting battle with a fresh enemy. Rather, they should return home and disembarrass themselves of all they had acquired, before renewing the campaign. But when the Romans discovered the Gauls were on the move, they set off in pursuit. Rather than retrace their footsteps, the Gauls decided to follow the Etrurian coastline, which not only provided an easier passage when encumbered with so much booty, but also afforded less risk of being surprised, especially as their left flank would be protected by the sea. The first warning they received of any impending disaster came when their foragers encountered some Roman troops as they approached the coastal town of Telamon. They sent their cavalry and some of their light troops to clear the Romans out of the way, and from one of the prisoners they took they discovered that the Romans in front of them were from a full consular army under Cornelius Atilius Regulus, recalled from Sardinia and recently disembarked at Pisae, further up the coast.

Trapped between the two armies with no way of escape, the Gauls formed two lines back-to-back, with their chariots on the extremities of both wings and the booty placed on a neighbouring hill to be guarded by a small detachment.

Polybius described how the Romans' initial joy at having trapped the Gauls turned to one of apprehension when confronted with the massed ranks of the enemy, their tumultuous and fearsome cries mingled with the blare of horns and trumpets, and their statuesque bodies naked to avoid being impeded in the coming struggle. But a combination of discipline and greed at the sight of the gold chains and bracelets with which the Gauls were adorned, are alleged to have overcome the Roman hesitation. After inflicting a considerable number of casualties on their opponents with a hail of javelins to which the Gauls had no response, the Roman legions advanced for close combat. Assisted by their cavalry who had broken those of the Gauls and after some desperate fighting, the Romans carried the day. Forty thousand Gauls were killed and 10,000 taken prisoner, with only a part of their cavalry managing to escape. The Roman losses are not known but they would have been substantial and according to some sources, included Regulus.

After clearing the battlefield and collecting the spoils, Papus led his army into Boian territory for a short but vicious raid, before returning to Rome. Determined to press home their victory, a second army was sent to clear all the territory around the Po, but though the Boii surrendered without offering resistance, the Romans were decimated by disease which swept through their ranks following a period of heavy rain. As a result the expedition came to nothing and it was left to the consuls of the following year, one of whom was Gaius Flaminius, the plebeian leader who had introduced the land reforms, to cross the Po in 224 BC and extend the war into the territory of the Insubres.

With his fellow consul Flaminius crossed the Po in its middle reaches, between Placentia (Piacenza) and Cremona, near where it is joined by its tributary the Adda with its source in the Alps. Instead of then marching directly against the Insubres, he made an indirect approach by turning east into the land of the friendly Cenomani, before swinging round to the north so as to re-enter Insubres territory unexpectedly from the direction of the Alps. Uncertain as to the loyalty of the Cenomani contingent when faced with actually having to fight a fellow Gallic tribe, Flaminius left them out of the battle when he located the enemy near Bergamo on the Clusius river. Burning the bridges behind him so that there could be no question of withdrawal, he attacked and gained a major victory.

After their defeat the Gauls sued for peace and offered to submit to almost any conditions, but their request was rejected by the new consuls, Gnaeus Cornelius Scipio and Marcus Claudius Marcellus, both of whom were to win distinction against Hannibal, who renewed the campaign in 222 BC. The Gauls were obliged to appeal for a second time to the transalpine Gaesati for help, who responded by dispatching 30,000 reinforcements. In an attempt to raise a continuing siege of Acerrae, an important supply base, which lay on the Adda just above its confluence with the Po. The Gauls dispatched a strong force to besiege Clastidium (Casteggio) and ravage the surrounding countryside. This, as they had anticipated, forced the Romans to react. At the head of two-thirds of the cavalry and all the light infantry, Marcellus marched from Acerrae to relieve Clastidium, leaving Scipio with the remainder of the army behind at Acerrae. What occurred in the ensuing battle is not clear, but it seems that the Gauls besieging Clastidium swept down on Marcellus' small force, in what was expected to be an annihilating attack. Their intention, by reason of their superior numbers, was to extend the front of their attack so as to outflank and encircle the Romans. According to Plutarch, and in view of the numerical inferiority, this is where his account lacks credibility, Marcellus matched the extent of his opponents' deployment and charged forward himself at the head of his cavalry to slay Virdumarus, the Gallic chieftain, in single combat. Outfought and disheartened by the loss of their tribal leader, the Gauls conceded defeat and abandoned the battlefield, leaving Marcellus free to rejoin Scipio. His fellow consul meanwhile had got himself into a near-desperate situation.

Scipio had managed to capture Acerrae, together with the large quantities of stores that had been accumulated there, and had then pursued the Gauls to Mediolanum (Milan) where they had taken refuge. For reasons which are unknown, but may have been due to his shortage of cavalry and absence of light infantry, Scipio then decided to return to Acerrae. This time there can be little doubt that he was overtaken by the Gauls and, lacking the means to secure his rear with an effective mobile rearguard, was surprised by an attack which inflicted heavy casualties among his rearmost heavy infantry, and panicked them into flight. According to Polybius, it was Scipio who rallied his troops and turned them round to face the Gauls. Though this may have been so, it is also possible that it was the arrival of Marcellus, after his victory at Clastidium, that turned the scales. Certainly it was the two consuls together who immediately after the battle pursued their foe and after taking Mediolanum by storm, forced the Insubres to surrender.

During the next two years, 221 and 220 BC, Cisalpine Gaul was conquered, and the last vestige of opposition was eliminated when the northeast corner of Italy, a strip of land between the Venetian and the

Julian Alps, was overrun and occupied up to the mountain passes. Two years later two colonies, each of six thousand settlers, were established at Placentia and Cremona to secure the crossings of the Po as a precautionary measure against the Insubres – but hardly had this been done before Hannibal's crossing of the Alps rallied all Cisalpine Gaul to his cause.

In summarising the lessons of the Gallic Wars, Polybius tell us that since the two opponents fought with equal bravery and both suffered heavy casualties, they were not mere sideshows but deserve their place in history. On the other hand he is dismissive of the wars as being trifling and contemptible because of the rashness with which they were entered into, and the senseless and absurd manner in which they were conducted. Although not explicitly so, his remarks appear to be directed at the Gauls as he goes on to criticise them for the impetuosity of their passions. Polybius' assessment can be readily accepted, since it recognises the futility of an unstructured tribal alliance attempting to challenge an organised military power in a set piece campaign.

The Gauls' first and disastrous tactical defeat at Telamon had its origins in their failure to maintain a clear operational aim. The original purpose of the campaign had been to capture Rome but, following the accumulation of plunder as they progressed southwards, the preservation of their booty took precedence and became an aim in itself. The Gauls were not forced to withdraw when Papus joined up with the Roman survivors of the battle around Clusium: they still dictated events as was shown by the leisurely detour they made before reaching the Etruscan coast and turning north with their booty still intact. But in so doing they lost the initiative which, except at the tactical level, they never regained.

The Romans' conduct of the war was marked by a far greater consistency of purpose than had been displayed in the First Punic War. This is hardly surprising, as it was conducted exclusively on land and directly involved the security of Rome. Originally defensive in their intentions, once the Romans had annihilated the Gauls at Telamon they moved onto the offensive and never lost the initiative. Though Cornelius Atilius Regulus could well have received general news of the Gauls' move, it is improbable that he would have known for certain that they were taking the coastal road. The way in which the Romans achieved surprise and the concentration of their armies at Telamon was therefore largely fortuitous, but the decision to disembark Regulus' legions at Pisae, which was not a natural port to use for communications with Corsica, rather than being panicked into a direct reinforcement of Rome, displayed considerable operational insight and courage. Subsequently, in spite of the criticism that has been levelled against him, Gaius Flaminius' decision to take an indirect route when advancing against the Insubres and in so doing, introduce an element of surprise through manoeuvre, indicates skilful generalship.

The duality of consular command does not appear to have caused any particular difficulties during the various campaigns. During the opening defensive stage, the two consular armies had been deployed separately to cover what was considered to be the Gauls' probable approaches. Though in the event the Gauls struck elsewhere, the Roman appreciation was sound and to have attempted to cover the whole frontier would have resulted in an unacceptable dissipation of force. Subsequently, when one of the consular armies had made contact with the Gauls, the other had wasted no time in moving to join it, even though in the event this proved too late. At Telamon cooperation had hardly been avoidable, in the initial stages because of the tactical situation and subsequently, following Cornelius Atilius Regulus' death, because Lucius Aemilius Papus was left in sole command. Though at Clastidium Marcellus could be criticised for having taken most of the cavalry and the light infantry, leaving Gnaeus Cornelius Scipio with only the heavy infantry, this must have been agreed by both consuls in view of the need to relieve the city as soon as possible. Thereafter the two consuls cooperated in the reduction of Mediolanum and their successes in the final conquest of Cisalpine Gaul.

At the tactical level, the besetting failure of the Romans appears to have arisen from a perpetuation of the weakness they displayed in the First Punic War, the lack of a really proficient cavalry arm. That the Roman infantry should have blundered into the trap set for them at Clusium and their failure to cover their rearguard when withdrawing from Mediolanum, though Scipio had only about a third of the available cavalry, indicates a failure to appreciate the need for both security and the gaining of information.

The tactical shortcomings of the Gauls mirror-imaged those they displayed at the operational level: an inability to achieve an effective coordination of their various contingents, including their infantry and cavalry. At Telamon the latter were employed in an ineffective and quite separate battle with the Roman horse when it must have been apparent enough that the main threat arose from their infantry. The cavalry could have been masked and the chariots on the wings reinforced. As it was, the Roman cavalry were able to maintain their naturally strong position on the high ground and cause the dispirited Gauls to abandon their infantry and seek survival in flight.

CHAPTER ELEVEN

THE ILLYRIAN EXPEDITIONS
229–227 BC

In spite of her eastern seaboard being separated from Greece only by the Adriatic, Rome had no formal contact with the Greek cities lying on the opposite shore line until 228 BC. This Illyrian coast, with its many islands and deep indentations, offered a perfect sanctuary for the many pirates who regarded the Adriatic as their undisputed hunting ground. As far back as the 5th century BC the Adriatic had had an unsavoury reputation for violence, and among the Athenians of that period 'to sail the Adriatic' was another way of saying 'to undertake a hazardous journey'. Though Roman vessels had not been spared and substantial numbers of Roman merchants had been killed or carried into slavery, the pirates' activities had attracted little attention from the Senate. After the First Punic War, however, the complaints became so numerous that two envoys were dispatched to Illyria to demand an explanation.

Following a period of rapid territorial expansion between 240 and 229 BC, the kingdom of Illyria had reached its peak, ruled over by its autocratic Queen Teuta. At this period the Illyrian boundaries stretched from Dalmatia in the north down to opposite the heel of Italy in the south, and incorporating, among other states, Epirus. The origins of Illyria are unclear but it seems that a single tribe, the Ardiaenes, had achieved a dominating position and established piracy as a form of livelihood that had developed into a national industry. The consequential accumulation of wealth had led to the formation of a navy capable of both brigandry on a grand scale and conquest of the adjacent coastal towns. It was while Queen Teuta was engaged in one such operation against the recalcitrant city of Issa (Lissa), on the island of the same name off the Dalmatian coast, that the Roman envoys arrived. According to Polybius, the subsequent meeting was a stormy affair with the Queen eventually reacting 'like a true woman; with much absurd passion and resentment; which carried her to such an excess that she ordered the envoys to be pursued as they were returning and in defiance of the laws of nations, killed the person who had spoken those words'. The person being the younger of the two envoys and the words being to the effect that if, as she had claimed, the Queen could not control the acts of her subjects, then the Romans would.

Such was the cause, if it really was quite so simplistic, of yet another war. That the Romans had not anticipated such an outcome is clear from the fact that only after this incident did they put in hand the necessary preparations for the campaign by raising a new army and assembling the fleet. That the Illyrians had not expected their relations with Rome to deteriorate so rapidly seems equally clear; they had, after all, been killing Roman merchants and seamen with apparent impunity for many years. Additionally, although Teuta must have realised that Rome was not a power to be trifled with, there had been no indication that the Romans ever wished to become directly involved with the people inhabiting the eastern shores of the Adriatic and Ionian seas. A Roman fleet had never entered these waters and Roman attentions seemed to be firmly fixed to the west and north in wars with the Gauls and Carthage.

Although the Romans ostensibly went to war because of Illyrian piracy and high-handedness, their previous apparent lack of interest in their Adriatic neighbours may well have masked a more substantial Roman concern. Up to then perpetual quarrelling among the Greek states had prevented any one of them from establishing themselves in a permanent ascendancy threatening to Rome. After the First Punic War, admittedly, anxiety over the rise of Macedonia had caused the Romans to offer assistance to Ptolemy III of Egypt in his war against a natural Macedonian blood ally, Seleucis II of Syria, but this potential threat to Rome had receded when the Macedonians had been dislodged from the upper Adriatic by the Aetolians and from the Peloponnesus by the Achaeans. However, the rapid territorial expansion and the accompanying aggressiveness of Illyria now denoted the emergence of a new and potentially hostile state that could come to serve Macedonian interests and aggrandizement. This danger therefore could well have been an underlying reason for the Romans going to war, even if the immediate pretext was Illyrian piracy and high-handedness at Issa.

The campaign that followed provides a good example of a war fought with a limited aim, one which was not exceeded even when

THE ILLYRIAN EXPEDITIONS

rapid successes could well have tempted the Romans into extending it. The potential Illyrian threat to Rome, and with it the piracy they practised, was to be removed by establishing Roman control over the eastern shore of the Straits of Otranto. To achieve this, it would be necessary to break the Illyrian domination of the Adriatic by defeating them in battle, but no attempt was to be made to subjugate them completely by occupying the heartland of central Illyria. The first move the Romans made was to dispatch a fleet of 200 ships, a number which may have been exaggerated, to Corcyra (Corfu) under command of Fulvius Centumalus. While on passage the consul learned that the Illyrian commander, the Greek Demetrius, had aroused Queen Teuta's jealousy, and fearing for his own safety had offered to hand the city over to the Romans and give them any further assistance they might require. Furthermore, on arriving at Corcyra, Fulvius was welcomed by the inhabitants and Demetrius alike.

The Romans then sailed to Apollonia, taking with them Demetrius, who remained with them for the remainder of the war as an adviser. At Apollonia the Roman fleet was joined by the other consul, Lucius Postumius Albinus, who had sailed from Brundisium at the head of 20,000 infantry and 2000 cavalry. Once again the Romans accepted the surrender of the city and occupied it without resistance. But almost immediately afterwards news that Epidamnus (Durzzo) was under seige by the Illyrians reached them, causing the two consuls to march to its relief without delay. Learning of their approach, the Illyrians fled and once again the Romans occupied a city that had surrendered to them as deliverers. But although the campaign had been successful, in that the Romans now occupied the coastal belt where the Illyrians had been establishing themselves, Roman authority had yet to be firmly imposed. The campaign was then extended further into Illyria, which induced many towns and districts, including the important Parthinian and Atintane tribes, to enter to treaties of friendship and alliance with the Romans.

Practically isolated, the Illyrians now found themselves under increasing pressure as the Romans continued to clear the Adriatic coast line steadily northwards. Issa, which was under siege from the Illyrians, was relieved and the only temporary setback the Romans suffered was at Nutria, which has not been located but may have been a distorted reference to Narona opposite Pharos (Lesina), where they suffered heavily when unsuccessfully attempting to storm the town. Content to consolidate their position, the Romans concentrated at Epidamnus before Postumius returned to Italy with the majority of the fleet and army in the autumn of 229 BC. Centumalus Fulvius had elected to remain behind, to ensure that there were no uprisings by the many tribes and cities which had been placed under Roman protection. The danger of this occuring cannot have been considered very great, as Fulvius depended mainly upon locally raised troops and some forty ships which he had collected together.

In the spring of the following year, 228 BC, Illyrian envoys arrived in Rome seeking peace, which was agreed on the following terms: 'The Queen should pay a certain tribute, and abandon all Illyria, a few places only excepted, and she should never again sail beyond Lissus (Lesk on the mouth of the Drin) with more than two warships, and those unarmed.' This restriction on Illyrian warships was of the greatest importance to all the Greek states and effectively ended acts of piracy in their waters, while guaranteeing the security of Roman shipping trading across the Adriatic from her southern ports around the heel of Italy. Illyria lost all her southernmost possessions and a number of cities along her northern coast, while Queen Teuta renounced her suzerainty over the Greek general Demetrius, who was not only restored to his hereditary domain at Pharos, but had his territory extended to form a minor state under Roman protection. In this manner Illyrian good conduct was to be monitored by Demetrius to the west, while Roman domination of the coastal area across the Straits of Otranto effectively achieved this to the south. Rome's authority was thus firmly established in the southern Adriatic, an achievement which fully accorded with her limited war aim of preventing a hostile power arising opposite her eastern seaboard. By this action Rome had erected an obstacle to Macedonian expansion into the Adriatic and Ionian sea, while eliminating Illyrian piracy. The next move was for Rome to placate her new neighbours.

Early in the same year, envoys were sent to the Achaeans and Aetolians to explain the causes of the war and relate the peace terms which Rome had made. This propitiating gesture was well received and the emissaries returned laden with gifts and expressions of good will. Further envoys were subsequently dispatched to Corinth and Athens where their diplomatic courtesies were equally well appreciated, the Corinthians going so far as to express their gratitude by inviting the Romans to participate in the Isthmian Games, a Panhellenic festival celebrated every other year in Corinth. This invitation was more than just a gesture of friendship, it implied that the Romans had been accepted as members of the Hellenic community. And although the Greeks continued to regard the Romans as a backward, if not barbaric, people, in this way the Romans established their first contacts with the Greek mainland. They also, if perhaps unfortunately, made no attempt to make contact with the Macedonians or any of their allied states, an omission which may have been no more than a recognition that the latent hostility existing between them was too great to be bridged in this manner. The risk of a humiliating rebuff was unacceptable; it was better to do nothing, even though this would inevitably make the Macedonians yet more suspicious and resentful.

Following the successful conclusion of their campaign, peace was to endure on Rome's eastern borders for ten years while she concentrated on her war with the Gauls. But this Roman preoccupation to the north and apparent lack of interest in developing her authority to the east encouraged Demetrius to extend his borders and to judge that his own interests would best be served by withdrawing from the hegemony of Rome and entering into a treaty with Antigonus, King of Macedon. But then, in 220 BC, just when the Romans had been forced to react to events in Spain by placing Saguntum, which was being closely besieged by Hannibal, under their protection and sending a stern warning to Carthage, Demetrius chose to flaunt Roman authority in a manner which could no longer be overlooked.

Together with his ally Scerdilaidas, Demetrius first of all invaded the territory of the Atintanes, whose independence had been guaranteed by the Romans and from whom they could accordingly expect protection, and then set sail to attack Pylos, a port in the extreme southwest of Greece. Having failed to take the city, Demetrius proceeded to ravage the Aegean coastline which, in spite of Roman preoccupations elsewhere, was an almost unbelievably reckless challenge to their authority.

The Roman response was devastating, both in its vigour and its rapidity of execution. In 219 BC two consuls, Lucius Aemilius Paullus, who was later to figure in the battle of Cannae, and Marcus Livius Salinator, descended on the Illyrian coast at Apollonia, or perhaps Epidamnus, both of which had remained loyal to Rome. Demetrius intended to hold firm in two principal cities, Dimalae on the mainland in the south, and his island capital Pharos in the north. The strength of the Romans is not known, but with two consular armies it would have been about 20,000, compared with the garrison of Pharos which we know numbered only 6000 picked troops. While the fighting quality and resolution of this garrison may, by Illyrian standards, have merited their being designated picked troops, their performance did not match that of the Romans and the city fell to Paullus by storm after having been invested for only seven days. The neighbouring cities and tribes were quick to renounce their allegiance to Demetrius and expediently offered to place themselves once again under Roman suzerainty. Their capitulation and change of heart was accepted by the Romans who treated them leniently, though no doubt extracting some retribution for the expense and trouble to which they had been put.

The Romans were now free to concentrate on the reduction of

Pharos; a task which was completed with skill and rapidity, in spite of the great natural strength of the city and, through being well provisioned, its ability to withstand a prolonged siege. Paullus succeeded by achieving surprise. He approached Pharos at night and disembarked the majority of his troops under cover of darkness, on a part of the island where the broken nature of the ground and woods enabled them to assemble near the city unobserved. The next morning he sailed towards the principal harbour of the island with a mere twenty ships. Deceived into thinking that this represented the entire Roman force, Demetrius hastened down to the harbour to contain and then destroy them. As the battle developed, more and more of the garrison was drawn out of the city until it was almost undefended. At this critical moment, the main body of Roman troops left their hiding place and seized a prominent hill lying between the city of Pharos and the contested harbour. Unable to retire and coming under vigorous frontal attack as Paullus' troops disembarked in ever-increasing numbers, the Illyrians broke and fled.

Demetrius was amongst those who managed to escape from the battlefield and, resourceful as ever, reached the ships he had kept concealed, just in case, in an out-of-the-way part of the island. When night came he put to sea and eventually sought refuge with Philip of Macedonia. Occupied by his struggle with Sparta and the Aetolians, Philip had done nothing so far to assist Demetrius against the Romans, but he now made him welcome and did not remain uninfluenced by that arch schemer's plans for revenge on Rome. Macedonian enmity towards Rome had been fuelled by the latters' invasion of Illyria, which provided another greatly resented example of Roman arrogant usurpation of Macedonian authority. This enmity was eventually to lead to the First Macedonian War when Philip entered into an alliance with Hannibal and attacked Rome's Illyrian possessions and Corcyra.

After the flight and annihilation of its garrison outside its walls, Pharos lay practically undefended and quickly fell to the first assault by the Romans, who then plundered and destroyed the city. In a campaign which had lasted only a few months, the Romans had re-established their protectorate in lower Illyria. They then, as had occurred ten years earlier, returned to Italy to focus their attention on more pressing developments. This time it was to Spain that they turned where the city of Saguntum was under vigorous siege by Hannibal.

The lessons to be drawn from the Romans' Illyrian expeditions are both political and military. First, they serve as instructive examples of a campaign being fought with strictly limited objectives. The military measures to achieve these objectives were accompanied by diplomatic moves, designed to ensure that the states bordering on Illyria understood the purpose and strictly limited nature of Rome's intervention. There was then a properly coordinated policy and the exercise of strict political control over the field commanders. The modern-day Korean War serves as an example of how difficult this can be. The UN forces, having restored South Korea's territorial integrity, then crossed the 39th parallel to complete the defeat of the North Koreans. However morally justifiable and militarily desirable this intent was, it introduced a further dimension into the war, the intervention of the Chinese, not only to save the North Koreans but to prevent what they saw to be the establishment of an American continental foothold on their very frontiers. This intervention in turn threatened a fateful extension of the conflict to involve the use of nuclear weapons. So care needs to be taken when employing military force: the powder train can run very quickly and in the most unexpected directions.

The second lesson to be drawn is once again that the effective exercise of military force requires a force structure which is appropriate to the circumstances. Illyria attempted to combine territorial expansion with piracy, an idiotic policy, its double and unrelated aims both requiring a maritime capability she manifestly did not possess. And thirdly, the overwhelming advantage to be achieved from surprise was clearly demonstrated by Paullus' use of darkness to land and conceal his main force at Pharos, before appearing at daybreak off the harbour as though this was where he was making his main assault.

We must now step back in time twenty years to 237 BC and see what, in the meanwhile, had been taking place in Spain.

CHAPTER TWELVE

THE CONQUEST OF SPAIN
237–219 BC

As we have seen, when the Mercenary War ended the peace party of Hanno was replaced by that of Hamilcar Barca, a party determined to restore Carthage to her earlier eminence and revenge the humiliations inflicted on her by Rome. The intent was clear enough but its implementation was fraught with seemingly insoluble problems. The Barcid party might be in power but the current of opposition still ran strongly and any faltering or the imposition of burdening taxation by Hamilcar, would quickly lead to his replacement. Yet if he was to attain his objectives and the vagaries of oligarchical reaction were to be avoided, Hamilcar's authority had to be absolute and his policy firmly supported by public opinion.

Hamilcar's first priority must have been to ensure that the war indemnity was paid to the Romans promptly and in full. Any failure there would have provided a pretext for the Romans to return to Africa and enforce yet sterner measures while Carthage still lay helpless. Secondly, if he were to raise an army capable of standing against the Romans, Hamilcar would have to rely on mercenaries and somehow obtain the money to pay them. The citizens of Carthage would have been neither willing nor able to provide the necessary manpower themselves. Equally, however, they would not have countenanced the cost of sustaining a large mercenary army while still paying off their debt to Rome. In addition to these local obstacles to his ambitions, Hamilcar had to face the danger that any overt preparations for war in Africa would inevitably attract the attention of the Romans and lead to their early intervention. Nor was it just a matter of raising an army; there would also be a need to construct a fleet for its eventual transportation to Sicily or Italy. Rejecting the strategically direct approach against Rome as being impracticable, Hamilcar, therefore, decided to move indirectly; he would establish a new power base in Spain.

The possession of Spain would enable the wealth of that country to be exploited, so permitting the Carthaginians to pay off their war debt to Rome and allowing Hamilcar to raise and maintain a mercenary army while remaining financially and – though he would not have said so – politically independent. There was to be no repetition of the predicament in which he had found himself in Sicily when denuded of support and abandoned. There was also another advantage to financial independence. If Hamilcar was to gain consistent support for his plans as they unfolded, there would have to be tangible benefits accruing to the citizens of Carthage: pockets would have to be lined. Hamilcar's friends and supporters would need to receive regular subventions.

Though wealth was only a means to an end, when putting forward his proposals to the Senate Hamilcar would have been unlikely to disclose his ultimate intentions, restricting himself instead to the financial benefits arising for Carthage. His justification for raising a mercenary army would probably have been based on the need to conquer a large part of Spain, in order to ensure an orderly administration and the proper exploitation of the country's resources of precious metals and raw materials. Hamilcar also probably pointed out that following the loss of Sicily, Sardinia and Corsica, the opportunities for profitable trading by Carthaginian merchants had been greatly reduced, while in Spain itself Carthaginian influence had declined. Pressure from Greek Massilia (Marseilles) had reduced the area held by Carthage along the southern coast to the Straits of Gibraltar and a small piece of land around Gades (Cadiz). If Carthage was to recover her position as well as meet her financial commitments, there could be no alternative to the conquest of Spain.

Hamilcar may also have put forward the argument that unless Carthage made this move, Rome certainly would. With the acquisition of Sardinia and Corsica Roman interest must inevitably be drawn westwards, in which event any subsequent attempt by Carthage to extend her Spanish possessions could be interpreted by Rome as a direct threat to herself. However implausible this may appear, as we have seen, this is exactly what occurred when the Carthaginians had taken steps to restore their authority in Sardinia after the First Punic War.

If Hamilcar did not disclose his ultimate intention to revenge himself on Rome, this is probably partly because at this stage he had not formulated any clear ideas as to how this ambition was to be achieved. Be that as it may, whatever plans he did put to the Senate,

Hamilcar gained their assent and was appointed to command the army. The appointment carried responsibility for the defence and security of Carthage's African Empire, a commitment which according to Diodorus resulted in him being created generalissimo of Libya for a short time. But Hamilcar's responsibilities for Africa must have rested fairly lightly on his shoulders since, although his son-in-law Hasdrubal had to return to Carthage in order to subdue a Numidian uprising, all Hamilcar's serious thoughts and energy seem to have been directed to the furtherance of his Spanish ambitions.

But before embarking on an account of his campaign, a portrayal of how Hamilcar might have viewed the opposition will provide some background to the undertaking.

The two principal tribes inhabiting the peninsula were the Celts and the Iberians. The former had been the original occupants of the central highlands and the western region of Spain, but they had been largely supplanted by the Iberians – who had previously been confined to the south and east coasts, to where they had probably migrated as a consequence of Gallic pressure on their ancestral homeland north of the Pyrenees. Some commingling of the two tribes had occurred to produce the wild Celtiberians, but it was the Iberians now inhabiting the highlands who were both the more primitive and the more warlike and recklessly brave. Their abiding defect, like that of the immeasurably more sophisticated Greek city states, was an inability to cooperate. The political unit was not the tribe, as with the Gauls, but the single settlement, frequently of insignificant proportions, which only combined with its neighbours when immediately confronted with a threat of unmistakable commonality. In the absence of any corporate identity, the Iberians were willing to be recruited as mercenaries by the Carthaginians but were equally prepared to serve in the ranks of the Roman legions. In spite of the ambivalence of their loyalties, individual Iberian settlements and townships defended themselves with a desperate determination that extended to cannibalism when enduring a long siege. The people who populated Spain, being hardy and brave, were therefore natural soldiers but politically and socially uncoordinated and economically naive, quite unaware of their country's wealth.

Hamilcar must have appreciated the limitations of the Iberians and Celts as opponents, while recognising their potential if incorporated into the disciplined ranks of his own army. Centrally directed purposefulness will inevitably prevail over disparate individualism on the battlefield; hence the danger which has been posed to freewheeling democratic societies by monolithic communism. In Hamilcar's case unity was achieved by the magnetism of his leadership and an identity of aspirations amongst his mercenary soldiers;

plunder, rapine and adventure. The Iberians on the other hand, though undoubtedly sharing the motivating instincts, lacked political and military cohesiveness.

As to the development of Hamilcar's campaign, since Carthage no longer had an effective navy, he had no alternative but to march his army along the northern Numidian coast to the Straits of Gibraltar, while a few ships kept pace with him, transporting supplies of food, and fodder for his elephants and cavalry horses. And in 237 BC he ferried his army across the straits, landing at Gades. From the outset he set about establishing that he and his close relations ruled by divine right, in the Macedonian tradition, and quickly transformed simple clan and tribal superstitions into a mystical theology centred on the Barcid family. In this way a dynastic religion was born that tied the loyalty of the army to Hamilcar and ensured the orderly transfer of command in the event of his death. Ambitious aspirants in Carthage would no longer be able to advance themselves for command of the army in Spain, and thus the political direction of events would remain with the Barcids. To give substance to this image of rule by divine writ and celestial guardianship, when he eventually succeeded to the command of the army Hamilcar's son Hannibal had coins struck portraying him and his father in close association with Melquart, the patron god of the whole Iberian peninsula whose sanctuary was at Gades. In this manner charismatic leadership was harnessed to divine inheritance and the resultant protection of the gods; all of which goes a long way to explain how Hannibal came to imbue his soldiers with such a degree of personal loyalty that they achieved seemingly impossible feats of endurance and courage.

Unfortunately Polybius deals with Hamilcar Barca's nine years of campaigning in Spain in only a most perfunctory manner, and from any other account that may have existed only a few details survive. According to these, Hamilcar's first move was to strike out from Gades to subdue the 'Tartessians', who were probably Celts, and the Iberians so as to occupy Andalusia. Diodorus refers briefly to two battles that ensued; the first was against the Celtic general Istolatius and his brother who, after being roundly defeated and taken prisoner, were executed together with many of their compatriots – though from the remaining prisoners, at least 3000 were recruited into the Carthaginian army. The second battle was fought against a 50,000-strong tribal army of unknown composition under Indortes, though most of them fled before battle was joined. Indortes himself was captured and blinded before being crucified, but the remaining 10,000 prisoners were treated leniently, being released to their homes. Following these two victories, many townships surrendered but others still had to be taken by force. It was during this period that the Numidians revolted and Hasdrubal was sent back to Africa by his father-in-law to subdue them; a task he carried out with ruthless efficiency, killing 8000 of them and taking a further 2000 prisoner.

Having secured southern Spain, Hamilcar's next move was to push the Carthaginian frontier up the eastern coast as far north as Cape Nao. To consolidate this advance and secure his right flank Hamilcar raised a dominating fortress on the steep rocky hill at Acra Leuce (Alicante), which was to remain the principal bulwark of Carthaginian defence in this area until replaced by New Carthage (Cartagena). This extension of Carthaginian territory was a matter of profound concern to Rome's ally Massilia, who saw the transgression of the recognised boundary at Cape Palus by nearly 100 miles as an erosion of their recently extended influence and trade monopoly in the area, and therefore a serious threat to their own position and prosperity. It was not long before news of their concern was judiciously conveyed to Rome, and in 231 BC an embassy was despatched to Spain to inquire into what was taking place. Occupied, as we have seen, with more pressing and immediate issues elsewhere, the Romans accepted Hamilcar's neat reply that he was only fighting the Iberians in order to obtain the means to pay off the war indemnity. Since Polybius states that the treaty with Saguntum was made many years before Hannibal's time, it may have been now that the Romans entered into an alliance with this important city lying some fifty miles to the north of Cape Nao; the later siege and capture of which was to lead to the Second Punic War.

In 229 BC Hamilcar set siege to Ilici (Elche), just south of Acra Leuce, but at the onset of winter he dispatched the greater part of his army into quarters, maintaining the siege himself with the remainder. While his army was dispersed in this manner, a tribal king called Orissus approached him with an offer of assistance. Though we do not know why or how this occurred, Hamilcar was caught off his guard when Orissus suddenly turned on him, forcing him not only to raise the siege but also to flee to Acra Leuce. Though there were two possible avenues of escape, it seems as if both necessitated crossing the intervening river which was in full spate. Ordering his two sons, Hasdrubal the younger and Hannibal, to take one route, Hamilcar took the other, which he may possibly have known was more hazardous. Certainly, while his sons escaped, he was hotly pursued and in attempting to ford the river, was swept from his horse and drowned.

By the time he died Hamilcar Barca had established Carthaginian domination over southern and eastern Spain. The cruelty which had been displayed towards those who had opposed him probably arose both from a determination to establish an orderly administration over the factious clans whose territory he now occupied, and from a need to serve warning on those he had yet to subdue. Certainly by 235 BC Hamilcar exercised complete control over the mines situated in the mountains surrounding the valley and headwaters of the Guadalquivir river. The silver extracted from these mines, being of an excellent quality and far superior to that being minted in Africa, was divided into three portions: one part was sent to Carthage, a second was minted at Gades by Hamilcar for his own purposes and the third, seemingly rather generously though it may have served other purposes as well, was given to the authorities of Gades in recognition of their loyalty.

As Hamilcar's two sons, Hannibal and Hasdrubal the younger, were too young to succeed him, on his death the army elected his son-in-law, Hasdrubal the elder; an appointment which was subsequently ratified by the people of Carthage. Hasdrubal's first action was to assemble against Orissus an army of 50,000 tried and experienced infantry, together with 6000 cavalry and some 200 elephants to avenge Hamilcar's death. No mercy was shown to Orissus and his followers. All those who were taken were put to the sword, and after the extinction of organised resistance, Carthaginian domination was extended as far as the upper Guadiana, which flowed some 100 miles to the north and broadly parallel to the Guadalquivir. In this way a broad sweep of territory was secured stretching inland from Gades in the west to Cape Nao on the east coast. But after this initial expedition of revenge and territorial expansion, Hasdrubal devoted most of his energies to consolidating the relatively limited Barcid empire and confirming its autonomy, thus fulfilling the role of a military governor more than that of a military commander. To strengthen his quasi-imperial role, Hasdrubal summoned a gathering of the Iberian chiefs and succeeded in having himself appointed as their overlord, a position he reinforced by marrying the daughter of a prominent Iberian prince.

The most significant step Hasdrubal took in both establishing and displaying his independence, was the founding of New Carthage: its magnificent harbour providing easy access to Africa, while in the surrounding hills lay further rich silver mines. Here Hasdrubal established his capital, built a palace fit for an eastern potentate and minted those coins which bore his own image with its divine association. His rule was harsh: the tribal princes and chiefs not only had to pay tribute, but also were forced to hand over their children and even their wives as hostages. Those suspected of plotting against Hasdrubal or Carthaginian administrations were either assassinated or seized and subjected to prolonged torture; and many of the lower orders were reduced to serfdom and forced to work in the silver mines under brutal conditions. Discontent was rife, but Carthaginian discipline and superior organisation ensured that order was preserved while the wealth of the country flowed in fulfilment of Barcid ambitions.

Once again the development of events in Spain drew the Roman's attention to the peninsula and a second embassy was dispatched in 226 BC, but some confusion exists as to what was agreed in the subsequent treaty. According to Polybius, 'they [the Romans] sent to Hasdrubal and concluded a treaty with him, by which, no mention being made of the rest of Spain, it only was agreed, that the Carthaginians should not pass the Iberus (Ebro) with an army'. Later on he is less specific, saying that 'they were content with having set some bounds to the progress of the Carthaginians by the treaty which was made by Hasdrubal'. The limit to Carthaginian expansion has understandably enough been accepted by most modern historians as being the Ebro, but as the Picards point out in *The Life and Death of Carthage*, were this so, Saguntum, which became a *casus belli* when attacked by Hannibal in 220 BC, would have been left isolated some hundred miles behind the Carthaginians' advance to the Ebro. The Picards argue that the treaty limit was more probably set on the Jucar, which would have confined the Carthaginians to some twenty miles north of Cape Nao, or as far as Hamilcar had initially advanced. That they are correct seems probable. First, the Romans would have been unlikely to have lamely countenanced the Carthaginians hemming in their ally Saguntum and effectively sealing it off by land from all outside contact or assistance. Second, Hasdrubal was primarily concerned with establishing a firm administration rather than embarking on further military conquests, about which no mention is made anyway.

In conforming to his role as an administrator and probably more motivated by a desire to preserve his empire than risk its extinction, Hasdrubal accepted the Roman terms, but in so doing Hamilcar's territorial acquisitions at the expense of Rome's ally Massilia were confirmed by the treaty: a further indication of Rome's desire to settle affairs in Spain by reasonable compromise because of more pressing concerns nearer home. Five years later, in 221 BC, Hasdrubal was murdered in his palace by a Celt, whose chieftain had been crucified for plotting against the Carthaginian Emperor King.

The Carthaginians delayed appointing a successor to Hasdrubal until the views of the army were known, but on hearing that Hannibal had been the army's unanimous choice, an assembly of the people was quickly called and his appointment confirmed. Hannibal was only twenty-five when he took command, but for the next twenty years he was to dominate events throughout the Mediterranean and come near to bringing Rome to her knees. His first enterprise was to mount a short expedition to subdue the Olcades, a tribe occupying the highlands some 100 miles west of Acra Leuce, after which he returned to his winter quarters in New Carthage, where the loyalty of his troops was ensured by the punctual payment of all that was due to them; accompanied by promises of further rewards to come.

In the summer of 220 BC Hannibal switched his campaign to the northwestern highlands against the Vaccaei, who inhabited an area extending round the middle waters of the Douro. Salmantica (Salamanca), some forty miles south of the river, fell quickly but Arbucale, which lay on the Douro itself, offered fierce resistance and after stoutly resisting a siege had to be taken by storm. On his return journey Hannibal was unexpectedly attacked by the Carpetani, a tribe occupying the very centre of Spain around Toletum (Toledo) on the Tagus, who had been stirred up by fugitives from Salmantica and the Olcades, the latter having been subdued only the previous year. That Hannibal was surprised at this development suggests that he had passed through the territory of the Carpetani unmolested when on his outward march. Now being greatly outnumbered, he was forced to withdraw behind the Tagus. Attempting to assault across the river, the Carpetani found themselves confronted by some forty Carthaginian elephants as well as their cavalry, and most of them were slaughtered before they could establish themselves on the opposite bank. Disorganised and demoralised, they broke and fled when Hannibal led an attack across the river in person. After this victory, except for the territory of the Celtiberians on the upper reaches of the Douro and Tagus, together with Saguntum, Spain lay open to the Carthaginians up to the Ebro.

Accounts differ between Polybius and Livy as to the sequence of events that now followed. According to Polybius, Hannibal again withdrew to New Carthage where he found some Roman envoys awaiting him. The Saguntines had repeatedly been sending anxious messages to Rome about Hannibal's rapid successes but the preoccupied Romans had largely ignored these warnings. But the Saguntine envoys were finally brought before the Senate and, alarmed at what they now heard, the Romans decided to send an embassy and see for themselves, to issue a warning to the Carthaginians not to attack Saguntum and to demand compliance with the treaty concluded with Hasdrubal, restricting the Carthaginians to south of the Ebro (considered to be the Jucar as discussed). In responding to the envoys, Hannibal posed as a friend of Saguntum and reproached the Romans for the arbitrary execution of some of the city's magistrates. In recounting these events Polybius asserts that Hannibal even went as far as to send messengers simultaneously to Carthage, relating how the Saguntines were sheltering behind their alliance with Rome to attack their neighbours, the Turdenti. In the event, the Roman envoys returned home convinced that Hannibal was intent upon war, but they had no suspicion that this would be fought elsewhere than in Spain; so once again Roman attention was diverted to what seemed more urgent and immediate concerns, this time in connection with Illyria.

Livy on the other hand, says that even before the Roman envoys had been dispatched to Spain, Hannibal had begun his attack on Saguntum. He then goes on to relate how the Senate debated the situation; some advocating that war should be begun at once, others that envoys should be dispatched to Saguntum demanding that Hannibal should immediately stop his attack. In the event of a refusal, envoys were to proceed to Carthage and demand his surrender for breaching the treaty between the two powers. The latter course was adopted, but Hannibal gave no satisfaction, and when the envoys continued to Carthage they were told that the blame lay with the Saguntines, and were advised not to let their concern for Saguntum take precedence over their long-standing treaty of friendship with Carthage.

Since it is not known which of these two accounts is correct, that of Polybius will be adopted in preference to that of the more unreliable Livy, whose conviction that the Romans were the greatest nation on earth tainted his presentation of facts, while his romanticism led him into some strange interpretations. According to Polybius then, in 219 BC, the year following the departure of the Roman envoys, Hannibal began his march from New Carthage to Saguntum while the Romans sent an army into Illyria, having no doubt concluded that in spite of Hannibal's ambitions in Spain the more immediate danger to their interests and authority lay across the Adriatic. Events in remote Spain would be left to run their course, even if this entailed a cynical betrayal of the Saguntines.

Saguntum lies on the eastern extremity of a narrow, high rocky plateau reaching out to the coast. At the time Polybius was writing, the city was rather less than a mile from the sea, but today this distance has been extended to at least three miles by the alluvial soil brought down by the Palancia. The surrounding countryside was rich agricultural land, the best on the peninsula, and was under intense cultivation. Saguntum was then not only of strategic importance, since its reduction would have been an essential prerequisite for any further advance northwards, but it was also a rich source of supply. So that Hannibal had only to offer his troops the prospect of sacking the city to arouse their fervour. Saguntum endured an eight-month siege, sustained by the hope of a Roman army coming to their relief. When the city finally fell by storm, the price of retribution was high; the Carthaginians took revenge in an orgy of butchery and looting.

With the reduction of Saguntum, Hannibal established the secure base in Spain which Hamilcar had sought in order to provide him with complete independence of action. Assured of a plentiful supply of hardy, battle-conditioned soldiers and an abundance of natural resources to maintain them, Hannibal could moreover guarantee to support Carthage if needed. But although he had also managed to arouse the enthusiasm of his soldiers for further adventure, few of them can have foreseen the immensity of the demands that would be placed upon them in the long, harsh campaign that lay ahead.

Hannibal had justified his attack on the Saguntines by accusing them of provoking a frontier quarrel with the Turdenti, a tribe allied to the Carthaginians, occupying the coastal region extending northwards to the Jucar. Such a justification seems thin at the very least. But, since we do not know for certain whether or not the territory of the Turdenti actually stretched as far north as the Jucar, nor even if the frontier dispute actually involved deliberate aggression, the question is not going to be resolved. All the same, given that the Saguntines would have been most unlikely not to have known of their ally Rome's heavy involvement in other theatres, it seems most improbable that they would have risked war with Hannibal for the sake of a trivial local quarrel. Taking this into consideration and recognising Hannibal's unconcealed ambition, it can reasonably be concluded that he engineered the war, the trigger for which was his attack on Saguntum. And the causes in fact lay far deeper: they can be traced back to the Barcid hatred of Rome, the annexation of Sardinia, and the humiliation of Carthage. Events at Saguntum were then no more than part of a progression of incidents, all leading fatefully to a war which, though it could have been delayed, would inevitably have broken out before much longer.

No attempt will be made at an overall appraisal, or to draw any particular lessons from the events which arose during this extended period. The identifiable causes of the Second Punic War have already been discussed. The interacting, yet divergent political interests of Rome, Carthage and the incipient Barcid empire in Spain are too diffuse to permit more than bland observations to be made concerning Roman shortsightedness or Carthaginian perfidy, observations which do little to suggest how war would have been averted. Similarly, accounts of the military campaign are too fragmentary and unconnected to permit any useful deductions. All that can be said is that Hamilcar and his son Hannibal were unswerving in the pursuit of their aim to take revenge on Rome. The aim can be deplored, but not the consistency with which it was maintained.

PART FOUR

THE SECOND PUNIC WAR
218–201 BC

CHAPTER THIRTEEN

FROM THE EBRO TO THE ALPS
218 BC

After the reduction of Saguntum, Hannibal went into winter quarters in New Carthage where he prepared for the coming war. First, he sent most of his Iberian soldiers back to their homes to rest until the summer campaigning season began. Next, he made the necessary dispositions to reduce the risk of revolt and ensure the security of Spain and Libya in his absence by cross-posting Iberians and Libyans. Hasdrubal Barca, his brother, was given responsibility for the management of affairs in Spain with an army of some 11,000 Libyans, 2000 Numidians and smaller numbers of other tribal troops, together with fifty quinqueremes and some triremes. About 14,000 Iberian infantry and other contingents were sent to Africa, some of whom were stationed in Carthage itself.

Hannibal had already sent messengers to the Gauls seeking their assistance for the passage of his army through their territory and across the Alps. As much information as possible was also obtained about the countryside through which he intended to march. Now, when the messengers reported back, they brought encouraging news; the Gauls were ready, in fact eager, to assist him against their age-old enemy. As for crossing the Alps, this would be laborious and difficult, but it would not be impossible. Judging by subsequent events, it seems that the messengers had contacted the Gaesati, the transalpine tribe who lived between the Rhone and the Alps. Even if, as seems probable from the nature of the reports he received, Hannibal did not contact the tribes to the west of the Rhone, the resistance he met from them after crossing the Ebro cannot have been unexpected in view of the known hostility of the pro-Roman tribes inhabiting this area.

Italy – To illustrate the Second Punic War

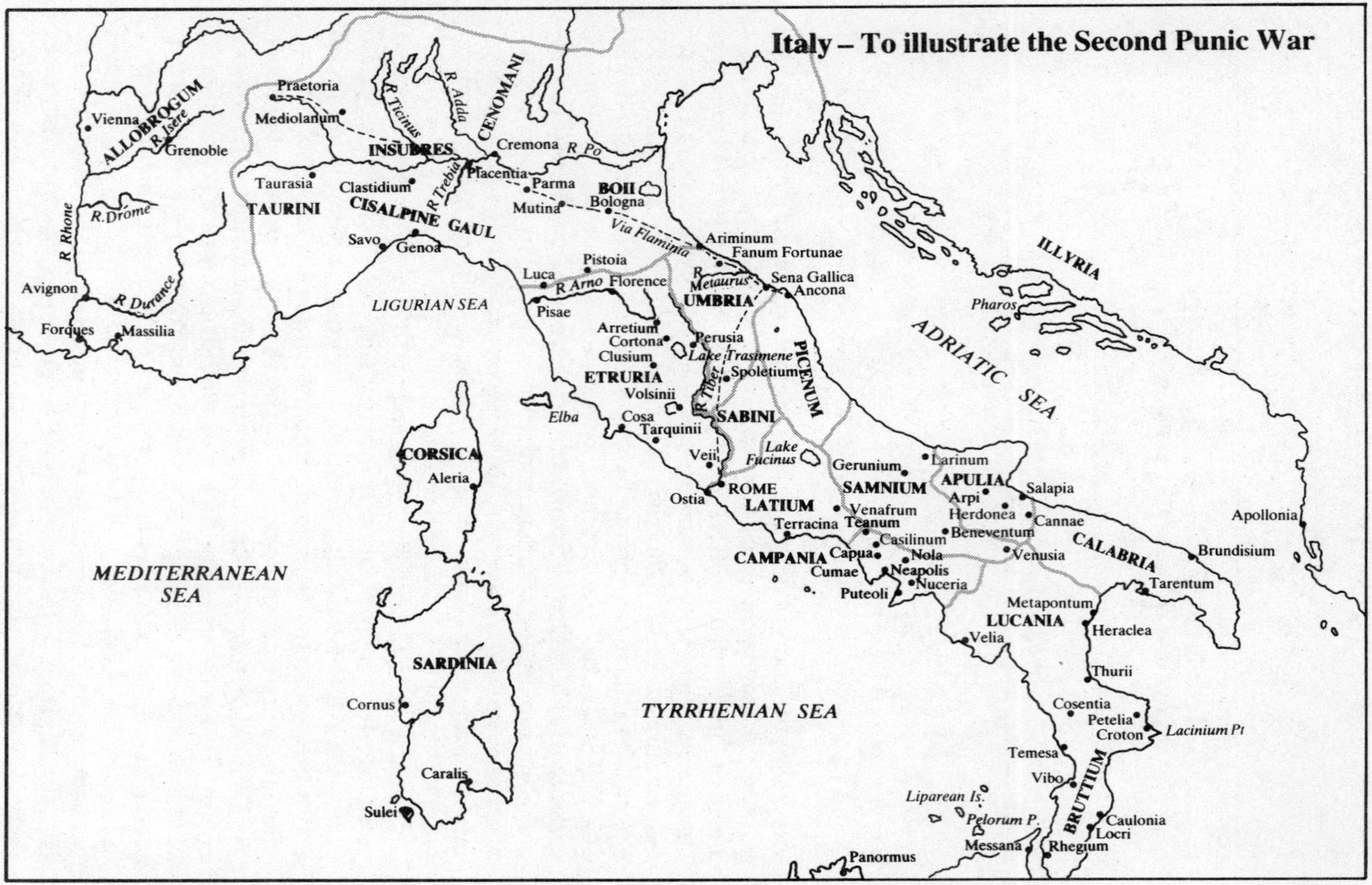

Reassured by his messengers' assessment, which was received shortly after the news of the Romans' ultimatum of war at Carthage, Hannibal assembled his army and unfolded the full extent of his plans for the first time. Perhaps to help overcome the natural anxieties which many of his soldiers would have felt, Hannibal described the richness and fertility of the countryside through which he was going to lead them, and reported the assured support of the Gauls. Furthermore, to arouse his soldiers' indignation, Hannibal told them how the Romans had demanded not only his own surrender into captivity, but also that of many of their own chieftains. The army roared its approval of his plans and its readiness to follow him.

However much he had stamped the imprint of his powerful personality upon the army, Hannibal remained dependent upon the intimate group of generals who commanded its various components. Following the example of his father, and the traditional Punic custom of nepotism, Hannibal appointed his close relations to positions of particular responsibility. As we have seen, his brother Hasdrubal Barca was to take charge of Spain, and his nephew Hanno was to serve with him as a field commander from the crossing of the Rhone, through Italy and on to Africa. Then there were the hardened old veterans, many of whom had served Hamilcar, and so must have played a part in his own election as commander-in-chief of the army following the assassination of Hasdrubal Hanno. Typical of these were Carthalo and Maharbal, commanders of the Numidian cavalry, who were later to protest against what they saw as Hannibal's excessive prudence after the battle of Cannae. There was also an unrelated namesake, nicknamed Monomachus, who is alleged to have advocated that his soldiers should be trained to eat human flesh, thus easing the army's logistic problems. Obviously he was a very practical fellow, but probably a bit short on realism, and one wonders what other ideas he may have had. It is possible that some of the cruelty later to be attributed to Hannibal by the Romans was in fact his, since the full title of this ferocious individual was Hannibal Monomachus.

While Hannibal had been making his preparations, the Romans had been active also. The consuls for the year 218 BC, who would have assumed office on 15 March in the usual manner, were Publius Cornelius Scipio, whose father had been a consul in the First Punic War, and Tiberius Sempronius Longus. The Romans intended to pursue a three-pronged strategy: Scipio, with two Roman legions and nearly 16,000 Italian allies, together with a fleet of sixty quinqueremes, was to open a campaign in Spain. Sempronius Longus was to assemble his somewhat larger army and a fleet of 160 quinqueremes in Sicily, and when they were ready, to sail from Lilybaeum to Africa. A third army, meanwhile, under the praetor Manlius Vulso, was defensively positioned in Cisalpine Gaul, ready to deal with any Gallic uprising. To secure their hold in this region, two Roman colonies, as has already been mentioned, were to be established on the northern bank of the Po at Placentia and Cremona.

The timing for the implementation of the Romans' strategy is interesting, in that it indicates their perception of its internal priorities. The first armies to be raised were those destined for Africa and entrusted with the security of Cisalpine Gaul. The Romans clearly regarded a threat to the latter as being highly probable: the colonists to be settled across the Po were given no more than thirty days to pack up their essential belongings, make the journey and be ready to receive their allotments of land from three commissioners appointed for this purpose. Scipio's army was the last to be raised – in fact he was still in Rome when news came, as often occurs to even the best-laid plans, that things had gone badly wrong. Possibly encouraged by reports of Hannibal's intentions, which they would have received from the Gaesati, the Boii and the Insubres had risen in revolt and were sweeping over the countryside. They had already dispersed the new settlers of Placentia and Cremona, forcing the survivors, who included the three commissioners, to seek refuge in the allied Etruscan city of Mutina (Modena), which was then besieged. The harried and unfortunate commissioners were then invited to a truce conference at which they were promptly seized and held against the Gallic hostages who had been retained by the Romans.

When news of these events reached the praetor Manlius Vulso, he set off with a legion to the relief of Mutina. Though most of the countryside was open and cultivated, Vulso's route took him through several woods, in two of which he was ambushed with the loss of some 1200 men and six standards. In his haste he appears to have neglected his security, but he eventually made his way to Tannetum, a village lying on the Po more than thirty miles from Mutina, where his advance was halted and he could do no more than defend himself. One of Scipio's legions, which can only just have been formed, together with one raised by the allies, was hastily sent to help him under another praetor, Atilius Serranus, while Scipio himself raised further levies to replace those just despatched. By now it was probably July and the Romans' plan had been completely disrupted. The best part of two armies had been sucked into a conflict with the Cisalpine Gauls, a third was still being formed and could not be ready for several months, while that of Sempronius Longus had also been delayed. The reason for this is not absolutely clear, though it was probably because of the dangerous situation which had arisen in northern Italy, together with the news of Hannibal's overland approach. Under the circumstances, not only would it have been impossible to provide reinforcements for Sempronius Longus' army while fighting in Africa, but even more importantly, the army might be required for the defence of the homeland.

Meanwhile Hannibal had completed his final preparations and in the spring of 218 BC, after going to Gades to offer sacrifice to Melquart, he set out from New Carthage for a campaign that was to last for seventeen years. Polybius says the army consisted of 90,000 infantry and 12,000 cavalry, and in view of the size of the contingent which Hannibal later sent back to Spain, and the number of casualties he suffered, these figures do not seem unreasonable.

The plan he had in his mind would have been developed over the years as a consequence of much deep reflection, but in essence it may have had it origins in the fertile imagination of his father. When the Carthaginian fleet had precipitously abandoned him in the closing stages of the First Punic War in Sicily, Hamilcar Barca had tasted the bitter consequences of placing overmuch dependence on sea power. Political irresolution, calamitous natural disasters and the ineptitude of others over whom he exercised no control, must have convinced Hamilcar that if he were to be master of his own destiny, he had better stick to the land, a line of thought which would have been inherited by Hannibal, and now confirmed by the fact that the Romans dominated the seas.

Having made the fundamental decision to travel overland to Italy, there were still many other matters Hannibal would have had to resolve, many of them on the basis of very incomplete knowledge. For one thing, apart from the sea/land factor, there may have been wider strategic considerations to be taken into account. After the successful conclusion of the Illyrian campaign, it will be recalled that Demetrius had abandoned his alliance with the Romans and gone over to the Macedonians, with whom he had taken refuge. Following their victory at Sellasia, Macedonia had re-established its authority over the Peloponnesus and now posed a threat to Rome's eastern borders. Although no suggestion of collusion is made by Polybius or other ancient historians, the possibility of Rome coming under attack from two directions, as later occurred, could well have been a factor Hannibal took into account. Timing too, was crucial: what resistance was to be expected, both from the hostile tribes and the Romans themselves? How was this to be overcome so that the Alps could be crossed before the worst of the winter? Ground would have been another factor; what were the major obstacles to be crossed and where were the crossing places? Would the most obvious passes be strongly guarded, and if so, would it be less expensive in lives and time to use subsidiary routes even if they entailed detours? These and many other questions must have been turned over in Hannibal's restless mind, and the answers sought by intelligence gathering and thoughtful analysis. But it was not just a question of how the march was to be conducted, there was also the problem of how such large numbers of both men and animals were to be provisioned.

As we are told that snow was falling when Hannibal began to cross the Alps, it must have been as late as April when he left New Carthage, the delay possibly being to allow the spring flooding of the Spanish rivers to subside. After crossing the Ebro, Hannibal had entered the territory of the tribes friendly to Rome, while further north lay the Greek coastal cities of Rhoda and Emporiae (Ampurias) which, being colonies of Massilia, were in alliance with Rome. Although neither Polybius nor Livy give any details of the fighting, the heavy losses Hannibal suffered were probably due to his having to carry the enemy's strongholds by assault, rather than starving them into submission, because time was at a premium.

After subduing the countryside up to the Pyrenees, and leaving Hasdrubal Barca with 11,000 men to deal with any smouldering resistance, Hannibal then further reduced the size of his army by sending home some of his Spanish mercenaries; possibly those who had most distinguished themselves in the recent heavy fighting, but more probably the deserters or the faint hearted. These measures, together with the casualties he had suffered, reduced his army to no more than 50,000 infantry and 9000 cavalry; a loss of 40,000 and 3000 respectively from when he had set out from New Carthage, though he still had his 37 elephants. From the Pyrenees to the Rhone, a distance of some 160 miles, progress was rapid. Hannibal was not intent on territorial acquisition or further conquest. All that he required was freedom of passage once he had crossed the Pyrenees, which he obtained by bribing the tribal chieftains and brushing aside what ineffective opposition he did encounter. Where Hannibal reached the Rhone is open to considerable speculation, but wherever it was that he chose to cross, he did all that he could to establish good relations with the local tribesmen first, purchasing their canoes of hollow tree trunks and the rafts used for the passage of goods, both of which were available in large numbers because of the extensive use made of the river by the inhabitants of the Rhone valley. Additionally, many of the soldiers preferred to trust their lives to their own devices, so constructed personal rafts of one kind or another. Within two days these preparations had been completed and the army stood ready to make the 1000-yard crossing. Time had passed, however, and their activities had not gone unnoticed.

While Hannibal had been on the march, Publius Cornelius Scipio had at last completed raising his consular army and had set sail from Pisae. After five days at sea, he disembarked his troops at Massilia on the easternmost bank of the Rhone's sprawling delta. Although Scipio knew that Hannibal had passed the Pyrenees, he did not know his present whereabouts and seems to have grossly underestimated the Carthaginians' progress. Restricting himself to sending a reconnaissance force of 300 cavalry up the eastern bank of the Rhone, Scipio settled down with his main force for a period of rest and reorganisation after their sea voyage. The delay was to prove fatal and as a result has been the subject of much unjustified criticism. Since Scipio can have had only the scantiest knowledge of Hannibal's movements, his disembarkation at Massilia was probably initially designed to do no more than obtain accurate information. As will be seen later, in Scipio's mind his primary task was to engage Hannibal. Had he really thought that his opponent was approaching the Rhone, the last thing he would have done would be to remain at Massilia opposite the Rhone estuary with its several waterways obstructing a possible passage to Hannibal. All that Scipio can be reasonably blamed for is failing to realise that Hannibal had made such rapid progress.

The Gauls in the meantime had assembled in large numbers along the eastern bank opposite where Hannibal was proposing to cross, and made every show of resistance. The territory of the tribe concerned, the Volcae, straddled the Rhone and their settlements studded the surrounding countryside. Those living to the west of the river had been willing enough to give the Carthaginians every assistance, if only to avoid having some 50,000 foreign troops in their midst for longer than was absolutely necessary, but those on the eastern bank were less amenable. This difference in attitude was probably due to the influence of Massilia, where Scipio was now sheltering. Additionally, the Rhone formed a natural barrier, so providing an obvious place at which to prevent the Carthaginians from entering their land.

Thwarted in carrying through his immediate intentions, Hannibal dispatched his nephew Hanno with a strong detachment, under cover of darkness and led by local guides, some twenty-two miles up river to where the Rhone is divided into two channels by an island. Hanno set out on the third night after the Carthaginians had reached the Rhone, and he was to coordinate his attack on the Gauls with that of Hannibal's crossing on the morning of the sixth day.

After making his crossing, Hanno started his approach down the opposite bank before daybreak on the sixth day, and when in position signalled to Hannibal by smoke that he was about to begin his attack. Hannibal in the meanwhile had completed his preparations and started to cross. The cavalry had been loaded onto rafts with the horses swimming astern, one man on each side guiding three of four of them with leading reins. Downstream of the rafts, and so to some degree protected from the current, sailed the canoes containing selected infantry, probably followed by those individuals making their own passage; all of them being cheered on by those waiting their turn to cross. At the sight of this mass of assorted craft approaching them, the Gauls ran down to the water's edge, confident in their ability to slaughter the disorganised Carthaginians before they could set foot on the shore. But at this moment Hanno's men fell upon their rear, and seized and fired the Gauls' camp. Complete surprise had been achieved and the Gauls' resistance was brief; they soon broke and fled.

Having cleared the eastern bank of all opposition, Hannibal spent the remainder of the day ferrying the bulk of his army across, though at this stage it did not include the elephants. The next day, having received reports of Scipio's landing, he dispatched a force of 500 Numidian cavalry with orders to locate the Romans and cover their movements. The rest of the army which had crossed the previous day was then assembled to hear an account by some Cisalpine chiefs of what lay ahead. Because of the varied ethnic composition of the Carthaginian Army, their address had to be delivered through interpreters but the fact that the chiefs had come to greet them was in itself an encouraging sign, and what they had to say was even more encouraging.

Guides would lead the Carthaginians through a fertile countryside where they would be amply provisioned and, when crossing over into Italy, they would find the Gauls ready to fight beside them against their common enemy. After the chiefs had finished speaking, Hannibal addressed his men himself, reminding them of their past achievements and reassuring them about their future. Some doubt, however, must exist as to whether around 50,000 men could really have been assembled and addressed through interpreters in this manner. In fact it would probably have been that the senior officers were paraded and then dismissed to brief their men in their own tongues.

Shortly after these various briefings had been completed, the Numidian cavalry returned from their reconnaissance in headlong flight, leaving about half their number behind either dead or wounded. While moving south down the left bank of the Rhone, they had encountered Scipio's cavalry approaching from Massilia in the opposite direction, and a fierce encounter had taken place. In view of the Numidians' natural superiority and numbers, 500 against the Romans' 300, they must have either been surprised or badly disadvantaged by the ground, since their opponents only lost about 140 men against their 250. The Roman cavalry then approached the Carthaginian camp and after making a thorough reconnaissance withdrew to pass information back to Scipio in Massilia. After loading his heavy baggage back on board his ships, Scipio marched out of his camp.

Aware that he had little time to lose, at first light the following day Hannibal deployed his cavalry to cover his flank against Scipio's advance, while his infantry were sent northwards along the river bank as though, as Polybius says, they intended to 'pass into the middle part of Europe'. Hannibal remained behind to supervise getting the elephants across the river. The method adopted, which must have been put in hand over several days, was to construct a pier about seventy yards long made from a number of rafts stoutly lashed together, and secured against the current by stout ropes fastened to trees along the river bank. At the end of the pier two larger rafts, again securely lashed together, were positioned with ropes leading from them to the boats which were to tow them across. The pier and the rafts were then liberally spread with earth and two female elephants were led onto them, followed by the bulls. How many could be taken over at a time is not known, but Polybius refers to several crossings being made, so it must have been a fairly protracted operation. The first elephants, though alarmed, made the crossing without incident. But some of those which followed panicked and tipped the rafts over. This proved fatal to their mahouts but not to the elephants themselves who, keeping their trunks above water, managed to struggle ashore without loss. Once all the elephants had been brought across, Hannibal formed men into a rearguard with some cavalry, and then set off northwards after his infantry.

It was not until three days later that Scipio arrived at the Carthaginians' deserted camp. He would have quickly discovered the direction taken by Hannibal, from the heavily trodden tracks of the marching column, and from the reports of the Gauls. Scipio can have had little hesitation in deciding against pursuit; not only did Hannibal have a three-day start, but it would have been foolhardy to have set off in precipitous chase into unknown country where he could find himself trapped at any moment into accepting battle on ground and under conditions of Hannibal's choosing. Additionally, in view of the hostility many Gauls felt towards Rome, there was always the danger of them seizing the opportunity to join forces with the Carthaginians against the two isolated and unprovisioned legions. Scipio must have correctly concluded that Hannibal's intention was to march up the east bank of the Rhone until he reached a major tributary which would lead him to its source in the foothills of the Alps. His destination was then clearly Italy.

Scipio wisely turned back to Massilia, but here he faced a far more difficult decision: should he continue to Spain, or should he return to Italy in order to oppose Hannibal? As we have seen, the disembarkation at Massilia had only been a temporary diversion from the intended Spanish campaign, brought about by uncertainty as to

Hannibal's movements. Scipio now took a bold decision: he sent his army with the fleet to Spain, under the command of his brother Gnaeus Cornelius, to undertake the task placed upon him by the Senate, while he himself set out for Italy. Scipio saw the main threat as Hannibal, whom he was determined to oppose himself, but he must have had considerable confidence in his standing with the Senate to have assumed he would be given command of another army in north Italy, rather than being arraigned for deserting his own.

After marching for four days Hannibal arrived at a place described by Polybius as being very fertile and heavily populated. The Rhone on the west side and the Aigues, one of its tributaries to the southeast formed two sides of a triangle, on the other side of which, to the northeast, was a range of mountains. The whole area resembled a delta which Polybius says was known as the 'Island'; an apparently rather loose description for an isolated piece of land liable to flooding.

Although the course of the Aigues and the Rhone may have changed over the last 2000 years such changes have probably been slight: modern maps show the 'Island' to be some eight miles long on each of the two sides formed by the Aigues and the Bois de la Montagne, while the base, formed by the Rhone, is about five miles in length. When Hannibal reached this area, he found two brothers in contest over its sovereignty and he was asked for assistance by the elder, Brancus, who no doubt made promises of support in return. Hannibal had little trouble in driving out the younger brother and was paid his due reward by the provision of supplies, clothing and footwear, but even more important, a strong rearguard to help cover the army while passing through the territory of the unpredictable Allobroges during his approach to the Alps. As a result of these additional reinforcements and the formidable Numidian cavalry, Hannibal was able to complete his ten-day march to the foothills of the Alps without interference. Although the course he followed is open to question, he undoubtedly crossed the Aigues and continued along the bank of the Rhone to the Drôme, a further fifty- odd miles further north. Here he probably turned east and marched along the river or, after crossing it, continued for about another twenty miles alongside the Rhone before encountering the Isère, which he then followed.

As Hannibal started his ascent of the Alps the escort provided by Brancus turned back, leaving the long column to begin threading its way through the towering mass of snowcapped mountains. The Allobroges hastened to occupy the high ground dominating a narrow pass that lay ahead and, had they attempted to conceal themselves and remain undetected, there is every possibility that they would have trapped and annihilated the unsuspecting Carthaginian army. But as it was, their conspicuous movement alerted Hannibal who was up with his leading troops, and all element of surprise was lost. Halting the advance, Hannibal sent forward a reconnaissance party of Gauls who had been acting as guides. On returning, the Gauls reported that the Allobroges occupied the heights by day, but at night they withdrew for shelter into a nearby town. Hannibal then closed up to the mouth of the defile and encamped, lighting camp fires to create an impression that he had settled for the night. Once darkness had fallen however, specially selected troops, stripped of everything but their weapons, were infiltrated into the pass and seized the heights temporarily abandoned by the Allobroges.

At daybreak Hannibal's main army started to enter the defile. The Allobroges, though they had lost possession of the more dominating heights, soon were able to find alternative positions amongst the broken ground which overlooked the densely packed Carthaginian column. While the marching infantry still presented a formidable foe, being able to turn and fight even within the restricted confines of the pass, the situation of the cavalry horses and pack animals was quite different; crowded together with no means of protection or room to manoeuvre, they were particularly vulnerable. Selecting their moment, the Allobroges struck the extended column in several places, nearly bringing about a total disaster for the Carthaginians as the wounded and terrified animals panicked. Some of the horses plunged into the depth of the gorge beside the path, others turned back, bringing chaos among those who had so far been shielded by the ground from the direct attack. Realising that the loss of his baggage train at the onset of winter would spell disaster, Hannibal turned about the detachments occupying the high ground seized the night before, and fell upon the Allobroges from the flank and rear. For a while the fierce close-quarter fighting swung to and fro amongst the broken crevices and rocky outcrops, but though the Carthaginians suffered heavily themselves, they eventually routed the Allobroges before advancing on the town used by them as a base and shelter at night. Here were found large stocks of corn and numerous horses and cattle, all of which went a long way to replacing the losses sustained in the morning's desperate fighting. Hannibal then closed his army up on the town and rested it that night and the following day, the third since it had entered the Alps.

The next day Hannibal resumed his advance and, after crossing the headwaters of the Durance, made uninterrupted progress for three days. But on the fourth he encountered some Gauls who, though bearing olive branches as a sign of peace, aroused his suspicions. When questioned, they said they had heard of the fate of those who tried to bar his passage, and they for their part only wanted friendship; tokens of which they provided by offering hostages, together with a large number of cattle and some guides to lead the Carthaginians over the next stage of their journey. For two days the march continued without incident but on the third, when the army was passing through a valley hemmed in on both sides by precipices, the treacherous Gauls suddenly fell upon the rear of the column. According to Polybius, the army might have been destroyed had Hannibal not placed the cavalry and the baggage in the van with the heavy infantry bringing up the rear. In the absence of any other information, it is not clear what overwhelming tactical advantage this particular deployment provided, since, in a confined space, the baggage train would have remained very exposed even if protected at the head and rear. But it enabled the Carthaginians to beat off the Gauls' attack, though not without heavy losses to both men and animals. The advance was then resumed but the Gauls continued to harry them, by moving along the mountain ridge and rolling and throwing down rocks and stones. During the following night the passage through the narrowing valley gorge was completed with great difficulty but without further loss. The next morning, as the army started to make the final climb to the summit of the pass, the main body of Gauls withdrew, leaving only raiding parties to harry the column and cut off any stragglers. The elephants now proved themselves particularly useful in covering the flanks and their very presence was enough to deter the Gauls' attacks.

On the ninth day Hannibal reached the summit of the mountains and here he rested for two days, during which time the whole of the army was able to close up and many of the animals which had broken free in the course of the various fierce encounters made their way safely into the camp. It was by now well into October, snow was starting to block the passes and as the conditions hardened, the army's spirit began to wane. To counter the mood of growing anxiety, Hannibal pointed out the fertile valley of the Po stretching out before them, and reminded his soldiers of the help which had been promised by the Gauls who lived there. He then ordered the descent to begin and although no further opposition was encountered, the losses of men and animals yet to be suffered were probably nearly as great as those incurred in the ascent. Livy gives a graphic account of the difficulties encountered as the snow was trampled into packed ice offering no foothold, and the animals died in frantic exertion or patient suffering. He relates one particularly desperate situation when a passage had to be cleared through a rock fall by the application of heat and moisture.

Large trees were felled and lopped, and a huge pile of timber erected; this, with the opportune help of a strong wind, was set on fire, and when the rock was sufficiently heated, the men's ration of sour wine was flung upon it, to render it friable. They then got to work with picks on the heated rock, and opened a sort of zigzag track, to minimise the steepness of the descent, and were able to get the pack animals, and even the elephants down it.

An epic account conjuring up a scene of heroic endeavour, though Livy's description invites a number of questions concerning the flammability of freshly cut tree trunks, the availability of copious quantities of vinegar, and the nimble-footedness of the elephants. It is never safe, however, to doubt a factual statement of a practical nature by serious classical authors.

Having finally cleared a passage, three days later, the fifteenth since he had started to cross the Alps, Hannibal at last reached the fertile expanse of the plains. But his army had been reduced to no more than a quarter of its size from when it had marched out of New Carthage some six months previously.

How and where these losses had been incurred, or whether the numbers involved are even correct, is far from being clear. To recapitulate briefly: according to Polybius, the total strength of the army on leaving New Carthage was some 100,000; it was then reduced to about 60,000 when setting out from the Pyrenees, and to 46,000 at the Rhone. After crossing the Alps, the numbers had been even more dramatically diminished, and only 12,000 Africans, 8000 Spaniards and 6000 cavalry survived. The modern mind shies away in disbelief from such figures, finding it almost inconceivable that an army could survive such casualties and remain able to take the field as an effective fighting force. But even if these figures can be accepted, the casualties which Polybius quotes for the various stages of the army's advance are disproportionally higher than is justified by the accounts he gives of the fighting; especially between the Pyrenees and the Rhone, including the crossing. What seems more probable is that massive desertions occurred during the long march and that the actual casualties suffered accordingly represented a much smaller proportion of the total losses than has generally been accepted.

But whatever the figures may have been and however they were composed, the Carthaginians had suffered cruelly and it says a lot for the stamina and recuperative powers of the survivors that, after only the three days allowed to them for rest and reorganisation, they were ready to open the campaign in Italy with such vigour and determination. But, it should be remembered, none of this would have been possible without inspired leadership.

CHAPTER FOURTEEN

THE EPIC YEARS
218–216 BC

An appreciation of Hannibal's strategy, operational plan and tactical thinking, will make it easier to follow the course of his campaign as he fought his way down the Italian peninsula during the next seventeen years. At the time of the Gallic invasion, which had flared out only two years previously, the Romans had been able to mobilise 700,000 men, whereas Hannibal's strength after crossing the Alps was only 26,000. Although the Cisalpine Gauls, principally the Boii and Insubres, had promised assistance and in fact had risen prematurely, not all the tribes regarded Hannibal as their saviour. Also considerable internecine antagonism existed, in particular between the Taurini and the Insubres, whose mutual antipathy was given a sharper edge following the Insubres' alliance with Hannibal. Under such circumstances, there would be a limit to the number of Gauls who would be prepared to accompany Hannibal, leaving their homelands open to reprisals from both the Romans and their rivals.

Even allowing for the fact that a large proportion of the Romans who had been mobilised were no more than elderly reservists, or garrison troops of little military consequence, Hannibal was therefore still greatly outnumbered. Given such a marked disadvantage, what was then to be his strategic objective? With certainty it can be stated that it was not to conquer and occupy the whole of Italy. With such a small force, even when strengthened by the Gauls, his aim would have to be far more restricted. From a later treaty drawn up between Hannibal and Philip of Macedonia, which has been recorded by Polybius, we know that his aim was in fact limited to breaking up the Roman Confederation. In this manner Rome would be reduced to being once again no more than one among a number of states, to be held in check by those who had just had their independence restored to them, as well as by the Gauls. Hannibal had reasonable grounds for believing that internal factions in a number of cities made their allegiance to Rome very questionable. In Capua, the capital of Campania and second only to Rome in importance, some of the city's leaders had openly begun to query whether the union with Rome was of any benefit. After Cannae, as will be seen, such voices became far more numerous and outspoken, leading eventually to Capua defecting to the Carthaginians. The same sort of tension existed in other cities such as Tarentum, whose prosperity had declined as a result of Roman hegemony.

The cohesive power of Rome lay in its army, so only if this could be destroyed would there be any chance of bringing about a general uprising. The problem Hannibal then faced was how to achieve this when the Romans were so much stronger?

Above all, in developing his operational concept, he had to avoid becoming involved in positional warfare that would permit the Romans to concentrate against him. This consideration alone debarred Hannibal from tying his army down in some prolonged endeavour such as a city's siege. The fact that he had no siege train was the result and not, as has sometimes been suggested, the cause of this restriction. Had he wished to obtain the necessary machines, he could have arranged for their construction or acquisition during the course of the campaign. As it was, Hannibal adopted a manoeuvre-based concept for the destruction of the Roman army through which he would avoid being drawn into a battle of attrition he could not sustain. He accepted that at times he would suffer severe casualties, but these would only be incurred when he had brought the Romans to battle on ground and under conditions of his own choosing. The resulting destruction of the Roman legions would then compensate for his own losses – and those could then be replaced from Rome's defecting allies and others wishing to join a winning cause. A war of manoeuvre demands a high level of generalship but this is exactly what Hannibal, with justifiable self-confidence, knew he could provide. Trained from the age of nine when he had accompanied his father to Spain, and drilled in the disciplined Spartan military tradition by his Lacedaemonian tutor, Sosilus, Hannibal knew he compared very favourably with the Roman consuls. Such army commanders, who were mostly amateurs and shared command on alternate days, would be overtaxed when confronted by a demanding and to them unknown form of warfare.

As for tactics, Hannibal undoubtedly respected the disciplined prowess of the Roman soldier in close combat, fighting under conditions which permitted an orderly progression of tactical movement, largely restricted at this stage to within the legion. He would have had scant regard for the Roman cavalry, however, which still continued to be looked upon as no more than an aristocratic adjunct to the cutting edge of the army, the legionary. This shortcoming restricted the Romans' tactical flexibility and speed of reaction, which in turn largely deprived them of the all-important battle winning factor of surprise. To counter the stolid solidity of the Roman legions, after the battle of Trasimene in 217 BC, Hannibal adjusted his own organisation to achieve a greater degree of flexibility. The most important innovation was to reorganise the heavy Libyan infantry, the bulk and backbone of the army, so that they were no longer to fight in the massed, hedgehog-like ranks of the phalanx. Instead of their spears, Hannibal equipped them with swords taken from the Roman dead, and the monolithic structure of the phalanx was adapted by the introduction of smaller tactical units, called *speirai*. In this way, while the ability to concentrate was retained, a looser structured framework gave the sub-unit and each individual the possibility of personal initiative. Additionally, the looser grouping made it possible to manoeuvre over broken ground and change direction, and most importantly it introduced a degree of elasticity into what had hitherto been a rigidly linear deployment. Flexibility constituted a vital element in Hannibal's tactical thinking, behind which always lay the aim of encirclement.

Once these organisational changes had been introduced, it was possible for the Carthaginian infantry to give ground in the centre, and then to advance their wings so as to enfold an enemy penetration. Both the Roman and the Carthaginian cavalry had traditionally always been positioned on either extremity of the front, from where they could engage their opposite numbers. But their role on the battlefield had never been properly coordinated with that of the infantry. As we have seen from Livy's account of the battle of Lake Regillus, the Romans even went so far as to misemploy their cavalry as infantry reinforcements – a perfectly acceptable tactic when conditions preclude mounted action, but not otherwise. Hannibal for his part seems previously to have used his Numidian cavalry to sweep their opponents off the battlefield, and then to dispatch them in pursuit of the fugitives, or on wide-ranging raids to dominate the surrounding countryside. But in future, having defeated the Roman cavalry, they were to be used to complete the envelopment of the legions. It was not always to prove possible to restrain the Numidians from undertaking the heady pursuit of a fleeing foe, but needlessly to wind horses in this fashion or to loot an abandoned enemy camp while the infantry were still locked in combat had no place in Hannibal's conduct of the tactical battle. All arms cooperation was then a precept he henceforth inculcated into the training of his army.

The campaign Hannibal now entered into can be considered in three phases. The first, which is the subject of this chapter, while only lasting for two years from 218–216 BC, was the most dramatic. It included the classic battles of Lake Trasimene and Cannae, and saw Hannibal's operational plan and tactical techniques unfold in an almost flawless manner. As a result, during this period the strategic objective of the campaign came near to being achieved, when Capua and a number of other cities deserted the Roman Confederation. This crisis having been surmounted by the Romans, the second phase began and lasted for four years between 216 and 212 BC, a period which saw a number of important developments. The Carthaginians temporarily held the strategic initiative and attempted to encircle and isolate Italy, while the Romans, though under great pressure at home, displayed commendable strategic clear-sightedness in breaking the Carthaginian hold, and though they nearly left it too late, also showed a readiness to adapt their military doctrine to meet changed circumstances. The final phase, which lasted for ten years from 212 to 202 BC, saw the consequences of the tide having turned decisively in Rome's favour.

To return to October 218 BC, when we had left Hannibal resting his army after its painful crossing of the Alps. His descent had taken him into the territory of the Taurini who, as has been related, were at loggerheads with Hannibal's allies the Insubres. Fighting had broken out between them, and after failing to negotiate a reconciliation he acted swiftly to take Taurasia (Turin), the chief town of the Taurini. This display of force and determination served to remind a number of other tribes of the obligation they had entered into with Hannibal, to rise against the Romans once he was in Italy. But before they could be mustered, the Romans marched through their territories crushing any signs of opposition. Had normal practices now been followed, as winter was now approaching active campaigning would have been suspended until the following year. But neither the Carthaginians nor the Romans could allow the other to retain their positions, so gaining domination over the Cisalpine Gauls, and thus possession of the whole of northern Italy. Both armies then remained in the field.

News reached Hannibal that the two legions approaching him had already crossed the Po near Placentia and according to Polybius, he was surprised to learn both this and that they were commanded by Publius Cornelius Scipio. But although the Roman consul had travelled nearly 1000 miles by land and sea from the Rhone in just over a month, it seems unlikely that Hannibal knew, or cared about, the name of the man he had briefly crossed swords with on the Rhone.

Moreover, he would in fact have been amazed had he *not* encountered the Romans on their northern frontier. Surprised or not, battle was now imminent and the two commanders assembled and addressed their respective armies. As has already been mentioned, the classical authors gloss over how these exhortations could have been conducted when such numbers and such a diversity of languages were involved. Yet the personality of the commander was all-important, and one only has to recall Field Marshal Montgomery's practice of gathering his troops around him to explain the situation, in order to appreciate this aspect of leadership.

The speeches over, the two armies advanced along the northern bank of the Po, Scipio westward from Placentia, and Hannibal in the opposite direction from Taurasia. On reaching the Ticinus (Ticino), the largest tributary of the Po, Scipio threw a bridge across the river and crossed over with his cavalry and light infantry. After advancing cautiously for the next two days, the Roman scouts reported the approach of the Carthaginian cavalry and Scipio deployed into battle formation. He placed his light infantry and Gallic cavalry in front and then, bringing the rest of his army into line, ordered them to move slowly forward. Hannibal had positioned his heavy Spanish cavalry in the centre and on the wings the Numidians, whose orders were to envelop the Romans from the flanks. On seeing one another, the cavalry charged and the Roman light infantry, fearful of being ridden down by friend and foe with equal impartiality, made their escape as best they could, not waiting to throw their javelins. Polybius says that in the ensuing contest many of the horsemen dismounted and that there was a mixed fight of horse and foot. As it is unlikely that cavalrymen would choose to fight in this manner, what may have happened is that a number of the Roman light infantry were caught up in the engagement, and the second horseman carried by the Spanish heavy cavalry had, as was the practice, dismounted. While the heavy cavalry were fighting it out in the centre, the Numidians succeeded in outflanking the Romans; then, wheeling round behind them, first rode down those of their light infantry who had managed to escape, before falling upon the rear of the Gallic cavalry. Though encircled, some of the Romans managed to cut their way out and escape, among them being Scipio in spite of having been wounded. According to one account his life was saved by a Ligurian slave, but Livy attributes this achievement to his eighteen-year-old son, later to win immortal fame as Scipio Africanus.

Although the Carthaginians enjoyed an overall numerical superiority in cavalry, it is not clear that they did so in this particular engagement; five hundred Numidians had been dispatched to ravage the territory of an adjacent hostile tribe, and others may have been occupied elsewhere. Livy merely comments that the battle clearly showed the Carthaginians superiority in cavalry, and made it impossible for the Romans to defend the country lying between the Alps and the Po. This cavalry action had clearly shown the ability of the Carthaginians to dominate the open ground, so giving them the freedom to manoeuvre at will. It also demonstrated on a small scale Hannibal's tactical thinking: using the wings of his line to achieve an encirclement.

Scipio at once withdrew across the bridge he had constructed over the Ticinus, which he then broke, evidently in some haste, as Hannibal was able to take some 600 prisoners from among the Romans who had been left as a rearguard. Perhaps the earliest recorded account of the dilemma facing a commander: when to order the demolition of the bridge during a retreat. If destroyed too soon, as occurred when the British 14th Army was withdrawing over the Sittang in Burma, large numbers of one's own troops can be lost, but if left too late, as happened to the Germans at the Remagen bridge over the Rhine, the enemy, in that case the Americans, secure themselves a crossing.

Thwarted in his close pursuit of Scipio, whom Hannibal had thought would turn and fight with his infantry, he now followed the Po in search of a crossing place. After two days' march, he found a suitable spot where he was able to construct a bridge with boats. Leaving Hasdrubal, his chief engineer, to marshal the army across, he went forward himself to confer with the Gauls, now flocking to join him with much-needed provisions. Once the army was assembled, Hannibal marched off downstream again to Placentia, intent on forcing the Romans to stand and fight.

While Hannibal had been searching for a crossing place, Scipio had completed his withdrawal to his base at Placentia, just east of the river Trebia which flows into the Po from its source in the Apennines to the south. Here, in a fortified camp outside the city walls, Scipio halted to rest his soldiers and give his own wounds a chance to heal; making no move when Hannibal arrived and demonstrated before his camp, challenging him to accept battle. This display of Carthaginian confidence and moral superiority, following the precipitous Roman withdrawal, made a powerful impression on the Gallic contingent serving in the Roman army. Sensing a change of fortune they decided to desert and, waiting until the early hours of the morning, fell upon the Romans quartered nearest to them. They decapitated the corpses, taking the heads with them as evidence of their new found loyalty when defecting to Hannibal, who was only too glad to welcome this unexpected gain of 2000 infantry and nearly 200 cavalry.

Concerned about the possibility of further acts of treachery when surrounded by Gauls whom he knew to be hostile, Scipio abandoned his camp the following night and after crossing the Trebia, established a new camp among the hills on the west bank. As soon as Hannibal heard of Scipio's move, he sent the Numidian cavalry in pursuit but they turned aside to plunder and fire the Romans' deserted camp, so allowing them to escape. Hannibal of course had no intention of attacking the Romans' newly fortified camp established on broken and difficult ground, any more than he would have contemplated besieging Placentia. He simply moved his own camp nearer to that of the Romans but without crossing the river, and waited while more Gauls came to join him, also bearing provisions. Shortly afterwards Hannibal took possession of the isolated Roman depot at Clastidium, which was surrendered without a fight by its garrison. Well stocked with corn and other stores, it satisfied Hannibal's immediate logistic requirements.

In Rome, disconcerting rumours of Hannibal's sudden descent into the Po valley had been confirmed by factual reports and frantic measures were put in hand to concentrate the legions. Sempronius Longus, who had been poised at Lilybaeum for an offensive against North Africa, was hastily ordered to return and reinforce Scipio. According to Polybius, having dispatched his fleet, Sempronius Longus made his legionaries swear on oath that they would march at best possible speed to Ariminum, which lay on the Adriatic coast at the southern edge of the Po valley. Having passed through Rome, the legions assembled at their destination forty days later, then promptly set off to join Scipio. Livy, on the other hand, says that the army went by sea to Ariminum, which certainly seems more probable since there would have been little point in sending the ships back empty, and to have marched some 840 miles from Lilybaeum with full equipment in forty days would have been a stupendously improbable achievement. Besides, Ariminum lay at least 220 miles east of Placentia, so it would have taken a further ten days for Sempronius Longus to have joined Scipio, even if he had been able to maintain the astounding rate of twenty-two miles a day. Polybius could, of course, have got the number of days wrong, but leaving that aside, what may have happened as a result of shipping limitations was that part of the army was moved directly to Ariminum, while the remainder was transported to Ostia, the port of Rome. From here they then marched the remainder of the way, some 200 miles.

However they travelled, on arrival Sempronius Longus' legions established their camp alongside that of Scipio's and the two consuls met to discuss their next move. Sempronius Longus was eager for a fight, but although he now exercised overall command as Scipio was still suffering from his wounds, he did not want to enter into a major battle without his fellow consul's agreement, and Scipio felt the legions would be all the better for a winter spent under arms. He urged caution, arguing that the Gauls who had gone over to the Carthaginians would soon desert them. Enforced inactivity and the lack of any new successes bringing plunder, would quickly blunt their enthusiasm and they would begin to drift off back to their homes. While still debating the issue, the Romans worsted the Carthaginians in a sharp cavalry skirmish, at which Sempronius Longus' determination to give battle hardened, a determination that may have been fortified by the thought that if he were to delay too long, he would be replaced by next year's consuls, so leaving himself open to the accusation that, having brought his legions to the battlefield in such precipitous haste, he was then too afraid to fight. Sempronius Longus then ordered his men to take the field, news of which soon reached Hannibal.

The consular army consisted of 16,000 Romans and 20,000 allied infantry, together with 4000 cavalry. Hannibal's army amounted to 20,000 Spanish, Gallic and Libyan infantry, as well as more than 10,000 cavalry, which included Gauls. The Romans thus had a considerable superiority both overall and in particular in their infantry – which, because of the hilly and broken ground to the west of the Trebia, effectively outweighed the disadvantage of their inferior cavalry. This was a fundamental factor for Hannibal to take into account when considering how to conduct the coming battle. If his cavalry were to be used to full effect, then the Romans would have to be drawn on to the open ground lying between Placentia and the Trebia, ground which Scipio had only recently abandoned. But this would run the risk of the Carthaginian infantry being shattered by the superior Roman legions. To risk defeat in this manner, or at best win a pyrrhic victory, would have run counter to Hannibal's principle of maximising his enemy's casualties at minimum cost to himself. The Romans' superiority therefore had to be redressed by the introduction of another element onto the battlefield: surprise. Hannibal's plan, like all good plans, was simple. The battle would be fought on the open plain but not far from the broken ground near the Trebia, through which the Romans would have to pass to reach it. Here a force of 1000 Numidian cavalry and a similar number of picked infantry, under the command of Hannibal's younger brother Mago Barca, would be concealed. They would be moved into position under cover of darkness and only emerge when the main battle had been joined. The Romans having been held to the front, they could then be attacked from the rear. A third detachment consisting entirely of Numidian cavalry was to display itself in insulting contempt in front of the Roman camp, so as to precipitate Sempronius Longus into premature action.

The battle developed much as Hannibal had planned. Stung by the flaunting audaciousness of the Numidian cavalry, the Romans poured out of their camp before the men had breakfasted or the horses had been watered and fed. It was a bitterly cold midwinter day, with snow in the early morning which later turned to sleet and rain. On reaching the Trebia, swollen by the torrential downpour of the previous night, the Roman had to wade breast high through the icy water. As delay set in and the day wore on, the lack of food and the cold began to take their toll; the light infantry and cavalry, who had been in the van and continually harried by the Numidians, were in a wretched state. In the meantime Hannibal had kept his army under cover, and only deployed for battle when he judged that the right moment had arrived. The Roman legions then advanced against the Carthaginian infantry holding the centre, and fierce fighting broke out along the entire line. It was then that Mago left his position and fell upon the Roman rear. While the battle raged in the centre, on the wings the Carthaginian elephants and cavalry forced back the Roman horse, which eventually broke and fled back to Trebia. Here the majority were caught while struggling to ford the river and destroyed. But in spite of being taken so unexpectedly in the rear and exposed on their wings, some 10,000 Roman infantry managed to break through the Carthaginian centre and seek refuge in Placentia, where they were joined by those who had survived the cavalry action. The remainder of the Roman infantry suffered the same fate as had the majority of their cavalry: they were forced back onto the banks of the Trebia, where most of them fell. The majority of the Carthaginian battle casualties had been borne by the Gauls; but only one elephant survived the intense cold and wet, which also killed off a considerable number of the pack animals.

After the battle Sempronius Longus attempted to hide the extent of his defeat, blaming a storm for depriving him of a victory. But it was not possible to conceal the truth for long, and the news soon broke that the survivors of the two consular armies had had to abandon the line of the Po, while the greater part of Cisalpine Gaul had gone over to Hannibal. Livy paints a picture of near panic in Rome, with the population convinced that the city was about to fall and the most desperate measures being contemplated. In the general disarray Sempronius Longus' defeat, as well as his subsequent deceit, was evidently overlooked as he was allowed to return and preside over the consular elections for the following year, before returning to Placentia. And it must have become apparent after sober reflection that the situation was not so desperate as had been imagined. Though Placentia and Cremona were admittedly having to be supplied by boat up the Po, they were still in Roman hands and fresh legions were being raised. For the coming campaign the Romans had ten legions; two were in Spain, one in both Sardinia and Sicily, two were in reserve in Rome and four were available for the northern frontier. There were also garrisons at Tarentum and other cities of strategic importance. The remnants of the four defeated legions in the north appear to have been re-formed into two, which were then moved to Ariminum on the east coast, while two fresh ones were sent to guard the central Apennines. To achieve this feat of organisation, not only had the Senate been extremely energetic but the consuls-designate, Gaius Flaminius and Geminus Gnaeus Servilius, had been busy courting the allies and raising new levies. They had spread their net widely, even seeking assistance from Hiero of Syracuse who provided a 1500-strong contingent which included 500 Cretan archers.

Flaminius we have met before, when commanding a consular army six years previously against the Insubrians during the Gallic invasion. A forceful leader, he was a powerful member of the plebeian Aemilian party opposed to the aristocratic Fabians, who dominated the Senate. His re-election after such a short time – a ten-year interval was the normal rule – indicated the seriousness of the situation and the regard in which he was held. In much the same way as he had not bothered to open the letter demanding his recall in that earlier campaign, he now scorned assuming the consulship in Rome, thus avoiding all the ceremonial paraphernalia of sacrifices on the Albion Mount and the taking of vows on the Capitol. Instead he took over command in the field while his fellow consul, Geminus Gnaeus Servilius, was still performing the traditional formalities. Small wonder that Flaminius was disliked by those in authority, who subsequently did all they could to blacken his reputation and minimise his achievements. He was obviously a powerful personality with an independent turn of mind, and a healthy disregard for the trappings of command. While possessing a sound sense of priorities, he was probably an unsettling figure for the more conventionally minded. About Servilius, nothing is known other than that he was a member of an old patrician family. Flaminius took over from Sempronius Longus, who disappears off the scene, and established himself at Arretium to block the main approach over the central Apennines into Etruria. Having completed his inauguration in Rome Servilius went to Ariminum, from where the east coast road could be controlled, and relieved Scipio, who sailed to Spain to resume command of the army he had left on the Rhone.

After the battle of Trebia, Hannibal used his Numidian cavalry during the remainder of the winter to dominate the surrounding countryside, the principal reason for Placentia and Cremona having to receive supplies up the Po. Hannibal himself went on to capture Victumulae, a Roman trading post near Placentia which, according to

Livy, was sacked in the most ruthless manner, 'as though it had been taken by siege rather than surrendering'. Conduct which, if reported accurately, was in striking contrast to Hannibal's treatment of Roman allied prisoners, towards whom he displayed great kindness, telling them that he had only come to fight the Romans and then dismissing them to their homes. Since Hannibal's policy was nothing if not consistent, the inhabitants of Victumulae may have been the victims of the outrageous Hannibal Monomachus or, alternatively, sworn allies of Rome of whom an example had to be made.

With the coming of spring Hannibal crossed the Apennines, not by the obvious route through Arretium where Flaminius lay but probably from Bologna, which brought him out probably some twenty miles north of Florence. Here the low-lying ground was no more than a marshy swamp, where sleep and rest were virtually impossible as the army struggled through the quagmire during the next four days. A considerable number of the horses lost their hooves which rotted in the perpetual wet, and many of the pack animals slipped and fell, never to rise again. It was not, however, just the animals that suffered: the Iberians and the Libyans managed fairly well as they were in the lead, but the Gauls had to follow them through what had become a leg-sucking morass. It was only because the cavalry brought up the rear, that many of the Gauls did not abandon the march and turn back. The whole army had suffered grievously and Hannibal, who had been riding the only surviving elephant, endured agony from an infection of the eyes, one of which he eventually lost. Livy gives an even more graphic account of the miserable deaths suffered by men and beasts, before the army finally ended its nightmare and emerged onto the firm ground below Faesulae (Fiesole). Here it was let loose to plunder the valley of the upper Arno, rich in grain, cattle and human habitation, an act which would have been designed to achieve two objectives: to provide much needed relief for the overtaxed troops, and to goad Flaminius into action.

Though Flaminius had been outmanoeuvred, given the attitudes and conditions of the times it is unreasonable to lay responsibility for this entirely on his shoulders. Obviously he can be criticised for not having used his cavalry to shadow Hannibal and provide early warning of the route he was taking, but the fault was not entirely of his own making. As has been repeatedly shown, the Roman cavalry was inferior and their light horse was particularly defective, lacking both the training and the *élan* to operate in small, independent groups for lengthy periods – unskilled and ill-prepared, they would have fallen as easy prey to the wide-ranging and vastly superior Numidians, who dominated not only the immediate vicinity of the battlefield, but the entire countryside around where Hannibal was operating. The fault lay with the Roman way of waging war, with their tactical doctrine rather than any particular commander.

Given the Roman weakness in their mounted arm, what should Flaminius have done when faced with an opponent who held the initiative? Eight years previously a similar situation had arisen when, as will be recalled, the Cisalpine Gauls had swept the Po valley clear of the Roman legions and after eluding those stationed to block their further passage had descended upon Etruria. Flaminius would have been well acquainted with the failure of the earlier Roman deployment, and so wanted not only to prevent such a potentially disastrous situation from arising again, but also to avoid the accompanying humiliation. The trouble was that both Flaminius and the Senate feared for the safety of Rome, and therefore assumed that the city was Hannibal's objective. The consular army under Geminus Gnaeus Servilius was kept at Ariminum away on the east coast, when the threat had been assessed as being to the west, because of the perceived need to keep a strong military presence in the area in order both to prevent Hannibal from using the coastal road to gain access to a number of routes crossing the Apennines and to deter the hostile Boii from taking the opportunity to invade this contested region – as well as ensuring the loyalty of the eastern provinces allied to Rome.

Lying between the Arno and the Tiber, Etruria was a prosperous and important ally of Rome, which served as a buffer against northern invaders. If Hannibal was again to force the Romans to react precipitately instead of combining their consular armies, how better therefore than to set about Etruria's devastation? Having identified his destination, Hannibal could now decide upon his approach. Livy says that Hannibal moved into Liguria and Sempronius Longus went to Luca, which would have put the centre of gravity for the coming campaign in the northwest. Polybius merely tells us that Hannibal camped in Gallic territory and places Sempronius Longus' successor, Flaminius, at Arretium. Several modern historians, however, locate Hannibal at Bologna, presumably because this is from where he began his march into Etruscany. This certainly seems to be the most likely position, since Bologna lies in the centre of the Italian peninsula and Hannibal was offered the choice of a number of routes over the central Apennines. The most obvious being blocked by Flaminius, Hannibal selected a relatively minor pass.

The problem facing Flaminius was that as there were a number of such passes, had he attempted to block them all the resulting dissipation of his strength would have carried the high risk of him being defeated in detail, an example of the truth of the adage that in attempting to hold everything one secures nothing. In summary then, the Roman misappreciation of how Hannibal intended to conduct the campaign, coupled with shortcomings in their tactical doctrine and organisation, led to Flaminius first being outmanoeuvred and then defeated.

From the upper Arno, Hannibal marched through Etruria, burning and ravaging the countryside, keeping the city of Cortona and the hills surrounding it to his left and making as though to pass Lake Trasimene to his right. Flaminius can have had few doubts that Hannibal's intention was to avoid an early battle in order to advance on Rome: why else would he have wished to elude him at Arretium and now be content to waste the countryside through which he was passing? Driven by this conviction, Flaminius decided not to wait for Servilius to join him but set off in close pursuit. When Hannibal reached Lake Trasimene after following the northern shoreline, he set an ambush along a strip of land between the Defile of Borghetto and Tuoro. Here, facing the lake, a semicircle of hills form a natural amphitheatre some five miles wide into which tumbles the Macerone, whose delta has steadily extended the land area. The discovery of 20-ft-deep cremation pits containing arrow and spear heads among the ashes, together with graves in which were found dismembered skeletons and shattered skulls, confirm that this must have been the scene of the battle. Furthermore, the accounts given by both Polybius and Livy can only be satisfactorily related to this piece of ground. It should also be remembered that in the last 2000 years, Lake Trasimene has undergone considerable change as a result of alluvial deposits being brought down by the Macerone. The water level has also been lowered following the construction of a canal in the 15th century, connecting the lake to the river Nector so that in 217 BC the shore area would have been less than it is today.

What then seems to have occurred is that Hannibal continued his march through the narrow defile to Tuoro. Here he established a camp and conspicuously positioned his Spanish and Libyan infantry on the long, exposed ridge. When his Balearic slingers and light infantry came up to this position, they were wheeled to the left so as to bring them on to the high ground at the head of the valley on either side of the Macerone. Here they were ordered to lie down and remain concealed. Similarly, the cavalry and Gauls were hidden in folds in the ground on the spur running down to the Borghetto defile opposite the ridge held by the Libyans and Spaniards. In this way the entire area encircled by the hills was dominated by the Carthaginians.

Flaminius, who had been in hot pursuit since learning that Hannibal had slipped over the Apennines, reached Lake Trasimene near Borghetto late in the evening, and at dawn the next morning the legions started to move through the defile across the valley floor. Though Polybius says that there was an early morning mist, from his

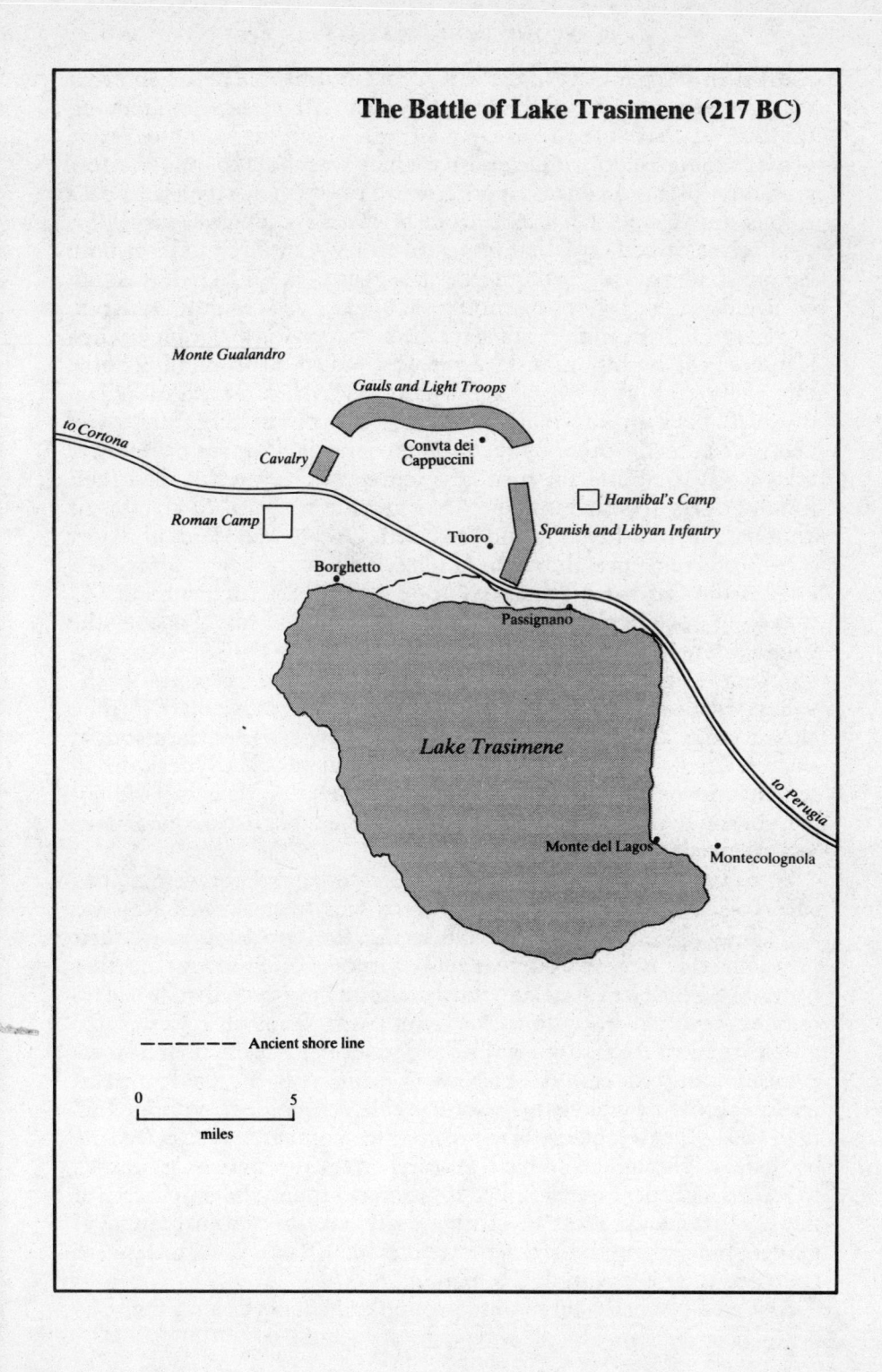

The Battle of Lake Trasimene (217 BC)

subsequent account of the battle it seems improbable it was so dense that it materially affected the course of events. The suspicion remains that this may have been a subsequent Roman embellishment to try and provide some excuse for the disaster which was about to follow. More probably, as the Romans approached Tuoro, they saw Hannibal's troops drawn up for battle in front of them and deployed into line themselves, gradually filling the entire valley until the bulk of both legions had passed through the Borghetto defile. Had this not occurred and the legions had still been in extended column of march, so many of them would not have been trapped in the valley when Hannibal sprang his ambush. As it was, sealed off from all possible means of retreat by the Carthaginian cavalry to their rear, assaulted on their left flank by the Balearic slingers and the light infantry, and hemmed in on the other by the lake, most of the Romans died where they stood. Some of them sought refuge in the water and in their frantic efforts to escape attempted to swim but weighed down by their armour, they quickly sank and drowned. Others waded out until just their heads remained above the surface, only to die begging for their lives as the Carthaginian cavalry rode out and dispatched them. As many as 15,000 Romans died, including Flaminius. About 6000 of the vanguard managed to fight their way through the Carthaginians blocking their advance and gained the high ground to the east of the valley. From here they looked back at the scene of desolation, then closed ranks and made for an Etruscan village where they sought shelter. The fact that the Roman vanguard were able to break out in this manner lends further weight to the contention that they did not stumble on to the Carthaginians in a thick mist, but had formed ranks and attacked in battle order.

After the slaughter, from which it is estimated there were 10,000 survivors, the Numidian cavalry were sent to deal with Romans sheltering in the village. But on seeing the hopelessness of their position, the Romans surrendered without offering any further resistance. As he had done previously, after telling them that he had no quarrel with anybody but the Romans, Hannibal released the prisoners taken from Rome's allies and sent them back to their homes. A resounding victory had been won which left the field open to Hannibal. Before making his next move, however, he re-equipped his men with the weapons taken from the Romans and cleared the battlefield. Though Hannibal had searched for the body of Flaminius to accord it proper funeral rights, it was never found and only thirty of the Carthaginians' most illustrious dead were buried in individual graves. Judging by the archaeological evidence, the remainder were cremated together with the Romans.

As a result of being lured onto ground of Hannibal's choosing, the

Romans had now twice been encircled and destroyed. At Trebia Hannibal had exploited the superiority of his cavalry on the wings, and achieved surprise in the centre by taking the Romans in the rear with a relatively small force of cavalry and infantry. Now, at Lake Trasimene, he had used the ground to encircle and destroy the best part of two Roman legions. The Romans' defeat on both occasions can be attributed to their misappreciation of the nature of the campaign Hannibal was conducting, both at the operational and tactical levels. In short, they were persistent in trying to fight the wrong sort of war, and it would take yet another crushing defeat before this fact gained general acceptance.

While still at Lake Trasimene Hannibal heard that Geminus Gnaeus Servilius was approaching from Ariminum to support his fellow consul, and had sent 4000 cavalry ahead of his heavily burdened legions, who themselves were already hastening down the Via Flaminia. Maharbal was at once dispatched with a mixed force of cavalry and light infantry to intercept this Roman contingent. In what must have been an effectively conducted action, nearly half the Romans were killed in the first encounter, the remainder being taken prisoner the following day. The first reports of the crushing defeat that had been suffered at Trasimene had hardly reached Rome when news of this second disaster began to filter in. The city was at once thrown into a state of near despair with the crowds thronging the public places as the wildest rumours spread. When the magnitude of the defeat was confirmed, demands were made for the appointment of a dictator with full imperium. Such an appointment had not been made since thirty years earlier when, following the naval disasters off Sicily during the First Punic War, Atilius Calatinus had been nominated as a dictator to command the army on the island for the remainder of the consular year. The most significant aspect of the powers given to a dictator was that, unlike a consul, he did not have to consult the Senate about his plans.

By means which are not clear but were apparently controversial, Fabius Maximus, an aristocrat but moderate member of the Fabian faction in the Senate, was elected as Dictator – an appointment which was balanced politically by nominating a member of the people's party, Marcus Minucius Rufus, as Master of the Horse. Thus the absolute power of the dictator which the people themselves had been demanding was curtailed for reasons of political rivalry. Instead of being able to select a second-in-command of his own choosing, Fabius had had to accept one who enjoyed degree of independence stemming from his different political allegiances. It was an uneasy compromise between the exercise of sole and dual command, as soon became apparent. A man of strong religious convictions, Fabius was in no doubt that the impiety of Flaminius had been the cause of Rome's disasters. His first act was to arrange for the Sibylline Books to be consulted, after which their direction as to sacrifices, the dedication of shrines and other propitiatory offerings were scrupulously enforced. More practically, the defences were put in order, and to hinder Hannibal's anticipated approach the inhabitants of unfortified towns were withdrawn into places of safety, bridges were broken and the countryside laid waste.

But Hannibal still had no intention of marching on Rome, and instead crossed the Apennines through Umbria into Picenum on the Adriatic coast. Here he rested his army while carrying out the reorganisation of his Libyan infantry as discussed earlier, in order to allow greater flexibility in their employment. These preparations having been completed, Hannibal moved south into Apulia, plundering and devastating the countryside as he went; but instead of renouncing their allegiance to Rome the towns along his route barred their gates to him.

Meanwhile Fabius Maximus had also completed his preparations, and marched out of Rome with two legions to join those of Servilius from Ariminum. Fabius then took over sole command sending the consul back to Rome with orders to prepare to meet any unforeseen emergency, particularly any Carthaginian attempt to land reinforcements in support of Hannibal – a necessary precaution in view of the fact that the Carthaginian fleet had attempted to contact him at Pisa and then harried the Italian coastline, before intercepting a transport fleet carrying supplies to Spain. Fabius then marched down the Via Appia with his four legions and closed up to Hannibal.

Although Fabius was now within reach of Hannibal, he was as firmly resolved to avoid a pitched battle as his predecessors had been determined to seek one. He had no intention of risking another defeat by accepting battle in circumstances of Hannibal's choosing. The plan Fabius adopted was one by which he would threaten and harry Hannibal until he could create a situation in which it was the Romans who dictated the terms under which the battle would be fought. Paradoxically, Fabius and Hannibal had then developed the same plan of operation, the difference being that the Carthaginian commander already held the initiative, so the Roman could only react. It was thus very difficult for Fabius to keep to his plan, since it entailed leaving Hannibal free to sack and burn his way though the lands of Rome's allies while a Roman army watched impotently, apparently afraid to intervene. In fact, all the Romans could do was keep to the high ground so as to nullify the superiority of the Numidian cavalry in particular. Acceptance of these Fabian tactics demanded great tenacity of purpose, unruffled patience, no little skill and – something that lay outside Fabius' control – an understanding of what he was doing by the allies, the Senate and the people. He might possess dictatorial powers, but these had not been given to him to pursue a course of action likely to be interpreted as cowardly by friend and foe alike.

When Hannibal learned that Fabius was in the immediate vicinity, he no doubt expected to be faced by another unbalanced and hastily trained Roman army, led by a commander who would be no match for his skill or the professionalism of his troops. But when it became clear that Fabius had no more intention than he did of being drawn into a battle not of his own choosing, Hannibal withdrew to his camp and when there were no signs that Apulia was prepared to abandon the Roman Confederation as a result of the devastation inflicted on the countryside, he set his army in march to recross the Apennines. With Fabius apparently hovering indecisively on his flanks, Hannibal entered into the rich heartland of Samnium, and passed the walled and unwelcoming city of Beneventum (Benevento) before capturing the open town of Telesia, alternatively identified as Venusia. He then turned into Campania to devastate the Falernus Ager, a fertile area which had been annexed by the Romans and was now cultivated by farmers who held their land on a yearly lease. Apart from its agricultural wealth, Campania contained some of the most famous and beautiful cities in Italy with Capua, the provincial capital lying on the Volturnus, being second only to Rome in importance. Girt by mountains on three sides and the sea on the other, Campania is described by Polybius as providing a sort of arena where the Carthaginians would display the terror of their power before the whole of Italy, making a pitiful spectacle of the Roman army's total inadequacy. Campania then became the keystone of Hannibal's strategy, and the way the province acted would be likely to determine the whole course of the war. If Capua could be persuaded to abandon her Roman alliance, other cities and even whole provinces could well follow suit. Given such circumstances, it might be thought that Hannibal would adopt a policy of conciliation, especially as savagery had not proved successful in Apulia, but this was not to be and the devastation continued unabated.

The allegiance of many of the cities to Rome, however, was not as solid as it seemed. Hannibal's revolutionary appeal had aroused the aspirations of the people's party, aspirations which the aristocrats in Rome vigorously countered by calling upon their peers in the allied cities to unite against the subversive threat they represented. Livy says that Hannibal had left Apulia and moved into Campania because, among the allied prisoners who had been released after Trasimene, there were three reputable Campanians who had assured him that he stood a good chance of winning over Capua. In the event, however, the advice they gave him about the policy he should pursue is unknown, and any hopes he may have cherished remained unrealised. Capua and Nola, together with the other major Campanian cities, remained loyal to Rome and in spite of the emerging signs of discontent surrounding his conduct of the war, Fabius maintained a consistency of purpose matching Hannibal's – even though, unlike Hannibal, he had to contend with the politically motivated protestations of his second-in-command, Minucius.

Something of a stalemate was beginning to set in, with Hannibal apparently incapable of achieving his strategic objective of isolating Rome by detaching her allies. Equally, after the initial successes of Trebia and Trasimene, his operations in the field were being thwarted by the evasiveness of Fabius, who had earned himself the title of Cunctator, or the Delayer. But the situation was not a matter of concern only to the Carthaginians, the Romans also were in a quandary.

Political controversy was bitterly rife in Rome and throughout the Confederation: here was a barbaric army marching with impunity throughout the length and breadth of the country, wreaking an appalling havoc wherever it went and now, having destroyed the best part of two Roman armies, exercising a fearful domination over a third. The aristocratic party which had brought about this catastrophic state of affairs must be replaced and the voice of the people heard. In the absence of any success, if Fabius continued with his present policy popular demand could sweep away the entire political and social fabric of the existing order.

With the summer drawing to a close, Hannibal had to decide where he was to pass the winter so as to be best placed to renew the campaign in the following year. Though Campania could furnish all his material needs and some nine coastal cities, including Neapolis (Naples), provided ready access to the outside world and Carthage in particular, Hannibal decided to move. No reason has been given for this, but a possible explanation may be that political and military considerations outweighed advantages of this strategically placed and well-provisioned province. The fact was, Capua was standing firm in her loyalty to Rome. There was also a military consideration. The longer Hannibal remained in Campania, the more difficult it was going to be for him to extricate himself through the limited number of passes. Though there were eight possible routes, since the Carthaginians were hemmed in north of the unfordable Volturnus, and since the only bridge north of Capua was firmly in Roman hands, the number actually available to Hannibal was three. It was not just a matter of extracting the army itself, there were also thousands of cattle as well as some 5000 prisoners – though the problem of the latter was resolved by ordering their execution rather than risk them attempting to overpower their guards during the march. News that Hannibal was preparing to leave Campania was probably not long in reaching Fabius, who must now have felt that the opportunity to make Hannibal fight for a passage would at last enable him to dictate terms. Minucius was sent to block the Via Latina, the northernmost pass, and another force was placed astride the course of the Volturnus to the east. Fabius positioned himself on the foothills on either side of the route running south of Teanum from where he could move to support his other two contingents. The scene was set and Hannibal was seemingly caught in the trap the Romans had been so long preparing. But Fabius had not counted on the ingenuity of the Carthaginian, who was once again to show himself to be the master of surprise.

For reasons which were probably connected with the ground and the alternative routes it provided, Hannibal decided to withdraw from Campania through the pass by which he had come. Assembling 2000 of the strongest working oxen, he had bundles of dry wood attached to their horns, and five or six hours before dawn, after setting the faggots ablaze, the cattle were driven up the slopes of the high ground rising above the Roman positions. Seeing the surging mass of lights above them, the Romans guarding the pass abandoned their positions and climbed up to intercept what they mistakenly believed to be the Carthaginians attempting to escape. The pass now being clear, Hannibal's long column marched through unopposed. Though alerted by the noise and the bewildering scene being enacted on the opposite side of the valley, Fabius made no move. Polybius ascribes his hesitation to fear, but Fabius was probably simply apprehensive of attempting to intervene in an unknown situation, and wisely so, across broken ground in total darkness. Prudently he remained in position until dawn, but by then Hannibal had cleared the pass and was entering the upper reaches of the Volturnus. Here the main course of the river made an abrupt left-hand turn and provided Hannibal with a number of routes to choose from for his next move. By first marching north towards Venafrum (Venafro), Hannibal rekindled the Romans' old fear that his destination was still Rome, so facilitating his unopposed passage when instead he suddenly turned east through Samnium, before crossing the Apennines into Apulia.

Back on his old campaigning ground, Hannibal seized the border town of Gerunium, some twenty miles north of Luceria, where he established a base for future operations. With the rich broad plains of Apulia stretching from the Apennines to the Adriatic coast, Hannibal's supplies were assured and he could manoeuvre freely. But though he had skilfully extracted himself from a potentially disastrous position and in so doing had further humiliated the Romans, their army had yet to be destroyed. In spite of the growing criticism of his policy and demands for positive action, Fabius still refused to be drawn into a battle not of his own choosing. Instead he remained in the foothills, while the Carthaginian foragers fanned out over the plains below to gather in the harvest. It was at this stage that Fabius was recalled to Rome, ostensibly on public business but probably also to answer his critics and give an account of himself. Upon his departure command passed to Minucius, an ardent critic of Fabius' indecisiveness and a powerful advocate of positive action. Although cautioned by Fabius, Minucius must have felt honour bound to act and, under the circumstances, he did so with considerable restraint.

At first Minucius kept along the line of the hills but, on learning that an increasing proportion of Hannibal's army was dispersed foraging, he descended onto the plain in Larinum to the north of Gerunium, where he then camped. Hearing of the Romans' approach, however, Hannibal reduced the size of his foraging parties and, with about two-thirds of his army, threatened Minucius by occupying a low ridge above his camp. But as neither Hannibal nor Minucius wished to engage in a major pitched battle under such conditions, only a series of inconclusive engagements ensued. Eventually, however, the Romans succeeded in killing a considerable number of the Carthaginian foragers, and thus decided Hannibal to withdraw into his base at Gerunium. Exaggerated stories of what had occurred were soon circulating freely in Rome, and Minucius was hailed as a hero. The Senate temporarily lost political control and the people took the unconstitutional step of elevating Minucius to be co-dictator with Fabius. So, for the first time in Roman history, two dictators had been appointed, perhaps an easier solution for the people than trying to obtain the removal of Fabius. On returning to the army in the field, Fabius insisted on persevering with his original policy and, on being opposed by Minucius, offered him a choice; either they would command on alternate days, or they would do so with separate armies. Flushed with his earlier success and the public acclaim he had received, Minucius elected to exercise an independent command and moved his two legions into camp a mile or so away from that of his fellow dictator.

Quick to take advantage of this divided leadership and deployment, Hannibal infiltrated some 5000 infantry and 500 cavalry in groups of 200–300 during the night into some dead ground behind a ridge which lay between him and Minucius. At dawn he then advanced his light troops and occupied the ridge in full view of the Romans. Minucius rose to the bait and advanced his two legions to the attack, but before he could close he suddenly found himself assaulted on his exposed flanks by the Carthaginians who had emerged from their hiding places. Once again the Romans had found themselves surprised and about to be encircled – a fate which they escaped from only through the intervention of Fabius, who had remained a spectator until it was clear that Minucius faced a crushing defeat. He then ordered the advance. Being off balance and in no position to fight what was now a superior force, Hannibal broke off the battle and withdrew. Minucius' legions had suffered heavy casualties as a result of his rashness, and there was no concealing that they had been saved only by the timely intervention of Fabius. Chastened by the experience, the Roman army chose to be reunited and Minucius voluntarily reverted to his subordinate role as a second-in-command, though this unified authority was not to endure. The six-month dictatorship of Fabius ended as the year drew to a close and two new consuls, Geminus Gnaeus Servilius and Atilius Regulus, took over command at Gerunium for the winter months until the elections of the following year. The former had been commanding the fleet before the approach of winter had caused it to be laid up, while Regulus had been Flaminius' replacement after his death at Trasimene.

In the bitterly contested elections of 216 BC, the People's party succeeded in electing their candidate, Marcus Terentius Varro. The son of a wealthy merchant, one of the classes hardest hit by the war, Varro was strongly opposed to the aristocratic leadership and its direction of the war. But he was more than a mere demagogue: he had held the posts of quaestor, plebeian, aedile and praetor, so had proven himself to be a man of some standing and competence. Moreover, on being elected consul, he took over the electoral proceedings and accepted the aristocratic faction's choice of Lucius Aemilius Paullus as his fellow consul. Paullus was a patrician who, during the closing stages of the Illyrian campaign, had shown himself to be a competent commander when driving Demetrius of Pharos from his kingdom.

The elections having been completed, the Senate next had to consider how the war was to be conducted. Fabius had saved the Romans from suffering yet another defeat, but he had not secured them a victory, nor had he prevented them from having to endure the economic consequences of Hannibal's devastation, as well as untold human suffering and loss of political standing. The allies could not be expected to continue their sacrifices if Rome was incapable of protecting them, so the fear that Hannibal might succeed in detaching them must have been one of the Senate's principal concerns. Positive and visibly determined measures were now required; Rome's full manpower resources would be mobilised and Hannibal would be crushed in accordance with traditional military thinking. Four legions were raised to reinforce those already in Apulia facing Hannibal, while

The Battle of Cannae (216 BC)

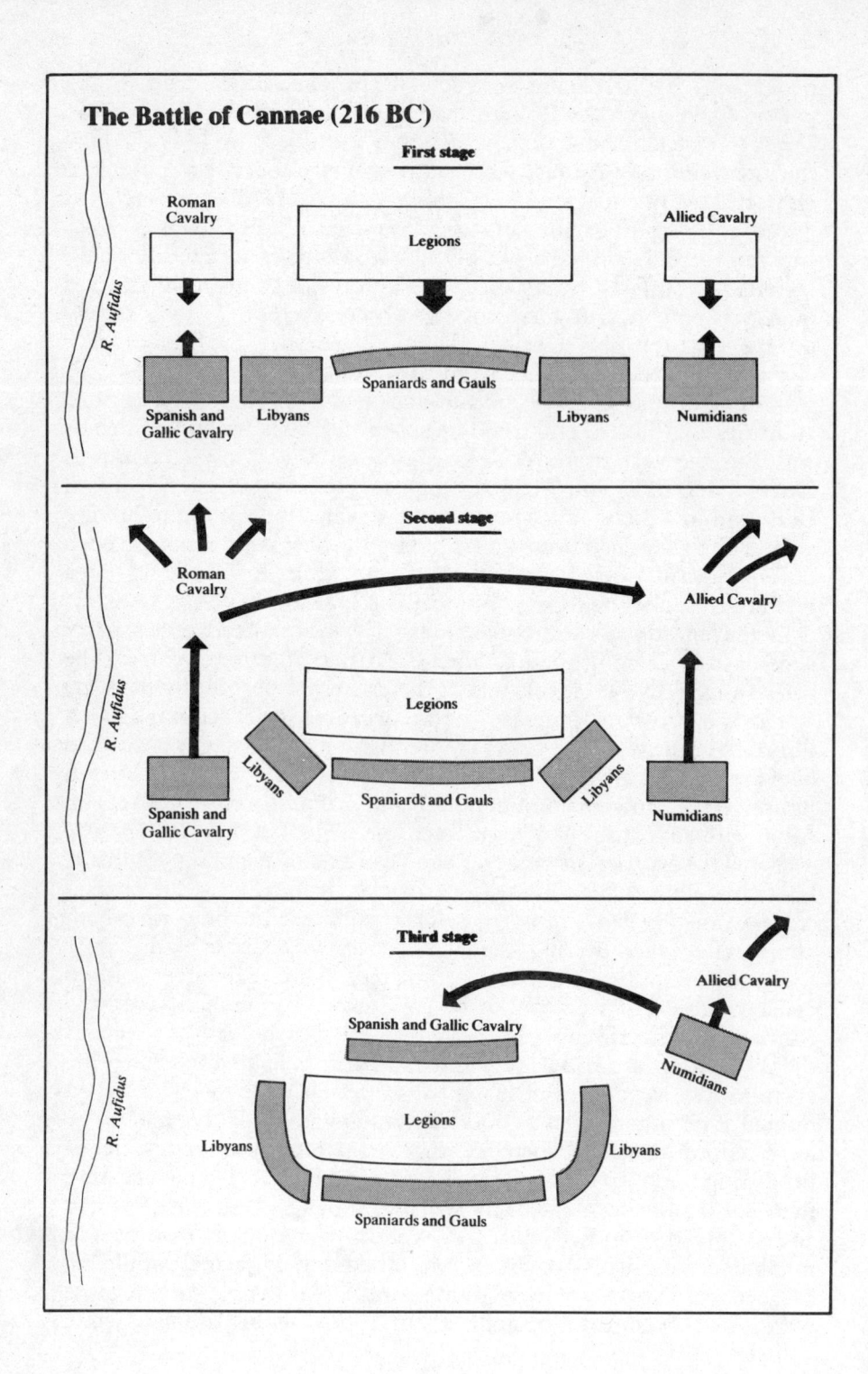

First stage

Roman Cavalry | Legions | Allied Cavalry

R. Aufidus

Spanish and Gallic Cavalry | Libyans | Spaniards and Gauls | Libyans | Numidians

Second stage

Roman Cavalry | Allied Cavalry

R. Aufidus

Spanish and Gallic Cavalry | Libyans | Legions | Spaniards and Gauls | Libyans | Numidians

Third stage

R. Aufidus

Spanish and Gallic Cavalry

Libyans | Legions | Libyans

Spaniards and Gauls

Allied Cavalry

Numidians

the size of the legions themselves was increased to the emergency strength of 5000 infantry. Never before had the Romans put such numbers into the field.

The winter and spring had seen little activity, but as the summer of 216 BC approached, Hannibal made a decisive move. He seized Cannae, a town which, although largely destroyed during the previous year's fighting, had a citadel still able to serve as a major support base for the army in the field. Its loss could not be overlooked and instructions from Rome were sought as a matter of urgency. If Hannibal's plundering was to be stopped, a major engagement must be undertaken. What were they to do? After prolonged debate the Senate passed a resolution that a battle should be fought, but not until Varro had arrived and eight full strength legions could be put into the field – by which time the conditions for crushing Hannibal by a massive concentration of force would have been created.

When the two new consuls arrived, Paullus addressed the army to explain the earlier reverses and to outline the future. The defeats which had been suffered could not be attributed to one or two mistakes, but had been due to a number of adverse circumstances which had had a cumulative effect. Now, however, they faced the prospect of a great battle in which they outnumbered the Carthaginians: all that was required was for every man to do his best and victory would be theirs. Seldom can a commander have so misled his men by such a faulty analysis of the causes of their defeat. The addresses over and the preparations complete, after a two-day march the Romans arrived within about six miles of Hannibal and pitched camp, while the two commanders met to discuss their next move. It was now that the first signs of serious dissension arose between them. According to Polybius, Paullus considered the ground to be too bare and so favourable to the Carthaginian cavalry. He therefore wanted to move into the hills further to the west, but Varro, whose turn it was to command the following day, insisted in remaining where they were – a determination which was reinforced when the Romans came off better in a skirmish with the Carthaginian cavalry. The decision to fight having been taken, the next day the Romans deployed on both sides of the Aufidus (Ofanto) where there was a ford, initially with the bulk of the army on the west bank and only about a third to the east.

For the next two or three days activity on both sides was confined to skirmishing, but tension slowly rose. Eventually the fatal day arrived and it was Varro who exercised command when, at first light, he moved the army across the river onto the east bank. He positioned the Roman cavalry on the right wing along the river, with the legions next to them and the cavalry of the allies on the left wing, while in front of the whole army were the light infantry. The Romans' total strength amounted to some 80,000 infantry and a little more than 6000 cavalry. Though the deployment adopted by Varro followed the conventional pattern, he made a significant change to the dispositions within the legions themselves, ordering the *maniples* to be brought much closer together and their fronts to be greatly reduced so as to achieve far greater depth. In this way, freedom to manoeuvre within the legions was removed and there was a reversion to the theory that sheer mass would conquer: the evolutionary developments which had taken place to provide greater flexibility were renounced and the rigidity of the phalanx was reinstated. Varro must have concluded that by achieving an overwhelming concentration of force in the centre, he would burst straight through the Carthaginian infantry who, being greatly inferior in numbers, could hardly even match his frontage; what then took place on the wings would be of little consequence. Had not the spearheads of the legions cut their way through the Carthaginian infantry at Trebia and Trasimene? They would now do so again but on such a massive scale that it would bring about a total disintigration of the Punic army. It must all have looked very simple.

At the same time as the Romans, were completing their deployment,
Hannibal brought his army into line. First he moved his light infantry and Balearic slingers across the river from the west bank to face the Romans' main force. Behind this screen and using two crossing places, he then moved the remainder of the army up behind them. Opposite the Roman cavalry on his left wing, resting on the river, he placed the Spanish and Gallic cavalry, next to them half the Libyan heavy infantry, then the Spanish and Gallic infantry, thrown forward to form a crescent with its arc towards the enemy, and beyond them the other half of the Libyans with the Numidian cavalry on the open wing. In total the army consisted of 40,000 infantry, of whom at least half were Gauls, and 10,000 cavalry. Unlike the Romans, who had concentrated their most effective arm, the infantry, in overwhelming strength in the centre, Hannibal gave his centre to the Gauls and the Spaniards, fearlessly brave but the most temperamental and unsteady of his troops, while the tough and resolute Libyans had been placed on either side of them. On the right wing where the open plain permitted total freedom of manoeuvre were the finest of all the cavalry, the Numidians, and on the left, where the fighting would be more cramped, stood the heavy cavalry. The outline of Hannibal's tactical plan was already apparent: the centre would give and the wings envelop. But everything depended on whether the Gauls and the Spaniards could hold out long enough for the encirclement to be completed and become fully effective. If not, then the army would be torn apart and any further co-ordinated resistance would be

impossible. Characteristically, Hannibal placed himself at the critical point, in the centre.

The battle started with indeterminate skirmishing between the light troops forming screens in front of both armies, but once Hannibal's Spanish and Gallic cavalry had charged those of the Roman's facing them on the river flank, or western wing, the battle began in earnest. It was a fierce fight but the Carthaginian cavalry eventually got the upper hand and when the Romans broke, they were given no quarter. While this cavalry action was taking place, the massed Roman legions were advancing against the Carthaginian thinly-drawn central crescent. For a while the Gauls and the Spaniards maintained their position, but eventually the sheer weight and the momentum of the closely packed legions began to force the crescent back until it first straightened, and then began to curve rearwards in the opposite direction. So compactly dressed was the Romans' massive concentration that their wings barely overlapped with the Libyan contingents, who then stood free beyond the immediate battle area. As the legions pushed further forward, so the Libyans were able to advance before wheeling inwards to fall upon the Romans' exposed flanks. In attempting to meet this assault from a totally unexpected direction, the Romans tried to turn and cover themselves, but the usual distances between the *maniples* had been so reduced that they could no longer wheel within the legions to face a flank. All that could be done was for individuals to turn and try to form an extempore new front. But it was a hopelessly inadequate endeavour, so cohesion was quickly lost, causing the relentless forward pressure on the overstretched Carthaginians to be relaxed and then contained.

While this situation had been developing in the centre, the cavalry on the wings had also been actively engaged. On the open eastern flank, the Numidians had not closed with the heavier cavalry of the Roman allies, but had tied them down by making as if to charge first from one direction then another, but always wheeling off at the last moment. But after annihilating the Romans facing him on the river wing, Hasdrubal had brought round the Spanish and Gallic cavalry to support the Numidians whereupon, seeing themselves greatly outnumbered, the Roman allied cavalry broke and fled. To ensure that they did not rally and rejoin the battle, Hasdrubal sent the Numidians in hot pursuit, while he fell upon the rear of the already embattled legions with his heavy cavalry.

The Romans were now completely surrounded and though they fought on in a desperate struggle for survival, the legions began to disintegrate and the casualties mounted as the circle around them remorselessly contracted. Finally all resistance ended. It is impossible to assess the Roman losses accurately. Polybius says that only 370 cavalry and some 3000 infantry managed to escape, while another 10,000 infantry were taken prisoner, leaving 70,000 dead on the battlefield. On the other hand Livy say that 19,000 Romans made an immediate escape, though some of them were later killed or captured, 4500 prisoners were taken and approximately 50,000 Romans fell. In view of subsequent accounts of the survivors being formed into two disgraced legions which were banished to Sicily on garrison duties, Livy's figures look the more probable. The absence of any reference to the numbers wounded perhaps can be explained by the fact that those who had been severely injured would have died anyway, while other Roman survivors, in the words of Livy, 'were dispatched by a quick blow as they struggled to arise from among the corpses'. But what is known for certain is that though Varro managed to escape, the consul Paullus, the previous year's consul Geminus Gnaeus Servilius, and the Master of Horse Minucius, with 29 military tribunes and some 80 men of senatorial rank, were among those who died. Against these staggering figures Hannibal's casualties, though severe in view of the fact that he could not replace the hard core of his army, only amounted to some 6000, of whom 4000 were Gauls, 1500 Spaniards and about 200 from among his cavalry. There was, then, no concealing where the brunt of the fighting had lain, and the fact that the Libyan casualties do not even get a mention underlines yet another of the battle-winning advantages of achieving surprise.

After winning such an overwhelming victory, Hannibal's strategic objective of breaking up the Roman Confederation appeared to be in reach. Rome's military inadequacy had been pitilessly exposed and her prestige had suffered what could prove to be a mortal blow. The run of defeats looked irreversible and the whole of Magna Graecia lay open to Hannibal; except for dispersed garrisons and the local auxiliaries, there was nothing to oppose him. Even in the north a Roman army under Lucius Postumius Albinus, which had been sent to Gaul to induce those Gallic tribesmen serving with Hannibal to return home, had been ambushed and annihilated only a few days after Cannae. Given such a situation, what should Hannibal's next move have been? According to Livy, his cavalry commander Maharbal urged him to march on Rome immediately, holding out the prospect of being able to dine on the Capitol within five days. But Hannibal was not to be drawn and delayed a decision – which, again according to Livy, was generally believed to have been the salvation of Rome and its empire.

The situation, however, was not quite so clear cut. As a start, news did not travel all that swiftly and time would have been needed too for the impact of the defeat at Cannae to be felt and assessed, in particular by Rome's allies. Though a number of cities, such as Tarentum in

Magna Graecia and others in Samnium, Apulia and Campania came over to Hannibal, none of this happened at once and the important city of Capua remained undecided for months. Additionally, the three great allied states surrounding Rome – Latium, Umbria and Etruria – remained loyal. Under such circumstances, Hannibal may well have recalled what had happened to Pyrrhus some fifty years previously when, having won a victory on the plains near Heraclea, he advanced to within forty miles of Rome only to have to withdraw when he could gain no popular support. Hannibal then remained determined to achieve the dissolution of the Roman Confederation by breaking his opponents' will rather than by attempting a direct assault on their principal and strongly fortified city. Maybe he was wrong and so missed a unique opportunity. But even with hindsight, it would be unwise to pass judgement on such a complex decision about which we have only the most rudimentary knowledge.

We must now turn to consider the course of action which Hannibal in fact pursued, but before doing so we should review what had been taking place in Spain, look at the wide-ranging strategic plan being developed by Carthage and finally, examine what was occurring in Rome.

The Campaign in Spain 218–216 BC

Though the Romans had considered it necessary to abandon their plan to invade North Africa and had recalled their legions from Sicily to defend their northern frontier against Hannibal, the second prong of their strategic offensive against Spain had been maintained. When Publius Scipio had decided on the Rhone that he should return to Italy in order to face Hannibal, he had dispatched his brother, Gnaeus Scipio, to Spain in accordance with the original plan. Although this expeditionary force never consisted of more than two legions, the campaign in Spain was a major factor in determining the course of the war as a whole. When they were eventually reunited, not only did the two Scipios firmly establish themselves in this independent power base of Hannibal's, but their early successes there served to counterbalance the string of disasters being suffered at home. Although only a general outline of the campaign is known to us, it is clear that the two Scipios displayed considerable political skill in their handling of the Spanish tribes, and no little military competence in the field against a superior enemy.

Gnaeus had disembarked in 218 BC at Emporiae, the important city port in northeast Spain closely connected to Massilia, Rome's influential Greek ally. From here he set about actively extending Roman influence down the coast towards the Ebro, courting the tribes and raising auxiliary contingents before marching to Terraco. Here Gnaeus encountered Hanno, Hannibal's nephew, who was responsible for the defence of Spain north of the Ebro. Perhaps stung by the indignity of the Roman presence and fearful of losing the whole area, Hanno decided to act at once and not wait for Hasdrubal, his fellow general responsible for the southern region, who was hurrying to join him. Thankful for the opportunity to engage the Carthaginians while they were still divided, Gnaeus closed for battle near Cissa, a few miles from Terraco. The Carthaginians suffered heavily, and after Hanno was driven from the field leaving 6000 dead behind him, he was captured when the Romans followed up in hot pursuit to overrun his camp. In all 2000 Carthaginian prisoners were taken, together with the baggage train left behind by Hannibal when setting out on his march to the Alps and beyond. It was shortly after this first disastrous encounter that Hasdrubal crossed the Ebro, but on hearing of Hanno's defeat, he turned off to the coast where he came across some marauding sailors from the Roman fleet. Killing a large number of them and scattering the remainder, Hasdrubal retired back over the Ebro. In barely two months the Carthaginians had lost possession of northeastern Spain, and the Romans had established a firm base for the following year's campaign.

During the winter Hasdrubal received over 4000 reinforcements from Carthage, and besides putting the thirty ships he already had into good order, he obtained a further ten. In the spring of 217 BC he was then able to move by both land and sea up the coast towards the Ebro. On hearing of this advance, Gnaeus decided, because of Hasdrubal's superior numbers, to avoid becoming involved in a major land battle. Instead, he concentrated against the Carthaginian fleet which had been located lying at anchor off the mouth of the Ebro, and set sail with his thirty-five ships, carrying some of the best soldiers from the legions. On seeing the Romans approach, Hasdrubal decided to fight close to the shore where he had drawn up his troops to give encouragement to the fleet. But the Carthaginian resistance was shamefully brief and their ships soon turned to run for the beach where the army had evidently been regarded as providing a safe haven rather than a stiffening to their determination.

Carthaginian maritime capability had in fact never been restored after the shattering defeats suffered in the First Punic War, either in numbers or morale. Hannibal had therefore acted wisely in not trusting himself to the sea when opening his Italian campaign. Other later naval engagements were to confirm this: a half-hearted challenge to Roman naval supremacy was mounted in 217 BC, when news of Hannibal's earlier victories prompted the Carthaginians to send a fleet of seventy ships in a display of strength to contact him. The fleet sailed to Pisa in the mistaken belief that this was where Hannibal was to be found. But reports that a Roman fleet of 120 ships was approaching caused them to make best speed home for Carthage. Other than the fortuitous destruction of a Roman supply convoy surprised on its way to Spain, as has been related, the appearance of the Carthaginian fleet had caused concern in Rome, and Servilius had been ordered to return to the city by Fabius as a precaution.

When the Senate heard of Gnaeus Scipio's naval success off the Ebro, they were encouraged to press the Spanish campaign with renewed vigour, and Publius Scipio was relieved of his command in Italy so that he could at last join his brother in Spain. Taking some 8000 reinforcements with him, he wasted no time in joining forces with Gnaeus, and after crossing the Ebro demonstrated before the powerfully fortified city of Saguntum. But even though Hasdrubal had withdrawn and was now at New Carthage, the Scipios lacked the strength to attempt an assault on the city, which showed no inclination to renounce its allegiance to the Punic cause. So the year's campaigning came to an inconclusive close.

The following year, the Cannae campaign in 216 BC was something of an anticlimax. Hasdrubal was fully occupied in a side issue, quelling a revolt by the Turdetani, whose territory encompassed the southern extremity of Spain, which today would be described as surrounding Gibraltar. According to Livy's account of the uprising, it was a fiercely contested affair and at times the Carthaginians were hard-pressed to hold their own, which makes the Scipios' inactivity during the year overcautious. But against this must be set the consideration that after Cannae there could have been no question of reinforcements reaching them for several years; they could then ill afford to risk seeing their successes rolled back by overreaching themselves. Besides, while the campaign in Spain was temporarily in the doldrums, political attitudes following Rome's reversal at Cannae were changing throughout the Mediterranean, giving the war not only a new character, but a wider dimension.

CHAPTER FIFTEEN

THE WAR EXPANDS
215–206 BC

After Cannae the Carthaginians held the initiative, but not all the cards. As we have seen, in Italy Hannibal could have tried to bring the war to a quick conclusion by marching on Rome, but instead chose to persevere with his policy of breaking up the Roman Confederation. In Spain neither the Romans nor the Carthaginians had the strength or the will to take the offensive unless reinforced; a course of action closed to the Romans until the situation in Italy could be recovered and new legions raised. But it was not only in these two theatres that the attention of the Carthaginians was drawn. Following Hannibal's victories their ambitions rose and the broad canvas of the war was extended.

While Hannibal had marched through the Italian peninsula, with Fabius Maximus doing no more than hover in his footsteps, it may seem remarkable that Carthage had assisted him merely with an ineffectual naval foray off the Etrurian coast. But the difficulties involved should not be underrated. To begin with, the Barcids had created their power base in Spain so as to be independent of Carthage and there is no evidence that Hannibal took the Senate into his confidence when he set out from New Carthage to cross the Alps. Given such secrecy and lack of trust on the part of Hannibal, the Carthaginians could hardly be expected to react positively to his victories, especially as they would not even have known where he was. As we have seen, at one time Hannibal was thought to be near Pisa, when in fact he was at least a hundred miles distant. To have risked running the gauntlet of the Roman fleet with heavily loaded transports would have been hazardous, while to have then landed reinforcements on an unknown shoreline with no clear knowledge of where Hannibal was would have been an act of considerable rashness. But after Cannae, despite the Romans' continuing superiority at sea, the whole situation had changed and by not acting vigorously the Carthaginians lost an opportunity to win the war.

News of Hannibal's victory at Cannae was brought to Carthage by his brother Mago Barca, who gave emphasis to his words by pouring out on the ground before the Senate a pile of gold rings taken from the Roman dead. A wave of enthusiasm for the war then swept through the city and the voices of those who had steadfastly opposed Barcid policy towards Rome were silenced. Well appreciating the risk involved, Hannibal did not ask for another army to be sent to Italy. Instead he put forward a new strategy which envisaged the encirclement of Italy, while he continued with the task of detaching Rome's allies. In essence he envisaged a double encirclement, both political and military. The Carthaginian Senate would carry the main responsibility for the wider envelopment, while Hannibal undertook that more directly centred against Rome itself. The imaginative sweep of Hannibal's strategy now extended far beyond his own campaign, which henceforth would only form a part of a larger mosaic. By forcing the Romans to defend their homeland, he hoped to prevent them from reacting to developments beyond the frontiers of Italy. Isolated and helpless, Rome would have to accept Carthaginian terms which would permit her survival only as a state of little consequence, dependent on the goodwill of others for its future existence. Whether in fact this plan was developed as a result of a measured intellectual appreciation or, as seems more probable, opportunistically and pragmatically, is not known. But however arrived at, it was both grandiose and imaginative in its design.

Practical measures to implement this strategy were now put in hand by the Carthaginians. The possibility of an alliance with Macedonia had long been one of their policy objectives, but the sudden death of Antigonus at the time of the Illyrian campaign had put such ideas in abeyance. The uncertainties surrounding Macedonian policies after the succession of the seventeen-year-old Philip V had prevented any formal commitments being entered into, while Philip's involvement in an alliance of Greek states against Rome's ally Aetolia in 220 BC had drawn his attention elsewhere. But following the blow to Rome's prestige inflicted at Cannae, and the termination of the Aetolian war in 217 BC, Philip's restless and warlike disposition made him ready to listen to new counsels and two such were ready to hand, from Demetrius of Pharos and from Hannibal. The former, having sought refuge in the Macedonian court after losing his possessions to the Romans during the Illyrian campaign, was ready with eager proposals for Philip to evict the Romans from the whole of the Adriatic seaboard, and Pharos in particular. Envoys were therefore dispatched to Hannibal and a far-reaching treaty of friendship between him and Philip was agreed, the details of which have been recorded by Polybius.

The commitments contained in the treaty were not lightly entered into, as is shown by the preamble which, in summary, says that the oath was taken in the presence of Zeus as well as all the gods of war, of the sun, moon and earth, of rivers, harbours and waters, and those who ruled over Carthage, Macedonia and Greece. In the six articles which followed committing both parties to war against Rome, the most important was the third, sworn by Hannibal, which promised to deprive the Romans of their possessions on the Illyrian coastline and return Pharos to Demetrius. Although no direct reference to Philip crossing over to Italy was made, that this was intended can be construed from the wording. The treaty also made clear that there was no intention to destroy Rome, but just to cut her severely down to size. The existence of the treaty, however, soon became known to the Romans when they intercepted Philip's envoys on their way back from Italy – a mishap which also caused considerable delay, until other envoys could be sent to finalise the arrangements.

While these events had been taking place during 215 BC, in Sicily Hiero had died at the age of ninety after a long and distinguished reign of fifty-four years, marked by moderation and stability. Although he had not been antagonistic to Carthage, as his willingness to send them much-needed supplies during the Mercenary War showed, he had remained consistently loyal to Rome. This loyalty had been further demonstrated after Cannae, when a course of prudent neutrality could well have been expected from him. As to his successor, his son Gelo having predeceased him, the throne went to his fifteen-year-old grandson Hieronymus who, under pressure from Hiero's two sons-in-law after they had dispossessed the Regency, authorised the pro-Carthaginian party in Syracuse to enter into negotiations with Hannibal against Rome. The price of the alliance required by Hieronymus was initially only the eastern half of the island, as far as the old Carthaginian–Sicilian frontier running along the Himera. But Hannibal's envoys eventually acquiesced to a demand for the whole of Sicily – probably secure in the knowledge that such matters could be adjusted more favourably once the war with the Romans had been won.

In 215 BC, too, the Carthaginians had sent an expeditionary force commanded by Hannibal the Bald to Sardinia. Here the violent Roman subjection of the whole island following the First Punic War had been in bitter contrast to the previous Carthaginian trading presence. As a result, several years of bitter and widespread resistance had followed before the Romans could impose their authority. Now, with the island garrisoned by only one legion, a renewed tribal uprising in support of a Carthaginian expedition could well provide an invaluable forward operating base covering Rome's western approaches.

Since the Romans had lost their entire consular army standing against the Gauls along the northern frontier in Italy during 216 BC, if they could now be cleared from Spain, Sardinia, Sicily and Illyria, Hannibal's outer encirclement would be complete. The inner ring only required him to continue with his seemingly effortless succession of victories before it would close relentlessly around Rome itself. Given a fair share of good fortune, and an adequate degree of competence in its execution, the chances of success for the Carthaginian strategy certainly looked reasonable in the aftermath of Cannae. The causes for its failure will now be examined theatre by theatre, but before doing so we must first consider the Roman response.

The crisis of Cannae acted as national catharsis, clearing the Roman mind of much of its political lumber. As a result the Romans were not only able to recognise the deficiencies in their direction of the war but also to introduce the necessary changes – an achievement which was accomplished without any high-sounding declaration pronouncements, but through a self-critical realisation that it was not just the military commanders who carried responsibility for their disasters, but the people themselves. The constitution, which permitted the people to disrupt the workings of the government, had served Rome well enough when it was little more than a provincial town, but now that it was the capital of a great empire, its inadequacies had been exposed. It was no longer acceptable that the appointment of field commanders and strategy they proposed to pursue should be determined by factional political considerations. Even the dictatorial powers granted to Fabius Maximus had been nullified by those given to his second-in-command, Minucius, after his contrasting policy had received popular acclaim. Paullus and Varro, whatever their share of individual responsibility may have been for the defeat at Cannae, held opposing views which reflected the political differences both within the Senate and between the Senate and the people. Time did not permit a fundamental revision of the constitution, even if this had been possible, but if the the war was to be won it would clearly have to be given a more purposeful direction and consistent execution. And this could only be achieved by ending the internal political strife between the ruled and the rulers.

Apart from a series of military disasters, there were also a number of mystical portents heralding yet further calamities, all of which added to the alarm sweeping through the city. Two of the Vestal Virgins were found to have been sexually active, an unforgivable crime befouling their sacred office, for which one suffered the traditional fate of being buried alive, while the other took her own life. As for the man involved, he was beaten to death. To cleanse this and other acts of impiety, supplication was made to the gods and the Sacred Books were consulted, together with the Oracle at Delphi. It was as a consequence of these deliberations that a pair of Greeks, male and female, as well as a pair of Gauls, had been buried alive.

To end the growing confusion in the city, Fabius Maximus then introduced some more practical measures. Public displays of mourning were banned, the city gates were barred against those attempting to flee, and the overwrought crowds were cleared from the Forum. The Senate's determination was further displayed when a deputation from the prisoners taken at Cannae seeking their ransom was curtly dismissed: the message was quite clear, there was to be no compromise with Hannibal. The further direction of the war was now in firm hands, and the air of alarm had been dispelled by sound disciplinary measures and the enactment of religious rituals. The great majority of Romans were now united behind the Senate in their determination to win the war, whatever the cost.

After being granted untrammelled freedom in their conduct of the war, the Senate acted with magnanimity. When Varro returned to Rome he could well have expected to be harshly received since, in the eyes of the Senate, he alone carried responsibility for the disaster at Cannae and had escaped with his life while Paullus, the Senate's man, had died a hero, fighting to the last with his troops. But even so the senators came to meet Varro at the city gate and publicly thanked him in front of a great crowd for not despairing of his country. He was then appointed to the command of a legion at Picenum, a less prestigious assignment but still one carrying command. It was an astute placatory gesture, designed to bridge the political divide and unify the people. Incidentally, the unfortunate survivors of the defeated legions which Varro brought back with him evidently lacked any political capital, for they were banished to Sicily in disgrace, to serve the remainder of the war there without home leave.

After Cannae and the decimation of the consular army in the Po valley by the Gauls, the Romans had only four full-strength legions left: two in Spain, one in Sicily and another in Sardinia, plus garrisons spread over a large number of cities elsewhere. Though two new legions were forming at Rome, to fill their ranks and expand the size of the army, as well as crew the fleet, was placing a heavy demand on Rome's already depleted manpower. This shortage was further accentuated by the loss of recruits from southern Italy, which included the cities of Magna Graecia, as well as those in Apulia, Samnium and Lucania. New and urgent measures were therefore introduced: the age of military service was reduced to seventeen, and the unprecedented step was taken to enrol slaves – 8000 were to be bought from their owners at public expense and placed under arms.

The strategy the Senate now adopted was courageously far-sighted but entailed considerable risk. Although Rome lay practically undefended and Hannibal was expected to march on the city, there was to be no withdrawal of garrisons from overseas. Instead Rome's hold on Sicily, Sardinia and Illyria would be maintained, the conquest of Spain completed and Hannibal defeated in Italy. This represented something of a victory for the Claudii, and the Scipio family whose interests traditionally lay in Sardinia and Corsica but who now were looking towards Spain. Finally, to implement this strategy and sustain her legions overseas, Rome must retain her maritime superiority. As an indication of what was achieved, four years later the Romans were able to put twenty-five legions into the field. Although the Carthaginians were to receive outside reinforcements and support, principally from Hieronymus of Sicily and Philip of Macedonia, Rome's superior utilisation of her manpower resources was to give her an ever-increasing advantage, while the Carthaginians were not able to maintain their campaigns in Spain, Sardinia and Sicily, as well as reinforce Hannibal in Italy.

We will now see how the two protagonists fared in the five different but interconnected theatres of war over the next fifteen years.

The Campaign in Spain 215–206 BC

After receiving 4000 infantry and 100 cavalry reinforcements, and being relieved by Himilco with a second army, who took over the task of suppressing the Turdetani, Hasdrubal marched north to settle accounts with the Scipios. The Romans were besieging Ibera, a strategically important town lying on the north bank of the Ebro opposite Dertosa (Tortosa), which controlled the coast road and the river passage into the interior. The coming battle would be of critical importance: after the slaughter at Cannae should the Romans be defeated here also there would be little hope of their renewing the campaign for several years, and by then it would be too late. For the Carthaginians, although a single defeat would not carry such disastrous consequences since Spain could always be reinforced, it would seriously disrupt their strategic plan to encircle Italy.

The two armies met somewhere near Ibera and, as far as numbers went, they were fairly equal, each being about 25,000 strong. The Roman legions probably adopted their normal formation; Hasdrubal for his part, in obvious imitation of Hannibal's tactics at Cannae, thinned out the Spanish infantry holding the centre, and concentrated the Libyans and the cavalry on the wings. But Hasdrubal was no Hannibal and the Romans broke through his line before the wings could close and envelop them. The Carthaginians suffered heavy casualties and were completely defeated, leaving the Scipios with the initiative.

But though the line of the Ebro was again in Roman hands, they were too weak to act offensively or penetrate too deeply into the south of the peninsula where Carthaginian power was most strongly rooted. For the next two years, 215–213 BC, they contented themselves with consolidating their position north of the Ebro, while gradually occupying more territory to the south, until eventually, in 212 BC, they secured the important city of Saguntum. The Carthaginians in the meantime, after quelling a rebellion by the Libyans, had been able to build up their strength to three armies. One of these was commanded by Hasdrubal, who continued to operate independently, while the other two, under generals whose names we do not know, combined together. The reasons for these arrangements are not known either. They could have been justified on logistic grounds, but equally they might have been no more than a reflection of the three commanders' inability to cooperate, a shortcoming which later was to be their undoing.

Though outnumbered, in 211 BC the Scipios divided their army between them and took the offensive. Gnaeus led one-third of their total strength against Hasdrubal, while Publius advanced with the remainder against the combined Carthaginian armies under Mago Barca and Hasdrubal Gisco. This division of strength, evidently intended to match that of their opponents, was mistaken. If the Scipios were not immediately able to concentrate against one or other of the Carthaginian armies, then they should have manoeuvred to make this possible or, as a very poor alternative, remained on the defensive until the Carthaginians made a move. In the absence of any marked superior fighting qualities, to have acted as they did was to invite the defeats that they both suffered.

Deserted by his Spanish allies, who went over to the Romans, Gnaeus attempted to break away but his army was caught and nearly annihilated on the arid plains around Ilotci (Lozqui) by Hasdrubal Gisco. Publius fared little better. After being surrounded in his camp by the Carthaginian cavalry, he attempted to cut his way out but his army also was largely destroyed. Thus the Roman offensive which had set out with high hopes ended in disaster. Two legions had been virtually obliterated and among their piled dead lay the corpses of the two Scipios. They had died in a valiant but futile manner – perhaps in answer to pressing demands from Rome for an early offensive, a situation not unknown to British commanders in the Western Desert during World War II. But when viewed overall, the Scipios' campaign was far from being a failure and, although not enough details are known to make a firm judgement, it may well have played a vital part in saving Rome. Above all, it forced the Carthaginians to reinforce their army in Spain at the cost of operations elsewhere, most notably in Italy where, following the diversion of his brother Mago to Spain, Hannibal was deprived of all but the most meagre support.

The brief opportunity offered to Hasdrubal and his two fellow army commanders to recover the whole of Spain came and went. All the territory up to the Ebro, including Saguntum, was easily reoccupied, but internal dissensions – reflecting the old political divide between the Barcids and those in power in Carthage – prevented any coordinated action to establish more than limited lodgements beyond the river, now only thinly held by the remnants of what had been the Roman army in Spain. So the opportunity slipped away and Roman reinforcements started to arrive, first in a trickle and then in a quantity and under a quality of leadership which was to reverse the situation. Gaius Claudius Nero, who had been commanding an army for two years in Italy, was the first to arrive with 4000 men, bringing the total Roman strength up to some 13,000, a number barely sufficient to hold onto the northeastern corner of the peninsula. But in 210 BC the young Publius Cornelius Scipio sailed from Ostia, the port of Rome at the mouth of the Tiber, at the head of thirty ships carrying an additional 10,000 infantry and 1,000 cavalry. He disembarked at Emporiae and then marched 100 miles down the coast to Terraco. Here he established his headquarters and set about recruiting 5000 additional Spanish mercenaries and preparing for the coming campaign. But before entering into an account of his sweeping victories, a short digression to introduce this latest Scipio is called for.

We have already met him briefly at Ticinus, when the Romans had first clashed with Hannibal after his crossing of the Alps. Publius Cornelius Scipio had been born in 235 BC, so was barely twenty-five when given command of the army in Spain. The son of Publius Scipio, who had died in battle with Hasdrubal the previous year, and son-in-law of Lucius Aemilius Paullus, who had fallen at Cannae, he had already, as we know, seen action at Ticinus when, according to Livy, he had saved his father's life. Though there is no record of the part he played in the actual battle, he was also at Cannae where, again from Livy's account, it seems he was among those who escaped across the river Aufidus to the Roman camp on the opposite bank. Then, rather than surrender, he was one of the undaunted 4000 who managed to elude the Carthaginian cavalry and reach Canusium. In recognition of his leadership during this desperate period, those who had escaped with him, who included four military tribunes, elected him to be their commander. The next event of professional consequence in Scipio's life was his election to the aedileship, an essential preliminary to higher office. He had unexpectedly presented himself as a candidate in the Forum, where his youthful vigour and ardent convictions had won the rapturous support of the people. There were others, inevitably, who resented this precocious youth, but after the dark years of defeat there was a popular yearning for an inspirational leader who could offer them hope for the future, and when he later presented himself as a candidate for consular command of the army in Spain, Scipio was elected.

On taking up his appointment, Scipio faced the task of welding a disparate lot into a cohesive fighting force: there were the dispirited survivors of the defeated legions, the raw reinforcements fresh out of Italy, and Spanish mercenaries of uncertain loyalty. No light task for a young man, especially one whose close relation had been so intimately associated with disasters. But Publius Cornelius Scipio (later given the cognomen Africanus) was remarkable. As Polybius says, he was 'perhaps the most illustrious man of any born before the present generation', and one of his first acts was to show his trust in Marcellus, the man who had striven so hard to rally the survivors of the two Scipios' shattered army, but who could now well be regarded as an awkward rival.

Such was the man who assembled his soldiers and exhorted them not to be dismayed by their earlier reverses, reminding them that no Romans had ever been beaten by Carthaginians in valour – the fault lay with the rashness of their commanders. As for the future, though the Carthaginians had three armies, because they were at variance with one another they could not fight as a unified whole. Having fortified the morale of his troops, Scipio then began to plan for the coming year's campaign. It was not his intention to embark upon a series of uncoordinated tactical battles, but to strike a single decisive blow.

During the winter months Scipio's agents had been active and he had acquired all the details he needed to know about New Carthage; this strategically important city with its spacious and sheltered harbour facing Carthage was garrisoned by only a thousand troops. The city also served as the main support base for the whole of the peninsula and therefore contained not only the bulk of the Carthaginians' provisions, but also their treasury and the hostages held against the loyalty of the Spanish tribes. Though the population was large, it consisted entirely of artisans, fishermen and tradesmen with no military training. Scipio also knew the layout of the city and, though there is much scholarly controversy over this, details of the tides which later were to prove of decisive importance.

The Punic armies were dispersed in three locations, all at least three days' march from New Carthage. Mago Barca was west of the Pillars of Hercules (Gibraltar), Hasdrubal Gisco was at the mouth of the Tagus on the west coast, while Hasdrubal was besieging a city in central Spain, not far from modern Madrid. The reasons for these dispositions are obscure, but it seems likely that, as Polybius' account of Scipio's address to his troops suggests, the quarrels and rivalries between the Carthaginian generals prevented them from agreeing to a coordinated campaign. Each went his own way in pursuit of personal ambitions, which would hardly have been fulfilled by electing to remain at New Carthage and ensure its security.

Scipio therefore decided to strike at New Carthage, seize it before relief could arrive, and only then turn to attend to the Punic armies in the field, a task which would be much less hazardous after they had lost their main base, were no longer holding hostages against tribal loyalties, and had been humiliated in front of their Spanish allies. Conceptually a master stroke, it was one which depended for its success on Scipio being able to achieve surprise though concealing his true objective, and then rapidly overcoming the city's resistance.

Scipio could reach New Carthage in seven days, two days quicker that could the two nearest Carthaginian armies lying near Gibraltar and Madrid. But the amount of time Scipio had in hand could be extended if his true objective were to remain concealed: before this became clear it was most unlikely that either Mago or Hasdrubal would attempt to intervene. Given the time news took to travel, at least another four or five days could then be gained, allowing about a week for the actual reduction of the city. But plans seldom survive the first contact of battle, and Scipio's timings were tight – especially if the Carthaginians acted with vigour. On account, therefore, of the need for total security, only Gaius Laelius who commanded the fleet was informed in advance of Scipio's plans.

Leaving 3000 infantry and 300 cavalry to secure his own base and pivot of operations at Terraco, in the spring of 209 BC Scipio marched on New Carthage with 25,000 infantry and 2500 cavalry, while the fleet moved down the coast to coincide its arrival with that of the army. On arriving before the walls of the city, he may well have found the task that lay before him even more daunting than his information had led him to expect. A jutting extension of the coastline formed a near circular bay to its south, the narrow mouth of which was partially corked by an island, leaving only two restricted channels on either side to give access from the sea. The bay itself was partially divided by a hilly promontory pointing out from the eastern shoreline; the inner half to the north forming a shallow lagoon, and the outer southern half a deep water bay. The city lay on the promontory, so was surrounded by water except for a 300-yard wide isthmus joining it to the mainland. Encircled by towering walls and well fortified, New Carthage did not lend itself to quick assault. Establishing his camp on the neck of the isthmus, Scipio first covered his rear by throwing up earthworks and digging a ditch from shore to shore, leaving his front facing the city open so that movement in that direction would not be hindered. The Carthaginian commander, another Mago, armed 2000 of the most stout-hearted citizens and posted them along the walls, concentrating the majority of them on the portion which covered the isthmus. His 1000 regular troops he divided equally between the citadel and an adjacent hill. Distances within the city were not great, so that were these two contingents to act as mobile reserves the dispositions would have been sound. But by all accounts they were not intended to be used in this manner, and instead were only tasked with making a last ditch stand. A hopelessly static tactical concept as events were to show.

The day following his arrival Scipio began his assault. After the fleet, which was well equipped with missiles of every description had encircled the city, a 2000-strong infantry detachment accompanied by ladder bearers moved out of the Roman camp. At the sound of bugles heralding the assault, the armed civilians were ordered to mount a spoiling attack. Considering their lack of training, and the single gate available to them, they fought well. But they were outmatched by the Romans who, having narrowly missed gaining the gate while it was still open, set about scaling the walls. The Romans suffered severe casualties under a hail of missiles, including heavy beams which swept the ladders clean, while other ladders broke under the weight of those swarming up them. When the landward battle was at its height, a party from the ships on the seaward side of the town put in an assault. But although their attack displayed great courage, as Livy dryly comments, 'it resulted, on the whole, in more smoke than fire; for in the course of making the ships fast, landing the men and ladders in a hurry, all being eager to get ashore the quickest way, the race to be first led not to speed but to mutual impediment and confusion.'

That Scipio had hoped to succeed in this first assault is evident, not only from the determination with which it was pressed home, but also from the fact that he was up with the most foremost troops. Protected by three shield bearers, he moved along the line of his attacking troops encouraging and directing them, and able meanwhile to assess the situation for himself – not the action of a commander mounting no more than a diversionary or holding attack. But as the day matured and the casualties mounted without either of the assaulting parties being able to achieve anything, Scipio sounded the retreat before making his next and what was to prove to be decisive move.

While still at Terraco, Scipio had learned from fishermen that when the water ebbed on the afternoon tide, the lagoon forming the northern half of the bay was fordable in a number of places. Under circumstances very similar to Hamilcar Barca's crossing of the salt flats outside Carthage during the Mercenary War, Scipio had already foreseen the possibility of using the lagoon. Now, leading a well-prepared 500-strong contingent directed by guides, he plunged into the receding water, while a simultaneous second attack was mounted along the entire length of the isthmus wall. Anticipating a repetition of the Romans' earlier efforts, the Carthaginians manning the walls were drawn into what they considered to be the critical sector. Scipio was then able to cross the lagoon unperceived and scale the hitherto unassailed northern wall. Once a foothold was secured, resistance crumbled rapidly and the untrained and ill-prepared defenders were either cut down or fled from their posts. The city was then ruthlessly put to the sword, a massacre which was only called off when Mago surrendered the central citadel, after what had in any case been no more than token resistance.

Scipio's tactics merit brief consideration since their combination of careful planning and tactical flexibility in the achievement of surprise has not always been appreciated. Had he relied entirely on the stratagem he was to employ in the afternoon, Scipio would still have produced a clever plan but one lacking flexibility and probably surprise, since Polybius tells us that in the beginning the walls were manned everywhere, so that the chances of being able to move unseen through the lagoon would have been greatly reduced. But as it was, in making what was obviously a determined effort to take the city by direct assault in the morning, Scipio drew the Carthaginians' attention away from the lagoon, so creating a situation which could be exploited later if necessary. The lesson is clear. If surprise can be achieved, by all means play the trump card straight away, but if surprise is uncertain, and the undertaking hazardous, then some preliminary play may well be advisable.

The booty taken in the city was immense and included catapults and great quantities of personal equipment, as well as fully stocked granaries of corn, gold and silver ornaments and coins; while in the harbour lay sixty-three merchant ships, eighteen of which were used to strengthen the Roman fleet. Those of the city's population who survived the butchery were set free – except for 2000 artisans who were decreed state slaves, only to be given their freedom if their work met Roman requirements. Having divided up the booty, Scipio withdrew most of his men from the city and after a brief rest, put them through a period of intensive training. Judging by the changed tactics he subsequently adopted, it was probably now that Scipio introduced the innovations which gave the Romans greater tactical flexibility. Polybius refers to the legionaries learning to run in full armour, and it seems that they also changed their short stabbing swords for the finely tempered, cut-and-thrust Spanish ones, substantial numbers of which would have become available from the city's arsenals, as well as from the Carthaginian dead. The training having been completed and a garrison installed in the city, Scipio withdrew his army and his fleet to Terraco.

In the meanwhile, the three Carthaginian armies had remained inactive in their dispersed locations, and the winter months passed uneventfully as Scipio prepared for the following year's campaign. Now that he was faced with what was inevitably going to be an entirely land battle, Scipio beached his ships and distributed the crews among his legions, so augmenting their overall strength by some 3000 men.

Early in 208 BC Hasdrubal started to make a move. Deserted by a number of the Spanish tribes who saw the Carthaginian hold slackening, cut off without a firm base and still at loggerheads with the other two army commanders, Hasdrubal decided to put everything to the test rather than suffer a remorseless decline. But before leaving his winter quarters at Baecula (Bailén) on the headwaters of the Guadalquivir, he learned that Scipio was advancing towards him. Shifting his camp for the coming battle, Hasdrubal positioned himself on an isolated plateau just south of Baecula, protected by ravines on both flanks, to the front by a valley through which flowed the Guadalquivir, and by one of its tributaries which ran partially round to the rear. Here he had a naturally strong defensive position which would help compensate for his numerical inferiority, probably 25,000 against the Romans 35,000 to 40,000. For two days the armies faced one another, Hasdrubal refusing to be drawn from ground of his own choosing, and Scipio uncertain as to how such a formidable position could best be attacked. On the third day, concerned that Mago Barca and Hasdrubal Gisco would intervene, Scipio moved. First of all he blocked the entrance to the Guadalquivir valley and the road leading out to the north from Baecula, thus providing for his own security and making Hasdrubal's retreat more difficult.

Across the valley from where the Romans stood, the plateau held by the Carthaginians rose in two pronounced terraces. On the lower of these Hasdrubal had thrown forward a screen formed from his

Numidian cavalry, Balearic slingers and some light troops, while the rest of his army was camped on the higher terrace. When the blocking troops were in position, Scipio sent forward his own light troops reinforced by some heavy infantry, against Hasdrubal's screen. After a difficult and costly assault up the slopes to the plateau they had little difficulty in driving back the Carthaginians, who had only been trained for skirmishing at long range and not for hand-to-hand fighting. After reinforcing his leading troops, Scipio ordered them to continue their attack. He then divided the remainder of his army into two; one half he led himself round to the Carthaginians' left flank, while Gaius Laelius, erstwhile commander of the fleet, took the other half round to their right. Hasdrubal, who had initially seen only the advance of the light troops, was slow to appreciate that this was more than just a skirmish and so failed to make a timely deployment, with near fatal consequences. While he was still assembling, first Scipio fell upon one exposed flank, then Laelius upon the other. But it does not appear that anything like all of the Carthaginians were caught in this enveloping movement since Hasdrubal, together with his elephants, baggage train and the greater part of the army, managed to withdraw unmolested and, furthermore, to avoid the blocking position in their rear. According to Polybius, Scipio did nothing further because he was 'afraid of the other two Cathaginian generals; but gave up the enemy's camp to his men to pillage'. The next morning 3000 prisoners, of whom 200 were cavalry, were rounded up, which suggests that a large number of them were Spaniards wishing to desert rather than escape. At any rate, all of them were later released without ransom after the tribal chiefs had assembled to offer their submission.

We have seen how Scipio had broken with the traditional Roman way of waging war in attacking New Carthage, rather than in seeking battle with the Punic armies. Now at Baecula he had broken with Roman tactical doctrine. Neither the ground nor the situation with which he was faced would have permitted Scipio to deploy and fight his legions in drilled and close formation. Although we do not know for certain, the vigorous period of training undertaken after the capture of New Carthage must have been at least partly in preparation for warfare in the broken, hilly heartland of the Iberian peninsula. Almost in imitation of Hannibal at Cannae, Scipio had advanced a weak centre to hold the Carthaginians, before enveloping them with two powerful wings. Though it is clear that the flanking movements had not been properly coordinated (and over such ground this was hardly surprising), there was a more serious failing. On reaching the plateau, control was not swiftly re-established, otherwise Hasdrubal would not have been able to withdraw in such good order. Confronted with the choice of plundering the Carthaginian camp or preventing Hasdrubal's escape, the legionaries succumbed to the temptations of personal gain. But this apart, Scipio's tactical innovations had loosened up the battlefield and, by permitting greater flexibility, had provided new means to achieve surprise.

Hasdrubal's objectives are harder to assess. Livy says that he had already decided to join Hannibal in Italy, but if this was so, the reasons for him electing to stand and fight at Baecula remain obscure. Once he had been defeated, however, he lost no time in abandoning Spain and setting forth. He probably followed the Douro up to its headwaters, before crossing the Pyrenees on the Atlantic seaboard. That Scipio let him escape in this manner has been the subject of much criticism. But after failing to trap him at Baecula, to have attempted a pursuit, always threatened by ambush through unknown, mountainous and hostile country, without any logistic provisioning, and leaving two fresh Carthaginian armies to his rear, would have been highly foolish. Scipio's father had desisted from pursuing Hannibal after he had set out for Italy on leaving the Rhone; the son was wise to follow his example ten years later. The only measure he could take was to block the eastern passes over the Pyrenees, possibly using garrison troops from Emporiae, though Polybius says he 'detached a body of men', implying that they were from his own army. As winter was approaching, Scipio then withdrew again to his base at Terraco.

Early the next year, 207 BC, the Carthaginians landed further reinforcements in Spain under Hanno who joined Mago Barca, then busy recruiting Celtiberians from what is now Aragon and old Castile. Scipio was now faced with a double threat. If he moved into the interior to break up the powerful army being formed by Mago and Hanno, he could find Hasdrubal Gisco, who had advanced from Gades into Andalusia, astride his rear. He therefore detached Silanus with 10,000 infantry and 500 cavalry to deal with this concentration. Marching with great rapidity Silanus achieved complete surprise. After first falling upon the camp of the Celtiberian recruits which, not being properly guarded, was quickly overrun, Silanus then turned to deal with the Carthaginians. But Mago was not prepared to give battle and withdrew to Gades. Hanno and a number of Carthaginians who had failed to escape were taken prisoner, and the Celtiberian recruits dispersed to the four winds. It had been a neat, well-executed operation which drew Scipio's unstinted praise, especially as it now allowed him to concentrate his forces against Hasdrubal Gisco. But the Carthaginian general avoided a major battle by splitting his army among the various cities, knowing that if he adopted a policy of passive defence during the winter, Scipio would be most unlikely to sap his strength in trying to undertake a series of costly sieges. A supposition which proved to be correct, when shortly afterwards Scipio withdrew to prepare for the next year's campaign.

In 206 BC the Carthaginians made a final great effort to recover their Spanish possessions, when Mago and Hasdrubal Gisco concentrated at Ilipa, some ten miles north of modern Seville, with 50,000 infantry and 4500 cavalry for a decisive battle. Scipio at once marched to meet them, though his army was considerably smaller: 40,000 infantry and 3000 cavalry. Encamping on some low hills, Scipio then paused to assess the situation. The fate that had overtaken his father's army had taught him not to rely overmuch on his Spanish mercenaries, yet the Roman legions on their own could not hope to defeat such numbers. Scipio then devised a plan whereby he would use the Spaniards to threaten and mislead the enemy, but leave the real fighting to his own legions. But while the Romans were still establishing their camp, Mago mounted a spoiling attack using most of his cavalry, including the Numidians under Masinissa. Ever mindful of security, however, and ready for such an emergency, Scipio had concealed his own cavalry behind one of the hills. Appearing unexpectedly at full gallop they threw the Carthaginians into confusion, and for the next few days the armies confronted one another across the valley from the two low ridges they had occupied, advancing as if to join in battle but always withdrawing. On each occasion Scipio let the Carthaginians make the first move, both to assemble and then at the end of the day, withdraw. In this manner Hasdrubal became familiar with the Romans' deployment; the legions were posted in the centre opposite the Carthaginian and Libyan regulars, with the Spanish mercenaries on the wings of both armies. But on the day he decided to give battle, Scipio changed his pattern.

After having been given a warning order the previous evening, the Roman camp was astir at dawn as the men breakfasted and the horses were watered and fed. When the light improved, skirmishers and cavalry were sent out to drive in the Carthaginian outposts and demonstrate before their main positions. Shortly afterwards, just as the sun was appearing above the horizon, Scipio marched out with the infantry and on reaching the middle of the plain reversed the order of his usual deployment, the Spanish mercenaries being moved into the centre and replaced on the wings by the legions. Startled by the sudden appearance of the Roman cavalry, the Carthaginians rushed to arm themselves and deploy; there was no time to have a meal, let alone to consider changing their own deployment to match that of the Romans. For the early part of the morning Scipio made no move, but let the skirmishing between the light troops continue. Eventually judging the critical moment to have arrived, he recalled his cavalry and light troops through the gaps between the *maniples* and positioned them behind his two wings. The light troops then stood immediately behind the legions, with the cavalry to their rear.

When all was ready, the advance was ordered but at different paces. From Polybius' account it is difficult to follow exactly how the two wings manoeuvered. Livy on the other hand, may not be correct in detail but at least has the merit of being comprehensible.

Ordering the Spaniards, who formed the centre, to advance slowly, Scipio, from the right wing where he commanded in person, sent orders to Silanus and Marcius to watch his extension towards the right and to match it by a simultaneous extension of their men to the left, and to bring their light infantry and cavalry into action before the two centres had time to engage. Thus with extended wings and three cohorts of infantry and three troops of cavalry with each, supported by light skirmishers, they advanced at a smart pace against the enemy, the rest following to complete the outflanking movement. The centre formed a concave line, where the Spanish auxiliaries were moving forward more slowly.

The only comment to be made on this account is that the battle plan must have been talked over between the commanders beforehand; had there been a need to give detailed orders, these would probably have become heavily distorted in their transmission.

Through manoeuvring in this manner the Romans were able to overlap the Carthaginians, who now found their only half-trained Spaniards on the wings being attacked frontally by the Roman legions, and on the flanks by their light troops and cavalry. The veteran Carthaginians and Libyans in the centre could only stand by helplessly, fearing to be attacked frontally should they turn to help their hard-pressed wings; while had they attempted to advance against the Spaniards, who were still out of missile range, they would have broken formation and left themselves open to attack from the rear. It is also extremely doubtful, after their army had been so completely surprised and was now caught up in mid-battle, whether such a decision could have been arrived at, let alone executed.

Now, as the wings crumbled, the Carthaginian army, which was already beginning to tire from hunger and fatigue, suffered a further blow when their elephants, maddened by the stinging attacks of the Roman cavalry on the wings, were driven in upon the centre. Thoroughly demoralised and confused, the Carthaginians started to withdraw. To begin with this movement was conducted in a reasonably orderly manner, but as the entire Roman line was brought into action, the Carthaginians broke ranks to seek refuge in their camp, sheltered by the hills, and a massacre was only averted by a sudden cloudburst which brought all organised movement to a mud-bound standstill. But this provided little lasting respite: instead of being able to get some much-needed rest, the Carthaginians were obliged to strengthen the defences of their camp against the inevitable Roman attack the next morning. As darkness began to fall, however, their Spanish allies started to desert in increasing numbers and Hasdrubal, fearful of seeing his army disappear altogether, quietly assembled his troops and slipped away during the night.

As dawn broke, the Roman forward outposts reported the Carthaginians gone and Scipio ordered the cavalry to begin an immediate pursuit, with the rest of the army to march hard on their heels. This time there was to be no repetition of what had occurred at Baecula. Though led astray by their guides when trying to get ahead of Hasdrubal by taking a short cut, the cavalry caught up with him and delayed his progress until the infantry were able, in the words of Livy, 'to turn what had been a battlefield into a slaughterhouse'. Only Hasdrubal and 6000 of his men escaped into the neighbouring hills, where they fortified one of the highest summits. Though reasonably secure, they were without food or water, their position was hopeless, and there was a constant stream of deserters. Finally recognising that all was lost, Hasdrubal abandoned his troops, made for the sea and eventually escaped to Gades. Seeing that the surrender of the remainder of the Carthaginians was only a matter of time, Scipio left Silanus with 10,000 men to wind up the battle while he withdrew to what, in view of his subsequent movements, was probably New Carthage, though Livy says it was Terraco. He spent seventy days on the journey, negotiating with the various tribes whose territory he passed through, before setting sail for North Africa. Here he sought to secure the support of Syphax and in so doing, narrowly escaped capture by Hasdrubal who was also bent on seeking the Numidian prince's support. But later, in the sanctuary of their host's camp, the two opponents sat down together on the same couch, being dined by a no doubt greatly intrigued Syphax.

The battle of Ilipa had been a tactical masterpiece, showing how a small army can defeat a sustantially larger one by manoeuvre; a capability which Scipio had been able to develop following his introduction of a more flexible organisation. As at Baecula, the Romans had fought in three separate contingents but in pursuit of a fully coordinated plan, which itself was remarkable for its skilful exploitation of surprise. First, the early deployment of the army and the unexpectedness of its dispositions threw the Carthaginians off balance, both mentally and physically, before the battle had even begun. Second, while the Carthaginians main fighting force was held in hopeless inactivity, their wings were crushed by a rapid and unexpected concentration of force. Finally, the Romans' vigorous exploitation of their victory caught the withdrawing Carthaginians totally unprepared.

Though after Ilipa no Carthaginian army remained to oppose them, it took another year of hard campaigning before the Romans could bring Spain fully under their control. Scipio acted with ruthless cruelty in suppressing those towns which now held out against him, or had sided with the Carthaginians in the past. In the Segura valley the entire population of Ilurgia (Lorca) was massacred after resisting fiercely and refusing to surrender; while further west at Astapa, the men immolated their families before sallying out to die in battle. Even if some severe lessons were necessary, and leaving aside the moral aspect, such extreme conduct would appear to be self-defeating. It was, however, no harsher than the punishment Scipio handed out to his own men. A mutiny among base troops at Sucro, suffering from inactivity and disgruntled by arrears of pay, was put to an end when they were lured to New Carthage with promises of payment, suddenly surrounded by loyal troops, and the thirty-eight ringleaders, after being paraded, were stripped, scourged and finally beheaded.

The last flicker of Carthaginian resistance occurred while Scipio was suppressing a tribal revolt north of the Ebro. Mago Barca, who had taken refuge in Gades, the one city of consequence still held by the Carthaginians, made a bold attempt to capture New Carthage but was easily repulsed. After being debarred from re-entering Gades, he retired to the Balearic Islands, and shortly afterwards the city voluntarily went over to the Romans, an act of submission which earned Gades the status of a free city. It was also at Gades that Scipio made contact with Masinissa, the great Numidian leader who was to dominate the scene in Africa for the next fifteen years.

Fourteen years after it had begun and the fifth since Scipio had taken command, the war in Spain was over. But to maintain their hold over the unruly tribes, the Romans had to retain an army of four strong legions year after year in the peninsula. The old Roman custom of not keeping men under arms for more than a year, except when faced with a national crisis, had to be abandoned. The long and arduous time spent in Spain led to discontent within the legions, and even mutiny when grievances went unredressed. Though they had acquired the wealth of Spain, the Romans found little respite as rebellion after rebellion broke out, every year requiring them to reduce some remote mountain area peopled with recalcitrant tribes. Other than fulfilling the overriding requirement to evict the Carthaginians, the conquest of Spain can have brought the Romans few benefits.

Much credit, however, should be given to the Senate and the Roman people for the determination and perseverance they had displayed, especially when faced with such a desperate situation at home. The Carthaginian hold on Spain had been irrevocably broken, resulting not only in Hannibal's loss of an independent base but also in the end of the Punic domination of the western Mediterranean. As for Scipio, he was not content to rest on his laurels but turned his thoughts to Africa. Like Agathocles and Marcus Atilius Regulus before him, he wanted to carry the war to the Carthaginians' homeland, well knowing that once this was done the remaining edifice of the Punic empire would collapse. But before these events are related, we must roll back the years and see what had been happening elsewhere.

CHAPTER SIXTEEN

SARDINIA, SICILY AND ILLYRIA
215–205 BC

Sardinia 215 BC

In 215 BC, the year after Cannae, Carthaginian activity in pursuit of their strategy to encircle Italy reached a peak. Following Hasdrubal's defeat at Ibera, two new armies under Mago Barca and Hasdrubal the Bald were dispatched to Spain, while a third smaller one sailed to Sardinia. Moreover in Italy, although Mago had been diverted to Spain instead of being able to join his brother as originally planned, Hannibal received some reinforcements which, after avoiding a Roman fleet off Sicily, were landed at Locri. But the expedition to Sardinia, under Hasdrubal the Bald, completely miscarried when it ran into a storm. Driven off course, the transports had to take shelter in the Balearic Islands, where they were hauled ashore for repair. A considerable delay followed as not only had the ships' superstructures been badly damaged, but their hulls had also been strained. Now alerted to the Carthaginians' intentions, the Romans reinforced the legion already in Sardinia with an additional legion commanded by Titus Manlius Torquatus, who knew the island well having served there previously as a consul.

Anticipating the arrival of the Carthaginian force, the Sardinians had risen in revolt but were scattered by Manlius Torquatus, who wasted no time in suppressing them once his own troops were ashore. Hasdrubal was eventually able to make a landing at Cornus and succeeded in rallying a number of the Sardinians to march on Caralis (Cagliari), but this force was too small and after being outmatched in a disastrous engagement, he was taken prisoner and the survivors fled to their ships, only to cross the path of a Roman raiding force returning

Illyria, Southern Italy and the Peloponnese

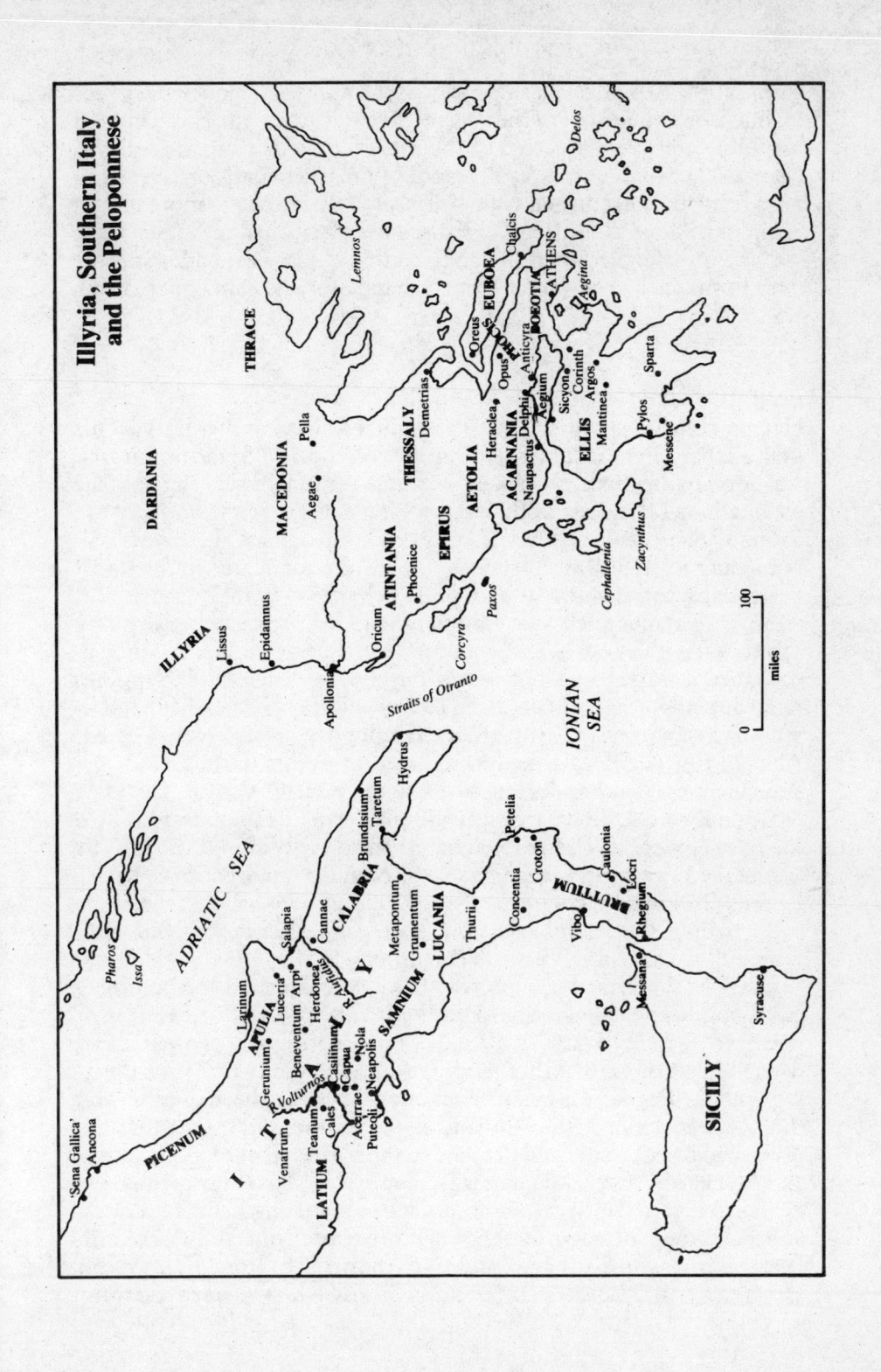

from North Africa; seven ships were lost and the remainder scattered. Hampsicora, the leader of the Sardinian revolt, committed suicide and his followers were subjected to the usual ferocious Roman reprisals. Manlius Torquatus soon had control of the island and, order having been restored, he returned with his legion to Italy, where more urgent business awaited them. The Carthaginian strategy had suffered its first setback. No further attempt to recover Sardinia was made, and the island remained securely in Roman hands for the remainder of the war.

Sicily 215–210 BC

Having concluded a treaty with Hannibal following the death of his grandfather Hiero in 215 BC, King Hieronymus of Syracuse himself was soon to die. In 214 BC a wave of popular reaction set in against the ostentatious behaviour of the young king and his desertion from the Roman alliance. While leading an expedition against the towns still remaining loyal to Rome, Hieronymus was assassinated in the midst of his army and the pro-Roman party seized power in Syracuse. But their arrogant conduct, and wanton cruelty towards those in any way connected with Hiero's family, so revolted the Syracusans that they in their turn were deposed. In the elections that were then held to appoint two captain generals, Hannibal's envoys Hippocrates and Epicydes, who had remained in Sicily after arranging the treaty, were elected. Already thoroughly alarmed at the turn of events in the island, the Romans sent another legion, led by the consul Marcus Claudius Marcellus who had been commanding an army in Italy, to reinforce the two legions which had been banished to Sicily after Cannae. The size of the Roman fleet was also increased and a hundred ships, under Appius Claudius Pulcher (son of the Claudius who had lost the battle of Drepana), were sent to demonstrate off Syracuse, but this only served to harden anti-Roman feeling there.

In 213 BC the Syracusans received a request for help from Leontini, a city lying near the front line with the Romans which was in fear of imminent attack. They sent Hippocrates with 4000 of their most determined troops to bolster the garrison, who soon started skirmishing with the Roman outposts. After one of these had been overrun and the occupants killed, the Romans informed the Syracusans that the peace had been broken and demanded the banishment of Hippocrates and Epicydes. After his demands were refused, Marcellus stormed the city and subjected it to the usual carnage culminating in the scourging and beheading of 2000 of those who had been the most active in bearing arms for Carthage, some of whom were Roman deserters. Hippocrates and Epicydes were among those who managed to escape to Syracuse, where they had little difficulty in inflaming the anti-Roman sentiments of the army and most of the population. The massacre at Leontini was then avenged by the butchery of those belonging to the pro-Roman faction. So Syracuse, great capital of western Hellenism, abandoned Rome for Carthage and after twenty-five years of peace, war returned to Sicily in a bloodbath of spiralling violence.

Flushed with their success of taking Leontini in the first assault, the Romans marched on the sprawling city of Syracuse. But here they faced more formidable defences. Syracuse had been founded by the Corinthians in the 8th century BC on the island of Ortygia (Quail Island), but as the city grew it had spread on to the adjacent mainland, where a massive rocky outcrop butted into the sea. Climbing the southern slopes onto the triangular shaped plateau of Epipolae, with its base running parallel to the shoreline, Achradina formed the first of the suburbs into which the city was now divided. In the 5th century BC two further suburbs were created, Neapolis and Tyche. The former by now had begun to encroach onto the western limits of the plateau, with the latter building up below it to the south; while Achradina had extended yet further to cover most of the coastal strip of land lying below the plateau's eastern seaboard. The whole of this natural defensive position was rendered almost impregnable during the 4th century BC by Dionysius, when encircling walls were raised around the lips of the plateau, with the fortress of Euryalus guarding its apex on to the west.

As Polybius relates, these already formidable defences were now yet further strengthened. 'The Romans did not take into account the abilities of Archimedes, nor calculate the truth that, in certain circumstances, the genius of one man is more effective than sheer numbers. However they now learned it by experience.' A friend and relation of Hiero's, Archimedes had designed a variety of machines capable of throwing the largest of boulders and an assortment of other missiles over varying ranges. Along the sea walls of Achradina, he had also positioned huge swinging beams capable of dropping immense weights, or alternatively grappling the bows of ships and after lifting them up vertically, releasing them stern first back into the water. Now an old man of seventy-four, Archimedes was about to supervise his machines in action.

After establishing themselves before the walls of Syracuse, the Romans mounted two assaults, one from the land and the other from the sea. Approximately in its middle the northern face of the plateau was broken by a ravine, up which ran a road giving access to the city. From here, where the break in the cliff face rendered the walls less formidable, Claudius Pulcher mounted his assault, only to be driven back by the determined resistance of the Syracusans. To the east

Claudius Marcellus had run his ships with their siege engines close against the walls of Achradina. But this was where the defences had been strengthened by the contrivances designed by Archimedes, so this second attack came to nothing and was called off after incurring heavy losses. Thoroughly startled, the Romans withdrew to lick their wounds and settle down to a prolonged siege.

Not all the Roman strength, however, was concentrated against Syracuse. Elsewhere there were cities in revolt which had to be suppressed, while others, such as Lilybaeum and Panormus, needed to be garrisoned. It was on duties such as these that the disgraced legions had so far been employed, and a plea for their wider use was curtly dismissed by the Senate. As for the Carthaginians, Himilco, who had been commanding the small Punic fleet off Cape Pachynus with orders to watch events, had returned to Carthage and urged resolute action in support of the Syracusans. In spite of the demands of Spain where two new armies had just been sent as reinforcements, and a revolt by the Numidians, an expeditionary force of 25,000 infantry, 3000 cavalry and twelve elephants was sent to Sicily, where it was landed on the south coast. Here Heraclea Minoa and the great city of Agrigentum, which had both been Carthaginian strongholds during the First Punic War, opened their gates to the invaders. Encouraged by this lead, a number of other towns quickly declared for Carthage and the Syracusans also decided that they should act. Leaving Epicydes to defend the city, Hippocrates with 10,000 infantry and 500 cavalry slipped out of Syracuse and through the Roman lines to join Himilco. But Marcellus, who was returning from an expedition to recover some of the inland towns lost to the Carthaginians, surprised the Sicilians as they were pitching camp. Only the cavalry with Hippocrates at their head managed to escape to Acrae, some fifteen miles west of Syracuse.

In spite of this tactical victory, the overall situation was deteriorating for the Romans. The Carthaginian fleet had gained a temporary dominance and thirty-five of their ships now rode at anchor in the Great Harbour of Syracuse. What had happened to the powerful Roman fleet remains something of a mystery. Perhaps a part of it had been used to carry the reinforcements which were later landed at Panormus, and some of it may have still been refitting after the assault against the walls of Achradina. But whatever the reasons for the Roman absence, the Carthaginian fleet had been able to break the blockade of Syracuse. Meanwhile, ashore, at the approach of Hippocrates, Marcellus had withdrawn behind the banks of the river Anapus, which ran from west to east a mile to the south of Syracuse.

But this Carthaginian ascendency was soon to end. Following the landing of a fresh Roman legion at Panormus, with their flank to the sea covered by the fleet, the Romans then avoided Himilco and Hippocrates who were waiting to trap them some eight miles west of Syracuse and marched along the northern coast road to Cape Pelorias, before turning south to Syracuse.

With the safe arrival of these reinforcements, the Roman strength in Sicily had now been raised to four legions, and the tide of the campaign started to turn against the Carthaginians. Bomilcar, the commander of the Punic fleet, no longer felt secure in the Great Harbour and withdrew to Carthage, while Himilco, seeing that he could not hope to raise the siege of Syracuse, moved away into the interior. Here the Romans had been reasserting their authority by ruthlessly exterminating any signs of opposition; suspecting that Enna was about to go over to the Carthaginians, they had recently seized the city and massacred the unarmed population. As winter approached and the campaigning season for 213 BC drew to a close, Himilco retired to Agrigentum, Hippocrates to the inland city of Morgantina, while Marcellus, after putting a garrison into Leontini, constructed a winter camp for himself at Leon, five miles north of Syracuse. To the south of the city, the Roman camp near the Olympieum was occupied by the legate Titius Quintus Crispinus, leaving Appius Claudius Pulcher free to return to Rome in search of a consulship for the following year.

In 212 BC the apparent stalemate was broken when a deserter to the Roman camp reported that the Syracusans had been celebrating the festival of Artemis for the last three days. Since the wine was flowing freely, and there were more unsteady legs around than clear heads, Marcellus decided to try and take the city by surprise. A scaling party mounted the northern wall under cover of darkness, and opened the Hexapylon gate to the remainder of the army just before dawn. By the time Epicydes learned of these developments, the Romans had swarmed forward to secure virtually the whole of the Epipolae, together with the suburbs of Neapolis and Tyche. But their further progress was barred by the old wall encircling the original settlement of Achradina, while the impregnable fortress of Euryalus dominated their right flank. After plundering Neapolis and Tyche, the Romans remained inactive for the next two days until the Greek commander of Euryalus lost his nerve and surrendered the fort in return for his life. The danger of Himilco encircling the Roman rear was then removed, and when he did arrive his attack on the Roman camp to the south of the city came to nothing; while a sortie by Epicydes from Achradina was also beaten back. Once more the Roman fleet had disappeared from the scene and Bomilcar, who had returned again to Syracuse, managed to slip out and return with a fleet of ninety ships which, favoured by a strong wind, entered the Great Harbour unopposed.

After leaving a part of his fleet to support the city, Bomilcar then sailed out once more bound for North Africa.

The whole situation in Sicily was now to change. Suddenly, as had repeatedly occurred during earlier stages throughout the centuries, a virulent plague swept through the armies. Camped on the low-lying ground during the oppressive heat of high summer, near the pestilential marshes at the mouth of the Anapus and probably none too concerned with sanitation, the Carthaginians were the hardest hit. Deserted by the Sicilians who had taken to the hills at the first signs of the plague, the Carthaginians were decimated, with Himilco and Hippocrates dying among their men. Though the Romans and the Syracusans holding out in Achradina and Ortygia also suffered, because they were on the high ground and further removed from the marshes they were not so severely afflicted.

In the spring of 211 BC, the Carthaginians made a supreme effort to relieve Syracuse. Bomilcar was once more dispatched with a fleet, this time of 130 warships and an even larger number of transports laden with supplies. After reaching the Sicilian coast near Agrigentum, these turned towards Cape Pachynus but were almost at once checked by an easterly wind. A further obstacle also appeared in the form of the Roman fleet, which had put to sea and was now lingering off the east coast between Syracuse and Cape Pachynus. Fearful of Rome's determination, Epicydes ran the gauntlet to impress upon Bomilcar the urgency of the situation and the need to force a passage. Bomilcar accordingly left the transports at Heraclea and closed the warships up to Cape Pachynus, where he waited for the strong easterly wind to abate. The Carthaginians were then the first to move.

Standing out to sea they started to double the cape, but the sight of the Roman fleet bearing down on him was too much for Bomilcar's nerves. Sending orders for the transports to return to Africa, he himself carried straight on out to sea before veering north and steering for Tarentum, where Hannibal was laying siege to the citadel. No doubt Bomilcar's arrival was of assistance in preventing further supplies from reaching the beleagured garrison, but his pusillanimous conduct can hardly be defended. Meanwhile Epicydes had taken refuge in Agrigentum, from where he was soon busy assisting Hanno with the fresh army he was to bring with him from North Africa. Hannibal meanwhile, no doubt concerned at the poor progress being made in the Sicilian campaign, had sent Muttines, one of his best cavalry generals, over from Italy. But the inadequacy of the Carthaginian fleet was not only to prove fateful to the campaign in Sicily but also, as will be seen, it was to impede the campaign being conducted by Philip of Macedon.

Abandoned and leaderless, the cosmopolitan garrison in Syracuse, which included many Roman deserters and others who could expect short shrift if taken alive, began to look to its own interests. A Spanish mercenary commander entered into negotiations with Marcellus and, by opening one of the gates on Ortygia, ended a siege of two-and-a-half years as the Romans poured in to secure the whole of the city. After taking possession of the royal treasures for display in Rome and, for some unknown reason, allowing the Roman deserters to leave unmolested, Marcellus gave Syracuse over to plunder by the troops. Three centuries of civilisation and high culture were uncomprehendingly ravaged and looted, while the population suffered a similar fate. Among those who died in the massacre was Archimedes, allegedly while still pondering over some abstruse geometrical problem. Those who did survive were spared the further horrors of famine by the action of the commander of the Roman fleet, Titus Otacilius, who had been raiding the city of Utica a few days before the fall of Syracuse from his base at Lilybaeum. He had seized 130 laden Carthaginian stores ships, probably belonging to Bomilcar's aborted relief fleet, and after returning to Lilybaeum had sent them on to Syracuse where, according to Livy, their timely arrival saved victor and vanquished alike.

The war in Sicily was now coming to a close as the leaders of the various cities accepted defeat and began to make their peace with the Romans; though there were some that still held out, well knowing the fate that awaited them should they be taken alive. During this unsettled period, Marcellus returned to Rome to give an account of his campaign – but because the war had not yet been won, he had to make do with an ovation rather than a triumph. It was, however, a fairly grand affair during which his battle trophies and the treasures recovered from Syracuse were given public display, a proceeding only marred by the news that yet another Carthaginian army had been disembarked in Sicily. These were the 8000 infantry and 3000 Numidian cavalry which had been brought over to Agrigentum by Hanno, and which Epicydes and Hannibal's cavalry general Muttines had joined.

This new display of Punic determination rekindled hope among a number of cities, leading them once again to rise against Rome. The Carthaginians initially met with considerable success, as the Numidian cavalry under Muttines wreaked havoc throughout the island, especially upon the agricultural land belonging to those cities in alliance with Rome – a task which was greatly simplified by the dissatisfaction, in many cases bordering on mutiny, felt by the legions which had not been allowed to return to Italy with Marcellus; while those which had recently arrived in exile after their defeat at Herdonea (Ordano) in Italy carried the additional stigma of not being allowed to winter in towns.

The situation was only restored in the late summer of 210 BC, when the consul Marcus Valerius Laevinus arrived to give renewed direction to the campaign. As for the Carthaginians, the specular successes of Muttines as he swept throughout Sicily at the head of his Numidians had aroused the jealous envy of Hanno, more prosaically left to garrison Agrigentum. Muttines was therefore deprived of his command and replaced by Hanno's own son. Such insulting behaviour was to complete the downfall of the Carthaginians and so to the irrevocable loss of Sicily. Following negotiations with Laevinus, the Numidians defected to the Romans and after killing the Carthaginian guards, opened the gates of Agrigentum. Hanno and Epicydes escaped from the city with a few of their closest followers to the harbour from where, after finding a small boat, they were able to continue their flight to Carthage. Fifty-one years after Agrigentum had submitted to the insenate blood lust of one victorious Roman army during the First Punic war, a second was now let loose on the unfortunate population. Thronging the approaches to the barred gates, those trying to escape were cut down while, rather more discriminately, the leaders of the city were subjected to the customary ritual of chastisement and decapitation.

Roman authority was soon firmly established throughout the island, and a senatorial committee arrived to draw up a new settlement. Those cities which had remained loyal to Rome throughout the war were given special privileges, with Messana, Tauromenium and Neetum receiving particular recognition in being granted both immunity from taxation and a near total independence. But less favoured parts of the island, which included sixty towns that had sided with the Carthaginians, suffered punitive confiscations, besides having to pay a tax in kind of 10 per cent on all their produce. These confiscations led to the accumulation of boundless estates by individual opportunistic Romans and Sicilians. The labour to work these new properties was readily at hand from among the survivors of the cities sacked by the Romans, who had then been either sold or forced into slavery.

Throughout the war the Senate, and in the field Marcellus, had displayed vigour and determination in its prosecution, but the part played by the Roman fleet is less impressive. As the tasks placed upon it are not known, however, care must be taken not to assume that it was necessarily incomptently handled by its various commanders. It is clear from both Polybius and Livy that the fleet was primarily based on Lilybaeum, where it not only protected this former great Carthaginian stronghold, but was available to raid the north African coastline. But the fleet appears to have been employed on such a variety of other tasks as well that it was incapable of fulfilling any of them thoroughly. While it had certainly deterred the Carthaginians from trying to recover Lilybaeum, it had repeatedly failed to intercept Bomilcar as he crossed to and fro from the ports of North Africa with what at times were huge and unwieldy numbers of ships. Cooperation with the army also appears to have been indifferent. Though flank protection was provided to the reinforcements disembarked at Panormus while they marched along the northern coast on their way to Syracuse, little was done to enforce an effective close blockade on the city. There were clearly many calls upon the fleet, including countering Philip's moves in the Adriatic and those of the Carthaginians off Sardinia, but this only made it all the more necessary to determine clear priorities. If blame is to be apportioned it must therefore lie with the Senate for not providing clearer strategic direction in the conduct of the war.

As for the Carthaginians, unlike their response during the First Punic War, they had made the most strenuous and consistent exertions to raise the necessary forces. Two expeditionary armies had been sent to Sicily, the first under Himilco and the second under Hanno, which together had numbered nearly 40,000 men. Additionally, a powerful fleet and a huge number of supply ships had been constructed, manned and put to sea. All this had been done while simultaneously conducting a major campaign in Spain. But these vast outpourings of manpower and wealth had achieved nothing of permanence in the absence of competent field commanders. Himilco had shown himself to be courageous and vigorous, but lacking inspirational leadership and professional skill. Hanno can be dismissed as a small-minded incompetent more concerned with his own image and safety than fighting. Bomilcar was little better: though undoubtedly an accomplished mariner, when it came to actually having to fight he proved himself a coward. Both he and Hanno were fortunate that the Carthaginians had discontinued their earlier practice of nailing unsuccessful generals to the cross.

Given such poor leadership it is then hardly surprising that the Carthaginians failed, but they had also suffered more than their fair share of bad luck. Had the Syracusans been quicker to decide where their allegiances lay, the Romans would not have been allowed the three precious years' breathing space after Cannae. Then there was the plague, and the sudden change of wind and weather which disruped Bomilcar's fleet when on passage to Syracuse. But even allowing for all that, the fact remains that poor generalship lost Sicily for the Carthaginians and, with its loss, their strategy of encircling Italy suffered an irretrievable reverse. The course of the war overseas had unmistakably turned against them.

Illyria 215–205 BC

Though the campaigns in Spain, Sardinia and Sicily had involved the local populations, they had all primarily been concerned with a direct clash between Roman and Carthaginian interests. But the campaign in lower Illyria introduced a new dimension. Philip of Macedon had been looking east far more than west, and his involvements there had to be concluded before he could honour his treaty undertakings with Hannibal. Macedonia was but one of the four great states in the east, the others being Persia, Syria and Egypt, but apart from difficulties in maintaining a power balance among them, there were also the Gauls and the Illyrians to contend with. Both of these had been pressing on Macedonia's borders, while to the south the Greeks were in almost permanent revolt against Macedonian oppression. In relation to her size and ambitions the population of Macedonia was sparse, the country having been largely depopulated as a result of the campaigns of Alexander the Great in the previous century and the subsequent policy of colonisation.

In 217 BC Philip was at war with the Aetolians on his southern frontier when he heard of the Roman defeat at Trasimene, news that had been brought to him by couriers from Macedon. Philip showed the letter to Demetrius of Pharos, who immediately urged him to invade Illyria and send an expedition to Italy. But before reaching such a momentous decision, Philip entered into discussions with his closest advisers and friends, and these resulted in him deciding to make peace with the Aetolians. There then followed a period of considerable uncertainty and deliberation throughout the Peloponnesus, as Polybius relates:

The affairs of Greece, Italy and Libya being connected as a whole; for none of the leading statesmen of the Greek cities made war or peace with each other with a view to Greek affairs, but were all fixing their eyes on Italy. Nor was it long before the islanders and the inhabitants of Asia were affected in the same way; for those who had quarrels with Attalus [Persia], no longer turned to Antiochus [Syria] or Ptolemy [Egypt], to the south or east, but from this time forth fixed their eyes on the west, some sending embassies to Carthage, others to Rome.

So the political separation of east from west was ended, with Philip leading the way.

Late in 217 BC Philip had decided that if he were to have the freedom of manoeuvre he required to wage war against the Romans, he would need to be able to move his army by sea. During the winter he therefore constructed a fleet of 100 vessels, designed to serve solely as rowed transports since he appreciated that there could be no question of him challenging Roman naval supremacy. Having had the vessels fitted out and undertaken a hurried period of training, in 216 BC he mounted an expedition against Apollonia on the Illyrian coast but turned his ships back in haste on hearing that a Roman fleet was approaching – even though this was before an open breach with Rome had occurred. After this fiasco there was near total inactivity until 215 BC, when the Romans took the initiative.

Having captured Philip's envoys to Hannibal and learned of the looming danger from Macedonia, the Senate decided that rather than wait on the defensive, they would keep Philip out of Italy by taking the offensive themselves. A fleet of fifty ships was assembled at Tarentum under Valerius Flaccus, who was ordered to do what he could to keep Philip occupied in Illyria. At the same time Marcus Valerius Laevinus was given command at Brundisium with instructions simply to repel any landing on the Calabrian coast. But when Philip captured Oricum and threatened Apollonia on the Illyrian coast directly opposite him, Valerius Flaccus acted swiftly. He recaptured Oricum and moved into Apollonia, surprising Philip in his camp outside the city. Forced to abandon his expedition, which according to Livy had been mounted only because these coastal towns would provide suitable bases for an attack on Italy, Philip now burned his boats and withdrew overland back to Macedonia.

As for the Romans, well pleased with this quick and easy success, with winter now approaching they retired to Oricum, where they were to remain until the following year. It was in 215 BC after the battle of Cannae that Philip and Hannibal had drawn up their treaty but no conflict of consequence arose in Illyria until 214 BC, when Philip attacked Messene in the extreme southwest of the Peloponnesus. His expedition failed and Demetrius of Pharos fell in the fighting, causing Philip to seek revenge by ravaging the surrounding country side with, as Polybius observes, 'more passion than reason'. Having thoroughly stirred up the Peloponnesus to no purpose, Philip now turned his attention to Illyria, and in 213 BC he acted with skill and vigour when he invaded Roman-held territory. After mauling two tribes in alliance with the Romans, he marched rapidly north to bypass Apollonia and seize the coastal town of Lissus. Philip achieved the capture of Lissus, which was no small feat, by concealing a part of his army, then luring the garrison out against what they thought to be a contemptuously inadequate force. The trap was neatly sprung, complete surprise was achieved and the citadel occupied with hardly a blow having to be struck. Though reducing the remainder of the city proved to be a more hard-fought affair, it was successfully completed the following day. Not only had Philip gained access to the sea, but by taking a notoriously well-defended city with such rapidity, he induced a number of others to surrender.

In 212 BC Laevinus moved to counter Philip's menacing stance by entering into negotiations to form an anti-Macedonian league from among the discontented Greek states. Headed by Rome's old allies the Aetolians, the league was quickly joined by Messene, Elis and, two years later, by Sparta, by Athens and by Attalus of Pergamun, on the west coast of modern day Turkey, as well as the Illyrian and Thracian tribes. Such an initiative represented something of a diplomatic coup which effectively bound Philip to Greece, while permitting the Romans to restrict their commitment almost entirely to their fleet. The Greeks then shouldered the main burden of the war which, as far as they were concerned, was to be directed primarily against Philip's Greek allies. The war then developed into a familar internecine struggle of Greek against Greek which, apart from keeping the Macedonians involved, had little direct bearing on the struggle between Carthage and Rome.

Realising that he must secure his northern frontier before being drawn down to the south, Philip exploited the powerful hold he had obtained in Illyria following the capture of Lissus. Moving suddenly, he marched down the coast to devastate the countryside around Apollonia and Oricum, driving the garrison back behind the city walls when they ventured out to engage him. Then turning north he moved with equal swiftness to capture Sintia, an unlocated Dardanian town which could have been used as a base from which to launch an attack on Macedonia. He then struck east to settle matters in Thrace and Thessaly on the Aegean seaboard, where news was brought him that, in the south, the Aetolians were attacking his allies the Acarnanians. Mere reports of his approach, however, were enough to frighten the Aetolians into withdrawing, so permitting Philip to return to the Macedonian city of Pella, not far removed from the Aegean coast. Philip had given a competent example of how to exploit interior lines of communication and, by rapid, concentrated action, inflict a succession of defeats on an encircling ring of enemies. The only battlefield success the Roman league had met with was the temporary capture of Anticyra in Phocis, lying to the north of the Gulf of Corinth. But their real achievement had been to tie down Philip in Greece, a situation which was to continue for the remainder of the war.

The next four years, from 210 to 207 BC, found Philip having either to respond to appeals for help from his allies, or to expel external aggressors inspired by the Romans. Marching from one crisis point to another, Philip fought repeated engagements with his old enemies the Aetolians; broke up a Roman landing near Sicyon on the Gulf of Corinth; was nearly killed in a sharp cavalry action outside Elis on the Aegean coast; and potentially the most serious of all, had to encounter a combined Roman-Pergamene fleet of sixty ships causing consternation along the entire Aegean seaboard. Landing on the island of Eurobea in 207 BC, Attalus of Pergamun took the unlocated city of Oreus after it had been treacherously betrayed by the commander of the garrison. But when attempting to capture Chalcis, which lay on the narrow channel separating the island from the mainland, the expedition was rebuffed before Philip could intervene. The misfortune of his late arrival prompted him to comment, 'It is a nice point whether in this war I have been more eager for a fight, or the enemy more determined to avoid one.' For a time it looked as though this abortive expedition had heralded an end to the war, since the Romans paid only scant attention to affairs in Greece for the next two years.

Apparently abandoned, the Aetolians were the first to sue for peace and accept a settlement on terms dictated by Philip. This, however, was a development which provoked the Romans into further intervention. They dispatched an expeditionary force of 10,000 infantry and 1000 cavalry which landed on the Illyrian coast under the consul Publius Sempronius Tuditanus in 206 BC. Originally intended to be sent in support of the Aetolians, this force had been diverted as a consequence of them having made peace without the consent of Rome. Sempronius Tuditanus now entered Apollonia unopposed, causing Philip to march there in all haste to prevent popular support for him arising among the neighbouring tribes. Deploying before the city, Philip offered the Romans battle but when this was refused, aware that he could not carry the city by storm, he contented himself with its encirclement. A wave of war weariness now swept through Greece which caused Philip, who had no wish to antagonise the Romans any further, to withdraw and subsequently agree to a negotiated peace settlement involving mutual concessions.

As for the Romans, they were only too relieved to end this scrappy campaign which had been thrust upon them, and had only served to divert effort from their major contest with Carthage. After the outbreak of hostilities, Philip for his part cannot have taken long to realise that, far from being able to undertake a campaign in Italy, he was going to be hard put to defend the territory of his allies and even Macedonia itself. Under such circumstances, he can hardly be blamed for coming to terms with the Romans after more than ten years of near constant warfare. Although he had consistently taken the offensive, it must have been a frustrating campaign for Philip, who had nearly always had to react to the moves of his enemies. Blame can be attached to him for his attack on Messene, but there is no evidence that this was more than a contributory factor in enabling the Romans to form an anti-Macedonian league. Philip's fault was not at the operational level of war nor, since he had won nearly all his battles, could there be any question of tactical incompetence. His failing was strategic: when going to war with Rome he had not appreciated the restricting nature of his position, or the limitations of his capability. His imagination, perhaps fuelled with the thought of becoming a second Alexander the Great and by the smooth blandishments of Demetrius, had led him into overreaching himself. Macedonian manpower resources were just not able to sustain a war on all four of the state's frontiers, let alone provide an expeditionary force for Italy.

Although there is little doubt that a competently led Carthaginian naval force would have given Philip greater freedom of manoeuvre, there are few grounds for thinking that it would have materially affected the outcome of the war. Roman activity would have been hampered, some local tactical successes could have been achieved along the Illyrian coast, and the means of transporting Philip to Italy would have been available. But there is little reason to suppose that the Aetolians and others would not have taken every advantage of Philip's preoccupations elsewhere, especially if he were tied down in Italy. The fundamental fact that Macedonian manpower was inadequate for such grandiose designs would still have remained.

But final comment must be reserved for the Carthaginians. The collapse of the war in the east had already been overshadowed by the loss of both Spain and Sicily; now, faced with the knowledge that the Romans were preparing to mount an expedition against North Africa the Carthaginians cannot have regarded events in Greece as being of much consequence. A sad epitaph for their grand strategic designs.

CHAPTER SEVENTEEN

THE WANING YEARS
216–211 BC

We have seen how the Romans reacted strategically after their defeat at Cannae by breaking the Carthaginians' hold on Spain and their attempts to achieve an encirclement of Italy. We have also seen how in Spain, at the operational level, Scipio's concept was to destroy the Carthaginian will by the capture of their main supply base, before turning to deal with their armies in the field, while at the tactical level he introduced flexibility onto the battlefield by organising his legions into contingents which could manoeuvre separately.

Like Hannibal, Scipio had developed warfare from little more than a gigantic trial of arms in head-on encounters, into an art where the destruction of the enemy's force was achieved by surprise arising from manoeuvre.

But in Italy there was not another Scipio, and the Romans made no effort to match Hannibal's tactical superiority; the dominance of his cavalry and the flexibility of his infantry, combined with his own genius, gave him an ascendancy which they dared not challenge. Instead, the Romans developed an operational concept which not only countered Hannibal's, but also largely nullified his tactical superiority. A fundamental new dimension had been added to the campaign following the secession of a number of Rome's former allies. In future Hannibal would have to protect them, and in so doing, he would lose the initiative he had previously enjoyed. If he were to win over more defectors, he would have to operate offensively, yet if he were to retain those cities he had already gained, he would have to act defensively. With an army which was not strong enough to undertake both commitments simultaneously, or to prosecute the campaign on both sides of the Apennines, the clarity of Hannibal's operational aim was diminished. The nature of his offensive operations also underwent a change, though care must be taken not to draw the wrong conclusions.

Polybius' *History* from 216 BC, from the revolt of Capua to the capture of Tarentum in 212 BC, has been lost, and only fragments of Diodorus Siculus have survived. We are then heavily dependent upon Livy, whose account of events always makes vivid reading but depicts Hannibal as being so completely outwitted and outfought by the Romans that it seems impossible he should have survived. Judging by Livy's account, however, it was no longer Hannibal's operational objective to bring about the break up of the Roman Confederation through the destruction of their armies in the field, but through the capture of the allied cities. This being so, there are three possible reasons for Hannibal adopting such a course. He could have anticipated the Romans' revised operational concept, which Carthaginian spies probably picked up quickly enough anyway; or he might have concluded that there was a hydra-like quality to the Romans' capacity to replace their losses which made further slaughter of questionable value; but most probably he had simply decided that the best way of inducing more cities to defect would be to act against them directly.

As for the Romans, the operational concept they developed had two elements. The purely defensive element was provided by the fortified cities which straddled the Italian peninsula, with a particular concentration in Campania. Here Acerrae, Suessula, Cales, Cumae, Nola, Teanum, Neapolis and others formed a defensive framework, much of it interconnected by the great highway, the Via Latina, in and around which the second element, the field armies, would operate. Further to the east in Samnium lay the cities of Beneventum and Venusia, and further east still in Apulia, were Teanum Apuli, Larinum and Luceria, which provided a similar though less compact framework for similar operations. In this manner, wherever Hannibal decided to campaign offensively, the Romans would go onto the defensive and revert to harrying tactics, but when he was not present, they would take the offensive against their former allies. In this way Hannibal would be forced to march and countermarch in pursuit of ever shifting and elusive objectives.

To exercise overall command, the Romans initially elected Marcus Claudius Marcellus and Tiberius Sempronius Gracchus, but after opposition from the Senate at the appointment of two plebeian consuls and, according to Plutarch, an inauspicious augury, Marcellus stood down in favour of Fabius Maximus, the Cunctator. In recognition of his qualities, however, Marcellus was given command of an army in Campania as a proconsul but was later sent to Sicily, where he distinguished himself by capturing Syracuse. He was very much a soldier's soldier who excelled in single combat and, according to Livy, was four times consul.

Turning to the north, one of the strangest aspects of the situation as it affected the Romans after Cannae was the inactivity of the Cisalpine Gauls. That they had not wished to risk provoking a Roman reaction immediately after Hannibal had left their territory was very understandable, especially as he had taken with him a strong Gallic contingent. But that this inactivity should have continued after Cannae seems almost incomprehensible. Yet all we know is that Lucius Postumius Albinus, one of the praetors in 216 BC, was sent to Gaul at the head of a 25,000 strong army of two legions, at the same time as Paullus and Varro marched into Apulia to confront Hannibal. Polybius specifically says that the purpose of Postumius Albinus' campaign was to create a diversion and induce the Gauls serving with Hannibal to return home. The expedition, as related, ended in disaster when the Romans were ambushed in a dense forest and annihilated only a few days after Cannae. Postumius Albinus died with his men, and on finding his body the Gauls cut off his head, gilded his skull, and used it as a holy vessel for the priest and temple attendants.

After this disaster and that of Cannae, when the Senate debated the critical situation facing Rome it was concluded that it would be impossible to replace the lost army in the north, and the Gallic campaign would have to be abandoned. Yet in spite of the obvious Roman weakness, the Gauls made no effort to follow up their victory by taking advantage of Rome's preoccupations elsewhere and so, as had occurred in the First Punic War, this vulnerable and usually turbulent region saw a period of tranquillity. Even the colonies of Placentia and Cremona on the middle Po, which had been established well in advance of the Roman frontier, were left unmolested. The first references to the Romans being able to take any precautionary measures on their northern frontier was in 214 BC, when Marcus Pomponius Matho was ordered to remain in Gaul and in 213 BC, when two legions were assigned to Ariminum covering Umbria and Picenum of the east coast. The inaction of the Gauls is all the more surprising since once the war was over, they then proceeded to attack Placentia and Cremona. Whatever the causes, this inactivity not only enabled the Romans to concentrate their attention in Italy against Hannibal, but also meant that Etruria and Umbria in particular, being the two northernmost states, were given no reason to revolt against the heavy demands being placed upon them entirely in support of Rome's ruinous war in the south.

The financial burden on Rome of prosecuting the war at this stage was enormous. Large tracts of land from which the state derived its revenue had been devastated or was in Carthaginian hands, the number of taxpayers had been greatly reduced following the slaughter of so many citizens in battle, and their families rendered insolvent through being unable to cultivate their properties. Though taxes were doubled, the Romans must have left considerable flexibility to their officials in deciding how to collect them. Whatever the needs of the State, to have overtaxed the already impoverished poorer citizens would have produced a sense of grievance and despair which could have destroyed the unanimity of all classes to sustain the war. As it was, however, the Roman Confederation in central and northern Italy held together, no doubt later fortified by the successes of the Scipios in Spain, and the dubious advantages to be gained from exchanging Roman domination for that of the Carthaginians.

In the closing months of 216 BC Hannibal divided his army into three groups. Two detachments were sent south to Bruttium and Lucania, where they were to stimulate a general uprising and draw recruits, while the main part of the army once again marched into Campania. Most of the population of Bruttium, an unruly province on the extremity of Rome's authority and in conflict with the coastal Greek cities, rose almost immediately in support of the Carthaginians under Hanno. But Petelia (Strongoli), lying on the southern coast, resisted Hanno fiercely and endured a siege of eleven months before it was finally starved into surrender. Meanwhile in Campania, Hannibal met with an early success in his endeavour to win over the cities lying to the south of the Volturnus. After envoys had been sent to both the Romans and the Carthaginians, and much debate, Capua defected from Rome; but the terms under which this second most important city in Italy did so had been closely defined. There was going to be no question of exchanging one master for another. No Carthaginian would have any jurisdiction over any Campanian; no Campanian would be obliged to serve the Carthaginians in any capacity against his will; and Hannibal would hand over 300 selected Roman prisoners, who could be exchanged for a similar number of Campanians serving alongside the Roman cavalry in Sicily. Having completed these arrangements, all the Roman and allied officials living in the city were rounded up and – under the pretext of assembling them for their own safety – were placed in the public baths and steamed to death. Since Livy had nothing good to say about Capua, however, this incident may have been the subject of some embellishment.

Elsewhere in Campania, Hannibal made two attempts to secure Neapolis, and so obtain a major coastal port giving ready access to North Africa, but on both occasions his ploys failed and he was forced to withdraw. He nearly succeeded in winning over Nola, where there was no lack of voices amongst the populace calling for defection, but the proconsul Marcellus was able to intervene and stiffen the senatorial party's resolution in their adherence to Rome. Hannibal must have felt supremely confident about his ability to dominate the military situation since, for the first time, he was now prepared to tie his army down to siege warfare. First Acerrae and then Casilinum were encircled: the population of the former managed to escape before this movement was completed, but Casilinum held out and the siege was eventually only raised following the onset of winter, when Hannibal withdrew into Capua.

From Polybius' earlier statement that the Romans had some 700,000 men under arms during the Gallic war, it seems probable that, even after the losses during the last few years, there were several hundred thousand troops throughout the length and breadth of Italy, employed in garrisoning the various cities. These would not just have been in Roman- and allied-held territory, but also in the largely Carthaginian dominated areas to the south, where such cities as Locri, Tarentum and Rhegium still stood with Rome. As for the active field armies, as the redeployment of existing legions and the creation of new ones was completed, fresh groups were formed. Unfortunately we have no indication as to the size or the composition of the Carthaginian army at this stage of the war. All that can be said is that the hard core of veterans with whom Hannibal had left Spain, or even Cisalpine Gaul, must have been considerably diminished. New recruits would have been obtained from the various cities which had defected to the Carthaginians and, except for the cavalry for whom Numidian replacements were received anyway, there is no reason for thinking that they should have been of markedly inferior quality. Hannibal was then unlikely to have been so disadvantaged, by either numbers or quality, that it impeded his conduct of operations.

In Campania, the Roman survivors from Cannae had been banished to Sicily in disgrace, together with sick and other inferior troops. They were replaced at Suessula, just north of Acerrae, by two newly formed legions, which had been raised in the neighbouring Campanian city of Cales between Capua and Teanum, and were now placed under command of Marcellus, who had previously been responsible for rallying the Cannae survivors. Their task was to cover Capua from the south and in so doing, lend support to Nola. Two more legions under Fabius Maximus, with a 25,000-strong allied contingent, whose organisation and suitability for employment in the field is not known, were initially positioned at Teanum, but were later moved forward to Cales, to cover Capua from the north. They were replaced by the two legions that had been raised from slave volunteers which, under Gracchus, were now moved to Sinuessa, west of Capua on the Via Appia running along the coast. From here they were to do what they could to protect the coastal cities, such as Cumae and Neapolis. As a consequence of the desperate situation, according to Livy, honour had given way to expediency and 6000 criminals and debtors had also been enrolled and armed with Gallic weapons captured by Gaius Flaminius in the war of 223 BC. There were, then, three armies of at least six legions in Campania which, in spite of their great numbers, were not to be used other than to bolster the determination of Rome's allies, and impede Hannibal without directly challenging him.

To the east, the two legions which had been replaced in Sicily were moved, presumably by sea, first to Luceria and later to Brundisium on the Calabrian coast where, under Laevinus, they received orders to counter the threat of invasion by Philip of Macedon. Terentius Varro, who had survived Cannae, was moved with a legion from Picenum into Apulia, though this legion was later sent down to Tarentum and Varro himself returned to Picenum to raise further reinforcements. Finally, in the north two legions were stationed at Ariminum to cover against the Gauls. But most of these dispositions were only completed during 215 BC, and in the meantime, Hannibal was virtually free to open offensives wherever he chose. In general terms, the campaign for the remainder of 216 and all 215 BC was restricted to Campania in the west and Bruttium in the extreme south. But the fighting also spilled over into Samnium, lying between Campania and Apulia, and further to the south, Lucania.

Following the defection of Capua, Hannibal had cut the great consular road, the Via Latina, running south from Rome through Campania into Lucania, so restricting Roman movement across the Volturnus while providing himself with easier access to the lateral road leading into Samnium. Capua had originally been an Etruscan city but in 340 BC had placed itself under the protection of the Romans who, after appropriating the rich Falernian plain, gave the city a considerable degree of political and administrative independence. But over the years with her growing affluence, Capua had come to resent even this limited inferiority and now, following Rome's humiliation at Cannae, she cut her ties completely. According to Livy, Capua was full of sensuality, soft luxury, and corruption largely attributable to the defects of character of the common people, who enjoyed unbridled freedom. Into this city, providing every form of pleasure, marched Hannibal to seek shelter from the harshness of the winter, and to rest his battle-hardened army before the rigours of the coming year's campaign. But, again in Livy's view, they were to emerge a very different body of men. Worn out and robbed of their strength, discipline and resolution by the excesses of wine, prostitution and idleness in which they had indulged themselves, they became little more than a pleasure-seeking rabble. At least Montgomery's decision in 1943 to keep the 8th Army in the desert outside Tunis will spare him and his troops from similar accusations by some distant historian.

There were three elements to the campaign conducted by the Romans and the Carthaginians during 215 BC: Hannibal's endeavours to win over further Campanian cities; the action Rome took to counter these moves and at the same time inflict the severest damage possible on those cities which had already defected; and in the southernmost extremity of the Italian peninsula, the landing of Carthaginian reinforcements. Hannibal's first move was to return to the siege of Casilinum which, following a spirited resistance, surrendered when the inhabitants were allowed to ransom their lives and freedom in gold. Though Casilinum was a relatively small town, it overlooked Capua from the north and gave access to the narrow passage over the Volturnus between the two cities. In recognition of its importance as a centre of communications, a 700-strong Carthaginian garrison was left in the city when Hannibal withdrew to his large base camp, established on Mt Tifata (Monte di Maddaloni) on the plain behind Capua. Two thousand years ago Tifata was very different from today; rich grassland and woods covered its triangular shaped plateau, providing grazing and shelter for the Carthaginian cattle, as well as a healthy, well-positioned base from which Hannibal could mount his operations.

While Hannibal had been occupied in the capture of Casilinum, the Capuans attempted to gain the city of Cumae, but Sempronius Gracchus had intervened and they were severely mauled and forced to withdraw. Cumae was an important seaport, and Hannibal seems to have tried to take advantage of the divided loyalties within the city and secure it himself, even though it was now garrisoned by Gracchus. But he did not persist for long before returning to his base camp at Tifata, and meanwhile the Romans under Marcellus in Nola had been punitively raiding the neighbouring territory of the Hirpini and the Samnite city of Caudium, both of which had defected to the Carthaginians and now urgently appealed to Hannibal for help. For the first time we see him having to respond to a Roman initiative and march on Nola, a city whose allegiance to Rome was only assured by the presence of its Roman garrison. That Hannibal took only a part of his army with him is clear from his other commitments; not only did garrisons have to be left in a number of cities, but his camp on Mt Tifata had to be defended, and he may well have also retained a reserve there. Hannibal was joined for a part of the siege at Nola by Hanno, who had been campaigning in Bruttium, and though we do not know the size of his force it cannot have been inconsiderable if he was able to undertake both the siege and protect his rear. Whatever his intentions,

Hannibal ended the siege with the approach of winter, sending his nephew back to Bruttium and moving into Apulia himself, taking up a position near Arpi, inland on the coastal plain not far from modern Foggia.

It was in 215 BC that Hannibal had met Philip's envoys, and had negotiated the treaty which would bring Macedonia into the war. Though on their return journey the envoys had been captured by the Romans off Cumae it is most unlikely that Hannibal would have known this, and his move into Apulia was then probably made in anticipation of Philip crossing the Adriatic the following year. With Hannibal's departure from Campania and Macedonia's clear intentions, the Romans adjusted their own dispositions. Fabius closed in on Capua and systematically ravaged the surrounding countryside, or gathered in the corn for himself; the size of the garrison in Nola was reduced and those no longer required were returned to Rome; Gracchus was moved with his two legions from Cumae to Luceria in Apulia, west of Arpi near the foothills of the Apennines, where he relieved Laevinus' legions from Sicily, which were then sent to Brundisium to defend the Calabrian coast against the anticipated Macedonian invasion.

Though all these tactical and other moves sound as though they were conducted with unimpeded precision, the part that religion played in deciding when, or even whether they should take place, should not be forgotten. Livy relates how Fabius was delayed at Cales when he should have been crossing the Volturnus, because he wanted to take fresh auspices and neutralise some ominous portents. Yet further delay was incurred when, according to the soothsayer, the entrails of the sacrificial victims indicated nothing but ill luck. The gods had to be propitiated and the needs of religion satisfied – which from all accounts was sometimes an unpredictable and lengthy affair.

While these events had been taking place, Bomilcar had landed in the far south near Locri with about 4000 Numidian cavalry and some elephants. These were the only reinforcements Hannibal was to receive from Carthage, the far larger force which it had been intended to send having been diverted to Spain with Himilco earlier in the year. After landing, Bomilcar marched to support Hanno in the successful campaign he was conducting in Bruttium and Lucania, where the reduction of Petelia and Consentia (Consenza) had ended resistance in the interior. Along the coast, Croton and Caulonia had joined Locri in defecting from Rome, leaving only Rhegium, which had been reinforced across the straits from Messana, in Roman hands. The campaign for 215 BC, then, drew to an inconclusive close; Capua and a number of important cities, particularly in the extreme south, had gone over to Hannibal, but the Romans had not suffered any further heavy battle casualties and they were rapidly building up their strength. With the prospect of Macedonian intervention, the centre of gravity for the war shifted from Campania in the west, to the eastern Adriatic seaboard.

Before the campaign season was due to begin in 214 BC, it seems probable that Hannibal would have learned of the misfortune which had overtaken Philip's envoys off Cumae. He would then have realised that there could be no question of him receiving Macedonian support that year, so once again he turned his thoughts to Campania – probably because he still thought it possible to break the Roman hold on the Campanian cities in this strategically important province and because of the distressed warnings he was receiving from Capua about the scale of Roman preparations to retake the city. In any case, re-established in his former base camp on Mt Tifata, he ordered Hanno to join him from the south of Italy.

The Romans meanwhile had shown their confidence in the prosecution of the war by re-electing Fabius consul, together with the previous year's proconsul, Marcellus. Continuity in command was then assured, with all that meant for the maintenance of consistent objectives. Fabius was still in Rome when he learned of Hannibal's approach, but he left at once to join the two legions which had already been assembled at Cales.

It is difficult to follow the Roman dispositions from the disjointed and incomplete account which Livy gives, but it seems that the following moves took place: Gracchus left Luceria in Apulia with orders to march to Beneventum, which commanded the road leading from just below Capua to southern Italy; Marcellus appears to have taken command of the two legions at Cales, since it was from here that Livy later says that he started when moved to Nola; finally, Fabius' son replaced Gracchus at Luceria with a newly raised fourth army of the standard two legions. With a field army remaining at Luceria to secure eastern Italy, Laevinus was free to use his troops at Brundisium offensively against Philip in Illyria, which he did by raising the Macedonian siege of Apollonia.

After assembling his army at Tifata and leaving a strong garrison to guard his camp, Hannibal descended onto the plains towards the coast and tried to seize Puteoli (Pozzuoli), the principal Roman supply base in the south, by a sudden surprise move. But the alert 6000-strong Roman garrison forestalled him, so he marched south to devastate the countryside around Neapolis, before once again trying to obtain possession of Nola. Here the old class conflict had flared up and the people had invited Hannibal to free them but – having been warned by the aristocratic party, and in spite of being delayed by the swollen state of the Volturnus – Marcellus managed to secure the city after a hurried march from Cales. Thwarted yet again, Hannibal withdrew, probably back to Tifata.

Before attempting to seize Puteoli, Hannibal had gone to offer sacrifices on the banks of Lake Avernus, the crater of an old volcano where, clothed in an aura of superstition and mystery, offerings were paid to the gods of the dead. While occupied with his sacrificial ceremonies, Hannibal had been approached by a deputation of five young noblemen from Tarentum, all of whom had been at Trasimene or Cannae and after being taken prisoner had been released to their homes. They now entreated him to march on Tarentum, which they assured him would surrender at the very sight of his army. With the prospect of gaining such an important city and its magnificent harbour, which would then be available to both the Carthaginians and the Macedonians, Hannibal listened attentively to the deputation before dismissing them with encouraging assurances. Attracted by the prospect of a new adventure offering such a rich prize, he then set out for Tarentum and with no attempt being made to stop him as he marched south, he burned and ravaged the land of those allies of Rome through which he passed.

But by the time Hannibal had reached Tarentum, the situation had changed and he received a dusty reception. Three days earlier a Roman officer, Marcus Livius, sent from Brundisium by Laevinus, had entered the city and, after enrolling all the men of military age, had posted them along the walls and at every gate. Tarentum was not going to surrender to Hannibal. This apparent reversal of the Tarentines' attitudes probably reflected a shift of influence between the political parties within the city. Marcus Livius is most unlikely to have been sent to undertake such an important task on his own, but would have been accompanied by a detachment of sufficient size to ensure that the pro-Roman party was restored to power. Livy would not have wished to suggest that there had been anything but willing support for the Romans from among the majority of the Tarentines, so the presence of troops with a coercive role was something best left unmentioned. The only apparent anomaly is that Livy says that the five young men who had approached Hannibal in the first place were noblemen. But since it was usually the aristocratic classes who were attached to Rome in the allied cities, he may have been careless over this point. Though frustrated once again Hannibal, with an eye to the future, made no attempt to take Tarentum by storm or revenge himself on its territory. Instead, he marched along the coast to Metapontum where he gathered in all the corn he required, before returning to Apulia and establishing his winter camp on the coast at Salapia. From here the Numidians rode out into the neighbouring countryside to restore the army's losses in mounts and pack animals;

4000 horses were rounded up, the best of which no doubt were broken in for use by the cavalry.

When Hannibal decided to march south to Tarentum, we do not know what orders were sent to Hanno who, it will be remembered, had been instructed to join the Carthaginian army concentrating at Mt Tifata. But whatever his instructions were, by the time Hannibal had set out, Hanno would have been well on the road to Beneventum. On reaching the city, he established a camp about three miles away on the river Calor, and engaged in the seemingly endless undertaking of devastating the countryside. At this moment Gracchus, whom Fabius Maximus had ordered to Beneventum from Luceria in Apulia, entered the city – but on hearing of Hanno's presence and activities he marched out again and camped a short distance off. After offering his slave volunteers their freedom if they fought courageously, the following day Gracchus led them out into the field. Hanno accepted the challenge and the ensuing battle was fought in the traditional manner; both armies lined up in close order, slowly advanced, clashed, and systematically set about butchering one another until, on this occasion, the Bruttians and Lucanians who constituted the bulk of Hanno's army could stand the toll of death no longer. They broke and ran. According to Livy, some 15,000 of them were left to litter the battlefield or to be taken prisoner, but as will be seen these figures, and so even the scale of the battle itself, were grossly inflated.

Meanwhile in Campania Fabius had moved against Casilinum which, because of its important position covering the northern approach to the Volturnus and Capua, was garrisoned by a 700-strong Carthaginian contingent, later to be joined by 2000 Capuans. Because Fabius was afraid that when assaulting the city he might be attacked in his rear by the Capuans, Marcellus had been ordered to leave a garrison in Nola and return to cover the siege. When the first attempt by the Romans to take Casilinum ended in costly failure, Fabius considered abandoning the siege altogether, arguing that there were more important matters to be attended to. Marcellus disagreed, maintaining that to admit failure severely damaged a general's reputation. The siege was then resumed, and when the various machines for the assault were brought forward, the Capuan garrison lost heart. They negotiated an agreement with Fabius that the city should be abandoned, in return for a safe conduct for them to Capua. But when the gate was opened and they started to leave, Marcellus fell upon them and an indiscriminate slaughter began, first around the gate and then within the city itself. Only about fifty of those who had been in the van of the withdrawal survived to reach Capua. Any other Capuans or Carthaginians who were rounded up, were dispatched to

Rome as prisoners and the city's inhabitants were divided up among the neighbouring communities, according to Livy, for safekeeping. But at least he had the honesty to admit this blot on the much vaunted Roman *fides*.

Following the capture of Casilinum, Marcellus returned to Nola where, due to ill health, he was obliged to rest for a while before being sent to take command in Sicily some time towards the end of the summer. Fabius for his part marched into Samnium to devastate the countryside, especially around Caudium, and to recover the cities which had seceded from the Roman alliance. The only reverse the Romans suffered was when Hanno caught some cohorts from Gracchus' army, allied troops from Lucania who like Fabius were conducting a reprisal raid, and were given a severe mauling.

So another year's fighting came to an end, and though no battles of great consequence had been fought, the ascendancy of the Romans was now unmistakable. However biased Livy's account may be, there is no disguising the fact that Hannibal had lost all sense of purpose in the conduct of his campaign. He might still exercise tactical domination over the Romans but they, with at least four armies in the field, were controlling events at the operational level. Moreover, according to Livy, public support for the war and the Senate's confidence were both growing: the owners of the slaves whom Gracchus had freed declined compensatory payment, at least until the end of the war; contractors carrying out public provisioning and works similarly offered to have their payments deferred; cavalrymen and centurions forwent their pay, and those who did not were termed mercenaries; while trust money belonging to wards and widows was paid to the treasury in return for bills, which were then treated as paper currency. The surge of public support also permitted action to be taken against all classes of citizens, though mainly the aristocracy and the wealthy, who had openly despaired of the State after Cannae, as well as against absconders and those who had failed in their duties on the battlefield.

In 213 BC Quintus Fabius Pictor was elected consul, with his distinguished father, the Cunctator, remaining to serve under him as a legate. Following the dispatch of Marcellus to Sicily and the siege of Syracuse, Gracchus was selected for the second time as the other consul. A council of war was then held in Rome to decide on the following year's campaign. Although once again the resulting deployments are hard to unravel, the dispositions of the armies appear to have been as follows: one was at Suessula in Campania, under the newly elected praetor Gnaeus Fulvius Centumalus; the second, under Gracchus, was near Venusia in Lucania, from where it could cover the great north–south road; two others were in Apulia, one under

Quintus Fabius Pictor at Herdonea, the second under the praetor Aemilius, being at Luceria; to the north at Ariminum in Umbria, was a fifth army under Tiditanus, another praetor; Varro was to remain with his one legion in Picenum; while to the south, Laevinus was to continue to operate against Philip from Calabria with a sixth army.

From Luceria in the north, through Herdonea to Venusia further south, there were, then, initially three armies loosely encircling Hannibal in Salapia. But they were soon joined by yet a fourth army, when Fulvius Centumalus marched from Suessula to join Fabius in attacking Arpi, Hannibal's winter quarters of the previous year. The city was taken after a 1000-strong Spanish contingent of the garrison had gone over to the Romans – but only under the condition that the Carthaginian garrison should be allowed to leave for Salapia unmolested. Unlike events at Casilinum the previous year, these terms were honoured.

How this opening move by the Romans took place without drawing Hannibal's intervention is not clear. A number of Roman sources allege that he became infatuated with one of the local beauties and dallied too long in Salapia; maybe this was the case, but in view of Hannibal's professionalism it seems highly improbable. Moreover, since his first move of the season was to march to Tarentum, it is quite possible that he had already left when Arpi fell. What is clear however, is that in marching south to Tarentum Hannibal had handed the initiative to the Romans in both Campania and Apulia. Though Gracchus saw some fighting against Rome's former allies in Lucania, it was only in Bruttium, where Hanno was able to achieve some local successes, that the Romans were faced with any serious opposition.

Hannibal spent most of the summer outside Tarentum. He took a number of small towns in the neighbourhood, but as the months slipped by his hopes for the city itself faded, and would probably have disappeared altogether had it not been for an act of extreme folly on the part of the Romans. When the Tarentine hostages held in Rome escaped – they were only loosely guarded, indicating a degree of trust which they clearly abused – the Roman reaction after their recapture was out of all proportion. The Tarentines were first scourged and then thrown to their deaths from the Tarpeian Rock. When the news of this reached Tarentum, the population was incensed and preparations for surrender were put in hand by a group of determined individuals. Two young men, Philemenus and Nicon, the leaders of the enterprise, made contact with Hannibal after leaving the city under the pretext of a hunting expedition, and the plot was hatched. In return for their assistance, the Tarentines would be free to enjoy their own independence, with only the Roman-occupied houses being given over to Hannibal.

In preparation for the city's betrayal Philemenus started making regular hunting trips, always presenting the self-indulgent commander of the Roman garrison and the guard on duty at the gate with generous shares of his game. The Romans then came to regard these regular expeditions as accepted practice. In the meantime, to allay Roman suspicions Hannibal let it be known that he was ill. Then, judging that the moment had come, he made his move. While the garrison commander was participating in a protracted party, Hannibal had four days' rations issued to a carefully selected 10,000-strong contingent of cavalry and infantry, and told them to march to Tarentum and conceal themselves in a deep river gully near the city. To ensure security, no further orders were issued at this stage, and the move was masked by a Numidian cavalry detachment which scoured the countryside around the marching column, giving the impression that they were on a raiding mission.

Although Tarentum was of Spartan origin its inhabitants, like the Sybarites, had suffered a decline through prosperity, pride and an excess of independence. The coastal city was built on a peninsula which ran from east to west, leaving only a narrow gap between its western extremity and the mainland, guarded by a citadel. The bay formed by the peninsula provided a magnificent harbour some sixteen miles in circumference, while the city itself, like Syracuse, had spread beyond its original confines onto the mainland. Hannibal's next move was to approach the eastern wall where it enclosed an extensive burial ground lying at the extremity of the city's inland encroachment. As darkness was falling, at an agreed signal Nicon and his compatriots within the city silently disposed of the guard and opened the gates, through which the Carthaginian infantry started to file. The 2000-strong cavalry detachment remained outside the walls as a reserve, ready to act against any external interference or unexpected developments within the city itself. Once inside, Hannibal advanced with his infantry through the deserted quarter of the tombs to near the market place. But he had not staked everything on this single entry point so he now halted until it was known how his other detachment, led by Philemenus, was faring. Accompanied at a discreet distance by 1000 Libyans, Philemenus pretended to be returning from one of his hunting expeditions, and on approaching the gate gave his usual signal before calling out to the guard to be quick, since he was carrying a particularly heavy load. He was then admitted through the small wicket gate with three companions, disguised as herdsmen, bearing a litter on which was stretched a fine wild boar.

More curious about the dead beast than Philemenus and his

companions, the unfortunate sentry suffered a quick death, so permitting thirty of the Carthaginian cavalry to pass through and set about killing the duty picket and cutting the bolts of the main gate. The Libyans were then admitted and the whole party joined up with Hannibal where he was waiting, still undetected, on the edge of the market place, the Tarentine conspirators who accompanied them telling their fellow citizens to return to their homes, and cutting down any Romans they encountered. Meanwhile Philemenus and some of his companions sounded the call to arms, whereupon the Romans turned out into the streets and were expeditiously dispatched. The more fortunate among them, including the garrison commander, were able to make their way to the citadel, which was hastily put into a state of defence.

Appreciating that the citadel was too formidable a fortification to take by assault, Hannibal decided to blockade it and at the same time protect the city from any Roman foray by constructing a ditch and a double wall. He then had the Tarentine ships, which were marooned in the harbour, dragged across the neck of the peninsula into the open sea and used to complete the blockade. Finally Hannibal left Tarentum and returned to his original camp three days' march from the city, from where the bulk of his army must have been covering his rear.

There has been some confusion over the date Tarentum was actually taken, either in 212 BC or the previous year, 213 BC, but this is something of a technicality: the important point is that the advantages to be derived from possession of Tarentum could not be realised until the citadel itself had been reduced.

Though Hannibal had displayed his usual ingenuity in obtaining possession of Tarentum through surprise, he left Hanno to undertake the campaign in Bruttium, and abandoned Campania and Apulia to the Romans. His reasons for risking the loss of all his gains in these two provinces by becoming tied down in what could well be regarded as a matter of secondary importance, can only be a matter of opinion since we have no firm information. But, as has been suggested may have been the case with Nola, perhaps he hoped that Tarentum would serve as a bait for the Romans and provide the chance to bring them to battle on his own terms. The key may possibly be found by considering the consequences of Tarentum's defection. First Metapontum and then Thurii, formerly Sybaria, followed her lead, then all the other Greek cities in Magna Graecia until only Rhegium, whose garrison had been reinforced across the straits from Messana, remained in Roman hands. The defection of Capua, on the other hand, had not led to other Campanian cities following suit, in particular he had failed to obtain possession of any of the ports, so essential if he were to receive reinforcements from Carthage, while the

Romans were able to maintain substantial armies throughout Campania and resupply them at will. There was then little to be gained in continuing to try and bring about the break up on the Roman Confederation through making Campania the primary theatre of operations.

But whatever his reasons for turning his attention to the south, Hannibal was fortunate that after the Romans had seized Arpi they took so little advantages of his absence. The near total inactivity of the four Roman armies throughout the summer of 213 BC was inexcusable, and judging by the changes they subsequently made among the commanders the Romans themselves thought so.

The previous year's picture which Livy had painted of national high morale, sustained by a self-sacrificing and resolute population united behind the war effort had, by his own admission, undergone something of a sea change. Now the 'alternations of success and failure were affecting men's minds', and a wave of superstition swept through the country as foreign cults replaced the old Roman forms of worship; prophets and priestlings came to the fore, especially in the cities which had become overcrowded with peasants fleeing from the ravages of war and famine; profiteering was rampant and lawlessness widespread. Clearly war weariness was gripping the population. In Spain, after the initial successes of the two Scipios, a stalemate had set in at the Ebro. In Sicily, Syracuse and Agrigentum had revolted and a powerful Carthaginian army had landed, necessitating the transfer of Marcellus, Rome's most vigorous field commander, and another legion to the island. In Illyria, Philip had conducted a skilful campaign in the interior against Roman allied tribes, before marching north to seize the important coastal town of Lissus.

The war was far from won, and the elections for the year 212 BC displayed the degree of dissatisfaction felt by the Romans at the ineffective leadership of their field commanders. Both Fabius and his son were replaced – though the latter probably never had much of a chance with his father overlooking him – as were all the other commanders in Italy with the exception of Gracchus, who was to continue to lead the slave army in Lucania. The new consuls were Quintus Fulvius Flaccus, who had been consul twice before in 237 and 224 BC, and Appius Claudius Pulcher, who had commanded as a praetor in Sicily since 215 BC. These sweeping changes reflected changes of influence between the various parties, as military ineptitude led to demands for commanders supported by the Claudii and Fulvii in particular. The appointment of commanders for party or other preferences may satisfy the needs of political expediency, but in an emergency, when military reverses have been brought about by incompetence, politicians usually regret their gerrymandering very

THE WANING YEARS

quickly. Though in this instance the Senate was able to preserve its monopoly of authority, they were also fortunate in being able to divert public resentments on to the Equites, the wealthy social order ranking just below the Senators themselves.

In spite of the difficulty the consuls were by now having in raising recruits, even though boys of sixteen were being enrolled, twenty-five legions were under arms in the different theatres of war, sixteen in Italy itself. With this massive concentration of force, the Romans decisively shifted the centre of gravity for the war to Campania and Capua in particular, though the fighting was to have focal points in other areas, among them Beneventum in Samnium, Herdonea in Apulia, and around the citadel at Tarentum. Between these battlegrounds Hannibal and Hanno, his stalwart lieutenant, were perpetually on the move either responding to a crisis or trying to take the initiative themselves. The first call for assistance came from Capua.

The Romans had only loosely invested Capua after the fall of Casilinum in 214 BC, but food stocks in the city were growing low and with Roman intentions to besiege the city becoming daily clearer, the Capuans sent an urgent appeal to Hannibal for help. Hannibal instructed Hanno to leave Bruttium and resupply Capua, setting out for the city himself once he had completed all that was necessary to ensure the security of Tarentum. Avoiding the Roman-held positions, Hanno camped near Beneventum and began assembling a convoy of some 2000 supply wagons, but before all was ready Fulvius Flaccus mounted a successful spoiling attack from Bovianum which forced Hanno to abandon the enterprise and withdraw again to Bruttium.

Both consular armies were now assembled at Beneventum, only one day's march from Capua, where Gracchus was ordered to join them with his cavalry and light infantry; the bulk of his army initially being left in Lucania under the quaestor Gnaeus Cornelius, with responsibility for maintaining order throughout the area. After setting out, Gracchus was betrayed by a Lucanian and was killed in an ambush. Diodorus says that Hannibal then celebrated his funeral with all the marks of honour and respect, and civilly sent his bones and ashes to the Roman camp. But Gracchus' death caused not only the dispersal of the force accompanying him, but according to Livy, also his two slave legions, who took their commander's death as the equivalent of a discharge and disbanded themselves.

Even so, the two consular armies had successfully prevented Hanno from resupplying Capua. They then closed in on the city and began its close investment but Hannibal arrived shortly afterwards, from Tarentum, the siege was raised, and the Romans withdrew on two separate routes; Flaccus towards Cumae and Appius Claudius Pulcher into Lucania. Hannibal hastened after Claudius Pulcher but was given the slip and, had it not been for the intemperate behaviour of a certain former centurion, Centennius Paenula, he would have achieved nothing. As it was, however, the Senate had agreed to Paenula's claim that he should be appointed to an independent command since he knew how to deal with Hannibal, and was given 8000 Roman and allied troops, possibly the remnants of Gracchus' army, which he had augmented by a similar number of local volunteers. This ill-prepared and poorly led collection of troops fell in with Hannibal's greatly superior army and inevitably was exterminated.

News then reached Hannibal that a Roman army under the praetor Cornelius Fulvius Flaccus, brother of the consul, based near Herdonea in Apulia and employed in repressing Rome's former allies, had become overconfident and slack following a run of easy successes. Here was an opportunity not to be missed, and after moving into Apulia Hannibal concealed some 3000 of his light troops during the night in the villages and woods to the rear of the Roman camp. He also blocked all the roads by which the Romans might seek to escape, and the following morning drew up the main part of his army for battle. Accepting the challenge Flaccus brought his army into line, but his troops were no match for the Carthaginians and 16,000 of the 18,000-strong praetorian army was destroyed. The Roman casualties may, however, have been fewer than those given by Livy, since he later relates how the survivors were rounded up and sent in disgrace to Sicily as reinforcements, under much the same conditions as the survivors from Cannae. After achieving these victories in Lucania and Apulia, Hannibal returned to Tarentum, but in so doing left the initiative to the Romans in Campania, who now prepared to resume the siege of Capua.

Claudius Pulcher divided his army between Puteoli and the mouth of the Volturnus river, presumably around Volturman, where they were given the additional responsibility of organising the distribution of the grain coming in by sea from Etruria and Sardinia – an indication of the shortage within Campania, following the devastation which had taken place. An inability to live off the land must then have also been a major factor affecting Hannibal's plans. No longer was he to have the freedom to operate as he chose; in future logistic considerations would determine where he could base himself and for how long he could provide direct support to Capua.

But to return to the Roman dispositions, while Claudius Pulcher was deploying his army, Quintus Flaccus began assembling material for the siege of Capua, and Gaius Claudius Nero was summoned to join him from Suessula. In each sector allotted to the three armies, preparations for the close investment of Capua were put in hand: a ditch, a double rampart round the city; and strongpoints at regular intervals along these defence works. But before everything had been completed, a Capuan deputation managed to slip through the Roman lines with another urgent appeal for assistance to Hannibal. Having found himself still unable to achieve anything against the citadel in Tarentum, Hannibal had moved to Brundisium, and it was here that the Capuan delegation contacted him and, according to Livy, received a very noncommittal reply before returning to Capua. Such was the situation as the year 212 BC drew to a close. Not only was the near overwhelming strength of the Romans making it increasingly difficult for Hannibal to maintain his support for Capua, but logistical limitations were now also becoming a major restrictive factor.

Though two new consuls were elected in 211 BC, Gnaeus Fulvius Centumalus and Publicius Sulpicius Galba, the previous year's consuls and the praetor Gaius Claudius Nero retained command of the three armies investing Capua. Four legions had either been destroyed or broken up in the course of the fighting during the previous year, but the Romans had been able to replace them and so were still able to field twenty-five legions. Two were now in Etruria, two were still covering against the Gauls, two freshly raised city legions were forming in Rome, four were in Apulia. The six legions in Campania, where the main war effort for the year was to be made, were concentrated against Capua and some time late in the winter the construction of siege works there, consisting of two lines, had been completed. The inner one ran round the city at a distance of about a quarter of a mile from the walls, the outer line was concentric with it, the enclosed space containing living quarters for something like 60,000 troops as well as all their stores. The work had been repeatedly interrupted by the Capuan cavalry, probably the Numidians who formed a part of the Carthaginian garrison under Bostar and Hanno. But by the time Hannibal arrived in the neighbourhood, the encirclement must have been virtually complete, though he evidently managed to get messengers into the city shortly before his actual arrival.

When responding to the appeal for help which he had received while at Brundisium, Hannibal had left most of his baggage train and heavier equipment in Bruttium. Nor did he take more than a part of his army with him to Capua, though the mixed force of infantry and cavalry he had formed included thirty-three elephants, probably those which had been landed at Locri in 215 BC together with his cavalry reinforcements. As Hannibal approached Capua he overran the Roman fort of Caleria, which guarded the upper valley of the Volturnus, before moving into his old camping area around Mt Tifata to complete his final preparations. At some stage the messengers who had managed to get through the Roman lines had delivered his instructions for the coming battle: these, in essence, were for the

Capuans to sally forth from every gate at the same time as he himself attacked. The problem facing the Romans therefore was that they dared not face the Carthaginian cavalry in the open field, while within their siege works they would have to defend themselves against attack from both directions. Appius Claudius Pulcher was responsible for the defence of the inner line and Flaccus for that of the outer, while Nero commanded the cavalry of all six legions which in fact had no useful role to play. The Roman horse were to the south on the Suessula road and those of the allies in the direction of the Volturnus, probably on the open plains to the west of Capua. But the forays mounted by the Capuans were contained without great difficulty, and even Hannibal's attack, which broke through the outer rampart to the west of the city and overran one of the Roman camps, was soon repelled.

Thwarted in his attempt to raise the siege of Capua by assault, and unable to supply his cavalry following the destruction of the surrounding pasture land by the Romans, Hannibal decided to try and relieve Capua indirectly. He would march on Rome and cause such alarm that the armies investing Capua would be called back to defend the endangered capital. There can have been no question of Hannibal hoping to take the city by storm, as had been the case after Cannae; the force he had with him was far too small and lightly-equipped for such a task. As they had been unable to break through the Roman field works encircling Capua, there was no possibility of their being able to penetrate Rome's far more formidable fortifications; nor in the absence of any inside collaborators, would there be any hope of gaining the city through betrayal or subterfuge.

Hannibal's move was, then, entirely a bluff and this being so surprise was essential if the maximum alarm was to be created. So he avoided the obvious approach up the Via Latina and instead took a circuitous route through Samnium; past Alba Fucens, fifty miles to the east of Rome where his passage is recorded by two roughly carved stone elephants; to Reate (Rieti), where he was still nearly fifty miles from Rome but now to the northeast. He then marched directly towards Rome, keeping the Tiber to his right, before crossing the Anio and camping some three to four miles from the city walls. From here he rode forward with 2000 of his cavalry to view the city for himself and casually inspect its defences.

CHAPTER EIGHTEEN

HANNIBAL IN RETREAT
211–205 BC

Hannibal's sudden appearance before Rome caused just the consternation he must have hoped for, as the wildest ideas and rumours gained currency – one even claiming that he would never have dared appear so near had he not already destroyed the armies at Capua. Polybius also records how while the men were sent to defend the walls, the women went to the temples and implored the protection of the gods, sweeping the pavements with their hair. By chance, however, Rome was considerably better-defended than usual, since not only were the city legions of the previous year remustering, but the new ones were being formed from freshly drafted recruits. There were thus four legions available, and though their quality must have been very uneven, a few days later they marched out of the city in a display of strength. But Hannibal was not to be drawn. He had already collected an enormous amount of booty, and he considered that news of his arrival before Rome would by now have caused the siege of Capua to be raised.

With nothing further to be gained, therefore, Hannibal began to withdraw, intending to reach the city before the Romans. But his progress was hampered by the Romans' destruction of the bridges over the Anio to his rear, and although the Carthaginians managed to ford the river they lost much of their booty and suffered several hundred casualties. Then, after five days' march, Hannibal learned that Capua was still under siege, so he decided to rid himself of the Romans who were following him. Allowing his pursuers to close up, he mounted a surprise dawn attack, killed a large number of them and drove the remainder out of their camp. Resuming his march and following a somewhat circuitous route through Samnium, Apulia and Lucania, Hannibal suddenly emerged in Bruttium. Here his arrival was so unexpected that he nearly managed to seize Rhegium, but having failed he withdrew into winter quarters.

Though there is no record of where Hannibal passed the winter, it has come to be accepted that this was in Apulia. Anticipating the events of the coming year, this then means that he marched back to Bruttium after the loss of Salapia, before returning to deal with Herdonea, which is highly improbable. It seems far more likely that he remained near Tarentum in his old camp, where he had left the remainder of his army when going to the relief of Capua.

Meanwhile in Capua the people had begun preparing themselves for their fate. Twenty-seven of the senators dined and wined themselves generously at the house of one of their number, Vibius Virrius, before taking their own lives by poison. Next day the Jupiter gate facing the main Roman camp was opened, and one of the legions with two squadrons of cavalry marched in to take possession of the city. Thereafter all weapons were collected and the gates barred to prevent anyone leaving, then the surviving Capuan senators were rounded up, scourged and beheaded in the best Roman tradition. Two other cities, Atella and Calatia, also surrendered and were subjected to the same treatment, bringing the total of those senators executed to seventy, while 300 aristocrats died more slowly in various prisons. The rest of the population were sold as slaves, all Capuan-owned land and buildings became Roman property, and the city was taken over by aliens, freedmen, small traders and artisans. Those electing to live in Capua did so purely as residents to be administered from Rome, possessing no political or civic rights. After their defection to Hannibal, the Capuans would clearly have been better advised to have striven wholeheartedly to ensure his ultimate victory, rather than have sought the most advantageous short-term gains for themselves.

The fall of Capua had been preceded by Marcellus' capture of Syracuse, but in Spain the two Scipios had died with their legions after crossing the Ebro to extend the campaign into southern Spain. In Illyria, after their capture of Lissus on the Adriatic coast, the threat of a Macedonian invasion had become more realisable, but the anti-Macedonian league led by the Aetolians, which Laevinus had put together during the previous year, had effectively reduced this danger by tying Philip down in Greece. In spite of Hannibal's continuing undisputed mastery of the open battlefield and freedom to manoeuvre at will, the year's balance of military events had tilted decisively in favour of Rome. Unless the Carthaginians could release resources for Hannibal from Spain by vigorously following up their victory there, superior numbers would inevitably lead to the Romans regaining possession of the whole of Italy. But Livy came to a different conclusion: 'For both sides everything hung in the balance,' he wrote. 'It was if, with all still to win and all to lose, they were only then beginning the war.' And he was probably correct in his assessment of the overall situation when viewed through Roman eyes.

Admittedly the reduction in the number of legions made available by the Romans for the following year could be taken as proof that they felt confident at the close of the campaigning season in 211 BC. There were only to be twenty-one instead of the previous twenty-five, and as a result of the dispatch of reinforcements to Spain as well as some disbandments, the number in Italy was reduced from sixteen to eleven. After the loss of the two Scipios and their legions in Spain, Gaius Claudius Nero had been sent from Capua with 4000 infantry reinforcements to secure the line of the Ebro. He was then relieved by the young Publius Scipio, with two legions released from Rome once Hannibal had withdrawn from beneath its walls, though they did not arrive until 210 BC. Elsewhere, time-expired soldiers were discharged and those legions which had been weakened, either through battle casualties or the provision of drafts for others, were amalgamated.

But serious difficulties broke out over the provision of rowers for the fleet, a requirement which had to be met, since without them Sicily could hardly be held, or Philip of Macedon contained. The treasury being bare, the consuls issued an edict that the cost should be borne by the public as a form of additional taxation. The outcry was shrill and sustained, the feeling among the people being that they had already been drained by taxation and had nothing more to give but their land, and that had been stripped bare. The Carthaginians had burned their houses, the state had taken the slave labour from their farms and since there was nothing more to give, there was no point in persecuting them with further demands. Angry complaints eventually led the senators, aristocrats, and others who do not appear to have been so hard hit by the war, to raise the necessary money themselves by handing in their gold and silver coins, jewellery and ornaments. They were, however, to be recompensed once the war was over.

Two experienced field commanders were elected for the year 210 BC: Marcellus, who had been in Sicily and was now to return there, and Laevinus, who had been conducting the Illyrian campaign but was now to command the armies engaged against Hannibal. As the allocation of responsibilities had been decided by the drawing of lots, when reports about the dismay of the Sicilians over Marcellus' return reached the Senate and found sympathy among the Roman upper classes, the roles were unceremoniously reversed. The Roman operational objective for the year was to continue with the recovery of the cities lost to the Carthaginians, and the weight of the campaign was to be shifted from Campania to Samnium, where Marcellus was to command two legions, and Apulia, where there were another two under the proconsul Gnaeus Fulvius Centumalus, a political appointee.

The Romans met with early success at the beginning of the campaign season: Marcellus recovered Narronea and Meles in Samnium, while in Apulia, Salapia voluntarily reverted to the Romans. Livy records how the 500-strong Numidian cavalry garrison in Salapia fought courageously to the end, with only fifty of them being taken alive. His account, however, does not ring true: separated from their horses and clearly taken by surprise, it sounds as though they were massacred, possibly while asleep. But however encouraging these successes may have been, by conducting their campaign in both Samnium and Apulia simultaneously, the Romans had separated their armies, a situation Hannibal was quick to exploit.

On learning that Herdonea was contemplating going over to Rome, Hannibal made a forced march from Bruttium, achieving complete surprise when he appeared before the town deployed for battle. Most unwisely, the inexperienced Roman commander Gnaeus Fulvius Centumalus ordered his two legions into the field, forming them up one behind the other. After holding the front of the foremost legion, Hannibal enveloped them both from the flank and rear with his remaining Numidian cavalry before cutting them down. Fulvius Centumalus, with eleven military tribunes and most of his army, was killed where he stood. Hannibal was probably unwilling to detach troops for garrison duties in Herdonea, so after executing those who had been negotiating with the Romans he moved the remainder of the population to Metapontum and Thurii and burnt Herdonea to the ground. Indeed, Carthaginian reprisals against those who wished to follow fluctuating fortunes by changing sides, would be as harsh as anything the Romans inflicted.

With the summer drawing to a close, after his victory at Herdonea Hannibal withdrew into Lucania, pursued by Marcellus who eventually caught up with him near Numistro. Livy then describes an inconclusive slogging match lasting all day, which is so out of character with Hannibal's subtle tactical handling of his army, that it can be discounted. It is more likely that there was no more than a sharp engagement which became greatly exaggerated in the writing. Certainly for what remained of the summer, Marcellus exercised considerable caution in following Hannibal, and was not lured into making a false move before the onset of winter, when he withdrew to Venusia in Samnium, while Hannibal returned to Tarentum, where the garrison was becoming critically short of food. But the situation there was saved when a Roman relief convoy, sailing from Ostia with both reinforcements and provisions, reached the town and enabled the garrison to maintain its stubborn resistance.

In spite of a few isolated successes, the Romans seem to have lost their vigour and determination in their prosecution of the campaign during 210 BC, in much the same way as they had done so two years previously. On that occasion it was the field commanders who paid the price by being replaced: now the consequences were to be more far-reaching. The legions which had been destroyed at Herdonea had been drawn mainly from the Latin colonies who, when the requirement for recruits was announced for the following year's campaign, now found themselves expected to provide their replacements. The demand met with an outcry of protest and twelve of the Latin colonies, among whom were some of the oldest and the most important, refused to send their quota. Livy depicts the depth of feeling aroused, as well as the narrow margin of confidence dividing military morale from the black despair of a civilian population overburdened by war:

For nine years now levies of money and men had been draining them dry; almost every year they suffered a grave defeat; some were killed in battle, others carried off by disease. Their friends who were drafted into the Roman army were more completely lost to them than prisoners of war in Carthaginian hands; for the enemy sent prisoners of war home without ransom, but the Romans dragged them off to fight outside Italy in what was more like exile than war. For seven years now the survivors of Cannae were growing old abroad, and they would be dead before the Carthaginians, now stronger than ever before, were forced to leave Italy. If soldiers never came home and new ones were always conscripted, soon there would not be a man left.

So spoke twelve of the Latin colonies approaching the extremity of war weariness in 209 BC.

The Romans were fortunate that the revolt spread no further and the remaining eighteen Latin colonies remained steadfast in their support of the war effort. Although no punitive action was taken at the time, the twelve colonies involved were duly punished in 204 BC, by being made to raise additional money and levies, when Rome was no longer constrained by concern for a critical situation. Once again we see that only with hindsight can 215 BC be regarded as a turning point in the war; in both 213 and now in 209 BC, the resolution of the ordinary people to sustain the demands being placed upon them had approached breaking point. As it was, however, Roman morale held up and their determination prevailed.

The consuls for 209 BC were Fabius Maximus, making something of a comeback and now being elected for the fifth time, and Quintus Fulvius Flaccus, who was to hold the appointment for the fourth time. The only significant change made to the deployment of the legions resulted from the winding-up of the Sicilian campaign in the previous year. Now that all opposition had ended, the island was to be garrisoned by the survivors of Cannae, Herdonea and other reverses, augmented by Numidian deserters and Sicilians, so freeing the two legions which had been sent there as reinforcements; these were now moved into Lucania and Bruttium under command of Flaccus. The events of the year 209 BC only make sense if they are seen to form part of a Roman double offensive. In a broad sweep stretching from northern Apulia, through Lucania and into western Bruttium, two armies would maintain the progressive squeeze being applied to those cities which had defected to the Carthaginians. But their objective was to be more than just to keep Hannibal on the move between one crisis point and another; he was to be held on the periphery of the area lying under his control, while a third army marched south to recapture Tarentum.

The Romans opened their campaign in northern Apulia. As soon as there was sufficient forage to be found in the surrounding countryside, Marcellus left his winter quarters in Venusia and moved to Canusium, where Hannibal was actively trying to induce the city to renounce its allegiance to Rome. Here Marcellus suffered another sharp reverse when he was caught off balance with one legion withdrawing, while the other was still moving forward to deploy. Livy records how they were flung into confusion, which turned into a rout as duty was forgotten in the general panic. Not very convincingly Livy then records that, following an impassioned exhortation by Marcellus, the legions rallied to fight again the following day, killing some 8000 Carthaginians for the loss of 3000 Roman and allied dead – as a result of which Hannibal started to withdraw to Bruttium. More convincingly, having administered another rebuff to Marcellus, Hannibal probably withdrew because news had reached him of Fabius' move into Bruttium. Meanwhile further to the west Flaccus was able to recover a number of towns in Lucania where, with an eye to recovering others in Bruttium, he treated the inhabitants with unusual clemency.

By keeping Hannibal engaged in Apulia, Marcellus had permitted Fabius Maximus to march unopposed on Tarentum, and to seize it through a Bruttian captain in the garrison who had a mistress whose brother was serving with the Romans under Fabius. The lovesick officer was prevailed on to betray the city and admit the Romans, who were then given free rein to butcher and loot at will. The suddenness with which Tarentum had fallen seems to have caught Hannibal by surprise since at the time he had been busy raising the siege of

Caulonia. Here a motley 8000-strong collection of Sicilian criminals and Bruttian deserters had been assembled and let loose by the Romans, with instructions to do as much damage to the countryside as they could and then to take Caulonia. Though Hannibal quickly rounded up these marauding brigands, in spite of undertaking a series of forced marches he was unable to reach Tarentum in time to save it from Fabius. With the summer drawing to a close, Hannibal provisioned his army by foraging, and then took up winter quarters in Metapontum.

Though the balance of advantage lay with the Romans, especially in Spain where Scipio had captured New Carthage, the year's fighting in Italy ended on a sour note, with Marcellus coming under particularly severe criticism. Tacitly confirming that his achievements had been exaggerated, Livy relates how the accusations levelled against Marcellus arose not only from his defeats in two successive battles, but also from his having billeted his troops in Venusia while it was still midsummer and Hannibal was ranging throughout Italy. The feeling was so strong that the people's tribune, Gaius Publicius Bibulus, introduced a bill to deprive Marcellus of his command. The accusations then seem to have become lost, however, in a wider indictment of the nobility's dishonesty and dilatoriness, levelled for class and party reasons, and leading to the demise of the Claudian party, and Quintus Fulvius Flaccus in particular.

That Marcellus should have survived this political crisis seems only reasonable. Though he was no match for Hannibal as a tactician, he was a vigorous commander who had at least kept Hannibal occupied in Apulia for long enough to enable Fabius to retake Tarentum. With a remarkable change in fortune, in fact, Marcellus was then elected consul designate for the following year, but before taking up his appointment he was sent to Arretium in Etruria, where there were growing signs of severe disaffection and possible revolt. His reputation and the authority he had received to withdraw the army from Apulia should this prove necessary, were initially enough to deter the Etruscans from giving any further expression to their discontent. But the trouble was more deep-seated, and in the spring of the following year hostages had to be taken from Arretium and held against the city's good behaviour when Varro, the survivor of Cannae, was sent to occupy it with one of the two city legions from Rome.

Unlike the year's fighting which had just ended, the campaign for 208 BC was to prove scrappy through lack of any direction by the Roman commanders at the operational level; and through Hannibal increasingly having to react to Roman moves rather than being able to gain the initiative himself. Though the usual change-round of Roman field commanders was undoubtedly a major cause for the lack of clear direction, with the appointment of Marcellus as one of the two consuls some positive leadership could reasonably have been expected. The causes for the Roman shortcomings were probably complex, but a number of contributory factors are apparent. Marcellus was obviously a fine fighting commander, but he seems to have lacked much imagination as a tactical commander and to have had even less understanding of the higher direction of the war. He was also a superstitious man, who Livy says was delayed from taking over his command by a succession of religious scruples. His fellow consul was Quintus Crispinus, who had served under Marcellus during the siege of Syracuse, so here was a commander probably wishing to display his new-found independence – especially since, according to Livy, his sole motivation was to gain distinction by emulating Fabius' achievement in obtaining possession of Tarentum the previous year.

Marcellus eventually took over command of his old army in Apulia, with Crispinus joining the army previously commanded by Quintus Flavius Flaccus in Lucania, and Claudius Flaminius being given Fabius' at Tarentum. While Marcellus was still occupied with his religious observances in Rome and his army remained passively at Venusia, Crispinus set off to try and seize Locri on the southern coast of Bruttium. So the campaign opened in a hopelessly uncoordinated manner, with the three Roman armies widely dispersed and acting in accordance with the whims of their individual commanders. But Crispinus wisely did not continue with the siege of Locri for long, since with no attempt being made to hold Hannibal elsewhere, the Carthaginians were free to move to the city's relief and send Crispinus hurrying back to join forces with Marcellus. Hannibal then also returned to Apulia and there followed one of those periods of sparring, during which he tried to manoeuvre the Romans into a false move. But the two consuls were not to be drawn and instead decided that another attempt should be made to take Locri. The fleet was ordered over from Sicily to block the sea approaches to the city, while a legion from Tarentum was to complete its encirclement ashore.

Unfortunately for the Romans, news of their intentions reached Hannibal, who acted with characteristic speed and decisiveness to intercept the legion marching from Tarentum. Laying an ambush near Petelia on the coast road, nearly midway between Tarentum and Locri, Hannibal awaited the arrival of the Romans. Inattentive to the hard-earned lessons which should have been gained from the disaster at Trasimene, the Po valley and elsewhere, the legion marched into the trap in close order. Two thousand of them were killed, 1500 taken prisoner and the remainder fled for their lives back to Tarentum. Hannibal then returned to Apulia, where Marcellus and Crispinus had apparently remained with their four legions in total inactivity throughout his absence.

It now looked as though the scene was being set for a major trial of strength, with the two Roman armies and that of Hannibal lying close to one another. But between the two camps rose a tree-covered hill, the tactical importance of which Hannibal was quick to appreciate. He secured it with his Numidian cavalry, and in the confused fighting which followed nearly fifty Romans were killed, including Marcellus, one of his military tribunes as well as one of the allied prefects, the other being taken prisoner; Crispinus received wounds from which he later died. With the loss of one consul and the incapacitation of the other, the Romans were in no mood to engage in a major battle, and withdrew into the mountains behind them.

Hannibal accorded Marcellus an honourable funeral, but then took advantage of possessing his signet ring by sending a letter to Salapia, which purported to come from the fallen consul, and announced his arrival the following night. Having been warned by the Romans about the possibility of such chicanery, however, the Salapians acted with equal cunning. When the Carthaginians arrived disguised before one of the city gates, the portcullis was partly raised to allow 600 of them to pass through, before being slammed down to seal their fate. Salapia was now firmly in Roman hands and if Hannibal had any other plans for the campaign in Apulia, with news reaching him that Locri was once again under siege, they had to be abandoned as he hurried south to relieve the city. The Romans besieging Locri came from the disgraced garrison troops serving in Sicily which had been augmented by Sicilians and formed into two armies, each consisting of the standard two legions. Hannibal had sent his Numidian cavalry on ahead of the infantry and as they approached Locri, the garrison made a determined sortie under their commander Mago Barca. Apparently the long period of reflection allowed to the legionaries during their banishment in Sicily had not greatly affected their attitude to danger; they now broke and fled back to the beaches and the safety of their ships. So another inconclusive year's fighting ended with the Romans apparently incapable of coordinating their superior numbers effectively; while the death of Marcellus, followed by that of Crispinus, underlined how correct Fabius had been in exercising the greatest caution when approaching Hannibal on the battlefield.

During the winter news reached Rome that Hasdrubal had left Spain and was wintering in Gaul with a 20,000-strong army, waiting for the spring before crossing the Alps. Feverish activity now ensued as measures to counter this new threat were put in hand, the first being to appoint the consuls for the coming year – not an easy task when so much was at stake and the field so restricted by death in battle and the

Roman politico-military system. Gaius Claudius Nero, a patrician who had commanded in Spain and Italy, was considered an obvious choice, though it has to be said that, judging by his recorded achievements, the reason is not immediately apparent. The trouble was, who should be his colleague? Marcellus, Paullus, Flaminius and Gracchus had all been killed; Fabius Maximus was another patrician, so that would make his appointment illegal, besides he was getting too old; Varro was still too suspect after Cannae; Laevinus, who had held command in Illyria and was now in Sicily looked a possibility, but he had offended the Senate two years previously by his opposition to Fulvius as dictator and anyway he came from a patrician family so was better left where he was; Titus Manlius Torquatus, whom Crispinus, as he lay dying of his wounds, had named dictator, was untried, did not want the job anyway, and so was a nonstarter; so the choice fell on Marcus Livius Salinator. Although he had become an unkempt and bitter recluse following his questionable condemnation for dishonesty when campaigning against Demetrius of Pharos in Illyria eight years previously, he was eventually prevailed upon to accept the nomination. There does not seem to have been any obvious reason for his selection, however; except for the unfortunate publicity attached to the matter of his dishonesty, the histories hardly give him a mention during the Illyrian campaign.

The consuls having been selected, the next step was to propitiate the gods. Following the occurrence of such untoward portents as lightning striking the temple of Jupiter and a vagrant wolf half-devouring a somnolent sentry at Capua, the proceedings initially endured for eight days. But further mishaps required an additional period of placation; stones were seen to fall like rain at Armilstrum, where the ceremony for the blessing of military arms was held, and a baby the size of a four-year-old was born at Frusino. How the poor mother fared is not related, but the prodigy itself was disposed of at sea and, homage having at last been paid adequately to the gods, the business of attending to military requirements could be put in hand.

By compelling the hitherto exempt coastal settlements to provide recruits, and by giving the consuls a free hand to supplement their forces from any source they chose, the number of legions to be put into the field was again raised to twenty-five. The latest figures for the available military manpower showed a 50 per cent drop to rather less than 140,000, and indicate the difficulties the Romans faced in meeting both military and economic requirements. But it should be remembered that many of the legions serving overseas, of which there were ten, were enrolling indigenous recruits, especially in Sicily.

As had been foretold, Hasdrubal crossed the Alps in the spring, according to Livy by the same route which Hannibal had followed eleven years previously, but without encountering any of the same difficulties or opposition. Hasdrubal's first move was to try and secure Placentia, but as he had no siege train it does not seem very probable that this was a serious endeavour, and the primary purpose of his delay before Placentia was probably to enable him to recruit the Cisalpine Gauls and Ligurians who now joined him, raising his strength to nearly 30,000. Having assembled his army, Hasdrubal then marched along the Po valley, probably following the line of the Via Aemilia to Ariminum on the east coast. Clearly some general understanding must have already been reached between Hannibal and Hasdrubal as to how the campaign was going to be conducted, but more detailed arrangements now needed to be made. Hasdrubal accordingly sent four mounted Gauls and two Numidians in search of his brother, bearing with them a letter stating his intention to march to Umbria where the two armies could be united. Having ridden through enemy territory along almost the entire length of Italy, the six horsemen mistook the route Hannibal had taken and approached Tarentum instead of Metapontum. Here they were picked up by a Roman foraging party and under the threat of torture, handed over the letter intended for Hannibal and disclosed all they knew.

In the meantime Hannibal, ignorant of Hasdrubal's intentions, moved from Metapontum to Grumentum in Lucarnia. Here he hoped he would be nearer to joining his brother in central Italy, while being able to watch against the Romans attacking his remaining bases in Bruttium. Apparently a brush then occurred between him and Nero, after which Nero decided to withdraw and was followed by Hannibal who, after another small action, then went on to Canusium in Apulia where he waited for news of Hasdrubal.

In the north Hasdrubal had marched past Ariminum and then followed the coast road past Fanum Fortunae, at the junction with the Via Flaminia which leads over the Apennines, before crossing the Metaurus river some three miles to the south. The Carthaginians had been shadowed by Lucius Porcius Licinus, commanding the two legions at Ariminum, who had been moving along the high ground to their right, not only to preserve his own safety, but also to ensure that should Hasdrubal decide to approach Umbria from this direction, he could fall back along the Via Flaminia. But Hasdrubal did not intend to cross the Apennines and resumed his march to the south, crossing the small river Sena (Cesano), some eight miles beyond the Metaurus. Here he found Livius Salinator, who had moved from Narnia, now camped before the little town of Sena Gallica.

Meanwhile to the south in Apulia, once he had learned of Hasdrubal's intentions, Nero had acted to ensure that the Romans implemented a properly coordinated plan. He at once advised the

Senate to send the city legions from Rome to block the Via Flaminia at Narnia, which had been vacated by Livius Salinator on moving to oppose Hasdrubal. Rome should be protected by moving the legion from Capua into the city. Nero did no more than inform the Senate of his own intentions, which were to leave his camp and a part of his army at Canusium under command of the legate Catius Quinctius, while he himself marched north with a selected contingent to join Livius Salinator. Assembling his best 6000 infantry and 1000 cavalry, and reporting his intention to storm a town in Lucania, Nero then set off south before turning north under cover of darkness to Picenum. These admirably deceptive arrangements seem to have been put at risk, though probably inevitably, by sending messengers along his proposed actual route with instruction to have provisions and additional horses ready as he passed through.

By making a series of forced marches, Nero is claimed to have covered the 240-odd miles to his fellow consul's camp within seven days, and then have been ready for battle the following day. Although doubtful, none of this detracts from the boldness of Nero's decision to achieve a concentration of force against Hasdrubal. The Romans at last had a commander in Italy with an understanding of how to direct war at the highest level. The test of his and Livius Salinator's tactical competence was now to come.

After falling out of the Apennines, for the last twenty miles of its course the River Metaurus flows through a wide, gently-shelving valley into the Adriatic. Over the millenia the river has secured a deep meandering passage of considerable width, so forming a sharp trough within the valley. The land on either side was probably thickly wooded, restricting both vision and movement so as to make the Metaurus a confusing obstacle, uncertain in its course and inaccessible over much of its length. After discovering that Livius Salinator had been joined by Nero, Hasdrubal attempted to withdraw by night. Abandoned by his two guides, he gave orders to follow the river until daylight would enable them to select a more direct line of withdrawal. It was an unfortunate decision. The weary column soon became confused by the winding turns of the river and made little progress. A halt was called, but as dawn broke they found themselves overtaken by the Romans. Nero was the first to arrive with his cavalry, followed by Licinus with the light troops, and finally Livius Salinator with the heavy infantry. Once the Romans had concentrated, they formed into line with Livius Salinator on the left, Licinus in the centre and Nero on the right. At the first appearance of the Romans Hasdrubal had started to prepare a fortified camp, but seeing that a battle was unavoidably imminent he ordered his troops to deploy.

Perhaps because of the nature of the ground, Hasdrubal drew up his army on a narrow front with correspondingly greater depth. The Gauls were positioned on the left flank, where a spur of the hills prevented any further extension of the line and before which was some broken ground. In the centre were his ten elephants, with the Ligurians just behind them, and on the right flank the Spaniards. Tactically the ensuing battle began unremarkably enough. Both armies met in head-on confrontation and set about the business of violent slaughter, aided by the maddened elephants who rampaged indiscriminately through the ranks, until killed by their own mahouts. But then Nero realised that because of the broken ground, the troops he commanded on the right wing were neither going to be threatened by the Gauls, nor be able to achieve anything themselves. He accordingly withdrew a number of cohorts, and after leading them round behind the Roman ranks beyond their left flank, he fell upon the Carthaginian rear so as to encircle the Ligurians. Seeing that this manoeuvre spelt the end of his army, Hasdrubal entered into the thick of the fighting and fell with his men.

Livy claims that 57,000 Carthaginians died and 5400 prisoners were taken, but Polybius more moderately assesses their casualties as being 10,000 killed and 2000 captured. Some 8000 Roman and allied troops also died, which were not inconsiderable losses; though not enough to deter Nero, once he had secured Hasdrubal's severed head, from starting back to Apulia the following night. Arriving before one of Hannibal's outposts, Nero had this trophy flung on the ground, while releasing two of the African prisoners to relate the disaster that had overtaken the Carthaginian army. Overwhelmed by the death of his brother and understanding that it signalled an end to all hopes of breaking the Roman Confederation, Hannibal withdrew to Bruttium.

When the two consuls later entered Rome in triumph the honours were accorded to Livius Salinator, since not only had the battle been fought in his province, but it was he who had been exercising command on the day it took place. Even if he was not given official recognition for the role he had played, it was Nero who had conceived the operational plan, who had been the first on the scene after Hasdrubal's withdrawal, and, though acting in a subordinate capacity, who had given the Romans victory by taking the initiative tactically. What is surprising about the career of Gaius Claudius Nero is that after two periods of undistinguished command in Italy and Spain, he showed such a flash of leadership as a consul, only to descend into total obscurity. He is not heard of again, so the suspicion arises that this proud and grim member of the Claudian clan had too many political opponents, represented in this instance by Livius Salinator and the ascendant Aemilian faction.

Hasdrubal for his part had probably done as much as could be expected of him under the circumstances. He was not his brother's peer, but as Polybius wrote: 'behaving on this occasion, as throughout his whole life, like a brave man, he died fighting, and deserves not to be passed over without remark'. There can be no doubt that it always was Hasdrubal's intention to join his brother and achieve a concentration of force, in which case he was undoubtedly right to use the Adriatic coast with its more open terrain and plentiful supplies. His decision to try to withdraw along the Metaurus is more questionable. If he had crossed the river already, why did not he and many others not know the way back? But leaving this point aside, to have attempted a night withdrawal through such an obstacle without having previously ordered his cavalry to find and secure a route, seems to have been a fateful omission. As for the conduct of the actual battle, it was not inspiring but the state of his army by then probably precluded him from attempting anything more demanding.

Nero and Livius Salinator had won the first clear victory over a Carthaginian army on Italian soil, and when the news broke in Rome expressions of relief were unrestrained. As Livy wryly remarks, while all was in suspense the women of Rome had wandered from shrine to shrine, 'giving the gods no rest from their vows and supplications'. Now that the agony of uncertainty had been lifted, the Senate decreed three days of public thanksgiving and the crowds thronging the public places behaved as though the war had already been won. This sense of euphoria was not restricted to the general population of Rome, it also spread among those responsible for the higher direction of the war. As a result no attempt was made to press the campaign against Hannibal who was at bay in Bruttium, whither he had withdrawn all his garrisons in Lucania and at Metapontum. As a result the whole of 206 BC passed militarily in relative inactivity and it was not until the following year, when Scipio stepped into the scene after his victories in Spain, that new life was breathed into the Romans' prosecution of the war.

CHAPTER NINETEEN

THE ROMANS CARRY THE WAR TO AFRICA
205–203 BC

In 205 BC we come to a period in the war when a fundamental shift in Roman strategic thinking occurred. As we have seen, up until now the Romans had pursued what amounted to a two-pronged strategy: first, to break the Carthaginian attempt to achieve an overseas encirclement, and second, to prevent Hannibal from isolating Rome by detaching her allies from the Confederation. Though they had acted offensively at the operational level, particularly in Spain, the Romans' strategic thinking had been basically reactive; it had been the Carthaginians who had held the strategic initiative by taking advantage of developments in Sicily, Sardinia and Illyria. Now it was to be the Romans who were to change the nature of the war, by adopting a strategy which was both offensive, in that it would carry the war into North Africa, and defensive in that it sought little more than the containment of Hannibal in Italy. Their strategy was then psychologically direct, striking as it did at the will of the Carthaginians to continue the war by extending it into their own homeland, but militarily indirect in that the obvious and pressing need to rid Italy of Hannibal was not going to be sought by confrontation.

But the apparent clarity of Roman thinking is deceptive, since their revised strategy was only arrived at after much bitter debate, and then was only to be implemented with half-hearted support. The architect for change was the imaginative military reformer Publius Scipio, now thirty years old; while the proponent of the orthodox was the doughty old traditionalist, Fabius Maximus, now about seventy.

While in Spain Scipio had been free of all political interference reflecting the interests and prejudices of powerful individuals or groups. The distances involved had precluded any demands for consultation, so the decisions he had taken were his alone. He had also been free from financial or logistic constraints imposed by others, since he had met all his requirements from local resources. Though only a proconsul, Scipio had exercised power and authority exceeding those of any dictator appointed in a period of high alarm to direct the affairs of Rome. But with his return to Italy in early 205 BC, this heady atmosphere was to change. It was common talk that Scipio intended to carry the war over into North Africa, and his confidence had no doubt inflamed the latent opposition within the Senate to this idolised young man and his pretentious ambitions. This was not to become immediately apparent however: as customary when a victorious general returned to Rome, the Senate greeted Scipio outside the city in the temple of Bellona, where he gave an account of his Spanish campaign (gravely underplaying the amount that still remained to be done before the unruly peninsula could be fully subjugated). In spite of the magnitude of his success, as he had never held a high magistracy Scipio was not entitled to a triumph. He therefore entered the city without ceremony and paid into the exhausted treasury 1432 lbs of silver, as well as a large quantity of silver coins. In the elections which followed, he was then appointed a consul, together with Publius Licinius Crassus, the Pontifex Maximus, who was responsible for religious affairs.

As will be recalled, Roman strategic thinking was powerfully affected by three of the most influential family clans: the Aemilii, who advocated overseas colonisation as a matter of general policy, but inclined towards the western Mediterranean; the Claudii, who favoured a southern expansion; and the Fabii, who largely dominated the Senate and whose interests lay in the north. We have seen how the Claudii suffered a reverse in the elections of 208 BC when Quintus Fulvius Flaccus had been dismissed. Though their man Gaius Claudius Nero had been elected the following year, the honours after the victory of the Metaurus river had been accorded to Marcus Livius Salinator, a member of the Aemilii clan, and Nero had been retired into obscurity. With the return of Scipio for the elections of 205 BC, the convergence of interests which had occurred ten years previously between the Aemilii and the Scipionic family, leading to Roman intervention in Spain, was further strengthened. They then posed a threat to the Fabii and their political dominance.

How far the opposition which Scipio now encountered arose from political rivalry and personal jealousy, as opposed to a genuine concern that his ambitions endangered the security of the state, is hard to assess. But as in the conduct of most human affairs at the higher political level, the former probably played a significant if not dominating part, while being masked by the apparent sincerity of the latter. From Livy's account of how Fabius placed himself above jealous rivalry when opposing Scipio's African campaign, it is hard to suppress the suspicion that like the lady, the Senator 'doth protest too much'. As for Scipio, when he came to make his reply, conceding Fabius' accusation that he was in search of fame, he admitted that his ambition was not just to rival the fame Fabius had won, but to surpass it. We therefore must lay aside the emotive factor and concentrate on the divergent strategies put forward first by Fabius and then by Scipio.

Fabius and those he represented wished to see the war ended, and the lost valley of the Po recovered so that it could be colonised by Roman farming settlements. His war aim, then, was strictly limited, both geographically and in intent: to be rid of Hannibal as quickly as possible. His opposition to Scipio's ambitions was based on a sincere conviction that the Roman people must be led back to their old simple ways, and this could be most expeditiously be brought about by evicting Hannibal from Italy.

After obtaining a day's grace for consultation and to enable him to consider his reply, Scipio reminded the Senate that there was a world of difference between devastating your enemy's country and seeing your own ravaged, and pointed out that merely removing Hannibal from Italy would not ensure any enduring peace for Rome. In exactly the same way as Hannibal had held his strategic objective to be the reduction of Rome's power and influence, so Scipio viewed Carthage. He was not bent on her total destruction; Hannibal would simply be forced to abandon Italy to defend his Carthaginian homeland, and that was where he would be defeated, not in Bruttium.

Though Fabius would probably have applauded Scipio's intention to reduce Carthaginian power, he then rose to express his fears at the social consequences for the Roman people, and at the prospect of a Roman army entering into a decisive battle against their formidable opponent, especially on his home ground. There was also the matter of public opinion to be considered; how would the Roman people and their allies react to the inevitable demands for additional manpower and resources to open up a new theatre of war? Twelve of the Latin colonies had already refused to make any further contributions, and the people had shown how near to total exhaustion they had become. Prudence and moderation were called for, not adventurism and glory.

Given its composition and fractional interests, that the Senate should have been unable to reach a decision is hardly surprising. The Senate first demanded to know if Scipio would openly declare whether or not he would abide by their decision as to the respective duties to be assigned to the two consuls. Somewhat evasively, Scipio replied that he would do what was in the interest of the state. The matter was referred to the people's tribunes, who ruled that Scipio would have to adhere to the Senate's decision. The Senate then decreed that whoever went to Sicily might then have permission to cross over to Africa if he judged it to be in the interest of the State. But as they well knew, being the Pontifex Maximus, Publius Licinius Crassus could not carry out his religious duties were he to leave Italy, thus Scipio was free to regard Sicily as no more than a stepping stone to Africa, so long as he could obtain the necessary resources.

In 204 BC Scipio openly began making preparations for his projected campaign; first by gathering all the information he could about the situation in North Africa and second by assembling an army, which included forming the nucleus of an effective cavalry army, obtaining the necessary shipping for its transportation, and collecting together the essential supplies. These were formidable undertakings but Scipio had for long anticipated his requirements and, in particular, had already begun his intelligence gathering. The politico-military situation in North Africa was complex but as it served as a background to Scipio's campaign, some understanding is required of the relationship between the principal native kingdoms with Carthage and among themselves.

In the west, where Morocco lies today, lived the Moors whose eastern frontier was bounded by the river Molcochatch (Meluchat), but they were too remote to play any significant part in the coming struggle. Next to them began the territory of the powerful Masaesyli Numidians, under their king, Syphax, with his capital at Cirta (Constantine), whose kingdom broadly corresponded to today's province of Constantine. Beyond them and bordering directly on the territorial extension of Carthage, were the Massylii Numidians ruled by their king, Masinissa, whose much smaller kingdom contained the inner mountains and plains of the Tunisian upper Tell, with its principal towns of Zama (Jama) and Thugga (Dougga).

These kingdoms had been created during the course of the previous century by an amalgam of tribes, now contained within their loosely defined borders. But their organisation was still very primitive and their relationship to Carthage resembled that of a protectorate, far removed from an alliance of independent states. To reinforce their influence, the Carthaginians had established a number of fortresses on Numidian territory, including the important city of Sicca (Le Kef). But generally Carthage maintained her authority by skilful diplomatic manoeuvring, playing off local tribal and kingdom rivalries.

The Massylii Numidians had been allied to Carthage from 213 to 208 BC, and had provided invaluable support during the Spanish campaign. But Syphax, king of the Numidian Masaesyli', had revolted against Carthage in 213 BC and is suspected of having been in contact with the two Scipios in Spain. He was then, however, brought back into the Punic camp by Hasdrubal Gisco, who secured his allegiance by giving him his daughter Sophonisba in marriage, as famous for her beauty as for her intelligence and culture. For reasons which are not fully known, though the betrothal of Sophonisba was allegedly one of them, Masinissa's fears of Syphax's intentions were probably the chief cause for his going over to the Romans. As has been related, after he had fought against Scipio at the battle of Ilipa he entered into negotiations with him at Gades in 206 BC. Now his timely offer would provide Scipio with the indispensable support of a truly proficient cavalry arm. But these hopes were suddenly dashed when Syphax responded to the overtures of Hasdrubal to seize Masinissa's kingdom and drive him into exile.

Even so, in the summer of 205 BC Scipio sent Gaius Laelius to North Africa to prepare the way for his coming expedition, to report on the relationship between the various tribes, and in particular to make contact with Masinissa. Though in exile, if he could bring his tribesmen out in revolt and encourage them to regard the Romans as their deliverers, Scipio's essential requirement for an effective cavalry arm could still be met, and with one considerable additional advantage. The Massylii would not be fighting for what could be regarded as being primarily Roman interests, but for their own independence and the restoration of their king. A firm alliance was then concluded between Laelius and Masinissa, which was to have far reaching consequences for the Numidian. But before these can be related, consideration must be given to Scipio's preparations for the raising of an expeditionary force.

Scipio had not been granted permission to raise fresh troops by the usual method of levy, but only by a call for volunteers – though this restriction appears to have been given a fairly liberal interpretation. When assigning the consular duties the Senate had, however, allotted thirty warships to the Sicilian Command, which Scipio now sought to augment by appealing to the allied communities for contributions to the construction of additional vessels, as well as providing supplies. In view of the resistance the Senate had met only a few years previously when asking for further levies and money, the response Scipio received was unexpectedly handsome, perhaps reflecting the respect in which he was held and his popularity outside the Senate. Etruria was particularly forthcoming, but other provinces and cities provided contingents of troops and crews for the fleet, classified as volunteers, as well as timber for the construction of ships, grain, weapons and assorted stores. Scipio was then able to lay down the keels of thirty ships which were reportedly completed, equipped and fully rigged in the remarkable time of forty-five days from when the timber was first felled. (According to Livy, though not when referring to this particular occasion, ships could be constructed of green wood so long as they were not left in the water throughout the winter.) Once they were ready, the vessels were sailed to Sicily with the 7000 volunteers embarked together with all their stores.

As soon as Scipio had arrived in Sicily, he began to take the measures necessary to ensure that the island gave him a secure base from which both to mount and to sustain his coming North African campaign. On entering Syracuse, he found the population in a turmoil of discontent arising from the war. The property of the Greek inhabitants had been seized by the covetous Italian community, and despite a decree by the Senate for its restitution, nothing had been handed back. As Livy relates, 'thinking the first essential was to honour the Senate's word', Scipio restored their property. This act of justice not only won the active support of the Syracusans, but ensured the tranquillity of this all-important city. Scipio is likely to have pursued a similar policy of moderation and reconciliation throughout the island, with generally comparable results. Sicily was then established as a dependable support base, while in the meantime the consul Crassus had joined the two armies in Bruttium, taking direct command of one of them himself.

The Carthaginians, too, had not been inactive. Having learned of Scipio's intention to invade North Africa, and after the alarm caused by the landing of Laelius at Hippo Acra, which had at first been thought to be that of Scipio, they had taken energetic measures to create such a critical situation in Italy that he would not be permitted to sail. Apart from the successful endeavour to win over Syphax which has already been recounted, three other measures were put in hand. Embassies were dispatched to Philip of Macedon requesting him to invade Italy – but following the peace he had just concluded with Rome a few months previously, he was not to be drawn – and at the same time Hannibal and Mago Barca were instructed to create diversions and do all they could to tie down the Romans.

A convoy of 100 ships carrying grain and other stores was sent to Hannibal, but it was blown off course into Sardinian waters, where it fell into Roman hands. Mago, who had taken refuge in the Balearic Islands the previous year after the collapse of the Carthaginian armies in Spain, was reinforced with some 7000 troops, seven elephants, money and twenty-five warships, with instructions to rally the Gauls into revolt. After assembling his expeditionary force, which he had expanded considerably, Mago set sail and descended on the coast of Italy with thirty warships, 12,000 infantry and 2000 cavalry, capturing the undefended city of Genoa. He then laid up ten of his warships, returning the other twenty to Carthage, where they were required to help counter the anticipated Roman invasion. From Genoa Mago marched into Liguria, lying between the river Po and Etruria, but though he received a considerable amount of support, he became involved in tribal disputes and nothing came of his venture, which was then sealed off by two Roman armies at Ariminum and Arretium.

While still undertaking his preparations in Sicily during the summer of 205 BC, Scipio became involved in Bruttium, where the campaign under the ineffectual leadership of his fellow consul Licinius Crassus had degenerated into little more than disjointed scrapping. After being approached by some Locrian exiles from Rhegium who wished to return to their city, Scipio ordered the praetor Quintus Pleminius to take a 3000-strong contingent from Rhegium and, aided by the exiles, to take possession of Locri. Although the undertaking was not of great moment, its telling provides a rare feeling for the occasional tensions lying behind the flint-like Roman disciplinary facade. Isolated on the very toe of Italy for the previous ten years of the war, for command and control as well as administrative reasons Rhegium had probably come to form part of the Sicilian military district – though whether Scipio had bothered to obtain Crassus' agreement to him attacking Locri, is another matter. But in any case, aided by their accomplices in the town, the Romans succeeded in storming one of the citadels, which led to skirmishing between Pleminius' troops and those of the Carthaginian commander, Hamilcar, who occupied the other one. Both sides were reinforced until Hannibal himself arrived on the scene which, had it not been for the loyalists gaining the upper hand and manning the city's defences, would have led to a speedy eviction of the Romans. As it was, Hannibal was unable to take any immediate action, so allowing time for Scipio to reach the city with further reinforcements from Messana. Realising that there was now no hope of recovering Locri without undertaking a major operation, Hannibal withdrew and left the city to the Romans.

Scipio's first act was to assemble the population of Locri and execute those who had been responsible for the revolt, turning over their property to the loyalists. As for the town as a whole, Scipio said that it was beyond his authority to pass judgement, so he ordered a delegation to be sent to Rome to receive the Senate's verdict. Taking the troops he had brought with him, he then returned to Messana leaving Pleminius in command at Locri. With his departure, discipline quickly broke down. Some of Pleminius' legionaries were restrained from looting by the tribunes, which led to a pitched battle between the troops of the different commanders. After being worsted, those of Pleminius ran to tell him how they had been treated and to display their injuries. In an uncontrollable rage, Pleminius had the tribunes seized, stripped and flogged, but while this summary justice was still being executed, the tribunes' soldiers arrived on the scene and set about Pleminius himself, leaving him half-dead, with his ears and nose mutilated. He seems, however, to have made a remarkable recovery, as when Scipio returned to the city after receiving reports of the disturbances, he was reinstated in his command. As for the tribunes, Scipio judged them to have been at fault and ordered them to be sent to Rome for trial.

Though following an admirable principle in supporting the commander, in this instance Scipio had made a bad judgement. No sooner had he started back to Sicily, than Pleminius had the tribunes dragged into his presence and tortured to death. With unbridled savagery, he then turned on those Locrians whom he suspected of having complained to Scipio about the ill-treatment they had received at his hands. The Locrian envoys had by now arrived in Rome to plead their case, which they did by relating how the Roman garrison's excesses outdid the Carthaginians'. Women, girls and boys were being dragged from their homes and debauched, while the holy treasures from the Temple of Proserpine had been sacrilegiously looted. These disgraceful incidents provided Fabius Maximus with an opportunity to criticise Scipio, not only for what had occurred in Locri, but also for leaving his command without the authority of the Senate, and for his Hellenic manner of life which the old senator found so depraving.

A Senatorial commission, headed by Marcus Pomponius Matho, was accordingly sent to carry out a thorough investigation. Skilfully turning the tables by impressing them with demonstrations by both his troops and the fleet, which indicated the extent and thoroughness of his preparatory training, Scipio managed to have himself completely exonerated. As for Pleminius, he was brought to Rome in chains and thrown into prison, where he died before he could be brought to trial. Few can have mourned his passing, or the ending of this sordid affair.

As a consequence of the favourable report their commission had given on Scipio's preparations, the Senate were induced to vote that he could select from the troops in Sicily any additional reinforcements he required – although even at this late stage, official support for Scipio's African campaign was grudging and half-hearted. It was, then, the 5th and 6th legions which Scipio, who did not regard the defeat at Cannae as being due to their cowardice, used as a core upon which to weld his volunteers; probably bringing them up to around 6200 infantry and 300 cavalry.

All now being ready, at dawn on a spring morning in 204 BC the army embarked at Lilybaeum, and after Scipio had called for silence by a herald he prayed to the gods and goddesses for their protection, cast the entrails of the sacrificial victim into the sea, and gave the command for the fleet to set sail by the call of a trumpet.

In all there were some forty warships and 4000 transports which, besides the troops, were loaded with water and rations for forty-five days, of which fifteen days' supplies were cooked. They were not troubled by the Carthaginians during their passage, and although fog closed in when the initially favourable breeze died down, as the sun rose the following morning the Hermaeum promontory (Cape Bon) became clearly discernible. Scipio ordered the pilot to head further to the west, but the fog descended to cloak them once again. Uncertain as to their position when darkness fell, and fearful of the dangers of collision or running aground, the fleet dropped anchor. The following morning the wind began to clear the fog as dawn broke, and the sweeping spread of the coastline lay exposed before the Romans' eyes. According to Livy, on being told that the nearby promontory was called the Cape of the Beautiful One, Scipio took this to be a good omen and steering towards it, ordered the ships to be beached. He had landed on what is now known as Cape Farina which, like Cape Bon to the east, projects northwards, with Carthage lying in the bay formed between them.

As soon as the army had been disembarked, a camp was established on some high ground which has been identified as probably being Porto Farino, about sixteen miles from Utica. The sight of the fleet and the thousands of troops pouring ashore caused panic among those living along the coast who, driving their cattle before them, blocked the tracks for miles around as they fled to safety. Soon the news reached Carthage where the gates were hastily closed, the citizens called to arms, and the walls posted. The next morning a 500-strong cavalry force was sent out to investigate the situation, the fear being that the Romans were already marching on Carthage.

But Scipio had other intentions: he had sent his fleet on to Utica and moved his camp further inland. The Carthaginian cavalry now clashed with Roman outposts and, after suffering a number of casualties, made a rapid withdrawal leaving their dead commander behind them. But the most welcome development for Scipio was the arrival of Masinissa with 200 of his Numidian cavalry. Now successfully ashore, Scipio advanced on Utica. Though today, as a result of the river Bagradas (Medjerda) having changed its course and its mouth having silted up, Utica lies some five miles inland, 2000 years ago it was a thriving port and an important city. It lay on the northern end of the long Djebel Menzel Roul ridge, which runs southwest to northeast before projecting strongly into the sea. Scipio now advanced and established his camp about a mile to the southwest of Utica, not far removed from where the fleet rode at anchor.

Although after the alarm caused by Laelius' landing in 205 BC the Carthaginians had attempted to resupply and even possibly reinforce Hannibal, as well as ordering Mago Barca to land in northern Italy and trying to persuade Philip of Macedon to do the same on the Adriatic coast, these significant offensive measures had not been accompanied by comparable defensive preparations around the home base. Certainly a fleet had been raised and sent to try and deal with the Roman squadron at Hippo Acra where Laelius had landed, more troop levies had been enforced within Carthage itself, additional African troops had been hired, and missions were sent to Syphax and other princes to strengthen the existing alliances; but if Livy is correct, these measures must have been imperfectly fulfilled, for he says that the preparations for the defence of the homeland were found to be hopelessly inadequate. New levies had to be hurriedly raised and an army formed under the command of Hasdrubal, while another delegation was dispatched to Syphax. The instructions given to Hasdrubal stipulated that his immediate priority was to increase the number of his cavalry, which he implemented by recruiting mainly Numidians.

When a force of about 4000 had been assembled, they were sent forward under Hanno, Hanibal's nephew, probably to cover and harry the Romans and gain time for Hasdrubal and Syphax. Hanno's first move was to seize the town of Salaeca (possibly Henchir El Bey), about fifteen miles west of the Roman camp. On hearing the news, Scipio is said to have exclaimed: 'What, cavalry under roofs in the summer? Who cares how many there are if that is the sort of leader they have?' He then sent Masinissa ahead with a strong cavalry detachment to demonstrate before the walls of the town and to draw out the enemy; but once the main force had been committed, Masinissa was to fall back by stages until Scipio himself intervened. The coming battle took place on the Djebel Roul feature, the actual site being known as the Tower of Agathocles where an old fort stood, built just over 100 years previously by Agathocles of Syracuse when, it will be remembered, he campaigned in North Africa and besieged Utica.

Having allowed time for Masinissa to provoke an engagement, Scipio moved his main cavalry force. Concealed by the hills rising up on either side of the track which they were following, the Romans wound their way up the ascending slope of the Djebel Roul. About two miles from their camp the ridge reached a peak from where it made a pronounced turn to the west, before falling away again so as to form a saddle. On approaching the summit of the high ground to the north of the saddle, Scipio halted his cavalry and ordered them to remain concealed behind the crest. Meanwhile Masinissa, by repeatedly riding up aggressively to the gates of the town, and then making as though to retire in timid confusion, had succeeded in drawing out successive detachments of Hanno's troops, until finally the whole force had been committed. Following Scipio's instructions, Masinissa then withdrew by stages along the southern slope of the ridge to where the Roman cavalry lay waiting. When he judged the right moment to have arrived, Scipio charged downhill to break into Hanno's column and encircle those in the lead, while Masinissa turned about to attack them frontally. Nearly 1000 of those who had been cut off were killed, together with Hanno himself, while another 2000 were either killed or taken prisoner in the ensuing pursuit that is said to have lasted for some thirty miles – an improbably long distance which suggests that the fugitives were subsequently overtaken in a far-ranging operation.

The next move made by Scipio was to carry out a devastating seven-day sweep through the surrounding countryside: villages were plundered, the inhabitants and their cattle were rounded up, and anything which could not be moved was destroyed. A swathe of destruction now encircled the Romans as Scipio turned on Utica, to acquire the city as his main base before winter brought active campaigning to a close. Utica was then put under siege with the fleet covering the sea approaches, while the army occupied the high ground of the Djebel Roul ridge where it almost overhung the city walls. Though Scipio had brought a number of siege engines with him, additional machines were required which were now constructed using local labour, while others were dispatched from Sicily together with further supplies. But even when isolated and under direct threat, Utica was not going to repeat its earlier disloyalty. It stood firmly with Carthage, enduring a siege of forty-five days which was only raised when Hasdrubal and Syphax threatened Scipio's rear with their combined armies.

Hasdrubal, who had fought Scipio in Spain and must have recalled the crushing defeat he had suffered at the battle of Ilipa only two years previously, had moved with great caution. After assembling an army of 30,000 infantry and 3000 cavalry, he had waited until Syphax was ready to join him with an additional 50,000 infantry and 10,000 cavalry. Even if Livy has exaggerated these figures, the Carthaginians now clearly confronted the Romans in overwhelming strength, so it is little wonder that Scipio broke off the siege of Utica and withdrew into a natural defensive position, a small peninsula about two miles to the east of the city. Later known as Castra Cornelia, the peninsula formed the northern limit of a ridge which ran inland with a slight westerly bias, and was to figure prominently in subsequent events. On this sea-girt promontory Scipio constructed his winter camp, raised his defensive works and beached his ships on the southern slopes, while receiving substantial supplies of grain and clothing from Sardinia to supplement the plundered stocks he had already accumulated. Livy refers to 1200 togas and 12,000 tunics, which broadly conforms to the earlier estimated size of the army.

On two separate hill features the Carthaginians now established their own camps, about seven miles from that of the Romans and two miles from one another. Hasdrubal's was to the east, so enabling him to maintain ready contact with Carthage, and Syphax's to the west, thus facilitating communications with his extensive kingdom. During the winter Scipio entered into negotiations with Syphax, hoping that he had tired of his new wife, Hasdrubal's daughter Sophonisba, and would be prepared to abandon the Carthaginians. But while Syphax made it clear where his loyalties still lay, he proposed that an honourable peace should be concluded, with the Carthaginians withdrawing from Italy and the Romans from Africa. After feigning to be interested in these proposals, Scipio sent some of his most experienced officers to accompany the envoys conducting new negotiations, which not infrequently lasted a number of days and so necessitated remaining in the Carthaginian camps quite long enough to spy out the troop dispositions and the ground, especially the approach routes. As a result of their reports, Scipio built up the same sort of detailed picture which had enabled him to achieve surprise and capture New Carthage by ruse. The two most significant pieces of intelligence Scipio acquired concerned the camps themselves, their construction and general layout. Hasdrubal's was built mainly of earth and dry wood, which had been foraged from the neighbouring farms; while that of the Numidians consisted almost entirely of reeds and thatch. Both, then, were highly inflammable. As for the layout, the Numidian camp in particular had been raised without regard to security, being scattered about according to the wishes of various groups and individuals. Scipio hatched his plan. A diversionary attack would be mounted against Utica, which would also serve to cover his rear from any sudden foray mounted from the city while the Carthaginian camps were being surrounded, fired and destroyed.

In the spring of 203 BC, Scipio started to implement his deception. His ships were launched and every indication was given that an assault was intended against Utica from the sea. With 2000 infantry he then reoccupied the high ground he had held the previous year, which commanded the land approaches and provided good observation over the city. Concealing his intentions still further, Scipio let it be known to his army that he intended to take Utica by storm, while giving renewed impetus to the negotiations being conducted with Syphax. His wish to conclude a peaceful settlement with Carthage was now considered to figure more prominently than ever in his mind; the overt preparations being made to assault Utica no doubt being presented as a last resort, should the talks break down. The Carthaginians having been both lulled and deceived, Scipio was ready to strike.

Assembling the tribunes at midday while his fleet demonstrated to seaward, Scipio briefed them personally as to his true intentions, ordering the legions to be ready to march that evening. A rearguard having been detailed to secure the camp, the Romans moved off after dark in two groups. The first, under Laelius and Masinissa, was ordered to attack and fire Syphax's camp and then, when this was well ablaze, the second group, commanded by Scipio himself, would assault Hasdrubal's and burn that to the ground. Dividing their force, Laelius and Masinissa converged on the camp occupied by the Numidians and while Laelius remained in reserve, ready for the unexpected and to cut off any escape, Masinissa entered the camp unopposed and soon had it in flames. Whereupon the troops in Hasdrubal's camp, seeing the spectacular conflagration and having no cause to suspect that it was anything other than accidental, either rushed to help or stood watching in astonishment. Their attention diverted, the Carthaginians could offer no resistance as Scipio fell upon them, firing the camp and slaughtering them at will. Both Hasdrubal and Syphax managed to escape, the former at first to a nearby town and then to Carthage, the latter to the neighbouring town of Abba, about eight miles away from the scene of the disaster, but their two armies had either been killed, taken prisoner or dispersed, and the survivors who still accompanied their two leaders numbered only a few thousand.

As for Scipio, it is possible that the idea of burning the camps came to him from a study of Agathocles' campaign in North Africa when, as Diodorus relates, a not dissimilar occurrence had previously decimated the Carthaginian army while conducting a siege. The Carthaginians were sacrificing the most eminent of their prisoners in gratitude for a victory they had just gained when a sudden fierce wind carried the flames from the altar to the sacred tabernacle, then to the generals' pavilion. From there it rapidly spread to the whole camp, which being made of reeds and straw, was soon a roaring inferno in which hundreds perished, with thousands more dying as a result of the ensuing panic. The Carthaginians would have done well to have reflected on this disaster a hundred years later.

When dawn broke the following morning, Polybius says, Scipio did not allow his troops any rest but at once started the pursuit of the fleeing Carthaginians. But the pursuit cannot have been conducted in great strength or with determination, since when the Romans approached the town where Hasdrubal had taken shelter, though he had only about 2000 infantry and 500 cavalry he was able to retire and make his way back to Carthage unmolested. Nor was any attempt made to dislodge Syphax from Abba, only eight miles distant, where he was soon busy collecting up the remnants of his widely dispersed army. After clearing the battlefield and stripping the dead, Scipio piled up the Carthaginian weapons he had collected and dedicated them to Vulcan by burning. The siege of Utica was then resumed.

When news of the catastrophe which had overtaken their army reached Carthage, the Senate met in alarmed debate to consider what was to be done. Initially it was feared that Scipio would march directly on Carthage, but once it was discovered that he was intent on the capture of Utica, calmer attitudes prevailed. Three courses were considered by the Senate: first, to send envoys to Scipio and treat for peace; second, to recall Hannibal from Italy; and third, to replace their lost army, while appealing to Syphax not to abandon them. Eventually the Senate adopted the third course. Enlistment was vigorously put in hand and Carthaginian resolution was fortified by the news that 4000 Celtiberians, who had been recruited from one of the toughest and most resolute of Spain's many warlike tribes, had arrived and were marching eastward. Together with the local levies raised in Carthage itself and the surrounding districts, the Celtiberians enabled Hasdrubal to begin forming another army. Syphax too had been active in collecting the dispersed survivors of his shattered army and raising new recruits. Assembling in the Great Plain which lies around Souk el Kemis on the upper reaches of the Bagradas, about eighty miles southwest of Utica, the new army was already beginning to take shape some thirty days later. But however proficient they may have been as individual fighters, the state of their collective training must have been as deplorably low as that of the army which had just been destroyed and whose fate they were about to share.

When news reached Scipio of these preparations, he decided to take the offensive before the Carthaginians were ready to move or more seriously, Hannibal had returned to Africa. Leaving the fleet and a contingent from the army to make as though the siege of Utica was being maintained, he led his legions in light marching order into the desert. In five days he had reached the Great Plain, where he established his camp on some high ground about four miles from the Carthaginians. For the next two days the two armies skirmished, no doubt taking the measure of each other, discovering as much as they could about their respective strengths and getting a feel for their dispositions. When finally ready, Hasdrubal placed the Numidians on his left flank, the Carthaginian cavalry on the right, and the Celtiberians in the centre. Following their normal internal dispositions with the *hastati* in the front rank, then the *principes*, with the *triarii* to the rear, Scipio placed the infantry of his legions in the centre opposite the Celtiberians, while his Italian cavalry faced Syphax's Numidians on his right flank, and Masinissa's Numidians stood before the Carthaginian cavalry on the left. At the first charge both of the Carthaginian wings gave way, so exposing the flanks of the Celtiberian phalanx. Though Livy says no more than that the Celtiberians were then encircled, it would seem that Scipio had used much the same tactics as he had employed at Ilipa, in which case he would have held the Celtiberians frontally, though this time probably engaging them directly, and then extended his line so that it could be wheeled in from the flanks; the envelopment being completed by the cavalry.

The Celtiberians died where they stood, fighting obstinately to the end, while the hastily raised and poorly trained Carthaginian and Numidian cavalry never stood a chance. In striking contrast, the core of Scipio's army had received a thorough period of training when in Sicily, while the remainder had been under arms for at least a year, were battle-hardened and, following their recent successes, of high morale. It was a foolish decision on the part of Hasdrubal and Syphax to stand and fight when so ill-prepared, but in a strange desert country, on foot and trained as they were for the set piece battle, it is simplistic to suggest that Hasdrubal should instead have used the Celtiberians, together with the raw Carthaginian cavalry, to fight a guerrilla war. Only the Numidians could have managed this, but even they would have been outmatched by Masinissa's superior cavalry. The fact of the matter is that Scipio surprised Hasdrubal and Syphax, catching them when they were in no condition to undertake any form of warfare.

Now, after this latest battle, Hasdrubal and Syphax mangaged to escape a second time, though there were problems over them being able to rally the survivors: the Celtiberians lay dead and the hastily-recruited Numidian peasants had probably made for their homes, which left only a few isolated groups of Punic cavalry to bear the news of this second calamity to Carthage. Like the Romans after Cannae, the Carthaginians now could have little doubt that Scipio's next move would be to march on their capital. In a state of high alarm, they feverishly put in hand measures to prepare the city for siege. The fleet, which had been specially built to intercept Scipio's supplies, was ordered to mount an attack against the Roman ships besieging Utica, and a delegation was sent to Hannibal recalling him and his army.

After dispatching Masinissa and Laelius in pursuit of Syphax, which strongly suggests that they had remained to encircle the Celtiberians, Scipio spent the next few days subjugating and plundering a number of adjacent towns. He accordingly found himself encumbered with booty and prisoners, which he sent back to Utica under escort while he himself marched on what was to be his primary objective, Carthage. As a preliminary step he occupied Tunis, lying some fifteen miles from the Punic capital, which had been abandoned and whose defences he now started to repair and improve. While the troops were engaged in this, the Carthaginian fleet was seen leaving Carthage and making towards Utica. Dropping their tools and seizing their arms, the Romans hastily assembled in their legions and the forced march back to Utica began. Here they found the Roman ships closely drawn up with their bows facing inland, heavily laden with siege engines and ill-prepared to undertake a naval engagement.

Had the Carthaginians acted with determination and speed even if Scipio had sent his cavalry ahead to give warning, there is every chance that the Roman fleet would have been annihilated. But only leisurely progress was made and after anchoring for the night, the Carthaginians stood off shore the following morning, in the expectation that the Roman fleet would sail out to fight a normal naval engagement. But by then Scipio had arrived and other ideas prevailed. Reversing the usual naval deployment, Scipio ordered the warships to be brought in close to the shore and the large transport vessels, secured firmly together and manned by 1000 troops, were formed up in four close ranks in front of them, so as to present a solid defensive wall. When the Carthaginians finally sailed in, they found themselves overlooked by the towering Roman transports and unable to get between them. By grappling their sterns with hooks attached to beams, however, the Carthaginians were able to break up the first line of transports and pull the broken sections towards the sea. But although many others must have been lost, only six vessels were triumphantly towed back to Carthage. Their arrival obviously did something to alleviate the air of gloom, but it represented a very limited success compared to what could have been achieved.

After following up Syphax for fifteen days Masinissa, accompanied by Laelius, had been able to enter his own kingdom of Massylia openly for the first time since his exile. But it was only to be a fleeting visit. Syphax had continued westward into Masaesylia where, according to Livy, following the entreaties of his wife and Hasdrubal, he had started to raise yet another army, once again formed from ill-prepared raw recruits. When brought to battle by Masinissa, in the ensuing cavalry action and while gallantly placing himself in the forefront of the fighting, Syphax was thrown from his badly wounded horse and taken prisoner. Masinissa now saw the opportunity to seize Cirta, Syphax's capital, so after obtaining Laelius' agreement and taking Syphax with him, he pushed ahead with the cavalry, leaving Laelius to follow on with the infantry. At the sight of their king in captivity, the garrison of Cirta offered no resistance and opened the gates to Masinissa, who after securing all the entrances, rode off at a gallop to take possession of the palace. Here he found Sophonisba, as irresistible a charmer as Helen and Cleopatra, who so rekindled his earlier passions that he married her on the spot; ostensibly so as to prevent her falling into Roman hands. As will be seen, however, this happy if somewhat precipitous arrangement was unfortunately abruptly terminated.

Although vast tracts of Numidia remained beyond Roman reach, the capture of Syphax and his capital and the strictly limited manpower resources of Carthage itself effectively precluded the possibility of raising yet another field army. Until the arrival of Hannibal and his troops, the end of all but the most forlorn resistance was in sight. But the Carthaginians were fortunate in that Scipio was consistent in his adherence to his original objective: he was not seeking the destruction of Carthage, merely the reduction of her power and importance so that she no longer posed a threat to Rome. Following the prisoners' arrival in the Roman camp with Syphax at their head in chains, Scipio's treatment of Syphax was courteous. No doubt recalling how only a few years previously he and Hasdrubal had dined together as the Numidian's guests, whose support they were both so assiduously courting, Scipio questioned him over his reasons for renouncing their former pact and friendship. If Livy is to be believed, Syphax unchivalrously blamed it all on Sophonisba's blandishments; her soft words and caresses had turned his mind and led him astray. Torn now by his hatred for Masinissa and overwhelmed by jealousy at the thought of his enemy's possession of his wife, Syphax warned Scipio that she would soon turn the young man's head in a similar manner. Scipio then took Masinissa aside and rebuked him for his precipitate marriage and the lack of self-control he had displayed. Torn between his passions and his sense of shame and duty, Masinissa decided that Sophonisba's death was the only way both to end his predicament and to deny her to anybody else. A poisoned cup was sent to the unfortunate young woman which she innocently drank as a bridal toast.

When Scipio heard of Sophonisba's death, he was concerned that the hot-headed young man's grief might drive him to some act of folly, so he ordered the troops to be paraded. Addressing Masinissa as King, he praised him for his achievements, presented him with costly gifts, and held out the prospect of him obtaining possession of all Numidia. Recognition, glory and the prospects of power were combined to dispel the pangs of unrequited love. Laelius was similarly praised before being sent back to Rome with Syphax as his prisoner, where the former all-powerful Numidian languished and died. Perhaps no more than a romantic fable further embroidered by Livy, it is nevertheless all perfectly possible. Women have played a larger role in the shaping of events than recorded history suggests.

Hasdrubal's fate is less certain. Though he escaped execution in spite of being sentenced to death, it seems that he committed suicide in 202 BC when persecuted during a demagogic reaction against those who had brought Carthage to such straits. The surprising thing about his career as a field commander is that he was allowed to perpetrate such an unbroken succession of disasters, extending throughout his time in Spain and now in North Africa. He appears to have been an able administrator, but to have been subject to a particular degree of political favouritism; not always a healthy portent.

His immediate business done, Scipio now returned to Tunis where he completed the work on the fortifications, so abruptly abandoned when the fleet was threatened at Utica.

The two military defeats they had suffered and the capture of Syphax brought about a realignment of political power in Carthage. After sixteen years the big land owners and wealthy merchants, who had always wished to avoid war with Rome in favour of their African territorial and commercial interests, returned to power. Even the Barcid faction which had supported first Hamilcar and then Hannibal, now appreciated that there was no realistic alternative to opening negotiations for peace; at any rate for long enough to allow Hannibal and Mago Barca to return. Thirty members of the Council of Elders, superior even to the Senate, came to prostrate themselves before Scipio, seeking his pardon and blaming Hannibal for the predicament in which they now found themselves. It sounds a thoroughly craven performance devoid of any dignity, and in replying Scipio said he had come to Africa in the hope of bringing home not a peace treaty but a victory. All the same, now that victory was in his grasp, he would consider terms, which he then laid down. All prisoners of war and deserters were to be handed over; all claim to Spain was to be renounced; the Carthaginian armies in Italy were to be withdrawn; all the islands between Italy and Africa were to be evacuated; only twenty warships were to be retained and the remainder surrendered; and a considerable indemnity in grain and silver was to be paid. Scipio then gave the Carthaginians three days to decide if they would accept the terms, in which case they were to agree an armistice with him and send envoys to Rome.

When the Elders reported these conditions, the Carthaginians were quick to decide that no terms ought to be rejected, especially as they wanted time for Hannibal to return. As instructed by Scipio, they then sent one delegation to conclude an armistice with him, while dispatching another to Rome which, according to Livy, was accompanied by a few prisoners and deserters strictly for appearance's sake.

CHAPTER TWENTY

VICTORY IN AFRICA
205–201 BC

In 205 BC we left two Carthaginian armies campaigning in Italy: with Hannibal in the south and his brother Mago Barca in the north. Mago had failed to obtain enough support from the Ligurians and Gauls to enable him to threaten Rome or join up with Hannibal. Instead, he had been contained in Liguria by two Roman armies; one formed from slave volunteers, which had been garrisoning Etruria before being moved to Ariminum, the other consisting of two city legions, which had been moved to Arretium. Mago's expedition had failed to have any effect on the Roman plans to invade north Africa.

Though in the following year there was no serious campaigning, it briefly looked as though the long-smouldering Etruscan discontent was going to break into open revolt in support of Mago. A number of aristocrats had approached him and declared their willingness to break with Rome, but their plot was discovered and all further prospect of assistance faded when those who had not yet been arrested fled into exile. Finally, however, in the summer of 203 BC Mago crossed the Apennines from Liguria into the Po valley, and in so doing faced the inevitability of having to give battle. There were seven Roman legions available to take the field against him; two were employed to prevent the Boii from intervening in his support, one was being used to secure the ruins of Genoa, while the other four marched to confront him in the territory of the Insubres. In the pitched battle which followed, victory appeared to be in Mago's grasp when his cavalry and elephants nearly broke the Roman horse and their twelfth legion found itself in serious trouble. But a courageous attack by the thirteenth legion, which had been held in reserve, together with the *hastati* of the eleventh, restored the situation. Mago was badly wounded in the thigh and had to be carried from the battlefield, whereupon his troops conceded defeat and withdrew. That night Mago was borne to the Ligurian coast, where he met the Carthaginian envoys who had been dispatched to obtain his recall as soon as possible. After listening to what they had to say, the army was at once embarked and set sail for Africa, but off the coast of Sardinia Mago died of his wounds and shortly afterwards a number of his ships were lost when intercepted by the Romans. Though now leaderless and probably dispirited by adversity, the remainder of the army made its way without further mishap to North Africa.

In the south during 204 BC, Hannibal had been involved in a series of relatively minor engagements with the consular army commanded by Sempronius, but nothing of military consequence occurred until the following year. Then several cities in Bruttium, sensing that the war was drawing to a close, surrendered to the second consular army commanded by Servilius Geminus. It was at this stage that the Carthaginian envoys arrived to recall Hannibal who, according to Livy, could hardly restrain his tears when hearing what was expected from him; but since his ships were already held in readiness, he must have largely anticipated the requirement. Embarking his army he then also set sail for Africa, to reach Leptis Minor without incident. With his safe arrival, the patriot party regained their confidence and former position of power; the death sentence passed on Hasdrubal was cancelled, and new negotiations were opened with Numidian tribal leaders.

During the same period, the Carthaginian envoys had arrived in Rome and been granted an audience with the Senate. After hearing what they had to say, the envoys were dismissed and the terms of the peace treaty offered by Scipio put to debate. Livy gives a thoroughly confused account of the proceedings, but three things seem to have occurred: first, some of the smaller political factions shifted their allegiances, so enabling the Claudii to regain their ascendency; second, an uneasy coalition was formed between the patriarchal families of the Claudii and Fabii to undermine Scipio's position; third, in spite of all the claims and accusations which were in consequence bandied about, the peace terms were finally agreed. Even so the political realignment against Scipio had been strengthened and intrigue against him continued unabated throughout this critical period.

While these machinations were festering, in 203 BC a violation of the truce occurred in Africa. One convoy of transports carrying supplies for the Romans from Sardinia had made the crossing without incident, but a larger one consisting of 200 transports escorted by thirty warships had not been so fortunate. Scattered by a gale, they were driven ashore within Carthaginian-held territory along the Cape Bon coastline where the citizens, probably feeling the effects of having lost so much agricultural land, forced the issue by demanding the seizure of the ships. Hasdrubal, the naval commander, was accordingly ordered to recover those he could and tow them back to Carthage, where their cargoes were soon dispersed. Now that Hannibal had returned, the confidence of the people and the aspirations of the War Party converged in a shared determination not to bow before the Romans.

In spite of his extreme indignation when news of this violation of the truce reached Scipio who had remained in Africa while the peace negotiations were in hand, he acted with moderation; envoys were sent to the Carthaginians to remonstrate and to demand the return of the ships and their cargoes. When the Roman envoys appeared before the Senate and the people, they spoke frankly, reminding the Carthaginians of their elders' abject attitude when seeking peace, and asking why the treaty was now being so flagrantly violated. If it was because of Hannibal's return, then the Carthaginians were being most unwise to place reliance on a general who had been driven into the very extremity of Bruttium, from where he had been fortunate to escape. Resentful at this plain speaking and reluctant to accede to the Roman demands, the Carthaginians dismissed the envoys without an answer. An escort was provided to ensure their safe return, but other forces were at work, and those wanting a resumption of the fighting at whatever price decided on a stratagem. The orders given to the two triremes provided as escorts were that they were to turn back on reaching the mouth of the Bagradas. Instructions were therefore simultaneously sent to the fleet now lying off Utica, that Hasdrubal was to intercept the Roman vessels before they could gain their base. Though the attack was beaten off, the Romans suffered a number of casualties, and were saved only by running their ships ashore.

This act of treachery served its purpose. Scipio was now determined to settle the long-drawn-out struggle between the Roman and the Carthaginian people. Since there was no chance of obtaining quick possession of Carthage by ruse, he first had to contend with Hannibal. And since as soon as the provisional treaty had been made, Masinissa had taken his cavalry, together with ten Roman cohorts, to complete the recovery of his own kingdom and take possession of Syphax's, Scipio now sent him repeated messages explaining that the Carthaginians had broken the truce, and requesting him to return and join him with strong reinforcements as quickly as possible.

Meanwhile, having taken measures to secure the safety of his fleet which he left under the command of the legate Baebius, Scipio set off up the broad valley of the Bagradas. Here he refused to accept the surrender of the towns and villages which lay in his path, but took them by storm and enslaved their inhabitants. Ironically, he was confronting Hannibal with a predicament not dissimilar to the one that had faced the Romans, most particularly in Campania. By ravaging and burning the Bagradas valley, he would force Hannibal either to ignore any appeals for help, or to react before he was fully ready. He was also being drawn away from the relative security of Carthaginian territory, towards that of the Numidians in hostile opposition, while facilitating Scipio's junction with Masinissa.

It was at this stage that the Carthaginian envoys returning from Rome reached the Carthaginian naval camp with an accompanying delegation sent by the Roman Senate. Baebius dispatched the Romans to Scipio's camp in Tunis but detained the Carthaginian envoys, who having heard what had occurred during their absence, had every reason to fear the worst. But though still outraged, Scipio was perhaps to some extent mollified by the news that the delegates brought with them: the Senate and the people had ratified the treaty terms, and eventually had acquiesced to his wishes in every respect. Confident in his authority, Scipio could now afford to pursue the course of political moderation he had advocated; orders were accordingly issued that the envoys were to be courteously treated and sent on their way.

In the meantime Hannibal had moved from where he had landed at Leptis Minor to Hadrumetum (Sousse), slightly further north along the coast towards Carthage. Here he rested his troops and refused to be drawn into precipitate action by appeals from Carthage to halt Scipio's destructive raiding. Though he was probably eventually forced to move before everything was ready, few commanders in history have ever enjoyed the luxury of unlimited time, and he was at least able to complete his negotiations with the Numidian tribal chief Tychaeus, a friend of Syphax's, who then joined him with 2000 of what were reputed to be the most warlike cavalry in Africa. He was also reinforced by 12,000 of Mago's troops who had arrived from Liguria. Assembling his army, Hannibal then marched to where Scipio was camped, in the vicinity of Zama some 100 miles southwest of Carthage, and established his own camp nearby. From here he sent out spies to report on the Romans' strength and intentions. These were quickly picked up, but instead of receiving the customary sentence of death passed on all those caught spying, they were led round the Roman camp and shown all that they wished to see, before being returned to Hannibal. The next day Masinissa, who had temporarily been sent away with 6000 infantry and 4000 cavalry rejoined Scipio with his men: the master of deception had been at work again. Though Livy says that Masinissa arrived in the Roman camp the very day that the Carthaginian spies were there, he must have made an error, for there is no reason to doubt the chronology of Polybius' account.

Hannibal for his part was so struck by the apparent magnanimity and confidence of his adversary that he resolved to meet him, so messengers were dispatched requesting a time and place. Scipio in reply told Hannibal he was agreeable to a meeting, and would let him know when he was ready. He then moved camp to Narragara, some fifty miles to the west which, as Polybius relates, while 'offering other advantages, enabled him to get water within a javelin's throw'. The 'other advantages' being that by distancing himself he had helped conceal Masinissa's presence, while drawing Hannibal still further to the west.

Scipio now informed Hannibal that he was ready for a meeting and the necessary arrangements were made. After moving his own camp to within four miles of that of the Romans, Hannibal confirmed the final details. The next day the two commanders came forward, each with a small escort; then, leaving these behind, they advanced towards one another, both accompanied by interpreters. As Livy says, 'they were not only the two greatest soldiers of their time, but the equals of any king or commander in the whole history of the world'. After exchanging the usual military courtesies, Hannibal was the first to speak. Paraphrasing Polybius' account, with which Livy generally accords, Hannibal began by expressing his regret that two great nations like the Romans and the Carthaginians had ever come to war in the first place – they should have restricted their ambitions to Italy and Africa respectively. But since they *had* gone to war through contesting Sicily and Spain, the conclusion he drew from his subsequent experience was that Fortune bestowed her favours in an unpredictable fashion; first one side was graced and then the other. So why should Scipio now risk everything he had achieved when a peaceful settlement could be reached? Rome could retain possession of all that she had gained, while Carthage would give a solemn undertaking never to go to war with her again. In replying, Scipio accused the Carthaginians of having perpetrated both wars, a fact confirmed by the way the gods had granted him an unbroken succession of victories. Though he was aware of the fickleness of Fortune, it was now too late to accede to Hannibal's proposals. These might well have been thankfully received when his star had been on the ascendancy, but not now, when it was on the wane. Moreover, after the Punic Elders had made earnest supplications, a peace treaty had been agreed much along the lines now being proposed by Hannibal. And this, after being ratified by the Roman people, had been perfidiously broken by the Carthaginians themselves. Under such circumstances, it would only be possible to refer the treaty back to

Rome if harsher terms were added: otherwise only two courses remained open to the Carthaginians – either they surrendered unconditionally, or they gave battle.

Accepting that such an exchange of views took place, it is quite clear where the moral ascendency lay. Scipio was a confident and successful young commander with a string of victories behind him, and now the prospect of another victory stood before him. The climax of the war had arrived; immortal fame lay within his grasp. Hannibal on the other hand had been campaigning for seventeen years and his epic successes, reaching a peak at Cannae fourteen years previously, had since been overshadowed by a succession of reversals. He had fought a desperate campaign against overwhelming odds with unparalleled skill and fortitude, but fortune had largely deserted him. Following a painful infection, he had lost the sight of one eye, both his brothers had fallen in battle, and his last few years in Bruttium had seen him penned in and on the defensive. Some thirty years after he had left his homeland as a nine-year-old, dedicated by oath to the humiliation of Rome, he now faced the prospect of his life's endeavour being ended with all his accomplishments brought to nothing.

No suggestion is made that Hannibal did not face the coming struggle with courage and determination, but in the many accounts of the battle of Zama that have been written, no regard has been paid to the possibility that at the time, Hannibal may have been suffering from mental and even physical exhaustion. Much emphasis is given to the stress factor in modern life, so just because it is not mentioned by classical historians, there is no reason to suppose it did not also affect earlier generations.

A battle now being inevitable, the next morning the two commanders drew up their troops and addressed them. As Polybius relates, both armies were led by skilled, well-trained generals of outstanding ability; the Carthaginians fighting for their lives and homeland, and the Romans for the supremacy of their empire. The battle would not just settle the destiny of Africa or Europe, but who were to become 'masters of all other parts of the world known to history'. Though the Romans had a superiority in cavalry, overall numbers were probably about equal, some 40,000 each. Hannibal drew up his army in three lines behind his eighty elephants, which probably covered his entire front. Immediately behind the elephants were some 12,000 Ligurians, Gauls and Balearic slingers from Mago's old army; the second line consisted of Carthaginians and Africans; finally, some two hundred yards to the rear, were Hannibal's own troops from Italy. The cavalry were posted on the wings, the Numidians on the left and the Carthaginians on the right, both covered by the elephants.

While Polybius explains the dispositions Hannibal adopted from the point of view of fighting ability, he gives no consideration to the tactical thinking behind them. There are, however, three points which should be noted. First, Hannibal had clearly instructed his second and third lines not to get sucked into a general engagement, but to maintain their distances and formation. Second, the third line, consisting of his old veterans positioned some two hundred yards to the rear of the Carthaginians and Libyans, were intended to act as a reserve. But Hannibal would not have formed such a reserve purely to prevent a Roman encirclement; it could also be used offensively as the battle developed. The same reasoning would have lain behind Hannibal's orders that the second line was not to be drawn into the fighting prematurely; they could then be employed to stand on the defensive, to reinforce, or extend the line as the situation required. By giving depth to his dispositions and keeping the three separate lines, Hannibal retained the flexibility to act either offensively or defensively, but with one qualification: he could not cover his rear. Third, by placing his elephants in front, Hannibal hoped to break up the Roman lines while protecting his own. His dispositions were thus designed to achieve flexibility and balance.

Just because Hannibal quickly found himself on the defensive, it is clearly not the case that this was his original intention. His invariable tactic was to throw his opponents off balance, then close for the kill; at Zama he intended to do this by the charge of his elephants, and when this failed he found himself simply having to react, the initiative had passed to the Romans.

The thinking behind Scipio's deployment is easier to understand. His army was drawn up in the usual three lines, with the *hastati* in front rank, then the *principes* and the *triarii* to the rear. The cavalry were positioned on the wings, Laelius with the Romans on the left, Masinissa with his Numidians on the right. The break with convention in Scipio's detailed dispositions was that, instead of positioning the *maniples* in the usual chequerboard fashion, the men in the second line were placed directly behind those of the first, so creating lanes between them for the advancing Carthaginian elephants. The distances between the three lines are not known, but there is no reason for thinking that sufficient room had not been left to allow the *maniples* to wheel within the legions in the normal manner. The *velites*, or light infantry, acting as skirmishers, were ordered to withdraw down the lanes between the *maniples* when pressed by the Carthaginian elephants. They were then either to fall back to the rear, or turn to right and left between the *maniples* from where they could harry the beasts as they passed.

After some initial skirmishing between the Numidian cavalry

facing one another, probably on the fringes of the flank, Hannibal gave the order for the elephants to charge. Whereupon the Romans sounded all their bugles and trumpets, possibly also following their usual custom of beating on their shields with their swords. The effect was all that Scipio could have desired. Startled beyond control, some of the elephants turned and fled, breaking into the Numidian cavalry and causing such disorder that Masinissa was able to exploit the situation by a sudden charge which drove them off the battlefield. The remaining elephants were either channelled down the lanes between the *maniples* – but not before they had inflicted considerable damage – or were deflected on to the other flank, where they were driven off the battlefield under a hail of darts from the Roman cavalry. Once the elephants were dispersed, Laelius' horse then outfought the Carthaginians opposing them who sought refuge in flight, only to be relentlessly pursued by both Laelius and Masinissa. In the opening round, Hannibal had then failed to break the hard glacis of the legions, his elephants had been neutralised, and his wings had been stripped of cavalry. But as the Romans had also, at least temporarily, lost their cavalry, the battle was far from over.

The opposing lines of infantry now closed on one another, except for Hannibal's veterans, who remained where they had been posted. The war cries of the Romans and the clashing of their shields were matched by the weird shouting of the various Carthaginian contingents, until both were drowned in the din of battle. For a while neither side gained any advantage as the ranks thinned and the piles of dead mounted: where the fighting was thickest, men toppled over one another to die from spear or sword thrusts, forming gruesome obstacles. But eventually, as Polybius relates,

The Romans, trusting to the steadiness of their ranks and the excellence of their arms, still kept gaining ground, their rear ranks keeping up close with them and encouraging them to advance; while the Carthaginians did not keep up with their mercenaries nor support them, but showed a thoroughly cowardly spirit. The result was that the foreign soldiers gave way; and believing that they had been shamefully abandoned by their own side, fell back upon the men in their rear as they were retreating and began killing them.

From the way the Carthaginians then fought, and the fact that the doughty Libyans also formed a part of the second line, though without getting a mention, it can reasonably be concluded that it was not from cowardice that the Carthaginians delayed joining the fight, but because they were complying with orders. Whether the mercenaries in the leading rank knew of these instructions, however, is another matter.

Their first line having largely disintegrated, the Carthaginians and the Libyans were ordered to charge the *hastati*, who fell back in confusion until reinforced and rallied by the *principes* of the Roman second line. After another period of carnage, the Carthaginians broke and on finding they could not gain shelter within the ranks of Hannibal's old army, who had menacingly lowered their spears, the survivors made for the flanks. In following the account Polybius gives of the fighting, some doubt must be expressed as to whether the Carthaginians and the Libyans really withdrew in such disorder. During the next phase of the battle when the reserves were engaged, Polybius says that the numbers on both sides were about equal; in which case a substantial number of the Carthaginians and Libyans, if not the mercenaries from the first line, must have participated.

The space between the two armies now being slippery with gore, obstructed with piles of wounded and dead, and littered with abandoned weapons, thus making any orderly conduct or further fighting virtually impossible, Scipio sounded the recall. He then had the wounded withdrawn to the rear and redeployed his army. The *principes* and the *triarii* threaded their way through the corpses and, after closing ranks, were arranged in line with the surviving *hastati* on either flank. What Hannibal was doing during this period is not known, and the question can legitimately be asked, why did he not attack while the Roman reorganisation was under way and before their cavalry returned? But however mentally and physically exhausted Hannibal may have been, he would not have just sat waiting for the Romans to make the first move. So there must have been other considerations which kept him fully occupied. Since there is no mention of the Romans extending their line beyond that of the Carthaginians, so as to be able to envelop them, they must for the next stage of the battle have been of broadly comparable lengths. Hannibal had then probably been redeploying the survivors of his two front lines of infantry.

Once their redeployments were finished, the two opponents, in the words of Polybius, 'charged each other with the greatest fire and fury. Being nearly equal in numbers, spirit, courage and arms, the battle was for a long time undecided, the men in their obstinate valour falling dead without giving way a step'. At which point Masinissa and Laelius, returning from their pursuit of the Carthaginian cavalry, now fell upon the rear of Hannibal's old army. Most of his men died fighting to the end in hopeless confusion which, as at Cannae and Trasimene, accounts for the disproportionately high casualties suffered by the vanquished. A few tried to escape across the open plain, but fell easy victims to the Roman and Numidian cavalry. According to Polybius, the Carthaginians lost some 20,000 dead and a further 20,000 were taken prisoner, while the Romans suffered only

VICTORY IN AFRICA

1500 casualties. As for Hannibal himself, he managed to escape with a few horsemen to Hadrumetum, from where he made his way to Carthage, arriving there after an absence of thirty-six years.

Polybius' verdict on Scipio's victory says it all.

Such was the end of the battle, fought under these famous commanders; a battle on which everything depended, and which assigned universal domination to Rome . . . He [Hannibal] had done in the battle all that was to be expected of a good and experienced general. First, he had tried by interview with his opponent to see what he could do to secure peace; and that was the right course for a man who, while fully conscious of his former victories, yet mistrusts Fortune, and has his eye to all the possible and unexpected contingenices of war. Next, having accepted battle, the excellence of his dispositions for a contest with the Romans, considering the identity of the arms on each side, could not have been surpassed. For though the Roman line is hard to break, yet each individual soldier and each company, owing to the uniform tactics employed, can fight in any direction. Those companies which happen to be in the nearest contact with the danger, wheeling round to the point required. Again, the nature of their arms gives at once protection and confidence, for their shield is larger and their sword will not bend; the Romans are therefore formidable on the field and hard to conquer.

Still Hannibal took his measure against each of these difficulties in a manner that can not be surpassed. He provided himself with those numbers of elephants and put them in the van, for the express purpose of throwing the enemy's ranks into confusion and breaking their order. Again he stationed the mercenaries in front and the Carthaginians behind them, in order to wear out the bodies of the enemy with fatigue beforehand, and to blunt the edge of their swords by the numbers that would be killed by them . . . But the most warlike and steady part of his army he held in reserve at some distance, in order that they might not see what was happening too closely, but with strength and spirit unimpaired, might use their strength and courage to best advantage when the moment arrived. Then, if in spite of having done everything that could be done, he who had never been beaten before failed to secure the victory now, we must excuse him. For there are times when chance thwarts the plans of the brave; and there are others again when a man though great and brave, has met a greater still. And this, we might say was the case with Hannibal on this occasion.

An opinion we will consider later when comparing the two commanders.

It is perhaps strange that two of the most illustrious commanders in history, whose battles had always previously been stamped by originality and subtlety, should have resorted to what was little more than a slogging match when encountering one another at Zama. The element of surprise was absent on both sides; the presence of Hannibal's elephants was obviously known to Scipio, and while Scipio may have deceived Hannibal as to the true strength of his cavalry, such deception was hardly significant. The redeployment Scipio, and probably Hannibal, undertook in mid-battle certainly displayed tactical flexibility of a high order, but it was less than subtle. One can only conclude that, given the limitations of the ground and the standards of training among the different national contingents within their armies, the two great generals had checkmated one another tactically. While at the operational level, in view of Hannibal's earlier example in Etruria which had led to Trasimene, and in Apulia to Cannae, Scipio had hardly displayed great originality in ravaging the Bagradas valley, so drawing Hannibal away from his own secure base into a hostile interior. That Hannibal had found himself having to fight on ground and under conditions not of his own choosing, was in fact an inevitable consequence of the far-sighted strategic decision by Scipio to transfer the war onto Carthaginian territory. The interesting aspect of the battle of Zama is, then, not in the way it was conducted tactically, but the interplay it shows between the strategic, operational and tactical levels of war.

After sacking the Carthaginian camp, Scipio ordered Gnaeus Octavius to march the legions to Carthage, while he took his fleet, which had been augmented by a further fifty warships, to Tunis, first inspecting Carthage from the sea much in the same way as Hannibal had ridden forward to satisfy his curiosity by having a close look at Rome. As he approached the Punic capital, Scipio was met by a Carthaginian ship decked with woollen filets and olive branches of supplication, carrying ten leading citizens sent by Hannibal to sue for peace. When they drew alongside the flagship and began to beg for mercy, they were curtly ordered by Scipio to report to him later in Tunis. Scipio then sailed on to Carthage and viewed the city more closely, before continuing his journey. While Gnaeus Octavius was still on the march, news reached him that Vermina, the son of Syphax, was on his way with substantial reinforcements for the Carthaginians. Octavius dispatched a part of his infantry and all his cavalry to deal with the Numidians who, after being surrounded, were cut to pieces and the survivors dispersed.

The Roman army then gathered in its old camp at Tunis, where it was joined by its commander, who shortly afterwards received the thirty Carthaginian envoys charged with suing for peace. In no hurry to allay their anxieties, Scipio kept them waiting for some twenty-four hours while he held a council of war to decide the Roman response. Recalling the treachery of the Carthaginians in breaking the earlier truce, there were many who called for the immediate destruction of Carthage, but their enthusiasm was tempered by reminders of the long and painful siege that would have to be undertaken, and Scipio's own powerful advocacy for a peace settlement.

The next day the envoys were summoned before Scipio to hear the peace terms. The Carthaginians would be free to live their lives according to their own customs and laws; they could retain all the territory and possessions they had held in North Africa before the war; and the Romans would cease all hostile acts once an agreement had been reached. But there was a price to be paid. All deserters, runaway slaves and prisoners were to be handed over; with the exception of ten triremes, all the warships were to be surrendered, together with the elephants, while the training of others was forbidden; the Carthaginians were not to make war on anyone, inside or outside Africa, without obtaining permission from Rome; a treaty was to be drawn up with Masinissa which restored all the territory and property that had belonged to him and his ancestors; the Roman army was to be provisioned for three months, and paid until the peace mission had returned from Rome; a large indemnity of silver was to be paid in equal instalments within fifty years; one hundred hostages were to be selected by Scipio from young men between the ages of fourteen and thirty; finally (and only according to Livy) the transports, stores and crews seized during the previous truce were to be returned, otherwise there would be no armistice or hope of peace. But in view of the time that had elapsed, an equivalent in silver could be paid for any of the stores that had been consumed.

The Senate's preoccupation with political diplomacy and military considerations to the exclusion of any clauses establishing commercial advantages, indicates the priorities and attitudes prevailing among the Romans. So it had been with Catulus' earlier treaty ending the First Punic War, as well as those made with Carthage during the 6th, 4th and 3rd centuries BC which, as has been related, while effectively shutting out the Romans from the whole of the western Mediterranean, only barred the Carthaginians from certain cities on the Latium seaboard. Though during these earlier periods the Roman fleet was of insignificant proportions, their subsequent acquisition of a substantial maritime capability appears to have been regarded as being of no commercial consequence. They even burned the Carthaginian fleet after it had been surrendered to them instead of using it for trading purposes.

With the return of the envoys to Carthage Hannibal, though vanquished, was also to display statesmanship, particularly by restraining the hotheads who argued against acceptance of the Roman terms. Inevitably the treaty was more severe than that which had been concluded previously: the number of warships allowed was halved, the indemnity was increased, and Punic military rights were drastically curtailed; Carthage was to be little more than a client state, utterly dependent on Roman good will for her future existence;

Masinissa was to be elevated to a position of unchallenged authority throughout the whole of Numidia and as a loyal ally of Rome would act as a powerful restraining influence on any future Carthaginian ambitions. Though probably she was no weaker than after the ending of the First Punic War, Carthage's potential for recovery had been drastically reduced with the loss of her overseas empire, and she had to recognise that her days as a major political and military power had ended. All she could do now was to concentrate on developing her trade and agriculture. Yet, however inglorious and humiliating the treaty's terms might be, Hannibal recognised the realities of the situation, and regarded the Roman conditions as providing at least an assurance of Carthage's survival.

After receiving Carthaginian acceptance of his terms, Scipio despatched a delegation from Tunis to Rome seeking the Senate's endorsement of these provisional arrangements. Meeting in the temple of Bellona, the Senate listened to an account of the battle, which was repeated to the crowds thronging outside, and then declared three days of public thanksgiving and threw open all the city temples. The election of the consuls for the following year were then held, resulting in the appointment of Gnaeus Cornelius Lentulus and Aelius Paetus, and the political infighting began.

Lentulus wanted to obtain Africa as his province and refused to allow any business to be concluded until this had been agreed, but his bid for self-aggrandisement failed when the issue was put to the People: Scipio was to remain in command of the army, and bring it home when the final arrangements for peace had been concluded; Lentulus had to content himself with command of the fleet, now an appointment of little consequence. This issue being settled, the Senate called upon the Carthaginian envoys to state their case for the treaty's acceptance, which they did in a manner that gained the support of the great majority. The thwarted Lentulus intervened once again to prevent the resolution being passed, but he was overruled by the People to whom the matter had been referred by two plebeian tribunes.

The peace terms having been agreed, the conditions which had been stipulated were then promptly put into execution. Livy says that 500 ships were surrendered, then towed out to sea and burnt; the elephants, runaway slaves and 4000 prisoners of war were handed over, together with the deserters who were given short shrift; the Latins being beheaded and the Romans crucified; finally, Masinissa was presented with the city of Cirta and all the remaining towns which had been captured by the Romans.

Scipio then embarked his army in Tunis and returned to Lilybaeum, from where he had sailed three years previously. Sending most of his troops on by sea, Scipio himself made his way through Italy to be tumultuously acclaimed by enthusiastic crowds along his route, and perhaps granted the greatest triumph ever on entering Rome. He was also accorded the title of Africanus. Now Scipio repeated the munificence he had displayed on returning from Spain; he presented the treasury with 123,000 lbs of silver, while additionally distributing 400 asses (about £34) to each of his soldiers. The war that had brought devastation to the whole of the Mediterranean during the previous seventeen years had come to an end. And although Rome had paid a terrible price in human lives and material destruction, she had finally established herself as an imperial power of unmatched military might.

CHAPTER TWENTY-ONE

POLITICAL FERMENT
201–149 BC

No sooner had peace been declared in 201 BC than the Gauls, as they had done after the First Punic War, reopened hostilities. As the war in Africa had been drawing to a close and Hannibal had withdrawn from Italy, Roman colonisation of the Po valley had been resumed and old Gallic fears revived. The Boii, who had been the most directly affected, and the Insubres, stimulated by a Carthaginian officer called Hamilcar who had been left behind following Mago's withdrawal, both rose in revolt. The two forward Roman settlements of Placentia and Cremona were attacked, and though Cremona was relieved after a major battle in which Hamilcar was killed, Placentia was taken by storm and ruthlessly sacked; the savage fighting then continuing until peace was declared five years later in 196 BC. Once again the Romans had been fortunate that following the defeat of the Carthaginians, the Gauls had not anticipated the renewed colonisation of their tribal lands. Had this been the case, Mago's expedition could have proved a far greater menace.

As has been seen, during the Second Punic War, and especially towards its close, Rome's direction of her strategic objectives was affected by the various political factions, each motivated by what were frequently conflicting ambitions. On his return to Rome after the victory of Zama, Scipio Africanus was undoubtedly the most powerful figure in the city, enjoying the rapturous welcome and support of the people, while the latent jealousy of many senators was masked by the need to show respect for a national hero. Though already during the war an individual's political interests had sometimes cut across family factions, with the advent of peace and the enlargement of Rome's imperial horizons traditional family loyalties appear to have been increasingly affected by the creation of wider groups. Sharing common interests and objectives, these associations formed what were virtually embryonic political parties, reinforced by the system of *clientela*, which has already been discussed in Chapter 2. But in any case, however based, opposition to the Scipio clan steadily grew, quietly at first while his reputation put him out of reach of overt attack, but more shrilly as the passage of time reduced such restraint, until in 184 BC Scipio finally withdrew from public life in disgust.

With the removal of his moderate and restraining influence, a more thrusting and uncompromising party came to power, to give a new face and direction to Roman policy. The leader of this new group was Cato, a well-to-do Tuscan farmer who, as Plutarch tells us, though observing the ancestral custom of working the land with his own hands, owned a large number of slaves, mainly prisoners of war. Articulate and pithy, he came to be known as the Roman Demosthenes, attracting broad support because of his unblemished integrity and conservative attitudes. Although he had been one of those most opposed to Scipio's African adventure, Cato had followed him to Sicily as a quaestor, or financial official, in 205 BC when, according to Plutarch, he had remonstrated with Scipio for his personal extravagance and the high pay he was awarding his volunteer troops. Having been dismissively told by Scipio that military preparations were the responsibility of the commander, and that he had no time for 'a niggling quaestor', Cato had returned to Rome where he lodged a formal complaint against Scipio.

This, as will be recalled, resulted in the dispatch of a commission to enquire into Scipio's command. After having been vindicated, Scipio then gave Cato charge of the supply of ships when the army crossed to Africa – which, though of vital importance, can hardly have been regarded as being the most prestigious of appointments. Cato was later to command the Roman garrison in Sardinia as a praetor in 198 BC where, once again according to Plutarch, he fell out with Scipio, who travelled to Spain especially to try and remove him from office. Nevertheless he served with distinction when commanding a province during the period of final tribal subjugation, and as a military tribune was also to fight against Antiochus in Greece at the battle of Thermopylae in 191 BC. Austere, condemnatory of all forms of ostentation, and despising Hellenism, this redheaded, grey-eyed senator's antipathy to Scipio must have been born in Sicily, early in his career, while his hatred of all things Carthaginian was instinctive and deep-rooted. So, as will be seen, can one man's attitudes exert a powerful influence on the course of history.

Largely as a consequence of the long and widespread war that had just ended, Roman expansion was able to continue. The acquisition of Spain led to the establishment of Provincia in southern France, later to serve as a springboard for Caesar's conquest of Gaul as far as the banks of the Rhine. Meanwhile across the Adriatic, memories of Philip's alliance with Hannibal, together with the allegations that he had sent an expeditionary force to North Africa, had turned Roman eyes eastward; leading inexorably to the Second Macedonian War. Taking advantage of Antiochus the Great's involvement with the Egyptians in Syria and Palestine, the Romans decisively defeated his ally Philip at Cynoscephalae in 197 BC. The Romans' fear that following his absorption of Thrace into his empire Antiochus would intervene in Greece and dispute their right to determine Hellenic affairs, led to a breakdown of relations in 195 BC. After five years of tension, the Roman legions eventually marched through Greece into Asia Minor. Here in 190 BC, Antiochus suffered a crushing defeat at Magnesia, when his massive phalanx, 16,000-strong and thirty-two ranks deep, which formed his centre, was outflanked and destroyed. Then, following Philip's death, the Romans alleged that the measures being taken by his successor Perseus to strengthen his kingdom were directed against them, and this led to the Third Macedonian War in 171 BC and Perseus' defeat at Pydna. Now, thirty years after Zama, the Romans had reduced Macedonia and Syria to vassalage and Egypt, the third great eastern power under its child king Ptolemy VI and the country's true ruler, the Queen Mother Cleopatra, tacitly acknowledged Roman hegemony. Affairs in the eastern Mediterranean having been settled, but stirred up by the implacable hatred of Cato, Roman attention once again slowly and fatefully turned to Carthage.

While these events had been occupying Rome, Carthage had been learning to adapt to her changed circumstances. Following the loss of her overseas possessions and the establishment of a united Numidian empire as a client of Rome on her doorstep, no longer was she a political or military power of any consequence. Devoid of allies herself and restricted in her freedom of action, Carthage's future existence depended upon the revival of her economy and most importantly, astute political skills. The Carthaginians had to overcome three interrelated problems: the first was entirely economic, to repair the war damage she had suffered, restore her commercial trade, agricultural production and mineral exploitation; the second was political and dependent upon the first, to give satisfaction to Rome by punctually paying off the war indemnity; the third was also political upon which her economic recovery ultimately depended; to contain Masinissa's territorial ambitions. We will now consider how far the Carthaginians were able to meet these requirements.

For the first few months of peace, Hannibal had remained in command of the remnants of the army and had striven to repair the damage inflicted on Carthage's war-torn rural areas; he then retired into private life as an ordinary citizen. For the first three years following the war, Carthage was ruled by the oligarchic party whose mismanagement, corruption and excessive taxation of the poorer classes seriously impaired economic recovery. As a result, the 199 BC war indemnity was paid in such poor quality silver that it was rejected by the quaestors in Rome. Any further such lapses carried the risk of Roman intervention into Carthaginian affairs with unknown consequences. Although this danger was averted, administrative and economic mismanagement continued until 196 BC, when Hannibal took office as a suffete and introduced far-reaching reforms. The searching inquiries he instigated and the fundamental changes that followed soon aroused strong opposition, leading to a direct clash with the all-powerful Assembly of the Hundred which was then dominated by a self-perpetuating oligarchic clique who exploited the perquisites of office to the full.

By appealing to the people over their heads, Hannibal was able to introduce a law requiring the Assembly's judges to be elected annually, and restricting their eligibility for selection to two years. His reforms soon showed that, if state expenditure were properly handled and the peculations stopped, excessive taxation was not necessary. Such measures met with general acclaim as the economy started to revive, and the discredited oligarchs not only found themselves financially accountable, but having to restore what they had corruptly obtained. The anti-Barcid party then started conspiring with their friends and contacts in Rome for the removal of Hannibal. Accusations were made that he had been conspiring with Antiochus of Syria and plotting against Rome, while reports were circulated that an army of Macedonian mercenaries was being formed. Using the whole weight of his prestige and authority, Scipio Africanus then condemned any Roman intervention in what was no more than a factional Carthaginian disagreement. But Scipio's powerful voice for moderation and reasonableness in Rome's relations with Carthage was stilled when, as we have seen, he himself became a victim of Roman political intrigue. In 195 BC a delegation was sent to Carthage, ostensibily to inquire into a boundary dispute with Masinissa, but in reality to bring about Hannibal's removal. Undeceived and realising that Carthage could be put into the position of having either to hand him over or face Roman wrath, Hannibal took refuge in flight. After making careful preparations, he slipped out of Carthage and by using relays of horses reached Thapsus, from where he sailed to Tyre and then on to Ephesus to join Antiochus – so confirming the worst of

Roman suspicions. When the senatorial delegation arrived in Carthage, formal charges were layed against Hannibal for plotting with Antiochus, and when demands were made that he should be punished, the Carthaginian Senate cravenly responded that they would do whatever the Romans thought best.

In fact, it will never be known if Hannibal had been in earlier contact with Antiochus. He may well have considered that Rome would eventually come into conflict with the Hellenistic kingdoms, from which Carthage would have been able to profit, and even if the defeat suffered by Philip of Macedon at Cynoscephalae in 197 BC was something of a setback, all was far from being lost. The disaster to be suffered by Antiochus at Magnesia still lay in the future and in the meantime, in the very year of Hannibal's flight, the growing tension between Rome and Syria had led to a breakdown in their relations. Whatever truth there may have been in the accusations made against Hannibal, he remained in the court of Antiochus for several years, and was not backward in giving his views as to how Rome could be defeated. According to Livy he put forward two proposals, the first in 193 BC and the other two years later. In essence Hannibal believed the war should be carried into Italy, where both supplies and willing reinforcements could be obtained. In this way the Romans would be forced onto the defensive and so be unable to mobilise their overwhelming resources for an offensive elsewhere. He asked that he should be provided with 100 ships, 10,000 infantry and 1000 cavalry with whom he would cross over to Africa and induce the Carthaginians to rise in revolt, he himself then being ready to land in Italy. In the meanwhile Antiochus should threaten to invade Italy across the Adriatic. The same year, one of his agents was picked up trying to engage Carthaginian support and prepare for his return. Hannibal's second proposal was only a variant on his first: he should sail directly to the west coast of Italy, then Antiochus should cross the Adriatic. But Antiochus evidently remained unconvinced and the venture came to nothing.

The effectiveness of Hannibal's administrative and constitutional reforms, however, is demonstrated by the continuing rise in Carthaginian prosperity even after his flight. In 191 BC, Carthage offered to pay off the whole of the war indemnity, while supplying large quantities of grain to provision the Roman armies – offers which either for reasons of hurt pride, or from a desire not to end symbols of Punic subservience, were disdainfully declined. No more than the fulfilment of her treaty obligations was expected of Carthage. But how far Carthage was prepared to go in order to placate the Romans and show her loyalty as an ally is indicated by the presence of

Carthaginian contingents fighting alongside them in their wars against Philip, Antiochus and Perseus.

The Carthaginians' third major requirement, to contain Masinissa, would necessitate exercising a finely balanced judgement: preventing his territorial expansion from undermining their economy, and at the same time avoiding acrimonious disputes which would offend Rome. Torn by conflicting factional interests, the Carthaginians were to find this balance impossible to achieve. At the end of the war Masinissa had been thirty-seven years old, vigorous and ambitious, strongly influenced by close contact with the Carthaginians in his youth, and determined to weld the Numidians into a united kingdom – and in so doing to introduce what he saw to be essential social and economic changes. The nomadic lifestyle of this horse-orientated warrior race was to be changed to one based on settled agricultural communities. But farmers require good, well-watered land for cultivation, much of which lay in Carthaginian territory, so that the more successful were Masinissa's reforms, the greater were the pressures on his boundaries with Carthage. Numidia had prospered under Masinissa's firm and clear-sighted direction, and although his further ambitions to extend its frontiers from the Atlantic to Egypt remained unfulfilled, substantial acquisitions were made at the expense of the Carthaginians. First of all the Punic western maritime colonies were absorbed, then in 161 BC one of the richest provinces, Emporia on the Gulf of Gabès. With age doing little to dim Masinissa's vitality – when ninety he would still be able to mount unaided and ride bareback, while at the age of eighty-six he had fathered his forty-fourth son – over a period of some fifty years his designs made a forceful contribution to the renewal of hostilities between Carthage and Rome. But apart from his reforming zeal and physical durability, Masinissa had also shown himself to be an outstanding administrator, and a skilful diplomat in playing off Carthage against Rome to his own advantage.

Given such circumstances, it is hardly surprising that a series of boundary disputes led not only to increasing friction between Masinissa and the Carthaginians, but to skirmishes of growing severity, then developing into reprisal raids which eventually led to war. The chronology of Masinissa's encroachments is not clear, but can in part be judged by recorded Roman reactions in the dispatch of various adjudicative boundary commissions. Since these generally favoured Masinissa, their findings must have served to further the sense of frustration and indignation felt by the Carthaginians, so stimulating overreaction. Two such commissions were sent between 193 BC and 161 BC without achieving any durable settlement, and the continuing dispute led to spasmodic fighting for five years. It was not until the commission of 155 BC that portents of the fate awaiting Carthage were clearly displayed.

The commission was headed by the doughty upholder of austere Roman virtues and opponent of degenerate eastern influences, the eighty-one-year-old Cato. Though he probably came with predetermined views, all Cato's instinctive distrust of everything Carthaginian was aroused by what he saw and heard. Though Carthage could not have been as prosperous as she had been in the previous century, the legacies of that wealth must still have been apparent in the splendour of her buildings, the richness of her temple shrines and the abundance of her works of art. The extraordinary speed of the Punic economic revival, indicated by the perhaps unwise offer to pay off the whole of the war indemnity some thirty years previously, would now have been readily apparent. The Carthaginians' workshops filled the overseas markets with products exhibiting the highest skills of craftmanship: furniture inlaid with ivory, woollen and linen goods pigmented with a uniquely indelible dye obtained from molluscs; glass, pottery, jewellery; and a whole range of non-precious metal objects of a practical nature, such as bowls, jugs, amphorae, hairpins and razors. But Cato would have noticed a more sinister side to this manufacturing capacity, for apart from producing a wide variety of domestic and hunting tools, such as knives, spears and daggers, the Carthaginians had also been able to re-equip themselves with a vast store of military weapons. Nor would the story have ended there; as a protagonist of the return to old standards, Cato would have noticed further indications of Carthaginian degeneracy. New forms of religion, less demanding and more personal, were replacing the old Carthaginian beliefs and customs. There was a greater reluctance to devote wealth to the gods and the dead. Living for today and not tomorrow was increasing the pace of decline. Carthage's prosperity, her manufacturing and military capability, and the decadence of her culture and citizens all posed an unacceptable and growing threat to everything that Cato believed Rome stood for.

Since Rome had just defeated the armies of Philip, Antiochus and Perseus, Cato cannot really have considered that Carthage posed a serious military threat. Though no doubt it was politically expedient to make use of this danger, the true reasons for Cato's hostility appear to have been his belief that the two races represented conflicting cultures, together with a liberal overlay of resentful envy at the disparity in wealth existing between them.

Whatever his personal motivations may have been, when he returned to Rome Cato was explicit in his condemnation of Carthage as a hostile military power on Rome's very doorstep. To illustrate the point, he contrived to drop some figs in the Senate House, and when the senators remarked on their size and beauty, he commented that the country which produced them was only three days' sail from Rome.

The only voice for moderation was that of Publius Cornelius Scipio Nasica, who managed to arrange that he should lead the commission of 152 and 151 BC, tasked with investigating the situation in North Africa. But although in his report the Carthaginians were criticised for the build- up of their forces, for the first time Masinissa had to yield some of the Carthaginian territory he had annexed. When the commission returned to Rome and gave their report, the Senate decided to refrain from war so long as Carthage demobilised and burnt their fleet. Before there was any question of these measures being implemented, however, the final climax broke. The pro-Numidian party in the Punic capital, which had been pursuing a policy of conciliation with Masinissa, was ousted from power and replaced by the War Party. This led to further border clashes and the eviction of Masinissa's supporters from Carthage, resulting in him attacking the town of Oroscopa. In the absence of any immediately enforceable restraint, the fighting escalated and in the winter of 151 BC, a 25,000 strong Carthaginian army under a hitherto unknown Hasdrubal marched into the plains of the interior with Masinissa withdrawing before them. They were joined by two of Masinissa's sons, who could not have anticipated receiving much in the normal course of inheritance, with 6000 Numidians. But Hasdrubal was worsted in a full-scale battle and, after having been surrounded, reduced to starvation and beset by disease amid their unburied dead, the Carthaginians surrendered. Only Hasdrubal and a few survivors managed to escape to Carthage, the remainder being massacred as soon as they laid down their arms.

In Carthage, news of this defeat and reports that the Romans had mobilised four new legions brought a realisation that things had gone too far. By waging war against Masinissa without first obtaining Roman approval, the Carthaginians had been in clear breach of the peace treaty. A display of penitence was necessary if the Romans were to be placated, so Hasdrubal and Carthalo, the commander of a small mercenary army, were promptly condemned to death. But Hasdrubal managed to escape and raise a new 20,000-strong army from the outer districts of Carthaginian-held territory. The Roman response was not favourable either, the envoys merely demanding to know why the culprits had not been condemned before, rather than after the war. Purposely concealing their real intentions, the Romans continued with their preparations for war. Sensing the fate awaiting Carthage, in 149 BC Utica sent envoys to Rome declaring her readiness to provide all the help at her disposal. This satisfactory development for the

Romans cannot have been altogether unexpected, since their agents had been busy in the city for several months.

When further reports reached Carthage that a Roman army and fleet were being assembled in Sicily, the Senate realised that there was no alternative but to submit unconditionally. Five envoys were accordingly sent to Rome with plenary powers, only to be told that war had already been decided upon. Realising that there was now nothing to negotiate, the envoys offered unconditional surrender, accepting the conditions which Polybius describes: 'those who surrender to the Roman authority, surrender all territory and the cities in it, together with all men and women in all such territory or cities, likewise rivers, harbours temples and tombs, so that the Romans should become actual lords of all these, and those who surrender should remain lords of nothing at all.'

The envoys were then summoned before the Roman Senate and its decision was made known. The Carthaginians had been well-advised to surrender as they had done, they would therefore be granted the freedom to live under their own laws, and allowed to retain all their property, both public and private. But certain undertakings were required of them in return. Three hundred hostages, selected from the families of the Senate and those of the Hundred, were to be sent to Lilybaeum within thirty days. Moreover, on their arrival in Africa further orders would be given by the consuls which must be obeyed.

In the debate which followed the return of the envoys to Carthage, their Senate expressed concern at the ominous reference to further orders, but decided that everything the Romans demanded should be accepted, unless any additional conditions were to be so oppressive as to make it impossible for them to be met. There was thus a realisation that the only alternative was between accepting total submission and facing the terrors of Roman retribution. Amid deep anxiety and sorrow, the three hundred hostages were then dispatched to Lilybaeum, from where they were transported to Rome and imprisoned in the naval dockyard. Shortly afterwards the Romans disembarked at Utica, the ranks of their legions having been swollen by volunteers anticipating easy and rich pickings. Further Carthaginian envoys now arrived in Utica, seeking clarification as to the further orders the consuls would be giving, and expressing an eager willingness to comply. After warmly commending them for their attitude, the Senate gave the envoys the details of its further orders: the Carthaginians were to hand over all the weapons in their possession. After vainly protesting that this would leave them incapable of defending themselves, the Carthaginians reluctantly surrendered 200,000 sets of arms and 2000 catapults. Without the need for any further dissimulation, the Romans then revealed their full intentions.

The Carthaginians must evacuate their city. They could settle where they chose, so long as it was at least ten miles from the sea; Carthage itself would be destroyed.

Though the Romans had given no assurance about the future of the city, the clear assumption had been that once the Carthaginians had handed over their arms it would not be sacked nor the population enslaved. Overwhelmed at such ruthless Roman duplicity, some of the Carthaginian envoys took flight rather than face the indignation and wrath of their countrymen. The remainder of the unfortunate envoys then returned to Carthage their gloomy faces portraying their dismay as they made their way in silence through the anxious crowds to the Senate house. Here they made their report among cries of disbelief and acrimony, with the news soon spreading to the overwrought crowd thronging outside. Bursting into the building, the infuriated citizens stoned to death all those held to have been responsible for the fateful negotiations. In a wave of fear and anger the crowd then turned on the city's Italian community, but as their emotions abated and more sober thoughts took hold, so their resolution hardened.

Once the fortifications of their city had been left behind the Carthaginians would stand defenceless, while the loss of this great harbour and their banishment from the coast would spell the death of their trade and prosperity. The extinction of the Carthaginian race would therefore follow as inexorably from accepting the Roman terms as it would from defying them. Better to die fighting for all that they most cherished, than to obtain an ignominious respite but suffer a no less certain death. The decision taken, the gates were closed, the slaves freed and the walls manned, while the temples and public places were turned over to the manufacture of arms. By toiling unceasingly, the Carthaginians were able to turn out 100 shields, 300 swords and 500 javelins every day. Social and other distinctions being forgotten in common adversity, among many other personal sacrifices the women of all classes offered their hair to make cords for the catapults and the men shared the calls for labour.

Two new generals were elected, the condemned Hasdrubal together with a grandson of Masinissa, and a truce of thirty days was requested to enable a further delegation to go to Rome; but the plea was rejected. Although the coastal towns of Hadrumetum, Leptis Minor, Thapsus, and Achilia, together with two inland cities, Usilla and Theudalis went over to the Romans, Hasdrubal was able to obtain the support of some of the Libyan tribes, and also rush provisions into Carthage. In the meantime the Romans were apparently content to watch developments, perhaps because considerable doubt existed as to Masinissa's response. To begin with he had been hesitant about providing support for the Romans, possibly thinking that to accept them in exchange for the Carthaginians would be unlikely to further his own ambitions. Also, since two of Masinissa's sons had sided with the Carthaginians, and now one of his grandsons had been appointed as a general, the Romans could well have considered it more prudent to clarify the situation before committing themselves to an assault on Carthage. But eventually, early in the summer of 149 BC the Roman legions marched out of their camp at Castra Cornelia, intent on the annihilation of the Carthaginian race.

PART FIVE

THE THIRD PUNIC WAR
149–148 BC

CHAPTER TWENTY-TWO

THE DESTRUCTION OF CARTHAGE
149–148 BC

As has been described (Chapter I), Carthage had been raised on a naturally strong defensive position and then extensively fortified. There were only two restricted land approaches, either along the 3000-yard-wide isthmus in the north, protected by three lines of massive defence works towering one above the other, or along the narrow spit of sand to the south, which terminated at the foot of the city walls. The two isthmuses were separated by the unfordable Lake of Tunis, and washed by the sea on their outer shores. The single twenty-two mile city wall enclosed the great harbour, the entrance of which lay just to the east of the southern sand bar, as well as the citadel constructed on the prominent Byrsa mound, not far distant from the harbour.

The Romans divided their forces between the two isthmuses and prepared for the assault. In the north, Manius Manilius established his camp on the isthmus itself, so blocking all entrance to and from the city along the principal supply route. Together with the fleet, Lucius Marcius Censorinus took up a position to the south, but suffered an early reverse when Hasdrubal's cavalry from his stronghold in the interior surprised a working party cutting timber and killed 500 men. Exercising greater attention to security thereafter, the Romans continued their preparations.

Either because he expected the Carthaginian resistance to be ineffectual, or because he lacked the imagination to do otherwise, Manilius decided to try to carry the main north and south defence works by storm. Not surprisingly he met with a bloody repulse in the north, but this did not deter him from trying equally unsuccessfully for a second time. To the south, Censorinus fared somewhat better.

By using huge battering rams propelled by several thousand sailors and soldiers, a breach was made in the city wall. But the assault troops were not ready until the following day, which gave the Carthaginians time to throw up fresh barriers during the night and man the surrounding rooftops. A hail of missiles now met the Romans who were driven back in confusion; a rout was averted only by the timely intervention of Publius Cornelius Scipio Aemilianus, the adopted grandson of Africanus, who was serving as a tribune with the fourth legion. Roman impetuosity was then sharply curbed and they settled down to the more prosaic business of blockading the city.

In the summer of the following year, Censorinus' army suffered severely from the heat and the unhealthy marshes where they were camped. As the death toll mounted, he was forced to withdraw the legions and the fleet to a site where they would benefit from the fresh sea breezes. The Carthaginians then cut loose fire ships to drift in on a favourable wind among the Roman fleet at its new anchorage and do considerable damage. In the autumn, with the approach of the consular elections, Censorinus set sail for Rome but on his way, no doubt so as to be able to claim some achievement, he broke his journey to capture the island of Aegimurus lying at the mouth of the Gulf of Tunis.

The Carthaginians now mounted a powerful raid against Manilius along the northern isthmus, but after catching the Romans by surprise they were driven back by Scipio Aemilianus, who made another timely intervention to prevent them exploiting their initial success. Alarmed at the mauling he had received, Manilius abandoned his forward position, and constructed a new fortified camp and protected anchorage for his ships further to the rear. The close investment of Carthage was thus raised, but – probably in an attempt to prevent supplies reaching the city – Manilius mounted a number of raids into the interior instead. When these proved ineffective and before the winter set in, he decided to undertake a full scale expedition, its target being Hasdrubal's stronghold in the hills around Nepheris (Bou-Beker), twenty miles south east of Tunis.

Hasdrubal had occupied high ground at the head of a steep and tapering valley, across the mouth of which ran a wadi. When the Romans reached this obstacle, Scipio advised that a well-fortified camp be constructed on the far side of the wadi, so as to provide a secure base from which to continue the advance. But in the council of war which followed he was overruled and the advance was resumed. In crossing the broken ground around the wadi, the leading legion had to break formation and was unable to re-form when it suddenly came under attack. Dispersing in every direction, it was only saved from annihilation by Scipio, who had stood ready, fully expecting just such a disaster. That night, when the troops were re-formed, it was discovered that three of the *maniples* had been cut off on the far side of the wadi; they were now encircled by the Carthaginians and had taken refuge on a hill. Acting quickly, Scipio moved a force of cavalry behind the Roman position while it was still dark, and by mounting a sudden charge was able to break the Carthaginian ring and relieve the beleagured *maniples*. Withdrawal towards Tunis then began, and although the majority of the fighting troops managed to reach the city, a large number of the less fortunate camp followers fell victim to the marauding Numidian cavalry. After this fiasco and with the onset of winter, Manilius withdrew even further west from Carthage, to occupy quarters at Castra Cornelia on the mouth of the Bagradas.

Ever since he had begun to appreciate the scale of their re-involvement in Africa, Masinissa's relationship with the Romans had been steadily deteriorating, and requests for his assistance throughout the winter had met with only vague promises. But the situation suddenly changed when Masinissa died in 149 BC, the same year as the death of Cato. Without Masinissa's powerful leadership, the unity of the Numidian kingdom which he had striven so hard to create started to unravel. The realm was divided between his three legitimate sons, the others having to content themselves with fiefs in the outlying parts, and Scipio, who curiously had been appointed as the old king's executor, was quick to take advantage of this new realignment of power. The most warlike of the three legitimate sons, Gulussa, who also commanded the army, was persuaded to assist in the destruction of Carthage. It is a poignant reflection on the conduct of human affairs that, while Scipio Africanus had laid the foundations for the creation of Masinissa's kingdom and won his trust, his adopted grandson on inheriting that trust should then have been largely responsible for the kingdom's dissolution. Further Numidian support was obtained when, following another expedition mounted by Manilius against Hasdrubal near Nepheris, his cavalry commander, Himilco Phameas, was persuaded by Scipio to desert in exchange for a free pardon.

The new consul to command in Africa for 148 BC was Gaius Culpurnius Piso, who had been defeated in Spain in 154 BC and came from an undistinguished background; the fleet commander was the legate Hostilius Mancinus, who does not appear to have been any more gifted. In consequence perhaps, the siege of Carthage was virtually raised, and the legions were dispersed in attacks against a number of small cities in the interior and along the coast of the Gulf of Carthage. A combined sea and land assault on Clupea failed and, though Neapolis surrendered only to be sacked, Hippo Agra stood firm. Following the destruction of their siege engines by a sudden sortie supported from Carthage, the Romans withdrew into winter quarters at Castra Cornelia, Africanus' old camp.

The obvious failure of leadership which had wasted the first two years of the war led to deep discontent in Rome, a situation the Scipionic faction were quick to exploit. Though Scipio Aemilianus, being only a tribune, had not had the chance to show the same brilliance as his adoptive grandfather, he had won distinction on the battlefield on at least three occasions. The support he received from the army was therefore enthusiastic, and when he sailed to Rome escorting Himilco Phameas the troops who came to see him off did not conceal their hope that he would return as their commander. Once back in Rome, Scipio soon gained the support of the people and, since just before his death Cato himself had lauded the youthful commander's achievements, Scipio was elected consul. A close friend of his former tutor Polybius, cultured and intelligent, Scipio raised fresh recruits, returned to Africa to assume his command, and arrived just in time to avert another crisis.

While Piso had been busy campaigning in the interior, the fleet commander Mancinus had discovered that a part of the city wall fronting the sea was only weakly defended, and so had landed with an assault party. After a brief fight, he had managed to secure an entry through one of the gates but, as no follow-up had been arranged, he soon found his men cut off and without supplies. On hearing of Mancinus' predicament, Scipio hastily embarked a strong contingent of troops and managed to re-embark the beleagured Romans and withdraw unmolested. After this incident, Scipio recalled Piso from the interior and brought a single clear aim to the campaign: the destruction of Carthage by close investment and assault. Discipline was tightened up, the swarm of hangers-on around the Roman base was summarily dispersed, the camp was then advanced towards Carthage, and its close investment began. A double line of earthworks was constructed across the isthmus, thus effectively preventing all supplies from reaching the city by land; it now only remained to close the sea route.

Using every available man and employing them in shifts round the clock, Scipio set his troops to work on the construction of a giant mole. The great harbour of Carthage consisted of two interconnected artificial docks, an inner circular naval yard and an outer rectangular mercantile dock, from the southern extremity of which a single entrance gave access to the sea. Scipio's plan was to completely block this entrance with a mole, reaching from the sand bar across the harbour mouth.

At first the Carthaginians did not believe that the Romans could succeed, but as the work relentlessly progressed they set about countering the project. Concealed from sight behind the encircling harbour walls, the Carthaginians worked with equal fervour to cut a new entrance giving access to the open sea from the east. Within the sanctuary of the harbour, capable of accommodating several hundred ships, the Carthaginians had also secretly constructed a new fleet. Now, as the Romans' mole neared completion, their new passage was opened and the Carthaginians could not contain their sense of achievement. Fifty triremes and a host of small craft sailed out in a triumphal display of contempt, flaunted themselves before the astonished Romans, and then returned into the shelter of the harbour. No doubt it gave them great pleasure to show the Romans that their prodigious expenditure of labour had been in vain, but by gratifying themselves in this manner, the Carthaginians had thrown away a chance to destroy the Roman fleet, which at that time had lain unmanned at anchor. Three days later, when they sailed out once again, the Romans were ready for them. An indecisive action was fought, but when the Carthaginians broke off in the afternoon and started to retire through the harbour entrance, they were closely pressed by the Romans. In their near panic to escape, a swarm of small craft blocked the harbour entrance, so forcing the triremes to take shelter against the outer quay. Here they turned their prows out to face the Romans, seeking protection from close assault under the cover of the rams and missiles positioned along the walls. But it was not until after dark, when the Romans had withdrawn, that the surviving Carthaginian ships managed to regain the security of the harbour.

Scipio's next move was to position his battering rams and other siege engines at the end of the now-completed mole. From here, working throughout the day, they concentrated their attack against the narrow head of wall protecting the seaward side of the harbour. A partial breach was made, but during the night a Carthaginian raiding party swam out to the mole and set fire to the closely-packed siege equipment. Utilising the respite that this gained, the Carthaginians worked feverishly to repair the damage and raise additional towers along the wall. But Scipio persevered with his attacks, finally succeeding in obtaining possession of the whole of the rectangle formed between the outer sea wall and that of the harbour. Though they had not gained access to the city itself, the outer wall of which still blocked their further advance, the Romans had taken possession of the new harbour entrance, so cutting Carthage off from both land and sea.

With Carthage's fate now sealed, Scipio turned his attention to clearing up the last pocket of Carthaginian resistance in the interior. Although Hasdrubal had been recalled to fight in the defence of Carthage, a considerable part of his army still remained in the field near Nepheris, under the command of one Diogenes, who must have been a Greek mercenary. Probably using no more than a legion at the most, Scipio moved some of his troops across the Lake of Tunis, while the remainder marched to where the Carthaginians had established their fortified camp. His preparations for the actual assault must have taken a considerable amount of time since, while they were under way, Scipio returned to Carthage more than once to check that the siege was being closely maintained. When all was ready, Scipio sent a thousand picked men round to the rear of the Carthaginian position, to remain concealed until the frontal attack had been fully developed. As had been intended, the Carthaginians rushed to man their defences against the Roman frontal assault, and so were completely surprised when suddenly taken in the rear. Abandoning their camp in panic, those who managed to escape made their way to Nepheris, hotly pursued by Gulussa and his Numidians.

Though the winter had by now set in, Nepheris was put under siege and fell some three weeks later to the Romans. With the destruction of the Carthaginian field army and Carthage itself closely invested, the remainder of the interior was quickly subdued. Now the last vestige of hope for relief that the Carthaginians may have held was irredeemably extinguished. To stiffen Carthaginian resistance Hasdrubal had already tortured and mutilated his Roman prisoners on the walls of the city before the eyes of Scipio's troops; whatever chance there may have been of coming to terms with the Romans had therefore been destroyed. Earlier peace feelers which the Romans had put out had also been rejected, their envoys not being permitted even to approach the city walls. The attitude of the Roman Senate had by now so hardened that Scipio had been expressly forbidden to show any accommodation. All that he was prepared to offer was the safety of Hasdrubal himself, of the garrison but not the field commander, of his own family and ten of his friends – terms which Hasdrubal was man enough to reject. There was now nothing more to be done except hold out until the Romans exacted their revenge through bloody assault or slow starvation.

The final assault was mounted from the harbour area, where the Romans had established themselves the previous autumn. After some desperate fighting they gained a foothold on the city wall, and then started to penetrate into the sprawling mass of dockyard buildings. As fresh reinforcements steadily extended the initial penetration and the Carthaginians' hold started to weaken, Hasdrubal ordered the whole area to be set alight. A new defensive line was then adopted, centred primarily on the citadel commanding the ridge of high ground extending east and west from Byrsa. When dawn broke, Scipio brought in a fresh legion to spearhead the advance against the citadel, but discipline broke down as his troops stopped to plunder one of the temples. The unimagined richness of the gold and silver ornaments and the heavily-adorned sacred statues led to a frenzy of looting, with the legionaries hacking the larger objects into more manageable proportions. But eventually the advance was resumed.

With the exception of the citadel itself, the defences of Byrsa were nothing like as formidable as those they had already overcome, but even so the Romans now faced some of the most ferocious fighting of the siege. The Carthaginians had turned every house surrounding the market place into a stronghold, each of which they then defended with a courage born of despair. To continue their advance the Romans had to clear the whole area, house by house and street by street. Some historians consider that the account by Appian, which gives a graphic description of the bitter fighting, was taken from Polybius, whose own eyewitness record has been largely lost.

The streets leading from the market square to the Byrsa were flanked by houses of six storeys from which the defenders poured a shower of missiles onto the Romans; when the attackers got inside the buildings the struggle continued on the roofs and on the planks covering the empty spaces; many were hurled to the ground or onto the weapons of those fighting in the streets. Scipio ordered all the sector to be fired and the ruins cleared away to give a better passage to his troops, and as this was done there fell with the walls many bodies of those who had hidden in the upper storey and been burned to death, and others who were still alive, wounded and badly burnt. Scipio had squadrons of soldiers ready to keep the streets clear for the rapid movement of his men, and dead or living were thrown together into pits, and it often happened that those who were not yet dead were crushed by the cavalry horses as they passed, not deliberately but in the heat of the battle.

For six days the battle raged. Then, on the seventh, Carthaginian envoys came out of the Byrsa offering to surrender but begging for their lives in return. After Scipio had granted their request, 50,000 terrified men, women and children nearing the limits of exhaustion and starvation, filed out to be sold later into slavery. But 900 Roman deserters, who could only expect crucifixion if taken alive, continued to fight on. At first they held out in the enclosure surrounding the temple of Eshmun, crowning the summit of the Byrsa; but as their numbers shrank, they fought in the building itself, then on the roof, before finally immolating themselves in the temple's flaming ruins. During this final stage of desperate resistance, Hasdrubal left the temple and surrendered to Scipio, who granted his life as an act of Roman clemency. But scorning her husband's cowardice, Hasdrubal's wife turned with her two children into the engulfing flames and died with the Roman deserters.

Reserving the gold, silver and sacred objects for the state, and excluding the legion which had stopped to pillage in mid-battle,

Scipio turned the city over to the troops to plunder. When appetites had been satiated and everything of value removed, the ruins of Carthage were levelled to the ground. A plough was then drawn over the site, salt thrown into the furrow and a curse pronounced that neither crops nor houses should ever rise again. The cities which had stood by Carthage to the end were also destroyed, while those like Utica, which had sided with Rome, were rewarded with their freedom and grants of former Carthaginian land. Further land was also given to Himilco Phameas and those other Numidians who had deserted to the Romans, while the remainder, some 5000 square miles, was annexed to form a new Roman province.

After some six centuries, Carthage had been destroyed. But the ephemeral nature of human endeavour was not lost on Scipio. To quote Polybius, who was there:

At the sight of the city utterly perishing among the flames he burst into tears, and stood long reflecting on the inevitable change which awaits cities, nations and dynasties, one and all, as it does every one of us men. This, he thought, had befallen Illium, once a powerful city, and the once mighty empire of the Assyrians, Medes, Persians, and that of Macedonia likely so splendid. . . . Though he did not name Rome distinctly, but was evidently fearing for her, from the sight of the mutability of human affairs.

Then grasping Polybius by the hand he added, 'Oh Polybius, it is a grand thing but I know not how, I feel a terror and a dread, lest someone some day gives the same order about my own native city.'

So total was the destruction wrought on Carthage that, though the Phoenician race was not completely exterminated in North Africa, it lost its identity through gradual assimilation and left no readily discernible religious, literary, political, or social heritage. An eastern civilisation had been planted in the western Mediterranean but, after a period of luxuriant growth, it had been violently uprooted and destroyed.

EPILOGUE

The Punic Wars provide such a wide diversity of political and military experience that for me to have withheld all comment to the end would have resulted in a confusing loss of textual relevance. The purpose of this chapter then is to draw together earlier comments, and put them into perspective. As Polybius pointed out, the study of history provides a means of learning from the experience of others, so avoiding some of the mistakes of our predecessors. Since I will also be considering naval matters, let me reinforce this opening statement by quoting Captain Mahan, of the United States Navy, who wrote at the end of the nineteenth century: 'History both suggests strategic study and illustrates the principles of war by the facts which it transmits. But if these lessons are to be of any value, they must be shown to have a practical application.'

Because we live in a material world which has changed immensely since the days of Rome and Carthage, we tend to measure our differences from them in terms of such developments as nuclear power, the exploration of space, aircraft and the host of everyday things with which we are surrounded, which inevitably make events which occurred over 2000 years ago appear irrelevantly remote. But since the fundamentals of life remain unchanged, to judge historical relevance through purely material comparisons, is to take a somewhat superficial view of history and what it can teach us. In spite of the codes of law and deterministic theories we have developed, providence remains as fickle as ever.

We can at least introduce an element of predictability in assessing the likely consequences of our actions by applying the lessons of the past, although care must be taken that those lessons are not reduced to dogmas. They should be regarded only as signposts or guidelines for future action, which can then be formulated into policy through debate. But before looking to the future, I will first summarise the main lessons that can be drawn from the wars between Carthage and Rome.

When considering the First Punic War, two factors were identified as making the war more probable. First, the Romans saw advantage to themselves in gaining a foothold in Sicily, and second they saw the Carthaginians were not prepared to oppose them. It should also be remembered, to keep events in perspective, that history did not begin for the Romans in 264 BC, any more than it does for us at today's date. Rome had already begun to extend her borders following her recovery from the Gallic invasion of 386 BC. She pushed north at the expense of the Etruscans, then of those Cisalpine Gauls inhabiting the southern half of the great Po valley, and south, against the closely related Latin tribes, such as the Sabines and Samanites, whom she eventually assimilated into a loose Confederation. Though the extension of Rome's northern border was largely checked by the Gauls, Roman domination over the length of the Italian peninsula south of the contested Po valley was largely completed with the surrender of Rhegium in 270 BC. There was therefore a momentum to Roman expansion, to which the Straits of Messana were only to provide a temporary check. After four years the Straits were crossed in pursuit of what was initially a limited objective, the instalment of a garrison in Messana. But the military successes which followed, crowned by the capture of Agrigentum, whetted the Senate's acquisitive appetite and eventually the whole of Sicily became a Roman province.

The Marmertine incident can then be seen for what it was, no more than one among many other steps taken by Rome in extending her boundaries. In fact, the Roman state went to war nearly every year, mobilising its army in the spring and attacking one or more of its neighbouring states as if through sheer biological necessity. Since every member of the Senate had to complete ten years' military service before even being eligible to hold office, the direction of Roman affairs was largely in the hands of an aristocracy schooled in warfare. Military service was generally regarded as not only being advantageous to the state, but as a means of gaining personal glory and advancement.

Though the Romans apparently showed little interest in expanding their maritime trade, the economic benefits which could result from war were certainly appreciated. Huge tracts of annexed land were settled by Roman citizens, and personal estates were established and worked by slaves. As will be recalled (Chapter VII), with the final eviction of the Carthaginians from Sicily at the end of the First Punic

War, the theory of state ownership was introduced: instead of the usual military service being imposed, a tribute was demanded. The economic benefits deriving from the employment of slave labour were enormous, and the flourishing slave trade must have brought considerable wealth to both the state and individuals. Even the austere Cato employed slaves on his land as a matter of course. Slaves formed an essential part of the economic system, so enabling the young men of Rome and those of their allies to serve in the ranks of the legions.

Christopher Donnelly, Director of the Soviet Studies Research Centre at the Royal Military College of Sandhurst, tells us how Marxist ideologists have attributed the cause of the Punic Wars to a dependence on slave labour, and the rivalry between the slave-owning classes of both empires. The Second Punic War certainly brought considerable economic benefits in its wake, including those accruing from slave labour. But to claim that Rome went to war for this purpose alone merely shows how history can be distorted to serve ideological requirements.

Polybius puts forward the theory that Rome went to war for purely defensive reasons. The Romans were afraid of Carthaginian aggrandizement, and concerned that the Carthaginians might occupy all Sicily and thus dominate the Italian coastline. Certainly the Carthaginians had attempted to annex the whole of Sicily during the 5th and 4th centuries BC, but during the 2nd century BC, Carthage had been content to maintain its hold on the western and central parts of the island, while retaining a small garrison, by invitation, in Messana. Although the Romans may not have liked having Carthaginian troops just across the straits, this hardly provides a justification for war. Moreover in 246 BC, Hiero of Syracuse provided a powerful counterweight to any Carthaginian ambitions, so that Polybius's assessment in fact looks somewhat contrived.

Discounting the self-defence and slave-ownership theories, we are left with the undeniable momentum behind Roman expansion which steadily expanded her frontiers through waging war. Periods of peace were temporary interludes, not unlike the pauses which took place over the winter months during a campaign. As we have seen, the First Punic War broke out for the most trivial of ostensible reasons, and would probably never have begun at all had it not been for Rome's expansionist ethos. An opportunistic act, with what was at least declared to be a strictly limited objective, soon became a war of annexation in which Sardinia was seized under the most flimsy of pretexts. The fact of the matter was that the island, lying off the long western seaboard of Italy, was of strategic importance to Rome, quite apart from being a considerable economic asset and source of slave labour. It was then conquered, and with its conquest were sown the seeds of the Second Punic War.

In the treaty which ended that war, one of the clauses stipulated that the Carthaginians and the Numidian king Masinissa, were to draw up a separate treaty defining the boundary between them. But in fact no agreement was ever reached over exactly where the border lay; even after the Romans had sent a number of commissions to arbitrate between the two claimants. This unresolved issue inevitably led to continued friction and eventually to the Carthaginians taking the matter into their own hands; first skirmishing, then raiding and finally, in full breach of the treaty, going to war. Judicially therefore, the Romans had right on their side when they intervened, but had there been any desire on their part to develop good relations with Carthage, the cause of her dispute with Masinissa could have been swiftly resolved. Indeed, even Polybius admits that the Romans looked for a suitable pretext to justify their action in the eyes of the world. What relevance has all this today?

Sir Michael Howard, lately Regius Professor of Modern History at Oxford, and now at Yale, who has probably done more than anyone to analyse the root causes of international friction, said in his David Davies Memorial Institute lecture (January 1983) entitled 'Weapons and Peace':

> The causes of war are as diverse as those of human conflict itself, but one factor common to almost all wars has been on the one side, or both, a cultural predisposition for war, whether this has been confined to ruling élites or widespread throughout society. This is a factor which has been so often overlooked by liberal-minded historians; the existence of cultures, almost universal in the past, far from extinct in our day, in which the settling of contentious issues by armed conflict is regarded as natural, inevitable and right.

Before turning to current events as they affect East/West relations, it would be helpful to consider the more recent past. Since the 16th century there has been a relentless Russian expansion: between 1917 and 1940 alone, ten countries or provinces with a total of over 100 million people were incorporated into the USSR. After 1945 it was the turn of Poland, East Germany, Romania, Bulgaria, Hungary, Czechoslovakia and the Baltic States to be subjected to Soviet thraldom. To understand how this occurred, we must examine the Soviet attitude of the period towards war. Were the Soviets, like the Romans, expansionist with a cultural propensity for war? Or were they quite different? We must also consider the most fundamental question of all: what has changed under Gorbachev? (Assuming he is still around when these words are read.)

In the West there is little interest in communist ideology, and so little understanding of the influence it exerts on Soviet thinking. This is not the place to attempt a lengthy presentation, but since ideology is such an important motivating factor behind the Communist Party and the USSR as a whole, a brief summary would seem appropriate. Marx's interpretation of historical development was materialistic; he saw the produce of human labour as dominating, and so determining, the whole of intellectual life. His intention was always to be scientific and rational, believing economic interests to be the motivating force behind all human activities – change economic circumstances and you change human nature.

If Soviet ideology had ended there, it would have been no more than just another political theory to be accepted or rejected as a matter of personal choice. But it did not, and when it became clear that the exploited classes in the West showed no inclination for revolutionary zeal, the benefits of communism had to be brought to them, if necessary by violence. To speed the attainment of this objective, every conceivable means could legitimately be employed: subversion and friendly assistance, intimidation and conciliation, military force and peaceful coexistence, intransigence and reasonableness. The tools of the trade are all to be used as the situation requires; if force is less appropriate than deceit for the moment, then its use may be renounced until circumstances change. Only a fool always tries to gain access with a sledgehammer, but that does not mean that you should not keep one to hand. With this in mind, it is as well to reflect on what Oleg Gordievsky, the former senior KGB officer, wrote in *The Times* in February 1990: 'We must not invent an imaginary Gorbachev, he is not trying to create a Western-style democracy in the USSR, but remains a profoundly convinced Communist.'

Therefore, to answer the questions posed earlier: yes, the Soviets have been expansionist like the Romans, but unlike them they do not have a cultural propensity for war. Their approach is more rational and sophisticated; war is just a tool of policy which, like all tools, can be laid aside when not appropriate. Meanwhile in the background lurks Clausewitz's dictum: 'the compulsory submission of the enemy to our will is a political object and war, being an activity carried out by military forces raised by states, is thus a continuation of state policy by other means.'

But if war has not always been seen as the appropriate tool to further Soviet policy, its spectre certainly has. Force has been applied indirectly to intimidate when the risks are high, as has been the case until recently in Europe since the end of World War II, or directly when the risks are perceived to be low, as in Afghanistan. But with the rapid advance of Western technology, principally that of the United States, the military tool has become too cumbersome and costly, while the threat of its use has proved to be counterproductive; the

NATO countries have been scared into spending more on defence, but without weakening their economies, as has happened to the Soviet Union.

In assessing the current situation, Gorbachev will have fully appreciated two facts. First, that it is only the strategic weapons of the United States which pose any real threat to Soviet security, and second, that the NATO countries simply do not have the numbers, equipment, higher-level training and logistic sustainability to undertake offensive operations of any depth or duration. The danger of the West provoking a war within at least the next ten years can then be discounted and, if necessary, or even helpful, the Warsaw Pact declared defunct. It is mainly for these reasons that Gorbachev has agreed to a united Germany joining NATO. It is a time for peace and goodwill when the economy can be revitalised. But unless communist ideology is renounced and the Soviet Union democratised, the West would be imprudent to assume that at some future date force would not again be applied as a tool of policy. So to answer the question, what has changed under Gorbachev? The answer is a great deal, though it is too early to be certain that in the long term it is in the way we would wish. Even in the short term Gorbachev may not survive, the most likely reason being that his reforms cannot meet quickly enough the expectations he has aroused. So let us see whether there is anything to be learned from the experience of Rome.

Following the Second Punic War (Chapter XXI), Scipio Africanus endeavoured to ensure that Rome's attitude to Carthage was one of moderation. But he did not survive the political infighting, and with his departure came a reversion, under the leadership of Cato, to the earlier policy of vigorous confrontation with Carthage. After being threatened and having disarmed to demonstrate their willingness to placate Rome under almost any circumstances, the Carthaginians were obliterated. The lesson here is writ large and clear. It is the long-term predisposition of states which should govern our relationships with them, not the ephemeral appearance of some charismatic leader. Then there is the question of unpreparedness.

Let us go back to the First Punic War. It is apparent from the scale of the operation and the haphazard way it was mounted, that in occupying Messana the Romans had not anticipated any effective reaction from Carthage. When Carthaginian unpreparedness and slow mobilisation led to further Roman successes, they saw a chance to annex the whole of Sicily. Though it is obviously impossible to prove that the Romans would not have undertaken the venture, had the Carthaginians been visibly prepared to react vigorously, there must be a strong presumption that this would have been the case.

EPILOGUE

As the causes of the Second Punic War are more complex and uncertain, the only deduction which can safely be drawn is that Hannibal was bent on war and Rome was not loath to accept the challenge. On the other hand, the Third Punic War clearly arose because the Romans were determined to erase Carthage. Although the Carthaginians were patently unable to offer prolonged resistance, what capability they did possess was radically reduced when they agreed to disarm as an act of submission. It can thus be deduced that when a marked disparity in military strength exists between rival states, in the absence of any external constraints, the temptation to exercise military superiority is high, while the fate of Carthage clearly demonstrates that unilateral disarmament does not ensure survival.

Michael Howard develops this contention a stage further in his examination of 20th-century experience:

> The argument that the more weapons there are in the world the greater the threat to peace (irrespective of the political intentions of both sides) and conversely, the fewer weapons there are the more stable the peace will be, does not stand up to serious examination . . . Stability comes from the relationship between forces, and not from their overall numbers, which in themselves mean nothing. Though as far as ensuring peace is concerned, the level at which military balance is achieved is irrelevant: it is however a fearful waste of resources if this balance is set unnecessarily high.

Having considered the causes and prevention of war, and concluded that a state which is visibly capable of defending itself is less likely to have to do so than one which is unprepared, we can move on a stage further in our study. Since a state's ability to deter aggression requires a war-fighting potential, we must next examine whether there are any deductions about the conduct of war to be drawn from the Roman and Carthaginian experience. Two conclusions are obvious: the first concerns force structure, the composition and organisation of a country's armed forces, and the second concerns the actual prosecution of war at the strategic, operational and tactical levels.

When the First Punic War started and the Carthaginians were caught unprepared, it was largely because their force structure was faulty. As a trading nation dependent upon the sea, they had a powerful fleet of well-designed ships, manned by skilled and experienced crews. Their naval readiness and potential were then high. But there were military disadvantages to being a seaborne trading nation: few Carthaginians served in the army and its actual size was kept to the absolute minimum. Only in an emergency was it expanded by the recruitment of mercenaries who, though often of high fighting potential, were of low readiness.

The Carthaginian force structure was then unbalanced: the fleet existed but the army still had to be raised. The only two commanders of any competence were both soldiers, so as the war progressed this imbalance was reversed. In North Africa, the Carthaginian army was reorganised by the Greek Xanthippus who, understanding the use of elephants and cavalry, drove the Romans out of the continent. Meanwhile in Sicily, the Carthaginian army maintained a guerrilla war under the inspired leadership of Hamilcar Barca, even when deprived of all support from the homeland. But at sea, through failing to adapt their tactics in order to counter the innovations introduced by the Romans, the Carthaginians' command of the Mediterranean was eventually lost and with it, the ability of the army to continue the war in Sicily.

In the Second Punic War, the potential of the mobile arm was exploited to the full by Hannibal, so enabling the Carthaginians to dominate the open battlefield. The Carthaginians also maintained a balanced force structure, but through poor leadership their fleet was never used to full effectiveness. The sense of inferiority at sea which the Romans had been able to impose on them in the first war, seems never to have been overcome. This demonstrates the importance of morale and underlines the fact that to possess the means with which to fight a war is not enough: the human requirements have to be given proper attention or the investment of resources is wasted.

The Romans on the other hand, entered into the First Punic War as a land power with no understanding of the need for a fleet. Even when overrunning the length of the Italian peninsula, no use had been made of the sea: the various campaigns were won by the feet and fighting prowess of the legions. After crossing the Straits of Messana into Sicily and extending the war throughout the entire island, the Romans were quick to appreciate the imbalance of their force structure. Unable to impose an effective blockade on the Carthaginians, they put in hand the construction of a fleet as a matter of urgency, and were gradually able to gain mastery of the sea, finally forcing the Carthaginians to sue for peace.

But the rapidity with which the Romans had identified the need for a fleet was not reflected in their recognition of the imbalance between the legions' cavalry and infantry. Only when Scipio was preparing for his African campaign in the Second Punic War, was due consideration given to the need for an effective mobile arm. Having identified the need to adapt force structure to changing requirements, we must now consider whether there is anything to be learned from examining the conduct of wars at their three levels, beginning again with the Carthaginians.

The Carthaginians' consistent strategic objective throughout the

First Punic War was to retain their possessions in Sicily. Had they utilised their fleet, they could have landed an army in southern Italy, very probably gained the support of the disaffected Greek cities, and prevented the Romans from massing against Sicily. Through not viewing the war in a wider perspective, the Carthaginians lost the opportunity to take the initiative. Moreover, when they were defeated at sea, while still trying to continue the war on land, they did nothing about replacing their lost ships until it was too late. After years of underprovisioning, their final great endeavour ended in disaster with the total destruction of their hastily mustered and ill-prepared fleet, so making it impossible for them to sustain the campaign in Sicily. Consequently, the initiative at operational level was left almost entirely to the Romans, until the Carthaginian army in Sicily was capable of doing little more than survive behind city walls or within its mountain sanctuary. At the tactical level, the Carthaginians' chief shortcoming was their failure to realise the potential of their greatly superior Numidian cavalry and thus to compensate for the inability of their infantry to face the Roman legions. The Carthaginians, then, lost the war through a combination of political inconsistency and poor generalship.

The Romans entered into the First Punic War with no strategic objective, the occupation of Messana being regarded by the Senate as a strictly limited undertaking. Carthaginian unpreparedness then encouraged the Roman disposition for aggressive expansion, which still had no clear long-term objective. Only as the fighting developed into a full-scale war did the Romans develop a strategic aim. Initially this was restricted to the annexation of Sicily, but later was widened to include the destruction of Carthage itself. After the failure of their African venture, however, their objective once again reverted to the annexation of Sicily, and remained so for the rest of the war.

Although they held the initiative because of their tactical superiority, the Romans initially failed to develop a coherent concept at the operational level. As a result, the legions were dispersed throughout Sicily in pursuit of uncoordinated tactical objectives: the capture of cities which turned out to be largely impregnable. The campaign then became a tactical stalemate, hence the change of strategic objectives from that of Sicily to North Africa. Only when forced to resume the annexation of Sicily as their strategic aim, did the Romans first pursue a clear operational concept: a coordinated land and sea offensive to capture the three main Carthaginian bases, Lilybaeum, Panormus and Drepana, in the northwest of the island. This aim, however, was not maintained and the campaign once again degenerated into a series of unrelated naval and land engagements, the war finally being won only when the Carthaginians belatedly attempted to revitalise the campaign and in so doing, lost their ill-prepared fleet and with it all means of sustaining their army. The Romans' conduct of the war was therefore gravely handicapped by a lack of a consistent strategic objective, brought about by ineptitude at the operational level.

When the Second Punic War began, Hannibal's strategic objective (Chapter XIV) was to carry the war into Italy and, by breaking up the Roman confederation, reduce Rome to her former status, no more than one city amongst many others. Probably recalling what had occurred in the First Punic War, Hannibal was not prepared to rely on the competence of the Carthaginian fleet. By crossing the Alps, he would strike at Rome's sensitive northern border region, where he was already assured of Gallic support. Following the battle of Cannae, however, the direction of the war was given a radically new dimension. Though Hannibal's ultimate aim remained the break-up of the Roman Confederation, the new strategy envisaged a wide encirclement of Italy by extending the war from Spain, through Sardinia and Sicily to Illyria, while within Italy itself the internal encirclement of Rome by detaching her allies would be continued.

Hannibal's operational aim was to destroy the Roman army, which he saw as the cohesive force holding the Confederation together. Because of the Romans' greatly superior numbers, he would have to avoid becoming involved in a positional war and instead conduct one of manoeuvre. Cities were not to be obtained by siege, but through destroying the Roman means of holding them under their domination. Plundering extravagantly and destroying what could not be consumed, Hannibal would force the Romans to react, so enabling him to draw them on to ground of his own choosing.

But as Hannibal's victories won over to him an increasing number of Rome's allies, he found himself on the horns of a dilemma. If he were to retain the loyalty of those cities which had joined him, they would need to be defended. But as his army was too small to defend and attack simultaneously, his operational aim gradually had to be abandoned and he was forced onto the defensive. When finally called to Africa, Hannibal found himself faced with precisely the same dilemma with which he had first confronted the Romans: should he permit Scipio to plunder and burn as he chose, or should he confront him in battle? By choosing the latter course in spite of the inferior quality of his troops, Hannibal suffered his first and ultimate defeat.

At the tactical level, Hannibal reorganised the solid formations of his army so as to introduce far greater flexibility. This enabled him not only to deploy his army so as to make full use of the ground, as at Trasimene, but also to manoeuvre and encircle an opponent, as at Cannae. Offensive action and the achievement of surprise, mobility and flexibility leading to encirclement, were Hannibal's hallmarks.

EPILOGUE

Initially the Romans' adopted a two-pronged strategic offensive for the Second Punic War, one directed at Spain and the other against Carthage itself. But when Hannibal crossed the Alps and seized the initiative by taking the war into Italy, the invasion of North Africa had to be abandoned, and the expeditionary army rushed up to defend the threatened northern frontier. Although the Spanish campaign was continued, it was five years before the army was reinforced and able to conduct operations with any degree of vigour. As the situation in Italy improved and Rome's mobilisation of her manpower resources began to take effect, so an offensive element returned to Rome's strategic thinking. Spain, Sicily and Sardinia would be conquered and in Illyria, Philip vanquished. Successful in all these endeavours and with Hannibal being confined to the toe of Italy, the Romans' strategic objective changed again, to one of defeating the Carthaginians in North Africa. Roman strategy can then be seen to have been both clear-sighted and appropriate to the changing situation. The same can not be said of their operational planning.

When Rome was forced to abandon the initiative at the beginning of the war and go onto the strategic defensive, her operational concept remained distinctly offensive: to close with Hannibal as quickly as possible, wherever he could be found, and to destroy his army. Ill-considered impetuosity based on a simplistic military doctrine led to defeats of increasing magnitude: first at Trebia, then Trasimene, and after tiring of Fabian caution, Cannae. Realising that they had nobody who could match Hannibal's generalship and tactical genius on the battlefield, the Romans' operational thinking became distinctly reactive, though admirably pragmatic. They would adopt a dual approach: wherever Hannibal was they would act defensively, wherever he was not, they would act offensively.

Hannibal was then slowly and inexorably penned into the toe of Italy, until he was finally recalled to defend the Carthaginian homeland. In North Africa the Romans' operational aim was the isolation of Carthage by the destruction of her army. After Hannibal had crossed over from Italy, this aim was to be achieved by drawing him away from his own secure base into territory under their domination, where he would be destroyed on a battlefield of their choosing. The parallel with Hannibal's operational aim at the beginning of his Italian campaign is obvious enough.

Until Scipio Africanus formed his expeditionary army in Sicily and introduced the organisational changes he had wrought in Spain, Rome's tactical thinking had not evolved. The cavalry remained an inferior arm and the infantry were too inflexible. Even after Cannae there were no signs that the need for greater flexibility was recognised until Scipio's reforms, but in spite of the brilliant way he handled his army, his organisational and doctrinal changes were no more than refinements of those pioneered by Hannibal: the creation of an effective cavalry arm as taught by Xanthippus, the reorganisation of the infantry into looser, more flexible contingents, and the achievement of surprise. These innovations were common to both the generals, but the one preceded the other.

Since leadership plays such a vital part in all we have discussed, before summarising the deductions to be made, it seems appropriate to consider briefly the qualities displayed by Hannibal and Scipio. Hannibal, like his father before him, was pre-eminently a warrior. But he was not a fanatic and he knew how to compromise in order to accommodate the wide ethnic diversity of the various national and tribal contingents which formed his army. He was therefore a leader who may serve as a model for all those holding international appointments. He led by example, fully understanding the capabilities and limitations of those he commanded. He was also mentally and physically robust, imaginative and so innovative, fearless without being foolhardy, unswerving in pursuit of his objective, outstandingly competent professionally through intelligent study, and ruthless when necessary.

Livy tells us he lived as an ordinary soldier when campaigning, and was to be found sleeping on the ground wrapped only in his military cloak. But after recognising his virtues, Livy goes on to list Hannibal's shortcomings, depicting him as being inhumanely cruel, with 'a total disregard for truth, honour and religion, for the sanctity of an oath and all that other men hold sacred'. Admittedly, therefore, Hannibal must have shared many of the characteristics of a harsher age. But as a professional soldier he was undoubtedly a genius, and his strategic vision threw the Romans onto the defensive and for the first five years of his campaign forced them to devote their resources almost entirely to the protection of their homeland.

Scipio, on the other hand, had been strongly influenced by Greek philosophy and literature. While perhaps displaying a higher appreciation of sensual pleasures than Hannibal, he was equally restrained in avoiding extremes of behaviour. Compared to his contemporaries, he must have been unusually liberal-minded, open to new ideas but still placing a high value on both intellectual and moral virtues. Perhaps Scipio accepted the belief that by performing just acts and acquiring good habits, a man's character is formed and the qualities required of a leader are established. His justice was displayed in his attitude to Carthage after her defeat, and his morality showed in his behaviour to women after the capture of New Carthage. On this occasion, a young woman of particular beauty was brought by some of his soldiers to Scipio who, as Polybius relates: 'was struck with admiration for her

EPILOGUE

beauty and replied that, if he had been a private citizen, he would have received no present which would have given him greater pleasure; but as a general it was the last thing in the world he could receive'. And Polybius also relates how after capturing New Carthage, Scipio refused to take anything for his own private use, and when returning from Africa allowed nothing which had been obtained there to be mixed up with his private property.

The self-confidence Scipio displayed was in part derived from a sense of direct communion with the gods; especially with Jupiter, to whom he displayed a particular devotion and from whom, reflecting the Roman religious belief, he could anticipate reciprocal favours. But this self-assurance must also have been inborn; though not particularly wealthy, Scipio came from one of the great aristocratic families, whose members would have been accustomed to exercising authority and commanding respect. He was, in short a born leader.

Although Scipio displayed a clear sense of strategic priorities in carrying the war to Africa, this was hardly an original idea. Rather, it was in his handling of the peace negotiations with Carthage that he showed his breadth of vision. As Basil Liddell Hart writes in a wider context,

> his peace terms alone would place Scipio on a pinnacle amongst the world's great conquerors, his entire absence of vindictiveness, his masterly insurance of military security with a minimum of hardship on the conquered, his strict avoidance of annexation of any state. They left no festering sores of revenge or injury and so prepared the way for the conversion of enemies into real allies, effective props of the Roman power.

At the operational level Scipio displayed imaginative insight and a full understanding of the need to look beyond the immediate battle. While in Africa, although he did no more than to adopt Hannibal's methods, his success in drawing his experienced opponent into an area of his own choosing was a major achievement not to be underrated. But it was at the tactical level where he had the best opportunity to display his ability. The distraction of the garrison's attention by a diversionary attack, and then the surprise crossing of the lagoon to seize New Carthage, sound so simple; but at Ilipa, he again demonstrated his skill in achieving tactical surprise; first by deceiving the Carthaginians through a pattern of regular deployment, then by the unexpectedness of his tactical moves, which ended in their envelopment. Finally, like Hannibal, Scipio well understood the need for good intelligence and the importance of security.

In comparing him with Hannibal, care must be taken not to overlook the different circumstances under which they both fought. Although Scipio's victories in Spain were achieved from a position of overall weakness, he had a secure base in the northeastern region and suffered from no obvious shortage of resources. Hannibal on the other hand had no such advantages. He had no secure base under his direct control, at any rate until he had established himself in the very toe of the Italian peninsula; he was always numerically gravely disadvantaged and after Cannae, he was never again able to rely on superior generalship to compensate for numerical inferiority. From fear that the Romans would achieve an overwhelming concentration of force, Hannibal's time for deployment was accordingly always limited. Surprise could only be obtained from the unexpectedness of his appearance on the battlefield as at Herdonea, and not by the sort of prolonged tactical deception which Scipio had practised at Ilipa.

When they met at Zama, the two generals appear to have cancelled out one another's tactical moves, so neither of them achieved surprise. In the final count, Scipio won the battle because of the superior fighting quality which his troops, and especially the cavalry, displayed in what was little more than a traditional slogging match. But however victory was achieved, Scipio vanquished Hannibal, which is the ultimate yardstick by which generalship must be measured. That said however, for innovative thinking and sheer achievement against superior odds, the laurels go to Hannibal.

After all he had done, Scipio spent his last years in exile at Liternum, a disillusioned and saddened man, neglected by his country which he had set on the path to universal conquest of the known world. He died quietly at the age of fifty-two in about 183 BC, and though there are memorials to him in both Rome and Liternum, it is not known where he was buried. Unless the vast hall of Valhalla is strictly reserved for heroes who die in battle, Scipio would soon have met up with his great Carthaginian opponent who died, also in exile but from self-administered poison, at much the same time.

Let us now sum up the conclusions to be drawn about the causes of war, its prevention, and if all else fails, being able to bring it to a successful conclusion. Though there were other contributory factors and many pretexts, the main cause of the Punic Wars was a Roman propensity for aggression in extending her boundaries and sphere of influence, and in the settling of disputes. In examining whether wars could have been averted, nothing positive can be identified but two important considerations emerge. In the first Punic War Carthaginian unpreparedness encouraged Roman opportunism, and in the Third Punic War although Carthage posed no real military threat to Rome, following her disarmament, she was destroyed. Though the argument cannot be reversed to conclude that preparedness will always prevent war, there must be a strong presumption that the more obviously ready a country is to defend itself, the less likely it is to be the object of aggression.

In our examination of the course of the wars, we have seen how both their direction and their conduct suffered from a lack of clarity and consistency. The causes for this were much the same in Carthage and Rome: direction by the Senate in both countries too frequently represented political factional interests and not those of the state. Moreover, the field commanders were nearly all political appointees, with little or no grasp of the conduct of war at its higher level. With politics having become virtually a secular religion in the Western world, care must be taken that it does not lead to those in high appointments being selected for reasons which are unrelated to professional competence. With modern conflicts being of such short duration, there will be no time to replace them when the going gets rough.

Once war has been decided upon, the national aim must be clearly defined at the strategic level. If this is not done or if it subsequently lacks consistency, then its prosecution at the operational level becomes virtually impossible. At all levels, which of course includes the tactical, the achievement of surprise throughout the conflict's duration is of paramount importance. In the military field, two further important deductions can be drawn. First, as far as it is humanly possible to anticipate them, force structures must reflect future requirements and not those of the past. Second, training in the higher direction of war is an essential requirement. Happily, though belatedly, this need is now being met in the British Army by the Higher Command and Staff Course; it did not have a particularly easy birth, but that is another story. Let us now try and relate these lessons to the future.

Whatever their public pronouncements to the contrary may be, we would be well advised to remember the Soviets' current doctrinal approach to war which supports the view of force as a tool of policy. What I have to say on this is founded on Christopher Donnelly's assessment, based entirely on Soviet open sources. All Soviet military policies and doctrines are, by their own definition, defensive because any military action they take can be defined as being in defence of socialism or revolutionary gains. But if the doctrine is defensive, the means by which it is implemented is most definitely not. Since the use of force is no more than the extension of policy, and there is no reason for thinking that the Soviet Army will not continue to be regarded as a military tool for the use of the Party, it is necessary to consider how it could be used.

Soviet politico-military doctrine places a high premium on obtaining surprise through deception, and ending a war rapidly by deep penetrations, designed to encircle whole groups of major formations, before the West has time to respond with nuclear weapons. Because of the country's historical development and its status as a vast continental power, the Soviet Union naturally views and organises its armed forces very differently from those of the West. It does not follow that their system is in consequence superior, but it certainly seems to be more readily adaptable to change. The Soviets integrate their forces to a far greater extent than does the West, organising them on a functional basis with combined staffs at the higher levels, while sharing a common infrastructure.

But however integrated and functional their military forces, it is the Soviet army which predominates, and so reflects the national priority accorded to the land battle, not just in the command structure but throughout the whole staff organisation. Consequently, though there is no attempt to produce a single integrated service, the direction of all three is tightly controlled by a single staff. Since, however, it is clear that the Soviet air force and navy have important roles to play, it would be simplistic to concentrate entirely on the land threat. So let us look at the current roles of the Soviet air and naval forces.

The bulk of the fixed-wing aircraft come under command of an army-directed headquarters, probably at theatre level. In Soviet eyes it does not matter who flies the aircraft, or to which service they belong; what is important is that they should be directed to fighting a fully integrated land/air battle. No doubt they face the same problem confronting all air forces, that of determining the right balance between aircraft and other delivery systems, and in particular, the right aircraft/missile mix, which requires some unusually objective thinking.

The position of the Soviet navy is even more complex, and it has had difficulty in fitting into the land-dominated strategy when it comes to war fighting. First, the navy has not been getting the priority it requires in the allocation of resources to counter the United States' determination to attain naval supremacy. Second, adverse climatic conditions and difficulty of access to the high seas force the Soviet navy into the unsatisfactory position of having to maintain and operate three essentially self-contained fleets. Third, the need to achieve strategic surprise before unleashing a land assault would have prevented the Soviet navy from deploying into the Atlantic before a war started. To undertake such a deployment once war had begun would be a pointless exercise, since even before it could be completed the land battle would have been decided. Except for those submarines and surface ships already at sea under a normal peacetime deployment, naval war fighting has then been virtually restricted to defence of the homeland.

EPILOGUE

The West's reaction to this Soviet threat is too well known to require more than a brief review. By maintaining an obvious war-fighting potential, while displaying the political will to use it collectively if attacked, the West has successfully sought to deter Soviet adventurism. Underwriting deterrence have been the twin strategies of Flexible Response and Forward Defence. If deterrence should fail, a flexible escalation of the fighting would begin, first through a conventional phase which, when no longer sustainable, would be followed by the employment of nuclear weapons of increasing size and scale. It has been a concept which has proved easier to ridicule than to replace.

Forward Defence originally applied only to the West's land frontiers with the Eastern Bloc, in particular to those of the Federal Republic of Germany, but its use became extended. Like their Soviet counterparts, British admirals have had difficulty in finding a convincing war-fighting role. Various ideas have been floated – broken-back warfare after the nuclear holocaust, war at sea before the land conflict began – but none carried any conviction and they had to be quietly discarded. Then came naval Forward Defence, the holding of the Soviet navy along a line drawn well north of the United Kingdom, behind which would flow the American seaborne reinforcements. Strangely enough, although there has never been any realistic possibility of strategic surprise being sacrificed by the Soviets deploying their fleet into the Atlantic, the concept was adopted. Even accepting the idea has some validity, the Royal Navy then had to face a further dilemma. If the American fleet had arrived, so would American troop reinforcements and war would probably be averted. But if the American fleet was not in the Eastern Atlantic, in spite of any proud words to the contrary, the navy would be powerless on its own and the war would be quickly decided on land anyway.

None of this should be taken to imply that there is no need for the Royal Navy; a nonsensical notion if only because the high seas cover the greater proportion of the earth's surface, and Britain depends on their free use as a trading island nation. But in spite of this, as the British White Paper on Defence for 1988 shows, identifying a war-fighting role for the navy has continued to prove very elusive. Recognising that NATO's land and air forces have a strictly limited war-fighting capability, and in view of the Defence White Paper's confirmation that the Soviets aim to achieve a quick victory, statements about, for example, the need for a large number of ships to protect the lines of communication across the Atlantic, seem somewhat illogical, while citing a situation which existed in the last two World Wars as a justification for future requirements illustrates just how difficult it is to stop trying to fight old battles, in this instance the Battle of the Atlantic, as if things had not changed.

The basic problem stems from the decision taken, when Britain withdrew from east of Suez, to give overriding priority to the support of NATO. Though undoubtedly correct as a broad policy statement, it has unfortunately been given an overliteral interpretation – an all too frequent occurrence – so forcing the navy to find a war-fighting role in order to obtain its share of resources. The fact that it has been so successful reflects a gut reaction that Britain needs a navy, rather more than any rational argument justifying such a role. But it is hard to assess how far planning to fight the last war rather than the next, has resulted in distorting British force structure.

It is not so much a question of whether the resources which have been allocated to the navy could have been more wisely spent elsewhere, as to whether they have been spent on providing the right sort of navy. However illogical the process, a better balanced fleet has resulted than might have been expected. To take an example: once again disregarding Soviet intentions about achieving strategic surprise, it has been accepted that the Marine Commando Brigade could be sailed to Norway before the outbreak of war. Amphibious shipping, essential for out-of-NATO-area operations, has therefore been provided which would not otherwise have been made available. But it is open to question whether such a seemingly haphazard way of determining force requirements, when combined with attempts to follow American doctrinal thinking, has provided Britain with the right sort of fleet.

A new chapter for Western security is clearly opening in the Europe of today. The Soviet Union could disintegrate; Denis Healey suggests a time span of ten years, while others think the pace of change is so great and the task Gorbachev has set himself so impossible, that it will be considerably sooner. Second, an orderly disengagement of the Soviets from Eastern Europe could well be put in hand, which may or may not be completed, depending upon its timescale and the Soviets' ability to reinvigorate itself.

As the political kaleidoscope begins to settle down and the way ahead becomes clearer, then Western security arrangements will also have to change. These will depend on any new alignments which may arise, and the nature of the rump of Russia which remains. What, for example, will have happened to the Soviet nuclear arsenal? It is all too unpredictable to draw any deductions, other than that we can be certain human nature will not have changed, and even if the need for armed forces may have diminished, it will not have disappeared. Until requirements can be assessed with some precision, the aim should then be to maintain balanced and flexible forces which, even if smaller, can be adapted as required. Once a capability has been renounced, it cannot be swiftly restored should circumstances change.

It can be argued, as Fukuyama of the Rand Corporation does when writing in the *National Interest*, that, 'What we may be witnessing is not just the end of the Cold War, or the passing of a particular period of post-war history, but the end of history as such: that is, the end point of mankind's ideological evolution and the universalisation of Western liberal democracy as the final form of human government.' After arguing his cause Fukuyama concludes: 'The Soviet Union, then, is at a fork in the road: it can start down the path that was staked out by Western Europe forty-five years ago, a path that most of Asia has followed, or it can realise its own uniqueness and remain stuck in history. The choice it makes will be highly important for us, given the Soviet Union's size and military strength, for that power will continue to preoccupy us and slow our realisation that we have already emerged on the other side of history.' Whatever one may think about having reached the end of history which, if only because of Iraqi aggression in the Gulf, seems somewhat improbable, few would disagree with Fukuyama that the Soviet Union will continue to exert a powerful influence over mankind's future. Fukuyama introduces a note of pragmatism that is not always present in the brilliant, but sometimes over-abstract, theories produced by the Rand Corporation. One only has to recall those of Herman Kahn and Thomas Schelling.

We can now briefly consider the military requirements in general terms. The Punic Wars demonstrate that achieving surprise by deception and manoeuvre is a battle-winning factor, a deduction given greater significance by the fact that Soviet doctrine stresses the same requirement. As it is a requirement that has endured for some 2000 years, we can reasonably assume it will remain relevant for at least the next few decades. There is another important factor to be borne in mind. The Soviets will seek by every means, arms negotiations included, to achieve what they term a favourable correlation of force, which can be obtained just as effectively by smaller numbers if the density (ratio of force to space) is reduced. Smaller forces look less provocative and menacing, yet can be concealed, deployed and employed more readily; surprise and deception then become easier, especially if mobility has been greatly increased. So we must not become euphoric about warning time.

Since the trend in most Western armies for the last seventy years has been for fewer troops having to cover greater distances, even without arms control reductions, there is every reason to expect this process to continue. Bearing in mind that an aggressor can always concentrate at the point of breakthrough, particular care will then need to be taken that Western forces are not so reduced in size and readiness that a favourable correlation of force is presented to the Soviets on a plate.

If we are going to be able to provide a coherent defence, two fundamental requirements will have to be met. First, the ability to concentrate firepower at the threatened area must be greatly increased. This can only be achieved by a combination of greater mobility and enhanced weapon effectiveness. The need for helicopters, both attack and support, to be integrated into fully air-mobile formations will then become of increasing importance, though not to the exclusion of heavier formations capable of conducting sustained fighting. The historical requirement for a balance between cavalry and infantry, again identified in the Punic Wars, will need to be reflected in future force structures, though under a different guise. Helicopters will be the cavalry arm, and formations of tanks and armoured personnel-carriers, the infantry. If regarded in this manner, there may be some chance of getting the balance right. Enhanced weapon effectiveness requires little elaboration. Ranges will have to be extended, with all that means for improvements in target acquisition, while accuracy and lethality must be greatly increased. With precise and more destructive weapons, the need to saturate targets with fire can be largely removed, and today's enormous logistic burden reduced.

With fewer troops and greater dependence on mobility the priorities, when allocating troops to tasks, must be to create mobile reserves, then to secure key terrain in the forward area, and to cover the gaps with small mobile units capable of calling for long-range fire support, and most important, the rapid laying of mines by remote delivery. Finally, command and control facilities will require refining and enhancing, the importance of electronic warfare be given greater recognition, and with the prospect of weapons directed from space, serious and long overdue attention should be paid to deception. It all costs a lot of money, but unless it is done we will find ourselves with a lot of outdated hardware just when the Soviets have completed their own modernisation programme.

But none of these enhancements in capability will be of any avail, if the air forces are not capable of first winning the air battle. Failure to identify and adhere to this priority would be to invite defeat. Thereafter enemy movement can be restricted and our own made possible, but as has already been mentioned, getting the aircraft/missile mix right will require some objective judgement. One broad yardstick might be to employ missiles against deeper, less time-sensitive, targets and aircraft against those nearer the battlefield itself. Fortunately land/air cooperation has reached a high level of joint understanding, except for the vexed question of collocation under certain circumstances.

The way out of the dilemma facing the navy would be to recognise the uncertainty factor in war, accepting that a range of general tasks will arise, and so allowing the navy to meet the challenges, outside the NATO area, identified by Professor Robert O'Neill at a seminar on sea power, held at King's College, London University: political instability among independent states important to the West, declaration of zones of peace, restrictions on the rights of passage, and the adoption of anti-Western attitudes by developing states. Although Robert O'Neill emphasises that naval intervention is very much a last resort, the navy still has an economic responsibility for maintaining the flow of trade. These proved to be prophetic words, and we have subsequently witnessed the Western world's naval contribution to keeping the Persian Gulf open to shipping. It can be deduced that the navy requires a general-purpose fleet less keenly focused on anti-submarine warfare. Loose claims about projecting sea power, however, need to be treated with caution. Only the Americans really possess such an independent capability; the rest of us need allies.

But to conclude on a note of hope: the longer Gorbachev's reforms are under way, the more irreversible they will come. Should this process continue, Marxist-Leninist ideology might be abandoned and the dominating role of the Communist hierarchy brought to an end, ideally, without engendering the dangerously strident turmoil which has occurred elsewhere. Desperate men tend to behave like Samson. In the meantime let us keep up our guard, which means getting our future force structures and priorities right, while remembering Cato and reflecting on what happened to Carthage through wishful thinking.

SELECT BIBLIOGRAPHY

ADCOCK, F.E.	*The Roman Art of War*
ARNOLD, T.	*The Second Punic War*
BLANEY, GEOFFREY	*The Causes of War*
——	*Cambridge Ancient History* (Vols VII and VIII)
CAVEN, BRIAN	*The Punic Wars*
CICERO	*The Offices*
DE BEER, GAVIN	*Hannibal*
DIODORUS SICULUS	*Corpus Historicum*
GRIMAL, PIERRE	*The Civilization of Rome*
HARRIS, WILLIAM	*War and Imperialism in Ancient Rome*
HERODOTUS	*The Histories*
LIDDELL HART, BASIL	*A Greater than Napoleon*
LIVY	*The Early History of Rome*
	Rome and Italy
	The War with Hannibal
	Rome and the Mediterranean
MAHAN, A.T.	*The Influence of Sea Power upon History*
MICHELET, J.	*The Histories*
MOMMSEN, THEODOR	*The History of Rome*
MOSCATI, SABATINI (ed.)	*The Phoenicians*
PICARD, G.C. AND C.	*The Life and Death of Carthage*
PLUTARCH	*Makers of Rome*
POLYBIUS	*The Histories*
	History of the Carthaginians, in 6 Vols
RIBICHINI, SERGIO	'On Beliefs and Religious Life,' in *The Phoenicians*
ROLLIN, M.	*The Ancient History*
SABINE, PHILIP	*The Future of UK Air Power*
SCULLARD, H.H.	*A History of the Roman World*
	Scipio Africanus

SHUCKBURGH, E.S.	*The Histories of Polybius*
SMITH, R.B.	*Carthage and the Carthaginians*
THIEL, J.H.	*A History of Roman Sea Power*
TILL, GEOFFREY	*The Future of British Sea Power*
WALBANK, F.W.	*Polybius: A Historical Commentary*

INDEX

Abba 279–80
Acarnanians 230
Acerrae 132, 234, 237
Achaeans 35, 136, 138
Achilia 309
Achradina 221–4
Acra Leuce (Alicante) 146, 149
Acrae 54, 222
Acragas 223
Acragas, (Biagio) River 55
Adda, River 131, 132
Adhubal vii, 83, 86–91
Adis (battle 255 BC) 72, 82, 104
Adriatic Sea 127, 130, 135–8, 184, 187, 200, 227, 240–1, 254, 264, 276, 302, 304
Aegates Islands 96, 98
Aegean Sea 139, 230
Aegimurus 314
Aegura 96
Aemilii family 27, 43, 177, 265, 268 (*see also* Papus; Paullus)
Aemilius (praetor 213 BC) 245
Aemilius, Marcus (consul 255 BC) 77
Aetolia, Aetolians 136, 138, 140, 199, 228, 230, 232, 254
Afghanistan 325
Africa *see* Carthage; Carthaginian state; Mercenary Revolt; theatres of war
Agathocles vii, 16, 37–9, 42, 64, 69, 72, 119, 217, 276, 279
Ager Gallicus 127, 128
Agrigentum 21, 36, 222, 223, 248; siege and battle (262 BC) 55–9, 63, 68, 84, 92, 322; burnt (254 BC) 80; stormed (210 BC) 224–6
Aigues, River 164

Alba Fucens 252
Albinus, Lucius Postumius (praetor 216 BC) 137, 194, killed in Gaul 235
Aleria 65
Alexander the Great 5, 21, 228, 232
Alexon (Greek mercenary) 84
Allobroges 164–5
Alps 127–8, 131–3, 155, 157–60, 165–7, 261–2, 330–1; Julian 132
Alsium 93
Alycus, River 90
Anapus, River 222, 224
Andalusia 145, 212
Anio, River 252–3
anti-Macedonian League 230–1, 254
Anticyra 230
Antigonus 139, 199
Antiochus the Great 301–6
Apennines 129–30, 173, 177–80, 184–5, 187, 240, 263–4, 286
Aphrodite 15
Apollonia 137, 139, 229–31, 241
Appian (historian), quoted 319
Apulia 195, 203, 296; Hannibal in (217 BC) 184–5, 187, 189; campaigns in (216–207 BC) 234–5, 238, 240–5, 247, 249–51, 254, 256, 258–61, 263, 265
Aquilius, Cornelius Florus (consul 258 BC) 65
Aradus (Ruad) 3
Aragon 212
Arbucale 149
Archimedes vii, 221–2, 225
Ardiaenes 135

INDEX

Ariminum (Rimini) 127–30, 174, 177, 179, 183–4, 235, 238, 245, 263, 273, 286
Aristotle 13
Armilstrum 262
Arno, River and Valley 127, 178–80
Arretium (Arezzo) 130, 177–80, 259, 273, 286
Artemis 223
Asculum (battle 279 BC) 21
Asina *see* Scipio Asina
Aspis *see* Clupea
Astapa 216
Astarte 15, 16
Atella 254
Athens 36–7, 61–3, 95, 135, 138, 230
Atintanes 137, 139
Attalus 230, 231
Aufidus (Ofanto), River 191, 206
Autaritus 117, 118, 121
Avernus, Lake 242

Baal Hammon 15–17, 38
Baebius (legate 203 BC) 288–9
Baecula (Bailén) 210–12, 215
Bagradas (Medjerda), River 275, 280, 288–9, 296, 315
Balearics 8, 112, 216, 218, 272; slingers from 180, 182, 192, 211, 291
Baltic States 324
Barcids 119, 142, 145, 147–8, 151, 198–9, 205, 284; *see also* Hamilcar Barca; Hannibal
battle formation 10, 68, 76, 87, 130–1, 170, 213–14, 280–1, 291–2 (*see also* tactics)
battles, land (principal): Cannae 191–4; Carthage 75–7; Great Plains 280–1; Ilipa 213–15; Metaurus, River 264–5; Montepulciano 130–1; Panormus 82–3; Trasimene, Lake 180–3; Trebia, River 173–6; Zama 291–5
battles, sea (principal): Drepana 86–8; Ecnomus 66–9; Hermaeum 77–8; Lilybaeum 96; Mylae 61–3; Utica 282
Beneventum (Benevento) 185, 234, 241–2, 249
Berbers 7
Bergamo 131
Berytus 3
Bibulus, Gaius Publicius (tribune 209 BC) 259
Blaesus, Cornelius Sempronius (consul 253 BC) 80–2
Boii 127–9, 131, 158, 168, 179, 286, 300
Bois de la Montagne 164
Bologna 178, 179
Bomilcar vii, 223–5, 227, 240
Boodes (Carthaginian admiral 260 BC) 61
Borghetto, Defile of 180, 182
Bostar (Carthaginian general 256 BC) 72
Bostar (Carthaginian general 211 BC) 251
Bosworth Smith, R. 12

Bovianum 249
Brancus 164
Britain *see* United Kingdom
Brundisium (Brindisi) 93, 137, 229, 238, 240–2, 251
Bruttium 236, 238–40, 243, 245, 247, 249, 251, 254, 256, 258–60, 263–6, 269, 272–3, 287–8, 291
Bulgaria 324
Burma 173
Buteo 93
Byblos 3
Byrsa *see* Carthage

Caepio *see* Servilius Caepio
Calabria 229, 238, 240, 245
Calatia 254
Calatinus, Atilius (consul 254 BC) 79–80, 183
Caleria 251
Cales (Calvi) 234, 237, 240–2
Calor, River 243
Camarina 78, 79
Campania 19–20, 169, 185–7, 195, 234–51, 256, 289
Cannae (battle, 216 BC) viii, ix, 25, 67, 76, 139, 157, 169, 171, 191–4, 197, 199–205, 227, 235, 237, 242, 250, 252, 257, 258, 274, 281, 291, 294, 296, 330, 331, 334
Canusium 206, 258, 263–4
Cape Bon 37, 39, 69, 77, 275, 288
Cape Farina 275
Cape Nao 146–8
Cape Pachynus (Passero), 90, 222, 224
Cape Palus 146
Cape Pelorias 51, 61, 79, 223
Capua 169, 171, 185–6, 195, 234, 236–42, 247, 249–55, 262, 264
Caralis (Cagliari) 218
Carpetani 149
Cartagena *see* New Carthage
Carthage, city (*see also* Carthaginian state): Acropolis 6, 7; besieged 72–7, 313–19; Byrsa 6, 313, 318–19; Council of Elders 284, 290; defences 6, 313; description 5–7; destruction 309, 316, 320, 329; economic revival 306; Eshmun, temple of 319; Gulf of 69; Hundred 13, 75, 119, 125, 303; isthmus 5, 6; lighthouse 7; Mapalian Way 7; Megara 7; People's Assembly 13; Sacred Band 9; Suffetes 13, 14; water supply 7, 37–8
Carthaginian state (principal references): armour and weapons 9, 10, 170, 182; cavalry 8, 72, 75–6, 82, 106, 162, 172–3, 175, 192–4, 252, 256, 275–6, 328–9; commanders 9–10, 73, 75, 99, 104–5, 119, 144–5, 157, 169, 172, 227, 295, 328, 329, 332, 334, 335; constitution and law 12–14, 125–6; economy and finance 92, 114, 142–

345

INDEX

3, 147, 304, 306, 323; elephants 9, 72, 75–6, 82, 106, 115, 160, 163, 166, 176, 214, 265, 291–3, 328; government and politics 13, 91–2, 119, 125–6, 142, 148, 199, 284–5, 302–4, 335; history and description 3–8, 270, 313; imperialism and colonies 14, 39, 42–3, 114, 128, 145, 148, 302; infantry 9, 170, 184, 329; mercenaries 8–9, 10–11, 55, 66, 72–3, 111–23, 143, 327; navy 8, 11–12, 41, 51, 66–7, 78, 96, 114, 184, 196–7, 224, 327–9; religion 14–17, 145, 242, 306; Senate 13, 75, 280, 297, 308–9, 335; society 12–13, 17–18; trade 7–8, 41–2, 44–5

Carthalo (general, First Punic War) 79–81, 88–90, 92

Carthalo (commander, Second Punic War), 157

Carthalo (general, Third Punic War) 307

Casilinum 237, 239, 243–5, 249

Castellacio *see* Heirkte, Mt.

Castile 212

Castra Cornelia 277–8, 310, 315, 316

Catana 54

Cato, Marcus Porcius vii, 301–2, 306–7, 315, 316, 323, 326, 343

Catulus, Lutatius (consul 242 BC) 95–7, 107, 111, 123, 297

Caudium 239, 244

Caulonia 240, 259

Celtiberians 144, 149, 212, 280–2

Celts, Celtic 84, 94, 128, 144–5, 148

Cenomani 128, 131

Censorinus, Lucius Marcius (consul 149 BC) besieges Carthage 313–14

Cephaloedium 58, 79

Chalcis 231

Chiana, Val di 130

China 141

Cicero: quoted 12, 28, 32

Cirta (Constantine) 270, 283, 298

Cissa 196

Clastidium (Casteggio) 132, 134, 174

Claudii, family 27, 43, 53, 88, 91, 97, 203, 248, 259, 265, 268, 287

Claudius, Appius (consul 264 BC) 49, 51–3

Claudius, C. (tribune 264 BC) 49, 51

Clausewitz, Karl von: quoted 325

Cleopatra 302

clientela 33, 34, 301

Clupea (Aspis/Kelibia) 69, 70, 75, 77–8, 315

Clusium (Chiusi) 130, 133–4

Clusius, River 131

Cocles, Horatius 20

colonies *see* imperialism and colonies

Confederation, Roman *see* Roman state

Consentia (Consenza) 240

Corcyra (Corfu) 137, 140

Corinth 138, 221; Gulf of 230

Cornelius, Gnaeus (quaestor 214 BC) 249

Cornus 218

Corsica 32, 41, 63, 73, 103, 129, 133, 143, 203 (*see also* theatres of war)

Cortona 180

corvus 61–2, 69, 86

Crassus, Publius Licinius (Pontifex Maximus 210 BC) 268, 270, 272, 273

Cremona 131, 133, 158, 176–7, 235, 300

Crete 177

Crispinus, Titius Quintus (legate 213 BC, consul 208 BC) 223, 260–2

Croton 240

Cumae 20, 94, 234, 238–41, 249

Cunctator *see* Fabius Maximus

Cynoscephalae (battle 197 BC) 25, 302, 304

Cyprus 7, 15

Czechoslovakia 324

Dalmatia 135, 136

Dardania 230

Delphi, oracle at 202

Demeter 16

Demetrius vii, 137–40, 159, 189, 199, 200, 228–9, 232, 262

Demosthenes 37, 301

Dertosa (Tortosa) 203

Dimalae 139

Diodorus Siculus (historian) 9, 17, 54, 55, 66, 73, 77, 78, 79, 81, 84, 85, 88, 89, 90, 96, 99, 144, 145, 234, 249, 279; quoted 10, 16, 37–8, 74

Diogenes 317–18

Dionysius 37, 221

discipline, 26

disease, 131, 224, 314

Djebel Menzel Roul ridge 275–7

Donnelly, Christopher 323, 335

Douro, River 149, 212

Drepana vii, 79–81, 84, 329; battle (249 BC) vii, 29, 86–90, 105–6; siege (249–241 BC) 91–7

Drôme, River 164

Duilius, Caius (consul 260 BC) 61–3

Durance, River 165

Ebro: River 148–9, 155, 160, 195–7, 203–5, 216, 248, 254–5; Treaty viii

Echetla 52–3

Ecnomus (battle 256 BC) viii, ix, 66–9, 70, 86

Egesta 36

Egypt, Egyptians 3, 5, 9, 136, 228, 302, 305

elephants *see* Carthaginian state

Elis 230

Elymians 35

Emporia (North Africa) 119, 305

Emporiae (Ampurias, Spain) 160, 195, 205, 212

Enna 66, 223

Ephesus 303

Epicydes 220, 222–6

346

INDEX

Epidamnus (Durzzo) 137, 139
Epipolae 221, 223
Epirus 21, 22, 135; see also Pyrrhus
Erbessus 56, 57
Eryx, Mt. 91, 94, 96, 97, 111, 115
Etruria (Tuscany), Etruscans 19–21, 29, 92, 127, 129–30, 133, 158, 177, 179, 195, 198, 235, 238, 250–1, 259, 271, 273, 286, 296, 322
Europe, Eastern 338–9
Euryalus 221, 223

Fabii, family 20, 27, 43, 53, 91, 93, 97, 121, 127, 177, 183, 268, 287
Fabius Maximus (Cunctator), Quintus vii, 25, 121, 183–9, 198, 201–2, 234, 237, 240–4, 248, 257–62, 267, 269, 274, 331
Fabius Pictor, Quintus (consul 213 BC) 244–5, 248
Faesula (Fiesole) 130, 178
Falernus Ager, Falernian Plain 185, 238
Fanum Fortunae (Fano) 263
finance see economy and finance
Flaccus, Quintus Fulvius (consul 212 BC) 248–52, 258–60, 262, 268
Flaccus, Cornelius Fulvius (praetor) defeated at Herdonea 250
Flaccus, Valerius (naval commander 217 BC) 229
Flaminius, Claudius (consul 208 BC) 260, 262
Flaminius, Gaius vii, 31, 127, 131, 133, 177–80, 182, 184, 189, 238
Flaubert, Gustave 6–7
Fleganae 93
Florence 178
Foggia 240
Frusino 262
Fukuyama (Rand Corporation) 339
Fulvii, family 248 (see also Flaccus)
Fulvius, Servius (consul 255 BC) 77
Fulvius, Centumalus (consul 229 BC) 137–8
Fulvius Centumalus, Gnaeus (praetor 213 BC, consul 211 BC) 244–5, 251, 256
Furius 31

Gabès, Gulf of 305
Gades (Cadiz) 143, 145, 147, 159, 212, 215, 216, 271
Gaesati 132, 155, 158
Gaul, Gauls, Gallic 19, 39, 64, 106, 117, 144, 202, 228, 251, 272, 302; Ager Gallicus 127–8; army 128, 134; attack in Po Valley (201–196 BC) 300; Cisalpine 132–4, 158, 162, 168, 171, 176, 179, 235, 237, 263, 322; Gallic invasion (241–220 BC) 127–34; Hannibal in (218 BC) 157–67; mercenaries 9, 55, 112, 178, 192, 194, 263, 265, 291; support for Carthage 155, 173, 261, 286
Gela 55, 90
Gelo 200

Gelon 36
Geminus, Servilius (consul 204 BC) 287
Genoa, Genoans 129, 272–3, 286
Germany: army 173; East 324; Federal Republic 337
Gerunium 187–9
Gibraltar, Straits of (Pillars of Hercules) 3, 12, 18, 143, 145, 197, 207
Gisco (father of Hasdrubal Gisco) 111, 113, 118
Glycia, Claudius (dictator, Sicily 249 BC) 88
Gorbachev, Mikhail 324, 326, 338, 342
Gordievsky, Oleg 325
Gracchus, Tiberius Sempronius (consul 215 BC) 234, 237–45, 248–50, 262
Great Plains (battle 203 BC) ix, 25, 280–1
Greece (see also Magna Graecia) 20, 124, 128, 136, 138, 144, 200, 202, 228, 230–1, 254, 302; civilisation 66, 332; mercenaries 84, 86, 112; religion 16–17, 29; Sicilian cities 7–8, 12, 36–9, 55, 58; trade 35–6, 55
Grumentum 263
Guadalquivir, River 147, 210
Guadiana, River 147
Gulussa 315, 318

Hadrumetum (Susa) 289, 295, 309
Halicyae 59
Hamilcar (commander, First Punic War) 37–8, 58, 63, 65–8, 72
Hamilcar (commander killed at Cremonia 201 BC) 300
Hamilcar (commander at Locri 205 BC) 273
Hamilcar Barca (father of Hannibal) vii, viii, 91–8, 111, 113, 115–26, 142–8, 157, 159, 209, 284, 328
Hampsicora 220
Hannibal (commander at the time of the Mercenary Revolt) 119, 122
Hannibal (commander in Sicily, First Punic War) 55, 57, 61, 63, 65
Hannibal (son of Hanno; blockade runner at Lilybaeum) 85
Hannibal the Bald 200
Hannibal (Barca) viii, ix, 9, 11, 21, 25, 132, 133, 139, 140, 327, 328; assessment of qualities 332–4; childhood military training 169; swears hatred to Rome 124; rules by divine writ 145; escapes to Acra Leuce 146; appointed to replace Hasdrubal 148; campaigns in Spain 149–50; conquers Saguntum 150–1; prepares to cross Alps 155, 157–60; marches through Spain and Gaul 160–6; crosses Rhone 161–3; crosses Alps 160, 165–7; strategy in Italy 168–71, 233–4, 330, 332; in Po Valley 171–4; battle of Trebia 175–7; crosses Apennines 178–9; marches into Etruria 179–80; battle of Lake Trasimene 180, 182–3; stalemate in Italy

347

INDEX

184–7; escapes from Campania 186–8; fights Minucius 188–9; victory at Cannae 191–5; treaty with Philip 199–200, 228, 229, 240; siege of Tarentum 224; campaigns in Italy (216–210 BC) 236–44, 249–52, 255–63; captures Tarentum 244–7; marches on Rome 252–3; learns of Hasdrubal's death 265; at Bruttium 266; at Locri 272–3; returns to Africa 281, 284–7, 288; meets Scipio 289–91; battle of Zama 291–6; returns to Carthage 295, 297–8; political moves 303; joins Antiochus 303–4; death 334
Hannibal Monomachus 157, 178
Hanno (commander, First Punic War) viii, 44, 51–2, 55–8
Hanno (the Great, Hannibal's political opponent) viii, 91–2, 95–6, 112–13, 115, 117, 119, 122, 126, 142
Hanno (commander, Second Punic War; Hannibal's nephew) 157, 161–2, 196, 212, 224–7, 236, 239–45, 247, 249, 251, 276–7
Hasdrubal (commander, First Punic War) 72, 82–4, 157
Hasdrubal (Hannibal's chief engineer) 173, 193
Hasdrubal (commander, Third Punic War) 307, 309, 313–19
Hasdrubal the Bald 218
Hasdrubal Barca (commander, Second Punic War; Hannibal's brother) viii, 146, 155, 157, 160, 196–7, 203–5, 207, 210–12, 218, 261–6
Hasdrubal Gisco (commander, Second Punic War) viii, 204, 207, 210, 212–13, 215, 271, 276–84, 287–8
Hasdrubal Hanno (politician) viii, 125, 128, 144, 147–9, 151, 157
Healey, Denis 338
Heirkte, Mt. 93–4
Helorum 54
Heraclea (battle 280 BC) 21, 195
Heraclea Minoa 56–8, 68, 80, 88, 89, 222, 224
Herdonea (Ordano) 225, 245, 249–50, 254, 256–8, 334
Hermaeum 77; promontory 275 (*see also* Cape Bon)
Herodotus 3, 27, 28; quoted 18
Hiera 96
Hiero viii, 42–3, 51–5, 57–8, 79, 82, 92, 97, 101–2, 105, 120–1, 177, 200, 221, 323
Hieronymus (grandson of Hiero) 200, 203, 220
Himera 200; battle (480 BC) 15, 36
Himilco (commander, First Punic War) 84–6, 88, 91
Himilco (comander, Second Punic War) 203, 222–4, 227, 240
Himilco Phameas 315, 316, 320

Hippo Acra (Bizerta) 7, 114, 117, 119, 122, 272, 276, 315
Hippocrates 220, 222–4
Hirpini 239
Hittites 5
Horatius *see* Cocles
Howard, Sir Michael 324, 327
Hungary 324
Hypas (Drago), River 55

Ibera 203, 204, 218
Iberians 144–7, 155, 178
Iberus, River *see* Ebro
Ilici (Elche) 146
Ilipa (battle 206 BC) viii, 213–16, 271, 277, 281, 333–4
Illyria 111, 128, 135–6, 150, 159, 189, 199–203, 241, 248, 254–5, 262, 267, 330–1 (*see also* theatres of war)
Ilotci (Lozqui) 204
Ilurgia (Lorca) 216
Indortes 145
Insubres 31, 131–4, 158, 168, 171, 286, 300
Ionian Sea 136, 138
Isère, River 164
Issa (Lissa) 135–7
Isthmian Games 138
Istolatius 145
Italy *see* Rome; theatres of war

Jeremiah: quoted 16
Jucar, River 148, 149, 151
Junius, Pullus (consul 249 BC) 86, 88–92
Jupiter 124, 333

Kahn, Herman 339
Kore 16
Korea 141

Laelius, Gaius 207, 211, 271–2, 276, 279, 281–4, 292–4
Laevinus, Marcus Valerius (consul 210 BC) 226, 229; negotiates anti-Macedonian league 230, 238, 240–2, 245, 254; in command in Sicily 255, 262
Larinum 188, 234
Latins, Latium 19–20, 40–1, 195, 297–8, 322; gods 29; revolt 257, 269
law *see* constitution and law
Lebanon 3
Lentulus, Gnaeus Cornelius (consul 201 BC) 298
Leon 223
Leontini 54, 220–1, 223
Lepanto (battle AD 1571) 66
Leptis Minor (Monastir) 122, 287, 289, 309
Lesina *see* Pharus
Libya, Libyans 40, 92, 144, 228, 309; infantry 170, 175, 180, 184, 192–4, 246–7, 292–4;

348

INDEX

mercenaries 9, 10, 38, 115, 117, 155, 178; trade 18, 39; unrest 73, 81–2, 204 (*see also* theatres of war)
Licinus, Lucius Porcius 263–4
Liddell Hart, Basil: quoted 333
Liguria, Ligurians 55, 127, 172, 179, 263, 265, 273, 286–7, 289, 291
Lilybaeum (Marsala) 39, 41, 59, 67, 80–97, 105–6, 111, 157, 174, 222, 225–6, 274, 298, 308, 329
Lipara 61, 66, 98; Islands 82
Lissus (Lesk) 138, 229–30, 248, 254
Liternum 334
Livius, Marcus (commander at Tarentum 214 BC) 242
Livius, Titus *see* Livy
Livius Salinator, Marcus (consul 219 BC) 139, 262–6, 268
Livy (historian) 24, 149, 150, 160, 170, 172, 173, 174, 176, 179, 180, 185, 194, 197, 205, 212, 225, 226–7, 229, 234, 236, 238, 240, 241, 243, 244, 249, 250, 251, 256, 258–60, 265, 269, 272, 275–8, 281–5, 287, 289, 297, 298, 304, 332; quoted 88, 166–7, 178, 194, 208, 214, 215, 248, 255, 257, 266, 272, 290
Locri 93, 218, 237, 240, 251, 260–1, 273–4
Longanus, River 42
Luca 179
Lucania, Lucanians 21, 203, 236, 238, 240, 243–5, 248–50, 254, 256, 258, 260, 263–4, 266
Luceria 187, 234, 238, 240–1, 243, 245

Macar (Medjerda), River 116–17, 122; bridge, 116
Macedonia, Macedonians 25, 136, 138–40, 145, 159, 199–200, 228–32, 240–2, 254, 302–3
Macerone, River 180
Madrid 207
Magna Graecia 20–2, 36, 39, 40, 103, 105, 194–5, 203, 247, 329
Magnesia (battle 190 BC) 302, 304
Mago (commander, New Carthage) 208, 209
Mago Barca (commander, Second Punic War; Hannibal's brother) viii, 175–6, 199, 204–5, 207, 210, 212–13, 216, 218, 261, 272, 276, 284, 286–7, 289, 291
Mahan, Captain A.T.: quoted 321
Maharbal viii, 157, 183, 194
Malta 7
Mamertines viii, 42–4, 49, 51, 101, 322
Mamilius Vitulus, Quintus (consul 262 BC) 55
Mancinus, Hostilius 315, 316
Manilius, Manius (consul 149 BC) 313–15
Marcellus, Marcus Claudius (consul 222, 214, 210, 208 BC) viii, 30, 132, 134, 206; takes Syracuse 220–6, 234–5, 237; defends Nola 239, 241, 243–4, 248, 254–60; killed in battle with Hannibal 261–2

Marcius Septimius, Lucius (second in command to Silanus at Ilipa 206 BC) 214
Marxist ideology 323, 324–5, 341
Masaesyli, Masaesylia 270, 282
Masinissa viii, ix, 213, 216, 270–1, 275–7, 279–83, 288–94, 297–8, 303, 305, 307, 309–10, 315, 324
Massilia 143, 146, 148, 160–3, 195
Massylia, Massylii 270, 271, 282
Matho (leader, Mercenary Revolt) ix, 113–15, 117, 121–2
Matho, Marcus Pomponius (praetor and Master of Horse 216 BC) 235, 274
Maximus, Fabius *see* Fabius Maximus
Mediolanum (Milan) 132, 134
Megara 54
Megellus, Lucius Postumius (consul 262 BC) 55
Meles 256
Melgarth 15
Melquart 145, 159
Meninx 81
mercenaries *see* Carthaginian state
Mercenary Revolt (241 BC) vii–viii, ix, 6, 111–23, 125, 200, 209
Messana (Messina) 36, 39, 42–4, 49, 51–4, 58, 60–1, 67, 79, 89, 98, 101–2, 120, 226, 273, 322–3, 326, 329; Straits of 22, 42–4, 49, 53–4, 101–2, 240, 247, 322, 328
Messene 229–31
Metapontum 242, 247, 256, 259, 263, 266
Metaurus, River (battle 207 BC) viii, 263–6, 268
Metellus, Lucius Cecilius (consul 251 BC) 82–3, 93
Michelet, Jules: quoted 17–18
Minoan civilisation 5
Minucius Rufus, Marcus 183, 186–9; killed at Cannae 194, 201
Molcochatch (Meluchat), River 270
Mommsen, Theodor 95
Montepulciano 130
Montgomery of Alamein, Viscount 172, 239
Moors 270
morale, problem of 84, 328
Morgantina 223
Morocco 9, 270
Motya 35
Mutina (Modena) 158
Muttines 224–6
Mycenean civilisation 5
Mylae (Milayyo) 62–4

Naravas 117, 119, 122
Narnia 263–4
Narona 137
Narragara 290
Narronea 256
NATO 325–6, 337–9, 342

349

navy (principal references): Illyrian 138, 141; Macedonian 228-9; Soviet 336; United Kingdom 337-8; USA 337 (*see also* battles, sea; Carthaginian state; Roman state)
Naxos 36
Neapolis (Africa) 315
Neapolis (Naples, Campania) 73, 186, 234, 236, 238, 241
Neapolis (Sicily) 221, 223
Neco 3
Nector, River 180
Neetum 54, 226
Nepheris (Bou-Beker) 314-15, 317, 318
Nero, Gaius Claudius (consul 207 BC) sent to Spain 205; besieges Capua 250-2, 255, 262-6, 268
New Carthage (Cartagena) 146-7, 149-50, 155, 159-60, 167, 197-8, 206-11, 215-6, 259, 278, 332-3
Nicias 36
Nicon 245-6
Nile, River 3
Nola 186, 234, 236-7, 239-41, 243-4, 247
Norway 338
Numidia 74, 92, 145, 270-1, 283-4, 287, 289, 320; cavalry *see* Carthaginian state; Roman alliance 298, 302, 305, 307, 315, 324; unrest 72, 81, 105, 115, 146 (*see also* Masaesyli; Massylia, Massylii)
Numistro 256
Nutria 137

Octavius, Gnaeus (fleet commander 202 BC) 296
Olcades 149
Olympieum 223
O'Neill, Robert 341-2,
Orethus valley 83
Oreus 231
Oricum 229, 230
Orissus 146-7
Oroscopa 307
Ortygia (Quail Island) 221, 224-5
Ostia 174, 205, 257
Otacilius, Titus (fleet commander) 225
Otacilius Crassus, Manius (consul 263 BC) 53-4
Otranto, Straits of 137-8
Ottoman empire 66

Paenula, Centennius (centurion 214 BC) 250
Paetus, Aelius (consul 201 BC) 298
Palancia, River 150
Palestine 302
Panormus (Palermo) 35, 61, 65, 79-84, 93, 94, 105, 222, 227, 329
Papus, Lucius Aemilius 129-31, 133-4
Parthinians 137
Paterculus, Sulpicius (consul 258 BC) 65

Paullus, Lucius Aemilius (consul 216 BC) viii, ix, 139-41, 189, 191; killed at Cannae 194, 201-2, 205, 235, 262
Pelias 93
Pella 230
Pellegrino *see* Heirkte, Mt.
Peloponnesian War 36, 61-3
Peloponnesus 136, 159, 228, 229
Pergamun 230-1
Perseus 302, 305-6
Persia 228
Persian Gulf 3, 341
Petelia (Strongoli) 236, 240, 260
Petra 80
phalanx (principal references) 10, 170
Pharos (Lesina) 137-41, 200; *see also* Demetrius
Philemenus 245-7
Philip V (King of Macedonia) ix, 140, 168, 199-200, 203, 224, 227-32, 238, 240-1, 245, 248, 254-5, 272, 276, 302, 304-6, 331
Phintias 67-8, 90
Phocis 230
Phoenicians 3, 5, 14-15, 35, 320
Picard, G. C. and C. 148
Picenum 184, 202, 235, 238, 245, 264
Pillars of Hercules *see* Gibraltar
Pisae 127, 130, 133, 160, 184, 197-8
Piso, Gaius Culpurnius (consul 148 BC) 315, 316
Placentia (Piacenza) 131, 133, 158, 171-7, 235, 263, 300
planning: operational 64-5, 101-2, 133, 169, 234, 329-31, 335 (*see also* tactics)
Pleminius, Quintus (praetor 205 BC) 273-4
Plutarch (historian) 25, 28, 132, 234, 301; quoted 30, 31
Po, River and Valley 127-8, 131, 133, 158, 166, 171-4, 176-7, 179, 202, 235, 260, 263, 269, 273, 286, 300, 322
Poland 324
politics *see* government and politics
Polybius (historian) 24, 25, 33, 39, 52-3, 56, 61, 66, 67, 73, 75, 77, 78, 80, 81, 84-6, 88-90, 97, 113-14, 120, 131-3, 145, 146, 149, 150, 159, 160, 164, 166-8, 171, 174, 179, 180, 185, 187, 191, 193, 200, 207, 209, 210, 214, 226, 234, 237, 265, 290, 292, 294, 316, 321, 323, 324; quoted x, 14, 22, 51, 60, 74, 119, 128, 136, 148, 163, 206, 211, 212, 221, 228, 229, 266, 279, 291, 293, 294, 295, 308, 319, 320, 332-3
Pompeii 20
Porsena, Lars (6th century BC Etruscan king) 20
Porto Farino 275
Provincia 302
Prussia 106
Ptolemy II 92

INDEX

Ptolemy III 136
Ptolemy VI 302
Pulcher, Appius Claudius (consul 212 BC) 206, 220–1, 223, 248–52
Pulcher, Publius Claudius (consul 249 BC) vii, 29, 86–8, 91
Punic Wars vii (*see also* theatres of war): First 42–97; Second 157–299; Third 313–20
Puteoli (Pozzuoli) 241–2, 250
Pydna 302
Pylos 139
Pyrenees 144, 160–1, 167, 212
Pyrrhus (king of Epirus) 21–2, 39–41, 52, 106, 195

Quinctius, Catius (legate 207 BC) 264

Reate (Rieti) 252
Regillus, Lake (battle 496 BC) 24, 170
Regulus, Cornelius Atilius (consul 250 BC) invests Lilybaeum 82–4
Regulus, Cornelius Atilius (consul 225 BC) wins battle of Telamon 129–34
Regulus, Marcus Atilius (consul 256 BC) ix, wins battle of Ecnomus 68; invades Africa 69, 70, 72–4; defeated and captured 76–8, 82, 92, 97, 105, 115, 119, 217
Regulus, Marcus Atilius (consul 217 BC) 189
Remagen bridge 173
Rhegium (Reggio) 19, 22, 40–1, 44, 49, 51, 101, 237, 240, 247, 254, 273, 322
Rhine, River 173, 302
Rhoda 160
Rhodian (blockade runner at Lilybaeum) 85, 95
Rhone, River 155, 157, 160–4, 167, 171, 177, 195
Ribichini, Sergio: quoted 15
Rollin, M. 18; quoted 17
Roman state (principal references): armour and weapons 23–4; cavalry 22–3, 134, 162, 170, 178–9, 252, 270, 276–7, 328, 332; commanders 24–6, 73–4, 106, 134, 177, 188–9, 241, 248–9, 259–62, 274, 332–5; Confederacy, Confederation 21, 42, 64, 125, 168, 171, 185–6, 194–5, 198, 234, 236, 248, 265, 267, 330; constitution and law 26–9, 188, 201; economy and finance 91, 95, 235–6, 255, 269, 271, 323; government and politics 27, 53, 91, 98, 183–4, 186, 201–3, 244, 248, 259, 267–70, 287, 300–2, 326, 335; history and description 19–22; imperialism and colonies 20–2, 28–9, 41, 44–5, 58, 92, 98, 127–8, 143, 216, 226, 257, 302, 322; infantry 22–3, 192–4, 328, 332; legion 23–4, 170; navy 40–1, 54, 60–1, 64–5, 78, 82, 84, 95–6, 103, 107, 196–7, 224, 226–7, 328; patronage 33, 301; religion 29–32, 128, 202, 240, 248, 253, 260, 262, 274–5; Senate 27, 43, 189, 202, 227, 249, 268–70, 274, 298, 335; society 32–4, 43; trade 322
Romania 324
Rome (city *see also* Roman State): Albion Mount 177; Bellona, temple of 268, 298; Capitol 63, 177, 194; defences 20, 184; Equites 249; Forum 20; Palatine Hills 19; panic at Hannibal's approach 183, 253; Patricians 26; Plebeians 26, 53, 98; Pontifex Maximus 30, 268, 270; Sibylline Books 128, 184; Tarpeian Rock 245; Tiber, River 19, 43, 179, 205, 252; Vestal Virgins 202

Sabines 19, 20, 24, 32, 33, 129, 130, 222
Saguntum (Sagunto, formerly Murviedro) 139–40, 146, 148–51, 155, 197, 204–5
Salaeca (Henchir El Bey) 276
Salamis (battle 480 BC) 66
Salapia 242, 245, 254, 256, 261
Salerno 20
Salinator *see* Livius Salinator, Marcus
Salmantica (Salamanca) 149
Samanites 19–22, 29, 53, 322
Samnium 185, 187, 195, 203, 234, 238–9, 244, 249, 252, 254, 256
Samson 341
Sardinia, Sardinians 7, 14, 32, 39–41, 58, 69, 73, 103, 118–20, 126, 129–30, 143, 151, 178, 200–3, 227, 250, 267, 272, 278, 287, 301, 323, 330–1 (*see also* theatres of war)
Sasinates 129
Saw, the 121
Scerdilaidas 139
Scipio family 203, 268, 301
Scipio, Gnaeus Cornelius (consul 222 BC) ix, 132, 134, 164, 195–7, 203–6, 236, 248, 254, 255, 271
Scipio, Publius Cornelius (consul 218 BC) ix, 157–8, 160–4, 171–5, 177, 195, 197, 203–6, 236, 248, 254, 255, 271
Scipio Aemilianus, Publius Cornelius (consul 147 BC) ix, 25; captures Carthage 314–20
Scipio Africanus, Publius Cornelius (consul 205 BC) viii, ix, 17, 315, 316, 330; assessment of qualities 332–4; religious beliefs 333; saves his father 172, 205; early career 205–6; campaign in Spain (210–209 BC) 205–10; captures New Carthage 206–10, 233; fights Hasdrubal at Baecula 210–12; campaign in Spain (207 BC) 212–13, 255, 259, 266; at Ilipa 213–16; treatment of mutiny 216; political opposition 267–70; preparations for African campaign 270–2, 328, 331–2; arrival in Sicily 272; takes Locri 273–4; crosses to Africa 274–5; successes around Utica 25, 276–84; peace terms with Carthage 284–5, 287–8; meets Hannibal 289–91; victorious at Zama 25, 291–6;

inspects Carthage 296; peace treaty 297–8, 333; returns to Rome 298–9; accorded title Africanus 299; opposed at Rome 300–1, 303, 326; death 334
Scipio Asina, Cornelius (consul 260 BC) captured at Lipara 61–2, 65, 79–80
Scipio Nasica, Publius Cornelius (consul 191 BC) 307
Segesta 59, 63
Segura valley 216
Seleucis II 136
Sellasia 159
Sempronius Longus, Tiberius (consul 218 BC) 31, 157–9; defeated on the Trebia 174–7, 179
Sempronius Tuditanus, Publius (consul 204 BC) 287
Sena (Cesano), River 263
Sena Gallica 263
Sentinum (battle 295 BC) 20
Serepta 5
Serranus, Atilius (praetor 218 BC) 158
Servilius, Geminus Gnaeus (consul 217 BC) 177, 179–80, 183–4, 189, 194
Servilius Caepio, Cornelius (consul 253 BC) 80, 81
Seville 213
Schelling, Thomas 339
shipwrecks 78, 90–1, 119, 218
Sicca (Le Kef) 112, 270
Sicels 35
Sicily 7–8, 73, 113, 129, 143, 157, 177, 194–5, 200–3, 218, 237, 244, 248, 255, 258–9, 267, 270–2, 281, 301, 308, 322–3, 326–31; history and description 35–9; strategic importance 41–2; trade 39, 42; (see also theatres of war)
Sicyon 230
Sidon 5
sieges (principal): Agrigentum 56–7; Capua 250–4; Carthage 72–7, 313–19; Casilinum 243–4; Clupea 78; Lilybaeum 83–6, 93, 106; Locri 260–1, 273; Nola 239–40; Panormus 79–80; Pharus 140; Saguntum 150–1; Syracuse 52–3, 221–5; Utica 277–81
Silanus, Marcus Junus (commander at Ilipa 206 BC) 212, 214–15
Silenus 82–3
Sintia 230
Sinuessa (Mondragone) 237
Sittany, River 173
slaves, in Roman army 203, 244
Soluntum 35
Solus 80
Sophonisba (daughter of Hasdrubal Gisco, married to Syphax) 271, 278, 283
Sosilus (military tutor to Hannibal) 169
Souk el Kemis 280
Soviet Union 324–6, 335–41

Spain 7, 9, 14, 41–2, 55, 111–12, 119, 126, 139–40, 155, 157, 159–60, 177, 184, 198, 201–2, 233, 237, 240, 248, 254–5, 261, 267–8, 271, 284, 331; (see also theatres of war)
Sparta, Spartan 10, 12, 13, 36, 74, 140, 169, 230, 246
Spendius ix, 113–14, 116–18, 121–2
Stalin 99
strategic objectives and considerations (chronological order): definition 101–2, 335; Sicily as springboard 41–4, 323–4; reprisals on captured civilians 57–8; inadequacy of land-based campaign 58–9, 328; expulsion of opponents from Sicily 64, 77, 104–6, 329; maritime supremacy 66, 95–7, 328; Roman lack of objectives 102–3, 326–7, 329; Hiero maintains balance of power 120; Rome's limited objectives against Illyria 136–7, 140–1; Hannibal depends on land forces 159; Hannibal aims to break Roman Confederation 168–9, 194–5, 198, 234, 265, 330; Rome maintains overseas forces 203, 331; Philip's flawed strategy 231–2; Hannibal put on defensive 233–4, 258, 330; concentration of Roman forces against Hasdrubal 264; Roman offensive in Africa 267–70, 331; Carthaginian submissiveness 308–9, 327
Sucro 216
Suessula 234, 237, 244, 245, 250, 252
Sulla (Sylla) 28
Sulpicius Galba Publicius (consul 211 BC and 200 BC) 251
supply, problems of 70, 89, 160, 247, 250
Sybaria, Sybarites 246, 247
Syphax ix, 215, 270–2, 276–84, 288, 289, 296
Syracuse, Syracusans 21, 36–44, 52–4, 58, 61–3, 84, 89–90, 97–8, 102, 200, 227, 246, 248, 254, 260, 272; armour and weapons 221–2; siege of (212 BC) viii, 220–5, 244; fall of 225, 235; see also Hiero
Syria 136, 228, 302, 304
Syrtis Minor 119

tactics: ambush 56, 158, 180, 182, 235, 250, 260–1; bridges, destroying 173, 184, 253; coordination 134, 170–1, 227; cross-posting 155; defensive 67, 69, 104, 133, 234, 337; delay 184–8; diversions 53, 58, 81, 252; encirclement 170, 183, 189, 192–4, 211, 265, 277, 281, 292, 330, 336; fire 279; flexibility 24–5, 76, 170, 192, 209, 212, 215, 233, 296, 330, 331, 337; guerrilla warfare 9, 94, 328; intelligence 155, 157, 160–2, 206, 271, 278, 289–90; manoeuvrability 10–12, 23–4, 72, 76, 117, 170, 192, 214–15, 233, 330; offensive 105, 133, 229, 234; planning 101–2, 335; surprise 83, 88, 116–17, 133, 141, 165, 170,

INDEX

175, 183, 187, 189, 209, 213, 229, 233, 247, 252–4, 256, 277, 330, 335, 340; training 107, 210–11, 229, 296, 335
Tagus, River 149, 207
Tanit 15–17
Tannetum 158
Tarentum, Tarentines 21, 22, 40–1, 73, 169, 177, 194, 224, 229, 234, 237, 238, 242–251, 254, 256, 258–60, 263
Tartessians 145
Taurasia (Turin) 171, 172
Taurini 168, 171
Tauromenium 54, 226
Teanum, Campania 187, 234, 237
Teanum Apuli 234
Telamon 130, 133, 134
Telesia 185 (*see also* Venusia)
Terraco (Tarragona) 196, 205, 207, 209, 210, 212, 215
Teuta, Queen 135–8
Thapsus 303, 309
theatres of war: Africa 70–8, 111–23, 270–85, 287–99, 313–20; Corsica 64–5, 123–5; Gaul 127–34, 156–67, 235; Illyria 135–41, 228–32; Italy 127–34, 171–95, 233–66, 286–7; Libya 80–2; Sardinia 64–5, 123–5, 218–20; Sicily 42–5, 51–9, 79–97, 220–7, 272, 274; Spain 128, 142–51, 195–7, 203–17, 259
Thermae 80, 82
Thermopylae (battle 191 BC) 301
Thessaly 230
Theudalis 309
Theveste 92
Thiel, J.H. 40, 60, 78, 84, 88
Thrace, Thracian 230, 302
Thucydides (historian) 36; quoted 35, 37, 62–3
Thugga (Dougga) 270
Thurii 247, 256
Tiber, River *see* Rome
Ticinus (Ticino), River 172, 173, 205
Tiditanus 245
Tifata, Mt. (Monte di Maddaloni) 239, 241, 243, 251
Timoleon 37
Toletum (Toledo) 149
Torquatus, Titus Manlius (commander in Sardinia 215 BC) 218, 220, 262
Trafalgar (battle AD 1805) 66
Trasimene, Lake (battle 217 BC) vii, viii, 170–1, 180, 182–3, 185–6, 189, 192, 228, 242, 260, 294, 296, 330–1
Trebia, River (battle 218 BC) 173–7, 183, 186, 192, 331
Trojans, Troy 35
Tunis 3, 7, 72, 113–14, 117–18, 121–2, 239, 282, 284, 289, 296, 298, 315; Gulf of 314; Lake of 5, 6, 313, 318
Tunisia 9, 270

Tuoro 180, 182
Turdenti 150–1
Turdetani 197, 203
Turkey 230
Tychaeus 289
Tyche 221, 223
Tyre 3, 5, 15, 16, 303

Ulbia 65
Umbria, Ubrians 129, 184, 195, 235, 245, 263
United Kingdom: air force 341; army 99, 173, 239, 335; defence policy 337–42; navy 337–8, 341
United Nations 141
USA 141, 173, 325, 326, 336, 337, 341
Usilla 309
USSR *see* Soviet Union
Utica 7, 18, 114–17, 119–20, 122, 225, 275–82, 288, 307–8, 320

Vaccaei 149
Val di Chiana 130
Valerius (Messana), Manius (consul 263 BC) 53–4
Varro, Marcus Terentius (consul 256 BC) viii, ix, 189, 191–2, 194, 201–2, 235, 238, 245, 259, 262
Venafrum (Venafro) 187
Venetians 128, 129, 132
Venusia 185, 234, 244–5, 256, 258–60
Vermina 296
Via Aemilia 263
Via Appia 184, 237
Via Flaminia 183, 263–4
Via Latina 187, 234, 238, 252
Victumulae 177–8
Virdumarus 132
Virrius, Vibius (Capuan senator) 254
Volcae 161
Volturman 250
Volturnus (Volturno), River 185–7, 236, 238–41, 243, 250–2
Vulcan 280
Vulso, Lucius Manlius (consul 256 BC) wins battle of Ecnomus 68, 70, 72; besieges Lilybaeum 82–4
Vulso, Manlius (praetor 218 BC) 157–8

Warsaw Pact 326
Western Desert 205
World War I 337
World War II 205, 325, 337

Xanthippus ix, 10, 74–6, 82, 104, 106, 328, 332
Xerxes 66

Zama (Jama) 270; battle (202 BC) viii, ix, 25, 289–96, 300, 334